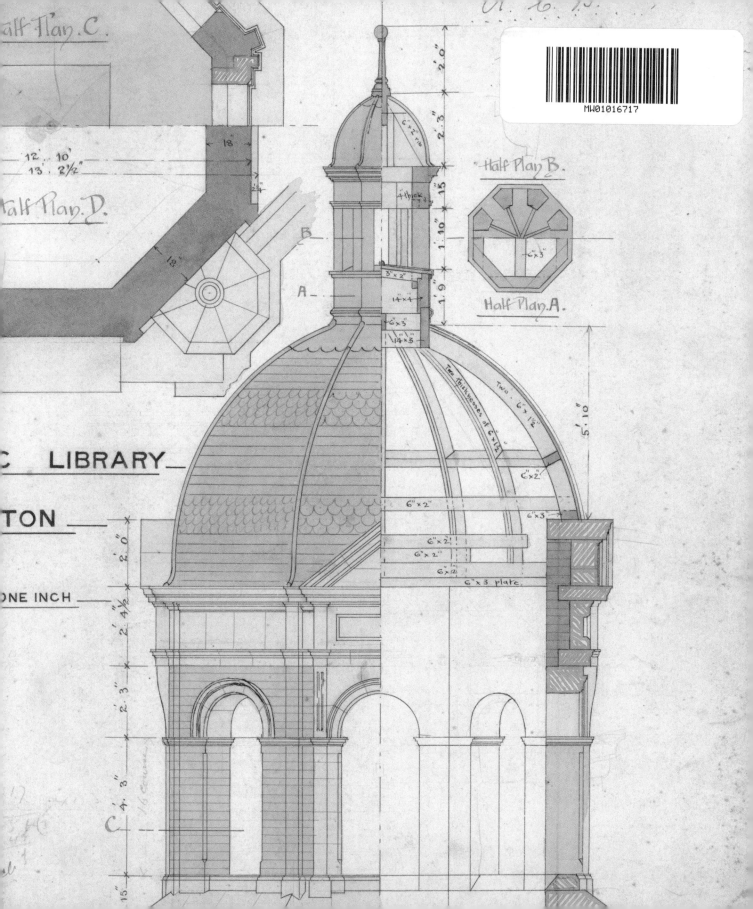

Half Plan. C.

12'. 10'
13'. 2½"

Half Plan. D.

18

24"

18"

B

A

Half Plan B.

6"x3"

Half Plan. A.

6"x2" rib

4 thick

3"x2"

14"x4"

6"x3"

14"x3"

Two thicknesses of 6"x1½"

6"x1½"

6"x2"

6"x3"

6"x2"

6"x2"

6"x2"

6"x12"

6"x3 plate

2'.0"

2'.3"

1'.10"

1'.9"

1'.9"

5'.10"

C LIBRARY

TON

ONE INCH

2'.0"

2'.4½"

2'.3"

C 4'.3"

15"

Grand-daughters of Te Puni, Te Wharepouri, and Edward Gibbon Wakefield, at the
1939–40 Centennial Exhibition. From left, Victoria Amohau Bennett (grand-daughter of
Te Puni), Ripeka Wharawhara Love (Te Wharepouri) and Lilian Priscilla Wakefield.

This book is dedicated with love to the memory of my late sister Gerda,
a true believer in the city of her birth.

Wellington
BIOGRAPHY OF A CITY

REDMER YSKA

REED

Endpapers: detail from Wellington Public Library building plans,
courtesy Wellington City Archives

REED PUBLISHING (NZ) LTD
TE KARUHI TÀ TÀPUI O REED (AOTEAROA)
Established in 1907, Reed is New Zealand's largest
book publisher, with over 600 titles in print.
www.reed.co.nz

Published by Reed Books, a division of Reed Publishing (NZ) Ltd,
39 Rawene Road, Birkenhead, Auckland 0626.
Associated companies, branches and representatives throughout the world.

Published in association with the Wellington City Council
and the Ministry for Culture and Heritage.

ISBN-13: 978 0 7900 1117 2
ISBN-10: 0 7900 1117 4

First published 2006

Yska, Redmer.
Wellington : biography of a city / Redmer Yska.
Includes bibliographical references and index.
ISBN-13: 978-0-7900-1107-3
ISBN-10: 0-7900-1107-7
1. Wellington (N.Z.)—History. I. Title.
993.63—dc 22

Edited by Jeremy Sherlock
Design by Jason Anscomb
Maps designed by Outline Draughting and Graphics Ltd

Printed in China by Nordica

Contents

Acknowledgements

Thanks to Ben Schrader for convincing me I was up to the task. I am grateful to the Wellington City Council for commissioning this project and to Bronwyn Dalley, chief historian at the Ministry for Culture and Heritage, for hiring me to tackle it. John Barton, Diana Beaglehole, Kent Clark, Katherine Coleridge, David Colquhoun, Peter Cooke, Neville Gilmore, Emma Hart, Terence Hodgson, John Martin, Hilda McDonnell, Joan McCracken, Greg McElwee, Geoff Park, Neil Pharazyn, Sue Piper, Donald Riezebos, Kevin Stent and Judy Siers variously supported this project. I am indebted to Adrian Humphris, Melissa Brown, Sophie Butcher (cheers for the chocolate with the 100th minute book!), Michael Biggs and Joanna Newman at Wellington City Archives. I am also thankful for the help of Gabor Toth, Anne Rewiti and Kerryn Pollock at Wellington City Libraries. Kynan Gentry, Gavin McLean, David Green, Fran McGowan, Jamie Mackay and Monty Soutar at the Ministry for Culture and Heritage all provided assistance. Thanks to Ali Carew for her editing. Special thanks to Ross Bly, John McGrath, Jack Morris, Neil Price and Peter Hunter at Wellington City Council. Walter Cook, Jean Drage, Morris Love and three Michaels (Bassett, Fitzgerald, Kelly) read the manuscript and made almightily useful comments. Hilary Stace was indefatigable in tracking down photographs. Thanks old friend. Ruth, Dan and Rosa provided great support at home. The greatest debt of gratitude is owed jointly to my supervisor Neill Atkinson and to Malcolm McKinnon, who read the draft chapters and kept the project (and the author) afloat with wisdom, humour and forbearance.

Abbreviations used in image captions

ANZ Archives New Zealand Te Rua Mahara o te Kawanatanga, Wellington

ATL   Alexander Turnbull Library, National Library of New Zealand Te Puna Matauranga, Wellington

WCA Wellington City Archives

Introduction

Wellington is the world's southernmost capital city, the only one located in the latitudes of the Roaring Forties. Since English settler ships first gathered off Petone beach early in 1840, the city's fortunes have risen and fallen as New Zealand itself has changed and grown. In this respect, the capital is not markedly different from the nation's other urban centres. But as a physical location, Wellington differs in its ability to seem at once cosy and unforgiving, concrete and unearthly. Maori tribal traditions tell of a landscape of buried supernatural powers.[1] It was here that early explorers battled with water-dwelling taniwha, distant cousins of the fanged fell-beasts that glowered from Courtenay Place facades at the end of 2003 for the final instalment of Peter Jackson's *Lord of the Rings*. Wellington has never been a place for the faint-hearted.

Unlike previous books about the city, this work explores the governance and growth of Wellington from 1839, the year in which the New Zealand Company bought up land for settlement from local Maori. By 1870, as the Wellington City Corporation was established, the city was embarking on a century of accelerated growth which saw a fundamental transformation of patterns of work, culture, and daily life. Geographically, the book confines itself to Wellington City, initially an amphitheatre stretching from Thorndon to Newtown, later taking in the four boroughs (Melrose, Karori, Onslow and Miramar), and Johnsonville and Tawa.

Describing itself as a civic biography, this is not one of those vanity works, popular with nineteenth-century Victorian municipalities as a means of lauding their city and attracting development. Nor is it an academic discourse on urban theory. As in any city history, the quest for better infrastructure — water, sanitation, transport, housing — dominates the narrative. But I have also tried to describe the context in which the city fathers (and later mothers too) formed attitudes and took difficult and expensive decisions. My aim has been to write a social rather than an administrative history of city governance in Wellington, describing the impact of Council activities on the people who lived here. Hence it has become a study of evolving relationships within a compact community.

Wellington's role as the seat of central government adds a unique wrinkle to the story: the inhabitants of Parliament Hill have long been cheek by jowl with the city's administrators. Moreover, parliamentarians often based their views about local government on what they saw from horseback, or as they drove by car about the capital. By 1900, Premier Richard Seddon in particular had embarked on a campaign to strip powers from local bodies, based on his negative perceptions of the Wellington City Corporation. It was a cause that would be taken up by his successors.

Politics is in the very air of Wellington, a fact that has always set its Council and its citizens apart from other civic communities. At times, national concerns have overshadowed interest in municipal affairs. In recent decades, however, community action has become a feature of the Wellington landscape as residents have mobilised against Council actions, drawing on the public servant's ability to influence. But despite the intertwining of national and local politics, the book does not cover Wellington's role as the personification of 'the nation' (as in 'Canberra signing an agreement with Wellington', rather than Australia with New Zealand), or as the home of the diplomatic corps.

Before European settlement, the land surrounding the harbour of Whanganui-a-Tara was thinly populated. The 'river of wind' squeezed through the gap between the mountain ranges of the North and South Islands has tended to disrupt human attempts to put down roots here. In the early nineteenth century, however, the harbour's ability to provide sanctuary for British sailing ships made it an attractive option for colonial settlement. Yet even as the raw township grew into a thriving metropolis, there was always that sense of living on a fault-line, of frail wooden houses clinging to hillsides that might throw them off at any minute. The saying that 'God made Auckland, but the engineer made Wellington' reveals much about the battle with geography and climate that continues to this day.[2]

This sense of precariousness, of transience, emerges as another important strand in the history of Wellington. From the moment the settlers arriving on the *Aurora* realised that the promised pastureland did not exist behind the wall of wet flax along Petone beach, keeping people here became a priority for city fathers. Damned as the 'town of precipices and earthquakes', the settlement in 1848 and 1855 saw the departure of terrified residents who had watched Mt Victoria 'dancing'. Economic downturn and conflict with local Maori during the 1860s brought fears that the entire population was going to leave. Many did. Only when the seat of government relocated to Wellington in 1865 did the city fathers relax.

Wellington then eased into a century of economic and political complacency. By 1918, the 'opulent' city was on such a roll that one commentator argued that moving the seat of government elsewhere would be 'no crushing disaster'.[3] Half a century later, the old dread returned as population growth stalled, and corporate head offices began moving north. Wellington was, in fact, crushed and humbled. While the incomes of public servants would always buttress the local economy, the quest for a firmer economic base would remain a key preoccupation for municipal leaders.

The rigours of the climate heighten the sense of precariousness. Wellington can probably lay claim to being the world's windiest capital. Thus weather is another theme of the book, even if, like a taniwha in the room, it is rarely talked about in polite company. In 1842 Bishop Selwyn talked of 'gentle breezes' and a 'ventilated' climate; the diarist Lieutenant Best was franker as the equinoctial winds were unleashed: 'I have heard of it blowing a gale, and half a gale, but if it ever blew a gale and a half it is doing so at the present moment.'[4] The boisterous wind is central to the personality of the city, playing havoc with the most glittering civic occasion. In 1953 a poet wrote sonnets praying for the forthcoming Royal Visit to be spared the 'vagrant winds' of summer, to no avail.[5] The gales of Wellington strip away certainties and stabilities; they humiliate its inhabitants, flinging them about and playing havoc with hairstyles and *haute couture*.

Yet arguably, the weather makes the people kinder because they all experience the same environmental outrages. People toughen up, refuse to be intimidated, put out more flags. They sit back and await the calm, luminous dawns and radiant days that invariably come. Are those who live in Wellington doing some form of cosmic penance? In Dante's *Divine Comedy*, those who have committed carnal sin are condemned to the second circle of Hell, to be eternally blasted by furious winds:

> The blast of hell that never rests from whirling
> Harries the spirits along in the sweep of its swath,
> And vexes them, for ever beating and hurling.[6]

The weather also forces people indoors to work and to create, thus helping to make the city a place of intellectual vigour, culture, and enterprise: this is the other main strand of the book. Because of its physical location, Wellington is known to Maori as Te Upoko-o-te-Ika ('the head of the fish'). The name also reflects the city's status as seat of government and repository of the nation's intellectual and cultural taonga or treasures. The Royal New Zealand Ballet, Te Papa, the New Zealand Symphony Orchestra, the New Zealand Opera, and the national dance and drama schools all base themselves in the city. The most important research and reference libraries and archives are also located here. The sprawling parliamentary complex constitutes an entire indoor, climate-proof village, stretching from Lambton Quay to Hill Street. Peter Jackson's network of film factories in the suburb of Miramar reflects the same spirit. The strong intellectual and cultural currents that drive the city have been noted by poet Lauris Edmond:

> You have to do and be, not simply watch or even describe.
> This is the city of action, the world headquarters of the verb.[7]

Research for this book drew heavily on the growing shelf of works on Wellington.[8] The extensive newspaper collections held at the National and Wellington City libraries yielded many gems. The mother lode, however, was the collection of largely untapped primary sources at the Wellington City Archives. The main focus of my research became 124 stout volumes of Wellington City Council (WCC) minutes, bound in leather and calf-skin, with gold-embossed titles on their spines. Here, in loving detail, first in copperplate and then, by the First World War, in purple typescript, lay the story of the Wellington municipality, from the Town Board of the 1860s to the present day. Reading some 65,000 pages of minutes might sound like another form of purgatory, but these debates and discussions were a mine of personalities and atmosphere. The minute books also led me on to other material: dusty memorandum and letter books, faded drainage reports dating from the 1920s, and rubbish furnace daybooks still smelling of smoke. Another vital source of information for the more recent era was the testimonies of mayors, officials and former councillors.

The book opens with Wellington's first 30 years of settlement, describing how the first wave of British migrants laid down the foundations for an instant township. Various layers of national, regional, and local administration were tried before a stable structure for a municipality was achieved. The second chapter covers the bumpy road to creating a working Borough Council. It also relates how, as thousands of settlers poured ashore in the 1870s and 1880s, Wellington's Maori inhabitants found themselves pushed to the margins. For half a century thereafter, the story of Maori in the city is one of absence.

Chapter 3 tells how continuing public health crises forced a niggardly municipality to pay for a sewerage scheme. The conservative Council faced further change in the 1890s, as local body franchise reform allowed non-ratepayers to vote. By 1900, as Chapter 4 relates, the municipality was in radical mode, running up debts to rebuild and extend the city. A socialist agenda led to public ownership of the electricity business, as Council-owned tramways turned wasteland into suburbs, setting the scene for amalgamations and a 'greater' Wellington. Chapter 5 charts the Council's central role in dealing with the 1918 influenza epidemic.

As the Depression of the 1930s intensified, the municipality used jobless people to rebuild the city, and nearly bankrupted itself running massive unemployment relief schemes. Return migration by Maori also began.

Chapter 6 explores the Council's role in running the 1940 Centennial Exhibition and helping the city adjust to war. The 1950s brought civic consensus, as an era of prosperity unfolded and Wellington settled into the role of sensible public service town. The 1960s, covered in Chapter 7, saw a municipality torn between the demands of the motor car and the constraints of a cramped and ageing city centre. The outcry caused by the routing of an urban motorway through an iconic graveyard forced the Council to become more transparent. The city was also forced to confront stagnant population growth and the mass relocation of businesses to Auckland. In the 1970s, an activist Council involved itself in large-scale social housing, while growing environmental awareness forced it to address the problem of sewage pollution.

Chapter 8 covers Wellington's emergence as a colourful and sophisticated metropolis. The economic revolution that followed the 1984 general election led to the loss of thousands of public service jobs and the biggest local government shake-up in a century. Meanwhile, a Maori resurgence showed itself in a public debate over a sewage treatment plant. The final chapter begins with the failed Sesquicentennial celebrations in 1990, and covers the wholesale restructuring brought about by local government reform. The story ends in 2005, on the cusp of civic reinvention. Buoyed by the economic impact and tourism potential of the *Lord of the Rings* film trilogy, the Council adopted a vision for the city as 'Creative Wellington — Innovation Capital'. As the exodus of corporate offices to Auckland continued, however, the municipality has since moved to shore up remaining businesses and to attract tourists, students and skilled migrants.

Commerce and economics are, of course, only one strand of the Wellington story. On Chaffers Street, between Te Papa and Oriental Parade, the Wellington City Council in late 2005 was uncovering the Waitangi Stream, once an important source of food and water for local Maori. By 1870, municipal engineers had forced all such harbour-side streams into underground brick culverts; and as the rivers vanished, so did their names. The Waitangi Stream is today the centre-piece of a new urban park: here it will surface to feed wetlands which will help remove pollutants, before flowing into the sea. Across the harbour, north of Queens Wharf, another lost stream, the Kumutoto, is resurfacing. As it heads into the future, Wellington City is reclaiming its past.

Wellington

circa 1840s

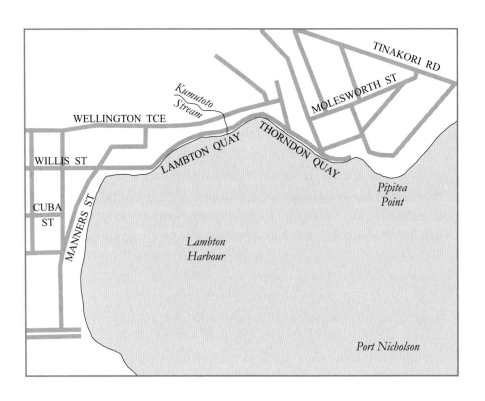

Colonial Settlement to Borough Capital

Chapter 1

1839–1870

When the tide was right and the sea was clear
you could see the lines go down
And each line had a bend in it that told
how time turns around.

Ian Wedde, 'Ballad for Worser Heberley'[1]

You can smell the sea from the old hospital steps between Moturoa and Moore Streets, on the lip of Thorndon Quay. But the winds that blow here, by the site of the old Pipitea Pa, are more likely to carry the whiff of petrol, liniment from a nearby gym, or a cigarette cupped in the hands of a passing student. Te Whanganui-a-Tara, the great harbour of Tara, lies half a reclaimed kilometre away, across the rusting railway tracks, out beyond the container terminal at Kings Wharf. Memories grow thick here on Pipitea Point, like the karaka trees that cling to the hillside.

Some 130 Te Atiawa people once occupied this corner of the harbour. Their cultivations covered several hectares, from today's Hawkestone Street to Tinakori Road, on the edge of the government quarter. Chief Te Ropiha Moturoa built his whare nearby, after migrating from Taranaki in 1827 with several of his brothers. Moturoa's potato patch stood by the present-day eastern boundary of Wellington Girls' College. The Pipitea Stream fed the crops; today its smelly waters are channelled through a culvert along Little Pipitea Street, past the AT&T Tower on Murphy Street. Down on Thorndon Quay, cars and buses speed along what was once a rocky beach. Across the road, in curious symbolism, stands an Early Settler furniture store, part of the Capital Gateway complex. Here the pa dwellers once beached their canoes, decorated with kokowhai and red ochre on ceremonial occasions. Pipi were harvested from the beds whose shells gave the pa its name.

In 1840, the lives of two European youths were spared here on Pipitea Point. It was a moment of humanity, of protection, typical of the small kindnesses that Maori and European often extended to each other in those early days of settlement. The details have faded, but the bones of the story remain. It began as a thousand British settlers from the first five sailing ships milled around on the sandy shores at Pito-one (Petone) early in the year, waiting to unpack the tin trunks filled with their possessions. The new arrivals argued about shifting their embryonic township, Britannia, to sheltered Pipitea, on the south-western side of the harbour. For Dr George Evans, a leading light in the New Zealand Company which developed the settlement, the latter location was 'a second Italy and a most picturesque spot'.[2] For the chiefs of Te Whanganui-a-Tara, there were strong motivations for selling land to the newcomers, namely the promise of trade and protection from their enemies. The people of Pipitea prepared a welcome. Their chiefs played a minor role in the land sales, but were nonetheless eager to host a powerful man such as Evans, believing that giving him protection and shelter would enhance their mana. Hence, in the late summer of 1840, a whare was built for Evans within the pa compound.

It was near this dwelling that the two youths nearly came to grief. One was a thirteen-year-old Londoner named Thomas (Tommy) Wilmor McKenzie; the other was Edwin Ticehurst, a carpenter. Like Dr Evans, both had just arrived on the 640-ton *Adelaide*. The ship's appearance at the harbour entrance on Sunday 7 March had coincided with a sudden eruption of wind, lightning, and rain.[3] This might have served as an omen of what was to come. The growing influence of missionaries kept local Maori from paying a visit to the *Adelaide* on the Sabbath. But the next day, three Te Atiawa canoes paddled out to the vessel as it lay at anchor off Matiu (Somes Island), and exchanged cheers with the immigrants. After a voyage lasting six months, young Tommy and his associates were straining to get ashore. As a local newspaper recalled many years later:

> A few days after their arrival, Mr Turnbull (a surveyor), Mr Ticehurst (who afterwards settled in the Wairarapa) and young McKenzie went ashore at Pipitea to pass the night in a hut — on a spot between St Paul's Pro-Cathedral and Molesworth Street — erected by the Maori chief Porutu, for Dr Evans. The surveyor, however, did not like the look of the Ngatiawa, and he went back to the ship, leaving Mr Ticehurst and the boy ashore. Mr Turnbull's fears

were justified. Porutu, attended by two of his wives and some thirty natives, disturbed the two pakeha [Europeans] when the latter were preparing their beds of native grass, and started to dance a haka.[4]

The youths were at risk of being summarily killed. For Maori, a newly constructed building was prohibited territory until the tapu had been lifted in an elaborate ceremony.[5] The story handed down is that Te Rira Porutu, a prominent chief with unlimited power of life and death over his subjects, worked himself into a fury:

> Old Rira questioned whether the coming of the white man was advantageous to the Maori at all. Rira watched the disrespectful hi jinks with troubled gaze. When the two boys were about to cross over the threshold, old Rira with anger mounting in his heart grabbed Orokiwi (Horokiwi), his greenstone mere, and made to strike them.[6]

Rira's daughter-in-law, Ruhia, broke the spell. In an act of Christian compassion, she threw her taniko-bordered cloak over the boys and pleaded for their lives. She was also exercising the prerogative of a woman of mana to save a person's life in this way, as noted by a European visitor in 1835:

> A chief's daughter has that superiority over her meaner subjects, that if there were vengeance sworn by any person against another, and they were in the act of killing him, by such female running and putting her mat over such person's head, it would at once prevent the murder taking place.[7]

Old Rira spared the boys. It was an event that changed the lives of everyone involved. Ruhia's action became a kind of teaching. She later persuaded Rira to convert to Christianity, and the family would share a pew at the nearby Anglican church of St Paul's, built in 1844. The McKenzie and Porutu families became lifelong friends, with Tommy regarded as Ruhia's adopted son, and brother to her own son, E Piti (Harry Pitt).[8] Tommy McKenzie went on to lead a long, active life as one of Wellington's leading citizens. At age fifteen, he participated in the first local body election, and later became such a prominent printer, newspaper proprietor, and editor that he was known as the 'father of the New Zealand press'.[9] Importantly for this story, McKenzie was elected in 1881 to the Wellington City Council, and unsuccessfully contested the mayoralty. He masterminded the city's Jubilee celebrations in 1890, and by 1904 had been living in the same Ghuznee

Ruhia Porutu in the cloak she threw over Tommy McKenzie and his friend after they strayed onto a tapu site at Pipitea pa in 1840. Her intervention saved the boys' lives, and McKenzie later became a prominent Wellingtonian and city councillor.

ATL, PAColl-5345-1

The boy saved from death at Pipitea, Tommy McKenzie, in later life.

WCA, 00154:0:27

Street house for 65 years.[10] McKenzie's deliverance at Pipitea was recalled at his funeral in March 1911, when Ruhia's cloak was laid over his coffin.

The tale of Ruhia and her cloak speaks to the potential for human co-operation in a raw colonial setting. Although Maori and the new settlers saw each other as encroaching on valuable land, both were capable of putting their differences aside. Sadly, the goodwill shown that day at Pipitea would fade as settlement gathered pace. Covetous settlers were soon eyeing the surrounding land, which they named Thorndon Flat after the Essex estate of one of the dignitaries in the New Zealand Company. The pa area became Belsize Point, recalling a prestigious north London address. In no time at all, the arrogant behaviour of the settlers matched that of any feudal lord in the Old Country. Surveyors ran their straight lines over Pipitea and occupied the pa at Te Aro, Kumutoto and Tiakiwai, trampling all over traditional burial grounds and extensive cultivations in the process. The inhabitants of Pipitea resisted by pulling up the surveyors' pegs, thus infuriating New Zealand Company officials and ensuring that surveying activity continued under arms. The Protector of Aborigines, George Clarke, later condemned the New Zealand Company as 'foolish, hot headed people enough who were bent on forcing on a conflict between the races'.[11]

Midway through 1840 the Company unveiled its town plan, which showed 1,100 one-acre residential sections surrounded by public streets and civic amenities. Thorndon Flat became the 'official' precinct. In a show of steel, the Company's armed survey team commandeered sections of Pipitea Pa. The cultivation areas immediately behind the pa were turned into military and native reserves. The police office, courts and government office were erected inside the pa compound. A gaol and stockade were placed next door. The colonial hospital — a two-storey brick building — was later built near the current site of Wellington Girls' College. But the Company's actions backfired. In 1842, the Governor appointed Commissioner William Spain to investigate settler activity in Whanganui-a-Tara, such as the commandeering of Pipitea and another harbour-side pa, Kumutoto. While Spain's controversial determination cut back the Company's land holdings, much of the surplus ended up being sold off to settlers anyway. In 1844, Moturoa and the Kumutoto chief Wi Tako accepted compensation of £400.

A well-intentioned scam

The stories have been buffed into myth. The long, arduous voyage from Britain, the tempest-tossed ships, the weary joy at making landfall: all serve to give New

Zealanders of European descent an inspiring vignette of the 1840 settler experience. We can see it in the monuments of nationhood: the concrete prow of the *Aurora*, the first arrival on 22 January 1840, juts out from the wall of the centennial memorial on the Petone waterfront, in the settlement first known as Britannia. Inside the building (now the Petone Settlers' Museum), a depiction of the vessel's landfall is framed in tall windows as a home-grown version of the *Mayflower* story: British pilgrims in quaint costumes splashing ashore to a bright new future, leaving behind the dark satanic mills of the Old Country. Those first settlers even drew on the legendary 1620 declaration of union and obedience that had helped pave the way for mass immigration to North America. The stories are perpetuated in stylised murals such as the one in Victoria Arcade, in the heart of central Wellington. In this 1960s cartoon, based on Charles Heaphy's 1841 painting, a bearded colonist in frock-coat and tall hat surveys an orderly vista of settlement: a shoreline dotted with tidy buildings, green rolling pastures, and neat roads. The harbour-side pa of Pipitea, Kumutoto and Te Aro are nowhere to be seen. He is clearly an acolyte of the New Zealand Company, that coterie of Englishmen, part utopians, part property developers, with elaborate theories of colonisation. Next to his bonneted wife stands a chiefly Maori, in feather cloak and clutching a taiaha, who looks out over the barques and waka plying the calm blue waters. He turns away, his expression hidden from our sight, surveying a landscape that is already slipping from his grasp.

According to Maori tradition, the legendary Kupe explored this area a millennium ago and left many place names. Whatonga, a chief of the Kurahaupo waka, also came south to the region known as Te Upoko-o-te-Ika ('the head of the fish'), and named the large harbour Whanganui-a-Tara, after his son, Tara. The boy is said to have been delighted with this grand expanse of deep water 'at the very nostrils of the island'.[12] The region came to be populated by people of Kurahaupo descent, including Ngai Tara, Ngati Rangitane, Mua-upoko, Ngati Apa and Ngati Tu-mata-kokiri.[13]

For centuries, Tara's tribe dominated the region. Hilltop pa appeared on strategic sites such as the Miramar peninsula, where the fortifications of Te Whetu Kairangi and Te Rangitatau Pa are located. Rangitatau was important in the seventeenth century when the Ngai Tara chief Tuteremoana lived there. His daughter Moeteao married a chief of the Ngati Ira tribe of Hawke's Bay, thus setting the scene for intermarriage between Ngai Tara and Ngati Ira. This led to their amalgamation, to the extent at least that most Ngai Tara became known as Ngati Ira. The people of Ngati Kahungunu, Ngai Tahu, and Ngati Mamoe later joined Ngati Ira. Each tribe occupied distinct areas around the harbour, before most of Ngai Tahu and Ngati Mamoe migrated to the South Island in the sixteenth or seventeenth century.[14]

From the 1820s, a series of migrations from the north gradually pushed out the traditional inhabitants. The migrants included Ngati Toa from Kawhia, Ngati Rangitahi from near Taumarunui, and several groups from Taranaki: Te Atiawa, Ngati Tama, Ngati Mutunga, Taranaki and Ngati Ruanui. By the late 1830s, Ngati Ira and related groups were largely driven out, while Ngati Mutunga had moved to the Chathams. By 1840, the groups holding customary rights to the area were Te Atiawa, Taranaki, Ngati Ruanui, Ngati Tama and Ngati Toa.[15] These were rights established through conquest, occupation, and use of resources.

Then everything changed. In September 1839, Colonel William Wakefield (called 'Wide-awake' by Maori, after the broad-brimmed hats fashionable at the time) sailed into Tara's great harbour aboard the New Zealand Company ship *Tory*, and persuaded sixteen Maori chiefs to sign a deed of purchase. In the space of one week he acquired close to 110,000 acres of land for sale to British settlers, many of whom were already heading for the Pacific. Local chiefs were famously divided. The most prominent dissenter, Waiwhetu chief Wiremu Puwhakaawe (Puakawa), asked his fellows: 'What will you say when many, many white men come here and drive you all away into the mountains?'[16] But the paramount chiefs Honiana Te Puni-Kokopu, Te Wharepouri, Te Kakapi-o-te-rangi and Wiremu Tako Ngatata (Wi Tako) were ready to take the blankets and guns on offer. For Te Puni, who lived in Pito-one, and his Nga-uranga-based cousin, Te Wharepouri, land sales carried a promise of safety from hostile tribes in the area.[17] Unfortunately, the chiefs didn't own all the land they were selling. The deed for the transaction, known as the Port Nicholson Purchase, was signed on board the *Tory*, and provided for one-tenth of the land purchased to be reserved for the signatory chiefs and their families. This provision gave rise to the expression 'tenths', to refer to the land thus reserved for Maori around Port Nicholson. Although misspelled, the names of Te Puni and Te Wharepouri live on in the Lower Hutt suburb of Epuni, and in Epuni and Waripori Streets in the Aro Valley and Berhampore respectively.

In his land dealings with Maori, 'Wide-awake' was engaging in an elaborate if well-intentioned scam. For Maori, land could never be legally owned in the way Europeans understood it, with its former occupants forever excluded. Neither could Maori conceive of the sheer volume of the planned European migration. Te Wharepouri was filled with fear and disbelief as wave upon wave of settlers came ashore and Puakawa's fateful prediction was realised.[18] Wakefield's inept interpreter, hotel-keeper Dicky Barrett, also felt that the whole process was farcical.

Between two worlds

Wiremu Tako Ngatata, known as Wi Tako, remained a powerful force in Wellington during the first decades of European settlement. Born in Taranaki of Te Atiawa and Ngati Ruanui descent, he came to the shores of Cook Strait during the migration of 1832. Seven years later, this 'handsome young chief' participated in the controversial land sales to the New Zealand Company.[19]

By the early 1840s, Wi Tako was leader of the 50 people living in the large Kumutoto Pa, close to the present-day intersection of Woodward Street and Lambton Quay. He succeeded Honiana Te Puni as the paramount chief of Te Atiawa. The kainga (village), beside the main street of the new colonial town, became increasingly surrounded as the settlers' demand for land grew. After the 1848 earthquake damaged his brick house, Wi Tako moved to Ngauranga.[20] In the late 1840s he married Mere (or Mereana) Ngamai. After her death in 1852, he wed her sister, also called Mere. From this second marriage came Hohipine (Josephine), also known as Te Amo, who married Daniel Kiri Love. The couple were the founders of the Love dynasty.

Wi Tako grew resentful of the settlers' attitudes towards Maori, stating that 'the Europeans say we are only like dogs'.[21] He was unfairly accused of conspiring to attack the colonial township, after giving evidence to a hearing that later compensated the Kumutoto people for their lost land. Nonetheless, he continued to assist colonial governments and officials, drawing accusations from a rival chief during the land wars of the 1860s that he was more loyal to Queen Victoria than he was to the Maori King. He converted to Roman Catholicism around this time.

In 1872 Wi Tako was appointed to the Legislative Council. On his death in 1887 he was accorded a state funeral, attended by between 4,000 and 5,000 people.

Wiremu Tako Ngatata, photographed in the 1870s.

ATL, Railways Collection, G-3876-1/1

British settlers, too, felt cheated. Steep hills and wet, tangled bush were no substitute for the rolling pastureland promised in the Company's handbills. Instead of enjoying a warm Mediterranean climate, they unpacked their possessions in a stiff southerly breeze. One newcomer recalled the moment when the ship entered the harbour: 'the passengers were all on deck straining their eyes … disappointment was visible on the countenance of everyone'.[22] Many had sold up everything they owned to fund their voyage. On the tin trunks of those first thousand arrivals were names such as Majoribanks, Molesworth, Dorset, Fitzherbert, Woodward and Riddiford — cabin passengers whose names stand out like veins on a contemporary map of Wellington. Majoribanks wrote of being cast upon 'a barren, dreary and inhospitable shore'.[23]

Less celebrated were the reactions of the assisted labourers and their families who had spent the long voyage in often wretched conditions in steerage, below deck. Male labourers, promised a pound a week and rations, made up close to a third of the first arrivals. Many were farm workers with geographical affiliations to a cabin passenger. The single women tended to be domestic servants or seamstresses. Most settlers hailed from regions such as Cornwall and Kent, with one shipload coming from Glasgow. To qualify for free passage, they faced strict age limits — 40 years for married men, and 20 years for single people of both sexes. It was a youthful cargo: passenger lists show that the oldest settler was barely fifty.

A radical family

Pressure for the private colonisation of New Zealand had mounted early in the nineteenth century. Its chief proponent, the London-based New Zealand Colonisation Company, sent ships to investigate likely sites for settlement. In the early 1830s, Edward Gibbon Wakefield decided to make colonisation, particularly to New Zealand, his life's work. From a family with a radical streak, Edward shaped his theories while in prison for abducting — and later marrying — a fifteen-year-old girl. His younger brother William was also gaoled for his part in the abduction plot. The crime forced Edward to keep a low profile and to delegate to William. His recipe for colonisation involved buying up cheap land from indigenous owners, reselling it to wealthy settlers for a high price, and using the profit to fund the passages of handpicked workers who were keen to emigrate. A replica of a British farm town would be created, run by gentleman farmers, with labourers doing the work.

Town planning by candlelight

The reputation of the new settlement of Britannia was sullied when the British authorities learned of the formation of a 'council of colonists', complete with its own constitution and with William Wakefield as president. Constituted as the first municipal entity in the Colony, its self-appointed councillors voted themselves power to appoint Dr George Evans as 'umpire' (magistrate), to hold annual elections, to conduct law-making, and to levy rates and duties. Obtaining the blessing of local Maori for this arrangement was also judged important, at least initially. It was an issue that dominated the agenda of the council's first meeting, which took place on 2 March 1840 'in a wooden frame house belonging to Captain William Mein Smith, situated in the sand dunes about half a mile east of the Pito-one pa'.[24]

The council had been hatched on the poop deck of the *Adelaide*, as the ship readied to leave England. Members had mulled over how best to rule a town in a far-flung territory seemingly beyond the reach of British law. They looked to Britain's Municipal Corporations Act 1835, which had introduced greater democracy and accountability at local government level. Victorian ideals such as financial prudence and self-help also shaped the council's thinking. A 'law and order charter' was placed on the capstans of the first three ships, and all the emigrants endorsed the idea of a fifteen-man council. Council members knew that formal British political control was coming. Yet, in setting up this raw form of local government, the settlers were seeking to 'civilise' the non-settler population, both indigenous and European. Wakefield's nephew, Edward Jerningham, wrote of the disorderly conduct of the ragtag of Europeans already resident in the area:

> One, named Coghlan, had established a grog-shop half-way along the [Petone] beach, where a disorderly assemblage of sailors, stray whalers, and other bad characters from the different stations had become accustomed to assemble, and caused some annoyance to the quiet settlers by their drunkenness and wild orgies.[25]

He went on to describe how order was brought to the beachfront settlement:

> Measures were put in readiness for all sorts of public works; the appointment of officers, the regulation of finances, and the selection of sites for a powder-magazine, infirmary, and other public institutions, were considered; and the note of organization and arrangement sounded busily in all quarters.[26]

By mid April 1840, paid constables and their assistants had begun patrolling at Petone and Thorndon, presumably putting a stop to the grog-fuelled orgies. The council even called up a militia to deal with growing Maori resistance to the surveying activity at Pipitea and elsewhere. On 30 May, it was announced that all men aged between sixteen and 60 were to be ready for mustering and drill. One colonist wrote that the fledgling council 'as might be expected is extremely arbitrary and tyrannical — so much so that I find since my arrival here that the government is determined to put them down by force'.[27]

The rebel council found itself in hot water. From Waitangi, Lieutenant-Governor Hobson issued proclamations declaring British sovereignty over New Zealand, a move that gave him authority over the wayward settlers. Talking of treason, Hobson dispatched a ship to enter Wellington Harbour and show its guns. The council vanished in a flurry of white flags. Hobson had over-reacted, but Britannia knew it was time to submit, at least publicly. On 1 July 1840, councillors gathered at the Exchange building above Te Aro beach, where they agreed to offer a grovelling apology. Concerned that Hobson's anger would taint his own recent land purchase, Wakefield argued that his rebel council had upheld 'the peace and order of the settlement of 1,500 English people and 400 untutored natives'.[28]

Work began on carving up the land. Months behind schedule, New Zealand Company surveyor William Mein Smith prepared a plan of the settlement, drawn up by candlelight in a leaky whare. Impatient settlers clamoured for a glimpse. At its heart was a standardised grid with long flanks (evident today on The Terrace and, at right angles, from Vivian to Pirie Streets). Wakefield's so-called 'package' model of colonisation gave each land-owner a mix of a numbered town acre and 100 country acres. As directed, Smith separated the two areas with a long green belt, 'which you will declare that the Company intends to be public property, on condition that no buildings ever be erected on it'.[29]

The town-acre lottery began at the end of July, in a prefabricated schoolroom that later became Dicky Barrett's famous hotel. In the course of a tumultuous fortnight Smith personally supervised the draw, with 50 town sections being allocated each day. He set aside 'ample' public land, an acre for a Company immigration building, and native reserves based on 100 one-acre sections.[30]

Settlers promptly moved onto their allocated lands, summarily evicting the inhabitants of Pipitea and Kumutoto Pa from their homes and cultivations in the process. With nowhere else to go, Maori moved onto vacant town acres, many of which had absentee owners. The Company's energies then turned to allocating the country sections — the second part of the settlers' entitlement. Wakefield's vision of a grain-based economy flourishing on rolling arable land jarred with the reality of the bush-choked hills between Pencarrow and Porirua. The shortage of usable land led the Company to start a subsidiary settlement up the west coast at Wanganui — initially dubbed Petre. Wakefield, meanwhile, travelled to the Bay of Islands and asked Hobson to shift the capital to Thorndon. The Lieutenant-Governor disagreed, preferring Auckland's 'more genial climate and a more productive soil'.[31]

The Port Nicholson land purchase was approved, subject to an investigation that sounded like a formality. The New South Wales Governor, Sir George Gipps, who was then Hobson's superior, also agreed to let Wellington be governed in the spirit of Britain's Municipal Corporations Act. A proposed municipal charter offered 'the inestimable advantage of local self-government in all matters of a strictly local nature'.[32] Granting the settlers self-government would not only help Victorian values take root in the Colony, but also foster political apprenticeships *and f*ree up the Governor to get on with national issues. The Colonial Secretary spelled this out in a letter to Hobson in late 1840:

> Promise as far as possible the establishment of municipal and district governments for the conduct of all local affairs such as drainages, bye roads, police, the creating and repair of local prisons, court houses and the like, independently of the excellent uses of such institutions … It is of the utmost importance to withdraw from the Governor the care of these innumerable local petty details and to relieve the public treasury from the wasteful expenditure in which it must be involved so long as it is hindered with the double charge of collecting local assessments and of effecting local works.[33]

On 5 October in that landmark year, 1840, carpenter/publican William Couper opened the Thistle Hotel on Mulgrave Street. Not much more than a two-roomed cottage, it became a popular watering-hole in a township that, like many others, boasted twice as many pubs as churches, where a good fire, a hot joint of beef, and a glass of rum were always on hand. The Thistle soon joined the popular Barrett's Hotel as a favoured location for political meetings. When the Thistle opened, the settlement was still called Britannia. Seven weeks later Britannia was renamed Wellington, in promised recognition of the Duke of Wellington — British war hero, politician, and Wakefield's ally.

Mr Pickwick's council

By the summer of 1841, Wellington was mostly a collection of beachfront dwellings: several hundred raupo-thatched whare and prefabricated colonial cottages. Public buildings and facilities were sparse, the courts and the all-important port poorly resourced. In July 1841 Sam Revans, editor of the Wellington-based *New Zealand Gazette* and mouthpiece for the New Zealand Company, called on the townspeople to get a grip on local affairs:

> Work on the corporation question. It is beyond all things important to us — with it we shall make rapid progress. We shall be in the condition of a New York township. Without it we shall be … unable to act for ourselves, and be neglected by those who have the power to act for us.[34]

This view of Te Aro pa in the early 1840s, sketched in pencil by Edmund Norman, shows a carved canoe prow in the foreground and the masts of British ships in the harbour beyond.

ATL, A-049-001

The energetic Revans became Wellington's first 'booster' or promoter. His busy print-shop operated from a site beside Te Aro Pa, at the foot of Taranaki Street;[35] among his staff of printers and compositors was the young apprentice, Tommy McKenzie.

In 1841 New Zealand was declared a Crown Colony in its own right, independent of New South Wales, with Hobson as Governor. Executive and legislative councils were duly appointed in Auckland. Members of Wakefield's 'rebel' council now

became justices of the peace on the Wellington bench, the nucleus of an elite group that would go on to dominate regional politics. Hobson's name, however, continued to be mud in Wellington. At a public meeting in Barrett's Hotel on 29 July 1841, settlers accused him of leaving them defenceless. Local government came to be seen as a way to keep a remote and fickle colonial authority at arm's length.

Work began on drafting the promised ordinance for local government, its wording hammered out at a series of pub meetings attended by settlers in their hundreds. Labourer and capitalist worked together: 'There is no distinction of ranks here. All are seen carrying wood, trunks, boxes, driving pigs and in short doing many things that they would not do at home. A new colony is a strange place.'[36] In the final wording of the draft ordinance, the working men of the town demanded as much say as the so-called colonists. Hobson received the document when he visited Wellington in August 1841, and it passed into law the following year. Without fanfare, local government in New Zealand was born, making citizens active participants in local democracy and public affairs.

At the end of May 1842, Wellington (the only settlement with the requisite population of more than 2,000) was declared the Colony's first incorporated borough. An elected Mayor and eleven-member Council were charged with administering public lands within the town's boundaries. The municipality had powers to make bylaws, carry out public works, raise loans and levy property taxes (rates) on all proprietors and occupiers. Any adult male could vote, as long as he paid the £1 registration fee (more than $80 in today's terms), which excluded many potential voters.

There was a flurry of nominations for election to the new Council. During February 1842, meetings were held at public houses to determine election 'tickets' (lists of candidates) representing the interests of gentry and of working men. Each camp endorsed eighteen candidates, with seven names appearing on both lists.[37] Citizens registered on the so-called Burgess Roll, and the election was set for 3 October. At the time, the population was hovering around the 3,500 mark, with about 900 adult males eligible to vote. Tommy McKenzie, then barely fifteen, was an 'enthusiastic participant' in the elections on behalf of working men.[38] The campaign brought a dash of much needed colour to the settlement:

> Placards, advertisements, electioneering cards and squibs, were in as great profusion as on the occasion of a contested election for a borough in England. On the day of poll, flags and a band of music paraded the beach

with some of the popular candidates; distinctive cockades were worn; and the straw hut inside the *pa*, generally used as a police-office, but now as the booth of the returning officer, was surrounded by agents of both parties, eager to force cards with their own list into the hands of each voter as he arrived. All the usual tricks and intrigues were resorted to; and bribery, in the shape of glasses of grog, was largely at work. But notwithstanding many such tricks, the 'gentry' secured a very good Council.[39]

Each elector could vote for up to eighteen candidates, with the top twelve becoming aldermen, and a reserve list established. George Hunter topped the poll with 273 votes and automatically became Mayor. The Municipal Council of the Borough of Wellington was made up of five candidates who appeared on both lists, three others from each list, and one independent. Some of them — Hanson, Daniell, Johnson, Guyton, Wallace — are immortalised in the names of city streets and landmarks. Representing the non-gentry were auctioneer and 'man of the people' Johnny Wade (founder of Wadestown) and gregarious ex-New South Wales publican Robert Jenkins. The aldermen's first public act was to attend an Anglican church service. In their first month they met seven times, gathering at 10 a.m. in a room at the busy Exchange building above Te Aro beach, in the emerging commercial quarter. Funds were short: the entire Council budget of £370 12s 6d came from voters' registration fees. Close to a third of the budget went on road and street repairs, while almost another third was swallowed up by the salaries of officials.

Hunter got busy. Committees were set up to run and regulate the harbour, frame by-laws for slaughterhouses, and restrict the growing number of dogs. But procedural and financial questions slowed progress. Uncertainty grew around the date of future borough elections and the incumbency of aldermen. Problems also emerged with striking a rate, largely because of delays in property valuation and continuing questions about the Council's legal status. During an energetic sixteen months, Hunter paid special attention to the Town Belt. His Council also rented the water frontages to proprietors of private wharves, set up a market in beachfront Manners Street, and set aside land for a Botanic Garden. Prison labour was used to carry out public works, with swampy Manners Street being drained and bridges built for pedestrians.

The pa at Pipitea and Te Aro were targeted. Hunter's one and only ordinance involved a tax of £20 (equivalent to a prohibitive $2,000 in today's money) to be imposed on beachfront shacks thatched with raupo. This followed a major fire along the Lambton Quay waterfront on 9 November 1842 which consumed more than

40 dwellings, half of which were thatched. Alderman Fitzherbert later moved 'that fires, candles, and all lights should be extinguished in raupo houses immediately after sunset on pain of a heavy fine for neglecting to do so'.[40] The Raupo Houses Ordinance also gave Hunter an excuse to evict Maori from residential pa.[41]

By mid 1843, events across Cook Strait caused the Council to shift its attention to military matters. The township was rattled by a skirmish at Wairau between settlers and Maori which ended in a number of fatalities, including William Wakefield's brother, Arthur. A 400-strong militia was formed, and the defence of the

The Mayor with the beaming eyes

At 52, George Hunter was probably the oldest of the youthful crop of settlers coming ashore in the first months of settlement. He and his wife and their ten children lived on Tinakori Road, on one of three town acres where Premier House was later built. Before becoming the Colony's first mayor, Hunter operated a general merchant and shipping business with Kenneth Bethune.

On the voyage out, Hunter had met a carpenter named Samuel Parnell who was keen to escape oppressive working conditions in England. When he asked Parnell to build a storehouse, the carpenter made his celebrated assertion that he would not work for more than eight hours a day. Hunter scoffed, but with only three carpenters in town, he later agreed.[42] The eight-hour working day, born in

George Hunter, first mayor of the Wellington Borough Council, in his younger days.

WCA, 00510:0:1

Wellington, was later exported around the world, and is celebrated every year on Labour Day.

Hunter is remembered as 'painstaking, thorough, and sagacious'.[43] On his election in 1842, a new arrival named Mary Swainson, aged sixteen, recorded that his 'bald head, and circular spectacles' and 'beaming eyes' made him perfect for the role: 'Mr Hunter is … the fittest person in point of appearance — he exactly resembles Mr Pickwick.'[44]

Her reference to the popular 1837 novel by Charles Dickens was fitting: Hunter was a founding member of the Pickwick Club, whose gentlemanly members gathered in the Commercial Hotel on Willis Street in the early 1840s. Though mainly social, the club also tried, unsuccessfully, to set up the town's first library and museum.

borough became a Council priority. On 19 July, during one of the many meetings to express sympathy for the victims, Mayor Hunter caught a chill and a few days later died at his Willis Street home. By then interest in local politics had waned, especially as the British government had discovered problems with the law under which the borough was established. Hunter's replacement was fellow merchant William Guyton, a man so briefly in the job that for years he was the only Mayor of Wellington for whom no portrait was available.[45] Guyton is best remembered for hosting a lavish banquet at Barrett's Hotel, soon after attaining office:

> The largest dinner party since settlement began was held for Mayor Guyton.
> By chance, the occasion happened to coincide with the demise of the mayoral
> office and of the corporation; within days notification arrived from London
> of the disallowance of the municipal corporations. Eighty unsuspecting
> people attended and again the dinner and the wines were excellent.[46]

A toast to an absent friend

In 1849 local Maori leaders were feted at a banquet at the Pipitea Street
hospital to celebrate the arrival of a framed portrait of Queen Victoria.

ATL, PUBL-0033-1850-084

Provincial fiefdoms

The demise of the municipality in 1843 put an end to any form of government that was truly 'local'. For the next twenty years, Wellington would be represented by national and later provincial authorities with fickle agendas, near-empty coffers, and interests beyond the township. To secure essential services and amenities — drains, sewers, drinking water, and refuse collection — its citizens, like those of other isolated colonial settlements, would be forced to improvise. Initially, the Auckland-based legislative and executive councils looked after Wellington's interests, but the national authorities were preoccupied with more pressing matters. In the meantime, government-appointed resident magistrates authorised local constables to maintain public order, and helped to organise essential street works.

Getting around the township remained difficult. Manners Street was a continuation of the Te Aro swamp, spanned by small bridges. Lambton Quay was

---

In April 1849, Queen Victoria made her symbolic debut in Wellington, as her framed portrait, beneath a 'splendid crown' of dahlias, was presented to the colonial hospital then located on Pipitea Street. The mezzotint engraving of the British monarch, resplendent in her robes of state, was a gift from the Colonial Secretary, Earl Grey, in recognition of the medical work of the hospital superintendent, Dr John Fitzgerald. As the *Illustrated London News* reported:

Underneath were two splendid native war spears, forming with the floor, a triangle, from the apex of which a magnificent 'mere pounamu', or greenstone club, was suspended; these, being emblems of New Zealand chieftainship were intended to represent the cessation of sovereignty to her Majesty the Queen. On each side of the picture were two meres (greenstone clubs) intended to represent their support of Her Majesty's Government. On

either side of the picture, also, but at some distance were two illuminated stars which had a most brilliant effect.[47]

After the function a lavish banquet was attended by a number of prominent Maori chiefs in European dress, including Moturoa and Porutu from nearby Pipitea Pa, Wi Tako from Kumutoto, Te Puni from Petone, and Otaki visitor Te Rauparaha.[48] Prominent legal and political representatives of the European settlers also attended, along with a crowd of spectators. Dr Fitzgerald led a series of toasts to Her Majesty, one of which asked that 'the White Man and the Maori … may continue to live together peaceably'. Te Puni, however, had the last word. Rising to his feet, he said: 'Listen to me; let us give our allegiance to the Queen; let us join with Earl Grey, with the Governor, with the white people. This is all I have to say.'[49]

little more than a muddy track, bisected by a bridge at Woodward Street where the Kumutoto stream flowed down the hill. The *Gazette* reported in 1845 that 'Beach Road between Kumutoto and Clay Point is in a vile state and has been almost impassable since the last rains'.[50] Yet many settler children relished the wildness and strangeness of their new environment. One later recalled it as 'a Robinson Crusoe kind of world':

> The freedom of the settlement was consoling; the fine white sandy beach, from Pipitea to Oriental Bay, was a precious possession, and as yet there were few bathing restrictions and fewer vigilant policemen bent on curtailing the enjoyment of young Wellington. Then besides sea-fishing there were numerous streams, with the Te Aro Swamp available where inungas and eels could with little skill and with very homely fishing outfit, be easily captured.[51]

By the late 1840s population growth had stalled, and economic activity was centred on whaling and flax. Many entrepreneurs had departed. Not enough grain was grown to feed the settlers, let alone export.[52] Wellington's remaining elite campaigned for an elected national legislature, with the debate played out in a vigorous local press. In 1845, at the age of eighteen, Tommy McKenzie and some fellow printers founded the Wellington *Independent,* a daily paper which advocated self-government for the township. The so-called constitutionalists battled on. In 1846, Britain produced a draft constitution, based on a series of provincial governments and municipal corporations, beneath a General Assembly — all to serve a total settler population of less than 13,000. The newly arrived Governor, George Grey, shelved the proposal on the grounds that it would disadvantage Maori, and once again the push for self-government stalled.

Few in the settlement shared Grey's concern for the rights of Maori. Lieutenant-Colonel William Anson McCleverty was appointed to obtain deeds from the tribes concerned, exchanging their settlements and cultivations around the harbour for land elsewhere. The McCleverty awards of 1847 were the final allocation of lands for Maori in the Wellington area. Pa such as Te Aro, Pipitea and Kaiwharawhara became less desirable as their food-growing areas were replaced by more remote land, mostly outside Wellington. With the threat of European settlers also encroaching on ancestral lands in Taranaki, return migrations took place. About 600 Te Atiawa went back to Taranaki in 1848; more followed as a consequence of the land wars in the province in the 1860s. Antipathy towards the remaining inhabitants of inner-city pa continued, with the authorities coming under pressure to evict them. In 1848, the *Independent* captured the settlers' feelings:

> Although these filthy kennels may not endanger the health by their noxious vapours or materially obstruct the promenaders, there is a possibility of being devoured by dogs … numbers can testify to the annoyance received on passing the pa's at both Pipitea and Te Aro.[53]

In 1853, the long-promised Constitution Act helped to set up a national parliament, buttressed by six provincial kingdoms representing the far-flung regions and the towns within them. These mini parliaments looked to the capital, Auckland, for much of their livelihood, with initiatives that fostered agricultural exports more likely to win support — and funding. Like the other provinces, Wellington was governed by a Superintendent, his bailiwick embracing land legislation, surveys, public works, harbours, hospitals, and education. Local services and amenities were not a priority: clean water and sanitation were shelved for the time being as expensive luxuries. Instead, politicians eyed Wellington's harbour as an outlet for wool and other agricultural exports. Reclamations were planned, and in 1862 an expensive deep-water facility was built at the Public Wharf (later renamed Queen's Wharf by Tommy McKenzie).[54] Bickering among regional politicians and growing conflict with Maori over land sapped the Provincial Council's energies — and its limited coffers.

The Wellington Provincial Council met in the government domain on Thorndon Hill. Parochial concerns, such as how best to maintain the township's muddy bullock tracks, vied with the bigger issues of economic development. Grants-in-aid, based on the Victorian ethic of self-help, emerged as the standard model for municipal works such as road-building. The residents of Abel Smith Street, for example, would raise half the cash for metalling their road, with the Superintendent paying the rest. The system necessitated a committee of volunteers going door-to-door asking for contributions, then calling for tenders. These neighbourhood committees can be seen as the forerunners of Progressive Associations.[55] Without a working municipal authority, however, their achievements were limited. The requirement for both energy and hard cash also meant that the less prosperous parts of town missed out. And even the wealthiest streets had householders who refused to contribute. Nonetheless, the absence of administrative costs and the use of prison labour made grants-in-aid a cheap and practical option during the 1850s.

The local economy remained unstable. Growth was evident, especially around the business precinct of Te Aro. In 1849, Mary Taylor founded a women's clothing and drapery shop at the intersection of Dixon and Cuba Streets, helped by brother Waring. She spent long days in the shop with her cousin Ellen: '[we] don't give over working till bedtime and take a new number of D. [David] Copperfield to bed with us and drop asleep on the second page.'[56] As a tough-minded single woman, she stood out in the Wellington of the early 1850s, and could be scathing about settler society in letters to her famous friend Charlotte Brontë: 'There is no one worth mentioning particularly. The women are all ignorant and narrow and the men selfish. They are of a decent honest kind and some intelligent and able.'[57]

The major earthquakes of 1848 and 1855 only briefly dented the confidence of a township already used to adversity. Early in 1840, new arrivals at Petone had watched fourteen cottages burn in 20 minutes, followed at dawn by an earthquake, and major flooding days later. The 1848 quake shook the townspeople awake and rumbled on for eight long days, sparking a legend that Mt Victoria was dancing. Three people died, and buildings made of brick and stone were destroyed. Mary Taylor managed to see the positive side: 'We have had occurrences here … lots of earthquakes … till they are quite commonplace. Two-fifths if not half of the houses in Wellington were shaken down by the [1848] earthquake and the town is vastly improved as a consequence.'[58]

A township rebuilt in timber was better prepared for the quake that struck in 1855, with a force equal to 8.2 on the modern Richter scale. Merchant John Plimmer recalled three distinct quakes, linked by a continuous quivering — the first on the Monday, another on the Tuesday, and then, just as he stood on a ladder helping to repair a neighbour's shop:

> I had hard work to regain a firm footing on the ladder, and I then saw that any attempt to descend meant certain death … I stood for a little while, and, looking round, saw that almost all the chimneys were down. The new Wesleyan chapel, which was in Manners Street, was very much damaged. The gabled end had fallen, and I saw a man in the ceiling joist, close under the roof. The most curious thing was the way in which the bog was moving. It was rolling like a heavy sea, but looking more like a field of corn in a high wind.[59]

The inhabitants of Te Aro Pa were particularly affected by the earthquake. The swamp encircling the pa was drained, removing a traditional food source and thus hastening their departure. Settlers' plans to construct a canal system leading to the Basin Reserve were dashed as the great swamp extending to Constable Street in Newtown dried up. The eastern side of the harbour was raised by nearly seven feet, with a five foot uplift at Oriental Bay. The shallows created across the harbour hastened the need for a deep-water wharf. But Wellington's most prized commodity — flat land — emerged. Some saw this as propitious. Shore platforms now encircled the harbour, sketching out the shape of future reclamations and creating natural routes for road and rail.

A new town board in a new capital

In 1862, Wellington's over-burdened Provincial Superintendent handed responsibility for basic civic services and amenities to a small board of works. Members introduced legislation to give the township the status of a city corporation, but the citizenry judged a town board more suitable for their current needs. This modest

Home of the brave

It was to be the site of an inner-city Venice, where horse-drawn barges transported goods to busy canal-side warehouses patronised by the people of Newtown. The great earthquake of 1855, however, raised the Basin Lake at the end of Kent and Cambridge Terrace by nearly six feet, and prisoners were soon set to work turning it into a public park.

At the end of 1866, the new Basin Reserve was formally enshrined as the home of Wellington cricket, although the first match was still a year away. In 1873, the Basin was vested in the City Council for public use; grass seed was sown, and an open drain running across the ground was filled in.

Other sports queued up to play here. At an 1876 rugby match, fans watched the Wellington team, in its new uniform of black and yellow, playing a side of visiting sailors. The *Evening Post* reporter considered that the team colours 'had an exceedingly comical effect, looking like so many magnified wasp bodies'.[60] One Friday night in June 1879, the Basin hosted a legendary night-time soccer match, at which the 'government electrician' demonstrated electric lighting for the first time to a crowd of 8,000. Glimpses of play were possible, before a power failure ended the match.

The Basin Reserve went on to host public events of all kinds, including the 1890 Jubilee celebrations, hot-air balloon landings, and a 1912 rally at which 3,000 supporters of striking Council tramway workers heard calls for a General Strike. The inaugural Carols by Candlelight concert was held there in 1949.[61]

Yet the Basin was always identified with cricket, with the first international test match being played there in 1930. Cricket tests and one-day internationals became regular fixtures until 1999, when the latter were moved to the larger WestpacTrust Stadium on the waterfront.

Timber town: The Terrace and Tinakori Hill from the back of the Oddfellows' Hall. Built on reclaimed land on the corner of Grey Street and Lambton Quay, this grand building hosted the first meetings of the Wellington Town Board.

ATL, F-31734-1/2

form of city governance did, however, mark an important separation from the 'mother' province. The two (later three) commissioners elected to represent each of the villages or wards of Lambton, Te Aro and Thorndon had much to catch up on after 'a blank of 20 years … during which time the affairs of the town were looked after, or neglected, by the Provincial Government'.[62]

The Wellington Town Board Act 1862 gave the six (later nine) commissioners the power to levy rates, to create streets and footpaths, and to undertake drainage and other public works, including fire protection. Another key brief was to survey the Town Belt and divide it into lots for leasing. A franchise based on the amount of property owned excluded most of Wellington's citizens — a far cry from the universal male suffrage that applied (albeit only to Europeans) at the 1842 Council election. This restriction would remain in force for close to 40 years. It meant that, from a population of 4,200 in 1862, barely 200 ratepayers were eligible to elect their representatives, with the wealthiest property-owners having four votes. The Act provided for an annual meeting of ratepayers at which they levied their own rate, provided it was less than two pence in the pound. The Town Board's income was supplemented through the grants-in-aid system and the occasional loan from the province.

Among the commissioners elected to the Board, notables such as Plimmer, Borlase, Pharazyn, Dransfield, Fisher, Buckley, Hunter, Mantell and Pearce would come and go. These busy men of independent means were the core of a mobile elite that revolved through national, provincial, and local politics. Left-wingers, such as the 'armed chartist' Robert Carpenter, occasionally joined this select club, but were in a minority. [63] Commissioners faced a thankless task, as the board increasingly found itself lacking the resources to meet ratepayers' demands and expectations.

During this period, Wellington consolidated its position as a central hub, strategically located between the seat of government in Auckland and the southern centres of Christchurch and Dunedin, which began to develop after 1848. The *Independent* coined the term 'Empire City' after Wellington secured the lucrative Panama mail and passenger service in 1866. The electric telegraph and the coach were connecting up the far-flung parts of the Colony. The discovery of gold at Tuapeka in 1861 saw Dunedin's population grow by 17,000 in a year. By 1863, Port Chalmers was the Colony's busiest port, and in 1865 Dunedin was elevated to the status of a city corporation. Wellington-based steamships left for Otago with full cabins, prompting Superintendent Isaac Featherston to crow: 'I doubt whether any province is reaping such a rich harvest from the Otago gold fields as this.'[64]

The other provinces worked hard to match Otago, their officials eager to gain a slice of the action. In Wellington, Featherston offered a reward of £1,000 to anyone who found a payable goldfield, and employed a geologist to cover the region. After minuscule quantities of gold turned up at Terawhiti, on the south-west tip of the North Island, Wellington's quartz rocks were compared to those found in Australian fields such as Bendigo. The town's hopes of joining 'the golden frontier' got off to a promising start after pay dirt was struck in, of all places, Lambton Quay. In March 1862 a man digging a well in the back yard of chemist Charles Barraud spotted the distinctive shine and, using a bucket, washed eight grains of gold. Barraud displayed them in his shop window, near present-day Panama Street, with a label: 'A specimen of gold obtained on the premises'. The *Independent* hailed this as 'another proof that gold exists in the neighbourhood of Wellington'.[65] Naturally, the news caused great excitement.

The Lambton Quay discovery was literally a flash in the pan, like most of the gold found in the region. The South Kaiwharawhara Stream, for example, was briefly invaded after the wife of a local landowner found gold in the gizzard of a duck she was preparing for dinner. Seat of government status, on the other hand, represented a genuine mother lode. In July 1865 one local newspaper described the decision to move the capital to Wellington as 'the tide which leads

Robert Carpenter, Molesworth Street bookseller, bookbinder, left-wing radical and village politician.

ATL, F-91021-1/2

onto fortune'.[66] Many Wellington citizens saw the move as their birthright, after Wakefield's assurances. In 1858 Featherston had a sprawling Gothic structure built on Thorndon Hill, bounded by Molesworth, Bowen, Sydney and Museum Streets, to house the provincial government. With chambers large enough to accommodate the Legislative Council and House of Representatives, it served as a costly enticement for a General Assembly divided on where to settle.

When Wellington won the right to host the 1862 session of Parliament, the government came south. In the process, boxes of records — and very nearly the entire Cabinet and its officials — vanished when the *White Swan* was wrecked on the Wairarapa coast. Despite the setback, Parliament opened on 14 July, with ranks of soldiers lining Molesworth Street and a band playing to greet Governor Grey. The town celebrated the visit with a glittering General Assembly ball, attended by the elite. Wellington worked hard to keep its political guests. In debates on the permanent location of the capital, members representing the Cook Strait region outmanoeuvred their opponents. Picton, Nelson and Wellington became the three options, as rivalry between Auckland and Wellington intensified. The final decision was assigned to a tribunal of Australians, who in 1864 chose Wellington.

The news was greeted with delight in the town's commercial circles, amid hopes that the deep pockets of central government would shore up the local economy. Moves were made to improve the appearance of Thorndon. In March 1865, town commissioners met with senior civil servants to discuss such matters as widening the streets around the government domain.[67] Concern was expressed about the new capital's primitive water and sewerage systems. The Town Board responded that without a corporation's powers to raise loans, little could be done. Weeks before the first session of Parliament in July, the domain overseer complained to the Board about sewage washing in from surrounding streets.[68] Before long, Wellington was routinely damned as the dirtiest town in the Colony.

The Bannister slide

From its beginnings the Town Board was hobbled by tough economic times. When 199 Wellington ratepayers met late in 1863, they levied themselves a meagre farthing in the pound. The Board's first meeting was held on 15 September in Lambton Quay at the private offices of William Allen, later its chairman. The first year was devoted to overdue works: repairing streets, building and clearing wooden drains, and issuing permits for erecting verandas and for butchering animals within town limits. Gangs of prisoners from Wellington Gaol initially

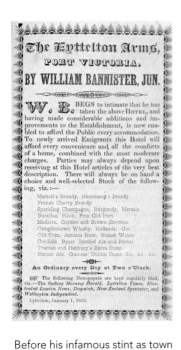

Before his infamous stint as town clerk with the Wellington Town Board, William Bannister Jr roamed the colony as a jobbing draughtsman, artist and hotelier. As this 1852 advertisement from the *Cooks Strait Almanac* shows, Bannister spent the early part of the 1850s as the landlord of the Lyttelton Arms, in the Banks Peninsula settlement then known as Port Victoria.

ATL, C-16071-1/2

did much of the work, later supplemented by squads of labourers. Directing the men were Board-appointed overseers with gun-toting assistants. Money was short: when the Board asked provincial lawmakers for a £500 cash advance against rates, Featherston talked them down to £200.[69]

The Board met on Tuesdays in rented rooms at the Oddfellows' Hall on the corner of Lambton Quay and Grey Street, one of the first pieces of reclaimed land in the township. In October 1863, the busy commissioners advertised 'for a youth to act as Clerk to the Board'.[70] Their desire to make a quick appointment would later backfire. William Bannister Jr was appointed on 27 October.[71] No youth at 44, he was a skilled draughtsman, artist, and sometime Lyttelton publican. His talent with copperplate handwriting is still evident in the Town Board's minute books. The *NZ Spectator and Cook Strait Guardian* noted that he 'excels in mapping and engrossing, and was employed during the sitting of the General Assembly last year to execute the addresses from both Houses to her Majesty the Queen'.[72] Commissioners set the Town Clerk's salary at a generous £100, with standard duties such as attending meetings and taking minutes. The position included responsibility for keeping accounts and collecting rates if so required. Seven days after he started, he was put to work assessing rating in the Te Aro ward. Within a fortnight he was appointed

Skill with a quill: a sample of William Bannister Jr's handwriting from the first Town Board minute book, 1863.

At a meeting of the Town Board held the 3rd Nov. 1863 at Mr. Allens Office Lambton Quay

Present Mr. Allen Chairman.

Messrs. Levy, Borlase, Moore, Plimmer.

Horner, Martin

Minutes of last meeting read and confirmed

The Chairman reported that the following names were proposed as Securities by Mr. William Bannister, viz. Mr. John Tompkins and Mr. Edwin Bannister, vide his letter of 29th of October 1863.

Moved by Mr. Levy. Seconded by Mr. Plimmer and that the securities proposed

Receiver of Rates, and was soon issuing summonses by the dozen for unpaid rates, collecting the money himself.

In the Board's first year, as it sorted out licences for slaughterhouses and made rules against removing clay, gravel or soil, £259 was prised out of ratepayers. Virtually all of the money raised in 1863 went on paying Bannister's salary.[73] By March 1864 he had billed and collected rates totalling more than £470. The new round of commissioners elected in September 1864 employed an engineer and a surveyor, and voted to raise Bannister's salary to £150. An iron safe was purchased, and a financial committee set up to prepare annual statements of accounts. No independent auditing system was put in place, however — an oversight that would have disastrous consequences.

Changes to Town Board legislation during 1864 distracted commissioners, and new terms of employment led to their mass resignation in August 'to avoid disputes and possible illegality'.[74] Commissioners' powers were enlarged, with each member receiving a triennial term, and one from each ward retiring each year. Occasionally, controversy emerged. Chairman Allen was challenged for pocketing a 5 percent commission from collecting rent for leased land on the Town Belt, without the knowledge or consent of other Board members.[75] He refunded the money before resigning. Meanwhile, Bannister continued to make himself indispensable.

In mid 1865, commissioners learned that their faith in Bannister had been misplaced. Hundreds of pounds in rates suddenly went missing, along with the Town Clerk himself. It was decided to sack him and recover the money. On 13 September, commissioners heard that the 'defalcations' of their former employee amounted to £428 — about $38,000 in today's terms.[76] The next day the *Independent* reported that Bannister had returned from Hokitika on the SS *Albion* and was ready to give himself up.[77] But when he appeared before the Resident Magistrate, charged with embezzlement, the magistrate ruled that there was not enough evidence to convict him — slippery record-keeping had seen to that. The charge of embezzlement was dismissed. The Board and its ratepayers were outraged.

> The prisoner … as he was leaving the court … was apprehended by Mr Inspector Atchison, for not having paid a fine of £20 for having scabby sheep. The prisoner pleaded for a little more time, which the Bench refused to allow, as he had shown an aptitude for making himself scarce, and he was then removed from the dock in custody.[78]

The commercial district, 1855. This sweep of private wharves and waterfront buildings on the Te Aro foreshore shows the Bethune and Hunter building on the far right.

One commissioner urged the Court to bring the Town Clerk back once the books had been examined. The magistrate refused. The dispute dragged on for years, with commissioners working behind the scenes to recoup the money through the sale of a house in Oriental Bay which Bannister had built with stolen money on land he didn't even own. Commissioner Pharazyn even travelled to England to persuade the absentee landowner to sell. The *Evening Post* played up the human side of the story, reporting that Bannister's wife had come to Pharazyn's Hobson Street house late the previous night, 'with tears in her eyes, and had begged him not to be hard with her and turn her out of the house which she now occupied'.[79]

The Town Board paid the absentee owner £100 for the land, and later sold the Oriental Bay property for £300. Thus, nearly three years after the theft came to light, barely half of the stolen rates money was recovered. The Bannister effect lingered in other ways, too. In 1868, as Joseph Dransfield took over as Board Chairman, residents of Hopper and Webb Streets complained that the Board hadn't fixed their roads. The Chairman's explanation was that 'the money in question had been subscribed in Bannister's time, and the payment to the Board could not in the meantime be traced'.[80] The reaction of the town's ratepayers to these sensational events is not recorded. Subsequent legislation setting up formal local government in the Colony did, however, reflect the need for independent auditing of annual accounts.

The Board did exact a revenge of sorts. In 1869, a letter of complaint was received about 'trees being cut and destroyed' by Bannister on reserve land he had leased on the Town Belt.[81] Six months later, commissioners resolved in an unusually public way, namely that 'if Bannister had not complied with the conditions of his lease that he be ejected at once'.[82] It is unclear whether this ever happened, but within three months, Wellington's first Town Clerk was dead. The official cause of death was diabetes, and the death certificate gave Bannister's profession as 'land agent'.

End of the beginning

Wellington's location on a major fault line produced a town built of shake-proof timber. Fire, fanned by the ubiquitous wind, remained a constant threat. On the morning of 8 July 1866, fire swept through the Thistle Inn, burning the original 1840 cottage to the ground. The alarm came early, but low tide put available water at Pipitea Beach out of the reach of fire-fighters. Neighbouring buildings were, however, saved. (The Thistle subsequently rose from the ashes as a two-storey timber building which still survives.) Such events prompted the Town Board to seek:

> the best means for rendering contiguous buildings, as far as possible fireproof,
> as with help of city surveyor, to draw up a code of regulations for the removal
> of dilapidated buildings and the erection of new ones, so as to render those
> in the main streets more uniform, substantial and fire-preventing.[83]

By the mid 1860s too, citizens and administrators alike were concerned about the state of the capital's drains. Wellington, of course, was not the Colony's only unhealthy urban centre. The Christchurch City Council, formed in 1862, had adopted a 'contour system' based on storm-water drains and levelling streets to help drain the notoriously swampy terrain. In January 1866, Town Board Chairman Edward Pearce went south to investigate, returning with lithographic plans of the Christchurch system.[84] Commissioners then set up a sanitary committee, 'to wait upon the government respecting the drainage of Lambton Quay and land about to be reclaimed'.[85] Options were explored for draining the government quarter, and a brick, egg-shaped culvert, three feet in diameter, was finally decided on.

The risks to public health became a talking point in Parliament, with dire warnings of possible consequences:

> The sanitary condition of Wellington was in a sadly defective state, and the malaria along the beach and even about the House was truly frightful, and would tell its tale some day. The miasmatic influence constantly going on may yet be the means of forcing on a fever or some other deadly disease, which will, with epidemic fury, sweep off the people in hundreds.[86]

The town's drains were even blamed for the sudden death of Lyttelton MP George Macfarlan in October 1868, less than a year after entering Parliament: 'Almost every member had been in ill health of account of the unwholesome state of the town; they had to lament the loss of one honourable member, and another was not yet out of danger.'[87]

In the late 1860s, as summer weather intensified the stench, the Town Board targeted home 'privies' (toilets). All cess-pits in the town were to be cleansed and filled in. But proper sanitation required running water, and the cost of laying pipes to the capital's 1,200 houses was £4 per dwelling.[88] Clean water was scarce in central Wellington, and had to be scooped up in buckets from deep clay wells or collected in rainwater tanks and barrels. Continuing problems with effluent, whether from human or animal sources, led the Town Board to appoint an Inspector of Nuisances (this being the euphemism then in vogue). An accepted part of the municipal landscape in Victorian England, its colonial equivalent drew rude comments and bad jokes. The *Evening Post* commented that a candidate needed to have knowledge of the 'science of stinks', and that the job would be 'to hunt the smells for £50 a year'.[89] The annual salary was raised to £150, and the job combined with that of Deputy Town Clerk. The *Post* outlined the tasks awaiting the appointee:

> We may mention the numerous poisoned dogs lying about the streets, the habit which appears to exist in Manners Street of making the footpaths and roadway a kind of cemetery for defunct rats, and the lazar pit near the Te Aro station house into which morning after morning are cast the carcases of starved cats, dead dogs, rats, mice and the emptying of dust bins. We might enumerate countless other nuisances …[90]

Prototype water closets were being used in parts of the town, drained into rough and usually open sewers, but they used large quantities of precious water. There was an alternative. The first Board meeting of 1867 heard about the outgoing Chairman's lavatory, patented as an earth closet or commode. The device involved a bucket below the seat, with a hopper behind it containing dry earth or ashes. The fact that the earth closet consumed plentiful dirt and not scarce water made it especially attractive.

A reliable water supply to help cleanse the town and also to fight fires became a priority for the Town Board. Early in 1867, Commissioner John Plimmer made efforts to locate the best site for a waterworks. Town Surveyor Nicholas Marchant suggested a four-acre reservoir in the Kaiwharawhara Valley, near Karori. But ratepayers baulked at the £25,000 cost of getting a private contractor to build a dam and pipe water into the town, and threatened to petition against it.[91]

By the end of the decade, Wellington's population was approaching 7,500. The Town Engineer warned about 'the manner in which town sections are cut by private holders and formed into narrow streets and bye-ways, reproducing on an equally pernicious scale the evils complained of in older cities'.[92] After nightfall, the streets tended to be dark and treacherous places. Citizens routinely fell into streams and open sewers. At the start of 1867, lampposts appeared within the government domain, spurring the Town Board to install 25 of its own along the main thoroughfares. The first gas lamps were lit on 14 June 1867.[93] But problems emerged with the Board's employees, especially those hired to light the lamps. According to Commissioner Mills, one was found to be intoxicated while lighting the lamps. Another commissioner commented that 'he was sorry to say that nearly all the servants of the Board were addicted to drinking'.[94]

By 1868 the Town Board, like the provincial legislature, was facing a financial crisis. The position was not helped by Bannister's 'defalcations', but the suspension of the grants-in-aid system was more serious. The Colonial Undersecretary then told the expectant town commissioners that the government would not pay rates on property occupied by the Crown. When they sent a deputation, he told them that the Crown was 'putting off' the payment of rates: 'There were too many demands on the Government and the session was so far advanced, he could provide nothing this year.'[95] Outraged, the commissioners plotted to 'select one of the owners of the property in order that the question of their liability for the rates may be tested'.[96] Nonetheless, the Board worked hard to keep the official end of town presentable, aware of the importance of the capital to the town's economy. In 1867, commissioners had resolved that 'the open drain in Charlotte Street requires covering in before the next sitting of the General Assembly'.[97] In the same spirit, Premier Stafford had made a diplomatic promise to provide half the money for widening the northern end of Lambton Quay.

A law change intervened. The Municipal Corporations Act 1867 standardised

Opposite

A studio portrait of the so-called 'Father of Wellington', John Plimmer.

WCA, 00138:0:13697

the structure of town boards, providing new powers for road standards, higher rates, and the raising of loans. At the time there were twenty incorporated towns in the Colony, almost all with different laws providing for their management. The Wellington commissioners supported the elevation of their town to an incorporated borough. But ratepayers, fearing that this new status would lead to expensive and unnecessary waterworks, raised a petition. *The Independent* hinted at anarchy if the petitioners succeeded:

> … is there to be no management at all? If the latter alternative be adopted, the evil will soon work its own cure. The streets, which in this wet weather are bad enough, would very soon, if totally neglected, become almost impassable, and the capital city of New Zealand would soon become as bad in its roads, as a canvas township at a new [gold] rush.[98]

The Town Board was wound up. By September 1870 Wellington had metamorphosed into an incorporated borough, its council able to raise loans and run as a business. The title Chairman of the Town Board was changed to Mayor; the commissioners became borough councillors. Commissioner Carpenter was typically unimpressed: 'The Town Board was a nuisance, and a Corporation would be a still greater nuisance.'[99]

Dodge City on Sea

Chapter 2

(1870–1885)

When our fair city boasts a Municipality
In a Government House are tenants of quality
Launched is a vessel from our Patent Slip
Loosened our energies from Maori grip
Inventive Genius can our flax prepare
Such as will with Native Article compare.

Steaming in harbour comes Webb's first boat
Tricker's JUST sentence utterly forgot
Realise the crazy dreams of finding Gold
Each street Gas Lighted as has been foretold
Employment found for all, and that well paid
Then still shall Harris rule the grocery trade.[1]

In a dozen lines of advertising doggerel, Willis Street shopkeeper Lionel Harris snagged many of the dilemmas facing Wellington in 1870. His acrostic poem, promoting his 'family and shipping' grocery business, spoke to an expectant population of 8,000 for whom the settlement era was a fading memory, and who looked to a rosier future for the town as both capital and commercial hub. It was time for the settlement to stretch out. The physical setting took the shape of a barbell, pushed out at Thorndon and Te Aro, and joined by a length of beachfront so narrow in parts that two bullock carts could barely pass. The barbell is also a fitting metaphor for the often heated contests between Wellington's elected leaders and the political 'kings' of the colony.

Harris's crystal ball envisioned a Wellington with full municipal status. He shared the view that a British-style borough with corporate powers was the best way to secure basic infrastructure and services. The first element of his vision was soon realised; others would prove more difficult to achieve. On 16 September 1870, the township was proclaimed a borough under the standardising provisions

45

of the Municipal Corporations Act.[2] Twelve days later, the elected members of the Wellington City Council (WCC), the controlling authority of the Wellington City Corporation, sat down together for the first time.

Economic downturn continued to test the Colony, although Wellington avoided the wave of bankruptcies that hit South Island cities in the late 1860s. Nonetheless, the number of insolvency petitions before town magistrates highlighted the fact that relocating parliament and the civil service was not necessarily going to make the population of the capital rich. The same edition of the *Evening Post* in which Harris's doggerel appeared described the fate of one of Harris's peers, whose stock of sauces, pickles and bottled fruits was now at the mercy of the auctioneer:

Dusty trails: until the 1860s, lower Willis Street was still part of Lambton Quay, the vital hub of commercial Wellington. The *Evening Post* was housed in the buildings on the right.

WCA, 00138:0:12497

A man named Duke, lately a grocer in Willis Street, was arrested for debt today in the Police Court, at the suit of a creditor. Immediately after being taken in charge by the bailiff, he was seized with a fit, and fell on the floor, where he remained for some time in a series of convulsions. As soon as he recovered, he was removed to the gaol, but had another fit on his way up. His sufferings, however, were powerless to move the stony heart of the bailiff, and he was safely lodged in durance vile.[3]

By 1870, Wellington businesses were fighting for the consumer sixpence, using marketing techniques such as newspaper advertising, handbills, and merchandising tie-ins. There was even an Old Curiosity Shop on Willis Street, capitalising on the Dickens bestseller from 1841. Willis Street resident J. H. Williams in his horse-drawn 'advertising van' plied the 'Beach', from Pipitea to Te Aro, calling out advertising slogans to the semi-amphibious township, which by now was filling up with oyster parlours, coffee stalls, theatres, churches, hotels and brothels, and a hundred stores supplying the settlers' needs.[4] Colonial horses, too, had their own emporia. Saddlers and 'horse repositories' catered to the beasts that in their hundreds dragged the buggies, omnibuses, dog carts, and Hackney cabs plying every few minutes from Queen's Wharf. The Victorian equivalent of an airport, the busy wharf precinct was a magnet for freewheeling children not sent to the private schools that dotted the township. Their behaviour shocked the *Evening Post*:

> The crowds of idle boys and sometimes girls are continually hanging about
> in the most exposed and dangerous situations they can pick out on the wharf
> — in everybody's way and of course running the risk of being knocked or
> falling off. Can no means be devised to keep the urchins away?[5]

The Education Act of 1877 solved the problem by providing the 'urchins' with free and compulsory schooling. The *Post* was right to be concerned: a number of unattended children had died from drowning and other accidents. In July 1869 a grocer's cart ran over and killed a cap-chasing child in Cuba Street, ensuring that speed limits on equine traffic would appear on the new Council's agenda.[6] The horse and bullock 'nuisances' that splattered the unpaved streets and fouled wells and streams also posed a threat to the lives of settlers and Maori. By 1870, animal and human waste was strongly (though not yet conclusively) linked with disease. At the time, sewage was routinely flung into streams and open sewers, dug into backyards or collected by night carts and dumped into the nearest waterway. This, combined with the stench of inner-city slaughter-houses and tallow-melters, gave the constant wind the status of friend rather than foe. Respectable Thorndon fared little better: its main sewer lay wide open to the elements.

Willis Street was the town's busiest thoroughfare, meeting Lambton Quay at prominent Clay Point (now Stewart Dawson's Corner). Close to the Post Office, banks and Queen's Wharf, it matched Lambton Quay as an important business district. In fact it was called Lambton Quay (South) until the early 1860s: early street directories show the Quay extending all the way to Bond Street.[7] A dusty bullock trail lined with wooden buildings, Willis Street in 1870 looked rather like the location for a Western movie — all verandas, narrow alleys, horse railings, and men in dark hats. But this was Dodge City on Sea: the buildings on the eastern side were literally beachfront properties. The absence of storm-water drains or footpaths meant that the street became a mud-bath after rain. From the earliest days of settlement, businessmen had set up shop here, and constructed private wharves or jetties to which small open boats called lighters ferried passengers and cargo from vessels anchored in deeper water.

Thirsty boatmen could always find their way to the landing steps of the Empire Hotel, recognisable from the water by lamps perched on statuettes. Located near where the Bank of New Zealand building now stands, the two-storey hotel was rebuilt in 1865 in anticipation of richer visitors to the capital. Known as Osgood's Empire, after its proprietor, it differed from its counterparts in its public bath, sited in an enclosure on the ground floor, its vast basement stables, and its watery back entrance.

signal –
" Signal expects every man to do his duty"

Episode at Mt Victoria
at Freemasons Picnic

Sophy Coates & Mr Nelson, that is
how it came about Mr Heaphy was
at the Picnic so must know

Wellington's unofficial civic emblem is a blown-out umbrella stuffed into a rubbish bin. As this Charles Heaphy cartoon from the mid 1870s shows, the phenomenon is not a recent one. Here, a man proposes to a woman during a wind-blasted Freemasons' Picnic on the summit of Mt Victoria.

ATL, A-147-015

Hotel guests could drop a fishing-line from an upstairs balcony, with excellent results.[8] The expected demand for luxury accommodation proved slow in coming, but an adjacent concert hall provided the Empire with a reliable income. Here, for two shillings, townspeople could watch entertainments such as Kin Foo — the first Chinese woman to be presented to Queen Victoria. And it was from the top of the Empire Hotel parapet that in June 1867 visiting trapeze artist Madame Tourneau walked her tightrope along Willis Street, over the rooftops of the town.[9]

Visually, the wider landscape provided little relief from the raw, windswept town. From the time of human settlement, fire and the elements had denuded the hills to the south and east of the harbour, apart from fragments of forest that survived in deep gullies. The north-facing slopes around the town, set aside 30 years before as Town Belt, were bare, apart from a few fallen tree-trunks lying in patches of scrub. The moister western hills, heavily forested at the time of settlement, had mostly been cleared by teams of sawyers with bullock-carts, and by the late 1860s had become steep, stump-dotted pastureland. It was an unforgiving setting for a settlement struggling to make its mark.

In the fifteen years covered by this chapter, Wellington was transformed from a sickly township into a thriving borough. Yet despite the ambitions of its founders, it was touch-and-go whether the settlement would survive beyond the late 1860s. During this period the township's annual population increase rarely exceeded 250, and some years saw an actual decline.[10] In 1869, Provincial Superintendent Isaac Featherston reported on the 'critical' situation of the national economy, saying he was 'unable to express even a hope of the colony emerging from its present difficulties'.[11]

At the start of 1870, Wellington province celebrated 30 years of settlement with banquets and bunting. The town's hopes were now centred on its deep harbour and busy wharves. Queen's Wharf, built off a reclamation adjoining Lambton Quay in 1862, and initially known as the Public or Deep Water Wharf, was later expanded to cater for the steam-powered ships coming from Europe. During the 1860s, the Provincial Council reclaimed 12 acres from the sea, forming a great wasteland between Customhouse Quay, the Cable Car, and the north end of today's Midland Park, so popular with lunchtime office workers. With the help of ten thousand

Mrs Pharazyn's diary

In the late 1860s, one of the shows at Osgood's Empire concert hall on Willis Street was an 'equestrian drama' entitled *Mazeppa, or the Wild Horse of Tartary*.[12] Written by composer Michael Balfe, it was one of the most successful plays of its day in Britain and the colonies. Few in the township who saw it, however, realised that poetess Jessica Rankin, who wrote the lyrics, was living in one of the mansions of Thorndon.

Jessica Rankin had arrived from London on Christmas Eve 1867. Early next morning, in St Paul's Church, she became the third wife of Charles Pharazyn, a prominent businessman and politician. Her 65-year-old husband then went straight back to work.

As the wife of a rich and powerful man, Jessica rubbed shoulders with the capital's social and political elite. Her unpublished diaries, with their sharp observations, confirm the growing mood of alarm and despondency in the capital. In May 1868, for example, she describes the bleak atmosphere at the opening of the Provincial Council, as Dr Featherston read his statement on the 'general welfare' of the province: 'Everything seems sadly depressed. There seems no money in the place; they must borrow again to keep going.'[13]

Subsequent entries show that economic concern was compounded by profound insecurities over the land wars raging in the central North Island:

Bad news again from the disturbed districts. Natives have burned a house not fifty miles off, and taken away all the half caste women and children. Commercial and financial affairs [are] in a terrible state of depression. People failing right and left and no money to be got — worse than the Old Country with all its faults.[14]

The windy, dusty town must have made a faltering economy even harder to bear. Jessica regularly walked from her Hobson Street home to Lambton Quay, known as the 'Beach', and complained of being 'blinded with dust, eyes quite inflamed in the evening'.[15]

She continued to live quietly in Wellington until her death in 1891, and is buried in Bolton Street cemetery. In the 1920s there were calls for the Wellington literati to recognise her achievements.[16]

barrow-loads of spoil, the waterfront retreated several blocks from the old Quay, loosening its ties with the harbour. This was just the start of reclamations that would push out much of the beach between Pipitea and Te Aro. On the precious flat land that emerged, the town's merchants erected three- and four-storey buildings to store the wool on which the regional economy depended.

Three-quarters of the citizenry now lived in Te Aro Flat, an area already becoming overcrowded. Whereas in 1863 one town acre in Tory Street might have two dwellings on it, a decade later there were fifteen houses, cheek by jowl.[17] At the same time Maori departures were increasing, as remaining unsold land in harbour-side pa came under pressure from settlers. But Maori were still a presence on city streets, as one new arrival noted in 1871:

> I got a bit of a shock as I was walking the quay, carrying my modest belongings, at seeing a couple of Maori women strolling down the quay smoking short black pipes … their heads and feet were quite bare. No one else appeared to notice any incongruity about these ladies; and they themselves seemed to be quite at their ease despite my unintentional rudeness in staring at them.[18]

Victorian notions of moral decency led to intolerance of the communal lifestyle of Maori. In the 1870s Charles Heaphy, now Native Reserves Act commissioner, argued that it was 'desirable to get the natives out of the town', ostensibly on sanitary grounds.[19] The pressure was such that by 1881 only 28 Maori were still living at Te Aro, and nine at Pipitea.[20]

The reference in Lionel Harris's poem to 'Maori grip' reflects a deeper insecurity, however. British troops had been stationed in the township since the mid 1840s, and their departure for England in the late 1860s brought growing unease. At around that time, Maori who had been taken prisoner in the land wars were landed at Te Aro beach and marched in chains up Cuba Street to the Mount Cook Barracks. For much of the decade, the politicians on Thorndon Hill were preoccupied by the protracted land wars.

Colonial Treasurer Julius Vogel soon helped to create a diversion. On 28 June 1870 he announced a £10 million cash injection into the economy. The aim of the Budget was to fund the Colony's next great leap forward. Premier Fox described the mission to the House in almost evangelical terms: 'The time has come when we should again recommence the great work of colonising New Zealand … the object of the Government proposals is, if possible, to re-illumine that sacred fire.'[21]

Hana Te Awhitu and her husband, Tamati Te Wera, on their porch in Franklin Avenue, off Nairn Street, around 1900. Hana was born in Te Aro, probably in 1831, and the couple had reputedly been the last two Maori to live at Te Aro pa.

WCA, 00340:0:485

Vogel launched an ambitious public works programme, based on borrowing to fund infrastructure and foster immigration. It included the building of 1,120 miles of railway track, 2,500 miles of telegraph lines, and — most significantly for the capital and its civil service — a number of public buildings. A Christchurch visitor sneered at the expectant mood in the so-called 'Empire City':

> Wellington remains in the memory as imperial only in the matter of artificial dressiness in everything. Your numerous gentlemen wearing long-faced hats, kid gloves and other fashionable attire … You bear away the palm of supremacy at the metropolis for leeches, drones and parasites, feeding on the public revenue. You have neither good water, except at Parliament House, nor gaslight, nor streets kept so as to do credit to a metropolis … Your buildings are 'imposing' in so far as they are a sham, with great pretensions to architecture of a solid character, which turns out to be as flimsy as a tin pot.[22]

Sorting the water

The visitor's barb about the capital's lack of proper street lighting and a decent water supply touched on two very sore points with the local populace. It was the water supply that preoccupied the new Council when it first met on 28 September 1870. Ten councillors were sworn in, with businessman and former Town Board Chairman Joe Dransfield elected Mayor by his peers. There was little prestige attached to the mayoralty at that time — the position was rotated annually, and amounted to little more than chairing a works committee. Formal city government was, nonetheless, a milestone, with the Council now able to make bylaws, levy rates, and, most importantly, raise loans. In an infamous editorial, the *Evening Post* touched on the high expectations surrounding the new authority, and the serious challenges it faced:

> [It is hoped that] a new order of things will be initiated, which will speedily remove from the Empire City the stigma under which it now labours in regard to municipal matters. Wellington, we fear, is pretty generally known as the muddiest, dirtiest, most dusty, worst drained, and worst lighted town in the colony.[23]

Two days later, a special committee sat down to consider 'the best means of providing a sufficient supply of water for the city'.[24] In the towns and cities of Victorian England, clean water and good sanitation were symbols of civic and social improvement. London's 'Great Stink' of 1858 saw parliamentarians authorising the local board of works to increase rates in order to fund a new drainage system, and to clean up the sewage-clogged Thames. The link between bad water and disease hardened opinion in Britain — and, in time, its colonies — that the supply of clean water was too important to leave to private enterprise. Dunedin's private water supply, launched in 1863, had proved expensive and unreliable, with the business later salvaged by its City Corporation.[25] Wellington's City Surveyor, Nicholas Marchant, argued that a clean water supply was both a municipal responsibility *and* a good civic investment:

> the Council must not overlook the fact that if it is not prepared or desirous
> of bringing water into this city, it will be absolutely impossible to prevent
> some private company from so doing. Under such circumstances, the loss to
> the city and ratepayers will be incalculable, as in a few years it would become
> more than self-supporting, and economically carried out, and administered,
> providing annually increasing revenue to the city.[26]

Revelations over water pollution helped spur the Council into action. Late in 1870, the prominent government scientist and Director of the Colonial Museum, Dr James Hector, agreed to inspect wells and streams across the township. Over the summer of 1871, he analysed 34 samples, drawn from eighteen privately owned deep clay wells, eleven rainwater tanks and barrels, and five streams outside the town. He detected 'organic' pollution equal to anything found in cities such as Manchester or London:

> No water collected within the crowded parts of the City, either from wells
> or house tops, is safe or proper for human consumption ... the waters from
> streams within the town are so obviously unfit for use that they were not
> analysed ... [A] proper water supply is urgently required for the city on
> sanitary grounds alone.[27]

Large quantities of human and animal excrement contaminated the water from inner-city wells. The worst pollution was found in a well in central Manners Street, close to cattle yards and fed by a nearby stream. The water was 'turbid, brown coloured, with a putrid odour'. Dr Hector also identified a major public health risk, especially to children, from the prevalence of intestinal worms.[28] The link between dirty water and disease, however, remained unproven. Dr Hector remained cautious, even as he discussed the suffering of worm-infested children:

> The connection between a defective water supply and the prevalence of this disease may not be established as cause and effect, but their constant association is undoubted, and there is no means found to be so effectual in arresting this plague, which abounds in Wellington, as an ample supply of wholesome water.[29]

Hector's findings caused a sensation. John Plimmer, a member of the water committee, revisited the earlier idea of a reservoir at the southern end of the Kaiwharawhara Valley. He urged his colleagues to agree to lease land at the back of Baker's Hill, in lower Karori, and 'to erect dams, reservoirs, laying of pipes, and other requisite for the works for the use and maintenance of a thorough supply of good water for the city'.[30] Marchant drew up a scheme, based on a future population of 47,000 each consuming 30 gallons of water a day.

Colonel James Hector, the prominent government scientist who exposed the deadly condition of Wellington's water, photographed on his wedding day, 1868.

ATL, F-110268-1/2

   Work began on a government bill to borrow £25,000 for the city water supply. The passage of the Wellington Waterworks Act 1871 was the next milestone in a long and difficult process that would drag on for a decade. The presence of gold claims over parts of the Kaiwharawhara Stream halted construction for two years, while the Council grappled with compensating miners pursuing the 'crazy dream'. Bush was felled, and a long tunnel dug to tap the stream. Early in 1874, the first water from the so-called Polhill distribution basin flowed through cast iron pipes. Ratepayers living within 100 yards of the mains were now liable for an extra shilling in the pound for the privilege of running water, plus the cost of connection. The arrival of water was not universally welcomed. Thorndon bookseller and councillor Robert Carpenter publicly expressed his views:

> I request you will order the sinners in your employ never to discharge Water on my premises — my shop is not lined — my Books are dusty — Water driven between boards turns dust into mud — in short, rusty water don't improve Dry Literature ... Liquors from vessels of Glass, not rusty waters from pipes of Brass, the dullest Government clerk will tell you is the correct liquid with literature.[31]

The new Karori supply was not enough. Fickle annual rainfall and variable demand forced the Council to raise a further £25,000 loan to fund a bigger reservoir of 35 million gallons, a filtering apparatus, and rising iron prices and labour costs. Allegations of corruption in the waterworks construction soon brought additional complications. A second Waterworks Bill was rushed through Parliament in 1874. Nor was this dam sufficient for the thirsty township. Hot summers with water restrictions, and weak mains pressure that hindered fire-fighting, led to calls for additional supplies.

By 1879 the Council was restricting to Sundays the practice of supplying water to all local churches to help power their organs. The Vivian Street Baptist Church alone got dispensation to continue using water for baptismal purposes.[32] The hunt for fresh supplies ended across Wellington harbour and over the eastern hills, in the massive watershed of the Wainuiomata River. In August 1879, ratepayers agreed to a £130,000 loan to harness this additional supply. Five years later, the Wainuiomata scheme was opened, and water was piped from its dam, across the Wainuiomata Valley, through the hill at Waiwhetu, and around the edge of the harbour, via pipe bridges across the Waiwhetu Stream and Hutt River.

This dreamy scene at Karori reservoir gives no hint of the scandals, resignations and engineering disasters that beset the establishment of a city water supply.

ATL, Burton Brothers Collection, G-3189-1/1-BB

At long last, Wellingtonians could safely drink water from a brass tap. The new supply also increased the use of flushable water closets, allowing wealthy Thorndon householders such as the Pharazyns to connect their 'utensil' to the mains. Costly sanitation infrastructure became the next priority for the Council. In 1873, its engineer was asked to 'devise a means of drainage and sewerage for the city, and the cost thereof'.[33] The idea was then dropped 'until the waterworks is in working order'.[34] A special rate was later imposed on owners of water closets, which helped to fund the first crude sewer pipes.

In the meantime, most dwellings relied on a weekly night-soil collection service provided by the Council, and involving 'nightmen' with horse and cart. Long drops were disallowed within the township's boundaries. Charles McKirdy held the lucrative job of main night-soil collector for years, supervising a horse and cart pick-up service that made regular drop-offs at 'manure depots' located in valleys on the outskirts of town. By 1874, three carts were serving a population of over 10,000; that same year, the Council voted to equip its nightmen with oilskins.[35] Some residents did not wish to pay (or could not afford) the levy charged. Residents of Wordsworth Street (now Aro Street) had to deal with the result — people dumping their nightsoil into Aro Stream. Early in 1874 the name of the night soil committee was changed to the sanitary committee — a symbolic victory for the public health movement gathering pace in England, and finding a voice locally in the Public Health Act 1872.

Current ideas about illness and sanitation were still dominated by the so-called 'miasma theory', whereby disease was believed to be spread by a noxious form of 'bad air'. According to this theory, improving sanitation helped get rid of bad smells, thus leading to a reduction in disease. Dead bodies were seen as a particular risk to health. Early in 1872, the Council moved to build a public morgue, where bodies could be stored before being collected by undertakers.[36] The city morgue which later opened by the Te Aro Market Reserve removed the need for so-called 'blood rooms' in city hotels, where dead bodies were stored to await the coroner.

In 1874, fears that 'putrefactive fermentation' of bodies was contaminating groundwater in the Bolton Street cemetery caused hysteria, prompting the introduction of a Wellington Burial Grounds Bill. Nearby parliamentarians were seen to be at risk from 'bad odours'. One politician referred to the need to 'more carefully provide for the sanitary state of the town in which the members of the General Assembly, for about a fourth part of their lives were compelled to reside'.[37] Although incorrect, the miasma theory did help to improve sanitation. The theory was overturned in 1884, when an English doctor established that cholera and typhoid were caused by micro-organisms in polluted water, which led to the so-called 'germ theory' of disease.

Proper sanitation was expensive. Despite the passage of the Public Health Act in 1872, the Council shied away from funding an effective sewerage system because of the likely burden on ratepayers. Two elaborate engineering proposals for such a system were commissioned during the 1870s, but the estimated £150,000 cost made them unviable. Councillors consoled themselves with the argument that the capital's temperate and 'ventilated' climate would dispel noxious gases. Yet the calls to fix the drains grew deafening, with the *New Zealand Times* suggesting that councillors' lives could be at risk if delays continued:

> The vital statistics of the city prove beyond a doubt that the time has arrived when sanitary reform admits of no further delay, unless we wish to see the inhabitants of this city exposed to the constant risk of decimation by an epidemic. If such a misfortune should befall the city … we may expect to see the City Council lynched by the surviving citizens.[38]

Ratepayers opted for a dirty city rather than an indebted one. Midway through 1879, John Plimmer articulated their concerns and shut down the debate — for the time being. He talked of the folly of spending £150,000 on a 'useless' drainage scheme, with annual interest payments of up to £13,000. For Plimmer, it was too much to pay when all that was required for the whole city was the daily removal of four or five carts of night-soil. He argued that the harbour, with its strong tidal flows, was the ideal dumping ground for sewage.

> I would say to you, as practical men who are entrusted with the government of the city, to set aside for a while that sentimental nonsense which has been made so much of late, of polluting the bay … when you come to think that the whole of the excreta that would be carried into the bay would scarcely be equal to a grain of sand in your water reservoir each day; and even that, according to my plan, would have a six hour's [sic] outrun with each night-tide, to be lost in the ever restless waters of the bay, you must, in the name of common sense, come to the conclusion that you nor anyone else would ever see any more of it.[39]

The municipality built open ditches for carrying both sewage and storm-water into the harbour. This primitive form of sanitation relied on the regular movement of water, not possible in flat areas such as Te Aro. Concern about people falling into open sewers at night prompted the Council to start lighting the town properly. As early as 1871, the Borough funded 24 additional gas lamps, to be located alongside newly laid private drains. Lamps were to be lit after midnight, on moonless nights only, and the annual gaslight budget was not to exceed £200.[40] The drains remained a hazard to public health, creating a stench during the summer months and overflowing in heavy rain, as in early January 1881:

> Last night's rain had the effect, as usual, in Wellington of choking all the drains, flooding the footpaths, and swelling the various streams, or sewers as they might with justice now be called, to the dimensions of turbulent torrents. In Lambton Quay pedestrians were compelled to avoid the footpath in favour of the road.[41]

The Council at work

The Council met weekly (later fortnightly) in an elegant room in the Provincial Council buildings on Customhouse Quay. In many ways it was the old board of works in a fresh suit of clothes: a closed shop of older businessmen and property-owners with the time, income and dedication to address those local body perennials: rubbish, roads, rats and rates. Hours were spent in committees, debating and voting on by-laws designed to keep the streets clean, control rubbish from shops, impose permits for fires, and restrict brothels, goats and gorse.[42]

Tucked away in their spacious offices, the councillors were insulated from the general public. A narrow franchise excluded the majority of citizens because they lived in rented dwellings; this was in line with the prevailing Victorian view that only those who paid annual rates should be entitled to a voice in the way their borough was run. Restricting the vote to property-owners was seen as appropriate, because these were the permanent residents who literally had a stake in their community. It was an all-male world, despite the fact that women ratepayers won the right to vote and stand in municipal elections as early as the mid 1870s. (Only a few widows and spinsters were involved.)

It was implicit that councillors would apply the principles of thrift and discipline to their deliberations. The philosophy of individual responsibility and self-help, celebrated in Samuel Smiles' Victorian bestseller of the same name, was underpinned by an even stronger reluctance at the local level to pay taxes and rates. Aspects of this *laissez faire* (without restriction) ideology could be seen at the national and provincial levels, with lawmakers funding only infrastructure that provided direct economic return. Local development tended to be left up to local residents, which called for high levels of public trust that were not always realised.

At the end of its third year, the Council was beset by claims of corruption. At a time when ratepayer participation in municipal business was minimal, newspapers such as the *Evening Post* (founded in 1865) took on the role of public watchdog. The fact that the paper's circulation had grown to 3,000 by 1876 shows it was reflecting a lively interest in local affairs.[43] Mayor Dransfield met his match in editor Edward Gillon, who gained a reputation as an anti-corruption campaigner. His editorial style was trenchant, as this extract from 1873 illustrates: 'Mr Dransfield's long monopoly of civic power had had the effect on him which any monopoly of power invariably produces on men of narrow mind and selfish instincts. In popular phraseology, he had grown too big for his boots.'[44]

'Jobbery at the waterworks'

Joseph Dransfield's mayoralty began well enough, as his Council addressed the urgent need for a town water supply in 1870. He led the purchase of Queen's Wharf and adjacent land, helping secure a lucrative investment for the city. But this Yorkshire coal importer, ship-owner and sometime Chamber of Commerce president always had bigger ideas, and was increasingly seen as representing the merchant elite of the town.

Dransfield saw the harbour as the key to Wellington's prosperity. During the 1860s, he had helped to found the town's first major commercial enterprise, the Wellington Steam Navigation Company. Based on a fleet of steamers, it was later overtaken by competition.

Securing the water supply led to Dransfield's downfall. By 1873 he was entangled in allegations

Joseph Dransfield, Yorkshireman, coal merchant and first Mayor of the Wellington City Council.

ATL, C-22072-1/2

of 'jobbery' at the waterworks, with his councillor cronies winning juicy contracts 'at their own price, and without the formality of calling for tenders'. The *Evening Post* alleged: 'The importation of the waterworks plant was given as a *bonne bouche* [titbit] to one councillor, the manufacture of a lot of extra plant, &c, has been entrusted to another at a price which … is nearly double what another tradesman in the town would have been willing to have done the same work for.'[45]

After being ousted in 1873, Dransfield returned to the mayoralty in 1878 to lead work on harbour reclamation.

In 1879 he left the Council, a bankrupt victim of the times, and retired to his palatial two-storey Italianate home at 335 Willis Street.

Evening Post editor Edward Gillon kept the spotlight on Dransfield, campaigning for the Mayor to be elected by ratepayers, not by his fellow councillors. At a heated Council meeting on 17 December 1873, Dransfield was voted out, as councillors agreed to mayoral elections by ratepayers. A bitter Dransfield railed against Gillon's editorials: 'You know the man who writes them, and I am quite prepared to pit myself against him.'[46] Dransfield's successor, Charles Borlase, an upright solicitor at the Provincial Council, was left to implement electoral reforms in the Wellington Mayors Act 1874. Thereafter, ratepayers were kept busy with two polls a year: ward elections in September and mayoral elections in December. Dransfield remained a councillor, the mouthpiece for a rich and powerful group of businessmen, and not above personal attacks on enemies through newspapers such as the *Independent*, and boycotting meetings to delay a vote. With the worthy Borlase in the chair, Council meetings became more decorous. At the end of 1874, William Moorhouse, a former Superintendent of Canterbury Province, was elected Mayor. The *New Zealand Times* would later describe the job as a thankless one:

> The emoluments of office are small, the dignity of Mayor is not very highly esteemed, and the cares and responsibilities entailed upon the chief councillor are very great. The salary is so small as to be quite out of proportion to the time and thought required adequately to discharge the duties. In addition to this, the style of argument adopted by certain members of the Council is hardly such as to make the office of Mayor a pleasant billet.[47]

Behind the scenes, officials worked to implement Council decisions and put in place administrative systems and structures. By 1875, the number of full-time Corporation staff stood at nine: the Town Clerk, the Collector of Rates, the City Surveyor and his assistant, the Inspector of Nuisances, the Collector of Fees, the Pier Master, a clerical assistant, and an office boy.[48] A town hall was proposed in 1873, after grumbles about having to share rooms with the Provincial Council. Land was set aside for what would be 'the handsomest and most compact public building in New Zealand', on the harbour side of Featherston Street, on a reclaimed reserve between Johnston and Waring Taylor Streets. The waterworks scandal, however, scuttled the proposal.[49] In 1876 councillors agreed to build a town hall and borough offices, but only the offices were constructed. A quarter of a century would pass before Wellington finally got its town hall.

Alongside its permanent staff, the municipality retained a small number of carters and labourers to carry out various public works. The bullock carts were dispensed with at the start of 1873 after their drivers demanded a daily pay increase from 10 to 12 shillings.[50] The Council later decided to let its permanent labourers 'be dispensed with as far as possible'.[51] But the Corporation could also show its compassionate side as an employer. Thanks to the intervention of Cr Robert Carpenter, half-pay was granted to a Mr Pickens after a work accident at the end of 1870. Employee Ben Reeves was also paid half his wages after 'debilitation by sunstroke', even though it was mid winter.[52]

The first purpose-built Wellington City Corporation building, located on the harbour side of Featherston Street, on a reclaimed reserve between Johnston and Waring Taylor Streets.

ATL, A-018-040

Gillon of the *Evening Post* continued to agitate against what he saw as shoddy Borough management. The 1873 accounts became a *cause célèbre* as he noted that salaries swallowed up more than a fifth of the municipality's total revenue. Further editorials demanded a staff restructuring, especially targeting cronies of the Mayor: 'To secure efficient and economical administration of affairs of the City, it is necessary that the departmental arrangements should be entirely reorganised.'[53] In 1875, Gillon himself stood for Council and was elected. His motion that all permanent staff be given three months' notice was unsuccessful; but within eighteen months the Council was considering a 'reorganisation', with the Dransfield-aligned Town Clerk one of the first to go. Cr Gillon lasted two years in the Council chamber.

Rate increases in the mid 1870s saw the emergence of embryonic ratepayers' organisations which made regular deputations to Featherston Street. The Ratepayers' Reform Association, representing large property-owners, was established in 1880 after Mayor William Hutchison called for a widened franchise and the abolition of plural voting.[54] Colonial politicians such as Sir Robert Stout pointed out the 'absurdity' of a man with £1,400 worth of property located across four wards having as many as twenty votes.[55] Hutchison highlighted the rival ideologies within the Borough, which later coalesced around political parties.

> The rate [paid by] the poor man was really to him of as much importance as the rate of the rich man was to him. The poor man was just as much interested in seeing that the administration of the city was well and properly carried out as the rich man; and he took as much pride and as much interest in his little dwelling, with its flower garden in front and small kitchen-garden behind, as the rich man did in his mansion.[56]

The municipality adopted a Corporation Seal in 1878, and the practice of ringing a bell if there was no quorum of councillors became part of standing orders.[57] Many of the Council's preoccupations were trivial. Members sparred over the cost of licences for peddlers, hawkers and the ubiquitous town crier. Another bylaw outlawed bathing 'in public view' between 7 a.m. and 7 p.m.[58]

The risk of fire in the inner city posed a more serious threat. As three- and four-storey warehouses and office buildings sprouted around the Queen's Wharf area, Wellington was forced to revisit its status as a 'timber town' straddling the fault-line.[59] Municipal fire and water inspectors were employed. Regulations first passed in 1867 to control the fire risk were strengthened a decade later, with four Borough districts established with different requirements according to building density. From June 1877, all new structures in the Number 1 district, spanning the so-called Golden Mile from Thorndon Quay to Taranaki Street, were to be clad in incombustible materials such as iron or slate, with party walls of brick, stone or concrete.[60] One businessman complained that the regulations threatened the city's growth, claiming that, in the current depressed times, 'businessmen were not in a position to incur the heavy expenses of erecting brick buildings'. He urged his fellow citizens 'not to vote for any candidate for the office of Mayor who would not pledge himself to the immediate and unconditional removal of such unsuitable regulations'.[61]

Meanwhile, the Town Belt came under pressure for development. The aim of the Wellington City Reserves Act 1871 was to hand responsibility for managing

Editor of the *Evening Post* and, briefly, a Wellington City Councillor, Edward Gillon was a one-man crusade in the 1870s.

WCA, 00154:0:23

The Duke of Edinburgh Hotel on the corner of Manners and Willis Streets, as seen from Boulcott Street in the 1870s.

ATL, F-2794-1/2

Wakefield's swathe of green acres to the municipality. Before guardianship formally moved to the Borough, however, the central and provincial governments joined forces to snatch 143 acres for a college, lunatic asylum, and hospital. The remaining land was then handed over, 'to be forever hereafter used and appropriated as a public recreation ground for the inhabitants of the city of Wellington'.[62] The new guardians proved to be no more principled, as elaborate plans were drawn up for building development. In 1882, 10 acres was targeted for a 'home for the old and destitute', but in a single decade the Town Belt had gained a sacred quality. The *New Zealand Times* voiced the people's outrage: 'however desirable, [the proposed home] does not justify an improper application of Town Belt lands vested in the citizens for all time as an open space to be reserved for the purposes of recreation and these alone'.[63] Citizens revisited Mein Smith's 1840 map, looked to the controversy over retaining Dunedin's town belt, and succeeded in winning protection for the remaining land:

> Let the thin edge of the wedge be allowed to enter, and the patrimony of our children will gradually disappear. It has been for all time considered a mean thing for a man to sell his birthright but how would the people of Dunedin, who wisely and jealously guarded their inestimable endowment for all time, chuckle to see the Wellington citizens do an incomparably meaner thing, through their Town Council? Sell the birthright of their children to the only piece of ground they may be able to call their own in the future.[64]

In the late 1870s, citizens began travelling greater distances to their place of employment. Hackney cabs were the choice of the wealthy, but working people used the horse-drawn omnibus services. In 1873, the municipality granted permission for a rival steam-powered tramway. On 21 August 1878, the Wellington Tramway Company dispatched three steam-tram engines, each hauling a trailer, from its terminus on Lambton Quay. A ride via Cuba and Vivian Streets to the company's King Street depot, off Adelaide Road, took half an hour and cost threepence. The impact was immediate: the horse-drawn bus and cab services lowered their fares. There was, however, a downside to steam-power: cinders emitted by tram boilers frightened the city's horses, and residents complained about having to leap out of the way because the trams glided through the streets so silently.[65] The competition led to financial difficulties, and as economic depression took hold in the late 1870s, the steam-tram business was regularly up for public auction. In 1882, horse-drawn trams came back into vogue, and proved so popular that the tram lines were extended to Courtenay Place — a move directly responsible for making it a transport hub for the city.

Harbour development and reclamation

By the mid 1870s, as Vogel's railways began to join up the remote peripheries of the Colony, the provincial kingdoms were readied for abolition. The assets and powers of Wellington Province were to be redistributed, with the Borough gaining additional status as the new territorial body. Throughout the 1860s, Wellington's Provincial Superintendents had worked hard to make the splendid harbour into a working port. The strong commercial sector saw an opportunity to secure lucrative waterfront assets and thus gain a steady income.

Part of the 'official precinct' of Thorndon in the early 1880s, seen from the railway wharf at Pipitea. The Thistle Inn (left of centre) and St Paul's Church (right of centre) are prominent; Thorndon Quay stretches to the right.

ATL, F-5777-1/2

The golden fleeces pouring in from the provinces secured the future of the port — and of Wellington. The city was building a bridge to its hinterland, preparing for its role as a transport hub. An early step was the opening of the first rail link to the Hutt Valley in 1874, part of a Wellington-to-Masterton line completed in 1880. By 1886, a private rail company connected Thorndon to the Manawatu. Queen's Wharf, with its steam-crane, night lighting, storage warehouse and wool-pressing facilities, became a main artery in the pastoral economy of the lower North Island. It literally provided a beacon for incoming sea traffic, with a powerful red light being hoisted at the end of the 400-foot-long wharf every evening at sunset.

By 1870, pressure was mounting to enlarge the narrow downtown area, squeezed between the tide and the crumbling clay slope of The Terrace. Flat land in Wellington was always a rare and valuable commodity. Since the 1850s, when the first reclamation widened Willis Street, the provincial government had claimed exclusive rights to retrieve land from the inner harbour. The emergence of new modes of transport placed pressure on land for inner city routes, marshalling yards, stations, and a connection to the south of the city.

Decisions about future reclamations and the administration of the port became urgent, as provincial structures were dismantled. The municipality seemed the obvious candidate to take over responsibility, but the influential Wellington Chamber of Commerce was known to prefer a separate harbour board structure. By 1870, Superintendent Featherston was keen to hand over all waterfront activities. Dransfield quickly persuaded his fellow councillors to buy up Queen's Wharf, the adjacent bond store and unsold reclaimed land for £50,000. The municipality then leased the running of the wharf to a local stevedoring company, a move that brought welcome rentals worth £675 a month.[66] Featherston meanwhile granted the Borough 70 valuable acres of the Te Aro foreshore for reclamation.

Attempts to secure more of the lucrative business on the waterfront would bring out the worst in successive mayors and councillors. As the money flowed in from Queen's Wharf, Mayor Borlase decided to extend it, build a dock, and start reclaiming the foreshore. His decision to raise a loan led to a public spat within Council, but the government in fact turned down the loan. In 1875, Mayor William Moorhouse revived the idea, but his visit to the Minister of Public Works proved a disaster. Parliamentarians attacked the greedy municipality, and threatened to build their own wharf.[67] Moorhouse then decided that the municipality would take over the running of Queen's Wharf.

In 1876 Mayor William Hutchison, a tough Scotsman and seasoned politician, took the loan request to the new Premier, Julius Vogel, with detailed plans for wharf extensions. Vogel expressed the view that harbours should be managed by harbour trusts, as seen in Auckland. Councillor Charles Pharazyn sided with the Premier: 'If the City Council gave up its Te Aro foreshore to a new body and confined itself to

Harbour railway: by 1884, Taranaki Street stretched to the Te Aro foreshore and trains rattled along the waterfront to the bottom of Tory Street. Here, the railway line can be seen in the foreground, with people walking along it.

ATL, F-8010-1/2

matters of drainage, lighting, water supply, and the streets, matters would be much simpler.'[68] Hutchison conceded, and later met with the Chamber of Commerce to work out the mechanics of establishing a harbour board. A Harbours Bill was prepared, although debate on the powers of harbour boards slowed its progress. The delays gave councillors time to rekindle their enthusiasm for waterfront enterprise, as revenue poured in from Queen's Wharf wool-pressing and warehousing. By 1877, the municipality was contemplating the riches to be gained from reclaiming the Te Aro foreshore, still an important source of kaimoana (seafood) for the remaining Maori at Te Aro Pa. The Borough was also behind moves to extend Taranaki Street through the middle of the pa to the sea.[69] As the land passed from Maori ownership, numbers at the pa declined dramatically.[70]

During 1878, Parliament changed its mind on the Harbours Bill, deciding that the municipality should absorb the additional powers of a harbour board. A Borough deputation learned that Cabinet wanted 'to hand over the charge of the harbour to the Wellington Municipality ... [as] they recognise that the Corporation has a very fair claim to the advantages of the foreshore'.[71] Joseph Dransfield returned to the mayoralty in 1878 to cement in this decision, but Premier George Grey meanwhile revisited the idea of a dedicated board to run the harbour. Midway through 1879, Dransfield left the Council for good, a bankrupt victim of the times.

In May 1879, councillors repeatedly told incoming Mayor Hutchison that setting up a board amounted to theft of Council endowments. Egged on by strong personalities like Cr George Fisher, members determined to dig in their heels. The powerful wharf committee started work on drafting a bill to turn the Council into a harbour board. The *New Zealand Times* scoffed, arguing that there 'were many things in connection with wharf management concerning which councillors had no skill or knowledge. The affairs of the harbour would be better managed by a board.'[72]

The Wellington Harbour Board Act 1879 created the eponymous board which, in 1880, met for the first time at the Borough's Featherston Street offices. The loss of Queen's Wharf was costly to ratepayers; the final six months of municipal ownership had seen profits reaching £2,524.[73] Councillors dithered over the sale price, as the *Evening Post* accused them of siphoning off profits to bolster their finances.[74] A cheque for £64,000 was later accepted.

The Te Aro seabed and foreshore asset remained in Council ownership, and a Te Aro Reclamation Act passed in 1879 allowed the municipality to reclaim its 70-acre endowment. It was the beginning of a saga that would last eight years, testing the tolerance of the populace, and raising serious doubts about the municipality's professional competence. Erratic leadership was provided by the 'difficult and divisive' George Fisher, an Irish-born printer, alcoholic and parliamentarian, who assumed the mayoralty in 1882.[75] The Harbour Board and the Marine Department challenged his reclamation plans, arguing that the resulting areas would be too large, too disruptive to shipping, and would encourage silting. Fisher fought back, but the plans were modified. The project then went into limbo for two years.

Work finally began in 1884. Three successive contractors went out of business. Claims and counter-claims flew back and forth, with various seizures of plant and stores.[76] The *Evening Post* attacked the municipality for 'its record of blunder upon blunder'.[77] Fisher called a meeting of ratepayers to authorise a £75,000 loan to finish the work. Relationships between the municipality and the Harbour Board were said to be 'as strained as those between England and Russia … [A] declaration of war was imminent'.[78] Fisher later introduced an unsuccessful private member's bill to reconstitute the Harbour Board. By 1889, the Te Aro foreshore extended out to the present line of Jervois Quay and Cable Street. A range of buildings, council yards, and depots would be built on the 40 acres thus reclaimed, with the municipality gaining long-term financial benefit from leases. But the Borough's attempt to muscle in on the waterfront had been a bruising experience for all concerned.

Hard times

In 1881, Wellington's non-Maori population reached 20,563, which allowed the capital to take on the coveted title of 'city'. The population continued to grow at the rate of a thousand a year until the mid 1880s.[79] To the newcomers, the grocer poet's dream of 'employment found for all, and that well paid' would have seemed a cruel joke. Vogel's £10 million spending spree was long over: public works had dried up as land and wool prices plummeted, businesses failed and the job market shrank. Lionel Harris himself left town, establishing a new career as a jeweller in the Hawke's Bay.[80] Here was the sting in the tail of immigration policies that enticed more than 140,000 people to the Colony during the 1870s. In late 1879 the *Evening Post* reported: 'Another shipment of the immigrants which a paternal Government is pouring into the colony to swell the number of unemployed, arrived today by the *Rakaia*, which brought no fewer than 300.'[81]

A salute to the Old Identities

The opening in 1879 of John Plimmer's Albert Hotel, on the corner of Willis and Boulcott Streets (the site of the Hotel St George), marked the end of the settlement era and celebrated the colonists who had helped to build Wellington.

A remarkable shrine to past and present grandees, the 50-room, three-storey hotel was topped with a painted statue of Edward Gibbon Wakefield. Carved wooden busts of prominent settlers appeared over the upper window keystones, earning it the nickname 'Wellington Old Identities' Hotel.[82]

Plimmer, a successful merchant, businessman and former city councillor, was often called the 'Father of Wellington'. He was among the notables depicted on the Willis Street facade, along with Councillor J.

John Plimmer's Albert (Wellington Old Identities) Hotel.

ATL, Tyree Collection, G-11618-1/2

S. M. Thompson, merchant J. H. Bethune, and the famous Johnny Martin, whose drinking fountain on Lambton Quay was a popular meeting place.[83] A bust of Premier Sir Julius Vogel was planned for the niche above the front entrance.[84]

John Plimmer is often and well remembered for his 'Ark' — the warehouse, the immigration reception station, and bonded store he had built from the hulk of the *Inconstant*, wrecked on the Pencarrow coast in 1849. He showed the same enterprising spirit in building the Albert Hotel, re-using sections of the old Union Bank, which dated from the 1840s, in its dining and sitting rooms. The hotel was demolished in 1929.

Without jobs or housing, the 'new chums' flocked to Te Aro Flat. By 1880 the area was crammed with undrained working-class cottages, boarding houses, and so-called 'places of entertainment', and criss-crossed by narrow private lanes. An angry group of unemployed immigrants protested on Mt Victoria in 1880, 'to furnish a chapter of their wrongs and disappointments to the public'.[85] By the late 1870s Lorne Street, off Cambridge Terrace, had 30 houses to the acre, matching the densest, grubbiest suburbs of London.[86] Sanitation was virtually non-existent. Little Taranaki Street (now Egmont Street, off Dixon Street) was described as 'a perfect sink of filth and hotbed of disease'.[87]

A few migrants found employment in public works at 3s 6d a day, but hundreds remained out of work. The Borough assisted unemployed married men, drawing on a £100,000 loan raised for road-building. The money 'provided employment for many who would otherwise have been compelled to leave the place'.[88] In 1880, a Council day labour relief committee reported on the building of Rintoul Street.[89] At the end of 1882, councillors met a deputation of 'sundry discharged Corporation labourers … seeking employment. They were informed that their case would meet with every consideration but that there was no work available at present.'[90]

Economic depression brought a more subdued approach to Borough politics. The *Evening Post* lamented that 'there was nothing approaching the life and earnestness which such contests possessed a few years back'.[91] In September 1881, Tommy McKenzie of Ghuznee Street was elected a councillor for Te Aro Ward, serving two solid but unremarkable terms. The lad once saved at Pipitea, now in his mid fifties, was more preoccupied with charitable and business interests, establishing the *New Zealand Mail* and merging his *Independent* with the *New Zealand Times*. Despite being a white-whiskered pillar of the establishment — a trustee of the Home for the Aged Needy, and a board member of St John's Presbyterian Church — Cr McKenzie still got himself into scrapes in pursuit of a good story. One occurred on the harbour as he tried to board a docking vessel:

> The enterprising pressman who was waiting in a boat for an opportunity to get on the deck of a newly arrived ship, seized a rope that was dangling from the mizzen-boom. The vessel at this moment was put about, and Mr McKenzie was left swinging in mid-air; he clung to his rope, however, and was first on board.[92]

With no end to economic depression in sight, the citizens lost interest in municipal politics, despite the appearance of colourful personalities such as George Fisher. Paradoxically, the economic gloom descended as a string of technological breakthroughs reached the city. In 1880 the Borough offices in Featherston Street were connected by telephone to the Manners Street yards.[93] Three years later, electricity lit up the new Government Printing Office, a late beacon of the Vogel boom.[94] The hydraulic lift made its Wellington debut in 1883 in the Bank of New Zealand Building in Customhouse Quay, thus starting a trend towards taller buildings.

By the mid 1880s, Wellington was no longer the ragged settlement of fifteen years earlier. The expansion of the port, the focus on infrastructure, and the forging of transport links to the hinterland all contributed to the change. Population growth, especially in the crowded parts of the inner city, would bring social problems reminiscent of the Old World. Still in its adolescence, the Borough would be tested as it made ready to become a grown-up city.

Illuminations

(1885–1900)

The New Zealand municipalities do practically nothing for the working man … nor does the working man expect them to do anything. He has fully grasped the idea of the central government being his agent for co-operative supply for the common wants, but he never applies this to town councils.

Beatrice Webb, 1898[1]

In June 1887, Queen Victoria's Golden Jubilee fired the imaginations of the citizens of Wellington, as in other outposts of Empire. On Thorndon Hill, the Government House tower was lit up by electric globes, with the letters 'VR' (Victoria Regina) glowing in the middle. On 20 June it was cold and wintry in Wellington, with rain clouds lurking all day. But as dusk fell, thousands poured into the city to watch the illuminations. The *Evening Post* described the activity in the choked streets: 'It seemed as if almost the whole population in town and suburbs had congregated there; and the coloured lights and fireworks which blazed in all directions gave a picturesque aspect to the whole scene.'[2]

Transparencies of the Queen were silhouetted in shop windows across the city, the images lit by incandescent flame and gas 'stars'. Out in the harbour, the SS *Ruapehu* 'was resplendent in blue lights, which were placed at the extremity of each yard, and from the deck and yards, rockets were let off and burst in the air with great beauty'.[3] The light show capped off months of lectures, poetry competitions, horse races, fetes, promenade concerts, sermons, athletic sports, military parades, and Highland dancing at the Opera House. The *pièce de résistance* was displays of electric lighting, seen as far superior to 'sickly yellow' gaslight.

A horse tram heads north along late Victorian Lambton Quay.

WCA, 00138:0:3186

By the late 1880s Mayor Sam Brown (pictured) and his Council realised they could no longer neglect the sewage-soaked and overcrowded inner-city slums. In 1890 alone, 77 locals, mostly from Te Aro, died from 'filth diseases' like typhoid and cholera.

WCA, 00154:0:26

Continuing economic depression, however, dampened the mood of official celebrations: the ailing government of Sir Robert Stout decided not to light up all public buildings in the capital because it would 'excite jealousy' in other towns.[4] The celebrations were, nonetheless, a much-needed tonic in tough times. This was the year when embattled Colonial Treasurer Julius Vogel noted: 'It appears that now the number of unemployed is larger than ever, and that there is a tendency in the "unemployed season" — if I may so term it — to extend each year, until now it really takes up the greater part of the year.'[5]

The Wellington municipality was determined to commemorate the Jubilee year in style. Councillors voted in March 1887 to bestow the name 'Victoria Street' on the muddy stretch of foreshore flanking Willis Street, created by its Te Aro reclamation. In August, Mayor Sam Brown read out a message from Buckingham Palace that the beloved Queen had received their congratulatory telegram on the occasion of her 50 years on the throne.[6]

Jubilee year also brought news that something was rotten in the unlit corners of the city. Te Aro Flat, home to many unemployed and single-roomed tenants, was known to be overcrowded and poorly drained. An *Evening Post* report, entitled 'Dens of Infamy in Wellington: A Raid on the Back Streets', confirmed the moral cost of the 'dirty alleys and black slums' that existed under the noses of respectable Wellington. It was easy to miss the single 'tombstone' column of 6 August, reporting a police raid on the Ghuznee Street brothel district. Constable Baskiville's lantern was said to have lit up a ghastly spectacle, as generations of a single family, a group of women prostitutes, and their clients all scuttled, blinking, from sack-covered, filth-strewn 'hutches' in a back garden.

Inspector Browne later told the Magistrates' Court that the slums of London were nothing to what he famously termed 'the Rabbit-burrows'. Charles Estall, his two daughters, two grandsons and a series of other low-life characters later appeared in the dock. Estall blamed his 79-year-old father, claiming that he rented out the 'hutches' in the quarter-acre garden. Police described them as measuring about four feet high and six feet long.

They were all alike, and a man could hardly turn around in them, for they were just like packing cases. There were six rooms in all, but if put together they could not make one decent room for a white man to live in …

[T]he homes were built of old boxes, with sacks thrown over them for a roof … [T]he occupants simply dossed down on the floor — in fact it was simply crawling.

As the Court jailed the Estalls and sent the boys to an industrial school in the South Island, councillors instructed the Inspector of Nuisances, Alfred Johnson, to clean out the 'hutches'. The *Evening Post* applauded their decision, commenting that the former dwelling had been left 'in a most filthy state', and describing the matter as 'likely to have an injurious effect upon public health'.[7]

The case exposed the city's dark underbelly, and the growing gulf between poverty and wealth. This chapter examines how the propertied elite running the municipality was forced to confront a public health crisis and, reluctantly, fund expensive sanitation infrastructure. The election of a Liberal government in 1890 with an agenda of municipal electoral reform was about to cause a major shake-up.

The 1885 mayoral elections were hard fought, as Cr Tommy McKenzie came up against grizzled campaigners such as Joseph Dransfield and the Browns, Arthur and Sam (no relation). Despite Sam Brown's elaborate handbill, his namesake Arthur took the mayoralty that year. Sam had his turn the following year, however, and was re-elected in 1887.

ATL, B-034-024

A capital eyesore: Grainger and Allen Streets were the heart of a notorious nineteenth century slum, jammed between Courtenay Place and the harbour. In 1899, after a land swap with the council linked to the last Te Aro reclamation, the Harbour Board embarked on a massive eviction and housing clearance programme — the biggest single rejuvenation of an area of Te Aro yet undertaken. The initial reconstruction took place between 1903 and 1907, but a number of buildings were constructed in the 1920s.

WCA, Wellington Harbour Board Collection, Grainger Street 002 & 003

Social evils

In 1887, the *Evening Post* carried revelations that a brothel was operating 'on one of the most public parts of Lambton Quay, under the guise of a tobacconist's shop and cigar divan'.[8] As the case went to the Supreme Court, colonial Wellington found it had unwittingly played host to an imported American vice, known as the 'cigar store battery'.

Ostensibly these were tobacco shops, but an uninitiated customer who entered would find a very meagre stock of cigars and a shopkeeper, often female, who did not appear interested in selling them. The knowing client, on the other hand, would be directed to the brothel in the rear or upstairs.[9]

The discreet backstreet brothel or 'disorderly house' had been a tolerated fixture in the capital since the 1860s. In 1879, when the Inspector of Nuisances was called in to investigate a visit to a brothel, his only concern was that a horse had been left unattended in the street.[10] By the late 1870s, however, the sex industry was increasingly coming to the attention of the city authorities. By 1881, Wellington's houses of ill fame were being targeted as a threat to property values,

prompting ratepayers to present a petition to the municipality:

We desire to bring to your attention the serious loss to property and annoyance and inconvenience caused by persons of ill-fame living in houses adjoining property owned by ourselves. In many cases, we are unable to find tenants for our houses from this cause, and when tenants are found, they only remain a short time.[11]

The authorities rightly suspected that drivers of the dozens of horse-drawn hackney coaches plying the city streets were in cahoots with brothel-owners. By the 1880s a council licence for such vehicles was compulsory, with the driver needing to be 'a fit person … of good fame and character'.[12]

The capital's prostitutes knew where the money was: Wellington's 'disorderly houses' tended to be within a stone's throw of Parliament:

Most of Thorndon's brothels were in tiny Fraser's Lane and John Street, while the south end of town had a brothel 'precinct' around Quin (later Sturdee) and Ghuznee Streets. In 1885, police returns showed Wellington had twenty brothels with about sixty prostitutes, the majority of them living in Thorndon.[13]

Although unemployment in the 'Hungry Eighties' ravaged much of the Colony, Wellington's busy port and the presence of the civil service and head offices protected it from the worst effects. The three-storey, red-brick Government Insurance Offices on Customhouse Quay exemplified the fine public buildings now gracing the city centre. Many of the capital's 2,000 civil servants worked in the four-storey wooden Government Building at the end of Lambton Quay, popularly known as 'the Big Matchbox', possibly because many feared in a time in which fires were commonplace that it might go the same way.[14] Despite the depressed economy and high unemployment, immigrants were still flowing through the gates of Queen's Wharf. Between 1891 and 1896, Wellington's population grew by 22.1 percent, compared with 12.3 percent in Auckland, although the latter still had more people. The capital's growth was phenomenal over this period: seven times that of Dunedin and three times that of Christchurch.[15] Wellington would continue to match Auckland's rate of population growth until 1945, with both cities increasing their populations eightfold.[16]

Like the newly minted word 'unemployment', the term 'public health' was gaining currency by the late 1880s. Wellington's Town Clerk had a parallel role as secretary to the local Board of Health, whose task was to confront the dangers of deadly infectious diseases such as typhoid and cholera. Removing nuisances and cleaning up accumulated refuse became an urgent priority: more had to be done. Three-quarters of the typhoid deaths in the early 1890s would occur in the sewage-soaked backyards of Te Aro Flat.[17] An 1886 amendment to the Municipal Corporations Act allowed local bodies to prevent 'the overcrowding of residents in houses to the danger of the public health'. The *New Zealand Times* urged councillors to act:

> Some efficient check is needed on the present wholesale erection of disrectifiable and unsanitary hovels or shanties grossly miscalled 'dwellings' or 'residences' — for they are utterly unsuited as human abodes, not merely for their cramped internal dimensions and defective arrangements but also to the way in which they are crowded together … In Thorndon, Te Aro and Cook Wards numerous cases may be seen of incipient 'rookeries' … Some sort of architectural censorship such as would allow the local authorities to stop the erection of dangerous or unsanitary buildings should be provided.[18]

Passing building bylaws was one thing; ensuring that land speculators, demonised as 'fat men', adhered to them was another. As we have seen, local body politics was dominated by wealthy elites wary of state intervention, which was anathema to the Victorian ethos. Most city fathers of the late nineteenth century were self-made men such as John Plimmer and Joseph Dransfield, closer in outlook to the average land speculator than to their poverty-stricken tenants. But the wider risks to social and economic well-being posed by shortcomings in the city's infrastructure helped to nudge municipal leaders away from the hands-off approach that led to the slums of Te Aro.

The private trams to Newtown — and beyond — would spirit families to healthier climes. Between 1878 and 1901, areas such as Mt Cook and Newtown accommodated more than half of the city's population growth.[19] The extension of electrified tramlines to coastal areas such as Island Bay helped to sow the seeds of suburbia. The wealthier classes, however, remained in the inner city. Engineers bolted the houses of businessmen and senior civil servants to the windy ridges overlooking Thorndon and Te Aro. The view from their sash windows, however, had changed little from pioneering days: the amphitheatre of treeless hills; the town itself, blasted by dust from unpaved streets; the raw new reclamations jutting into the harbour. Despite some relief on the western fringe, from affluent Thorndon along The Terrace to Upper Willis Street, where private gardens and some public parks provided patches of green, Wellington was regularly lambasted as the 'ugliest city in the colony' and 'a characterless and inelegant town'.[20]

But not even the most venomous editorial writer could fault Wellington's glittering harbour. This, its unassailable reputation as the 'Corner Shop' of the Colony and its position near the geographical centre made it the busiest port in the country by 1890.[21] Here was a hub for the import and export sectors, and for the influential coastal shipping network. As one historian has put it: 'The warehouses of reclamation Wellington were the sorting place channelling the exchanges between industrial Britain and frontier central New Zealand.'[22] The port was crammed with steamers, big and small, plying the provincial, trans-Tasman, and European routes. The Wellington and Manawatu Railway Company's route to Palmerston North opened with a fanfare in the mid 1880s. However, a large proportion of the thousands of tons of wool received at the Wellington railway wharf every year was still carried by the 'mosquito fleet' of coastal steamers, schooners and ketches.[23] Supplementing the wool-based economy were export staples such as dairy produce and frozen meat, made possible by new technology that would bring wealth to the young nation. On 25 February 1883, nine months after the *Dunedin*'s historic voyage, the *Lady Jocelyn* sailed out of Wellington carrying the capital's first London-bound refrigerated cargo of 5,794 sheep carcasses and 352 quarters of beef.[24] Meat-processing plants opened in the central city during the 1880s, before moving variously to Ngauranga and Petone.

The activity on the wharves — a 24-hour operation after electric lighting was installed in the mid 1880s — provided jobs for thousands in the city. Wellington also enjoyed a less predictable role as the Colony's fastest-growing manufacturing centre, its goods exported to Australia and sent around New Zealand. Thousands more people worked in nearly 400 registered factories and workshops. Edwin Arnold, for example, ran a basket and pram assembly enterprise, employing nineteen people and turning out 2,000 baby carriages and countless wickerwork objects every year. His business straddled the city: its ironwork was forged in a Courtenay Place smithy, above which the woodwork was assembled from kahikatea; meanwhile the willow osiers were woven in a building on Old Customhouse Quay, and the parts were finally put together, painted and varnished above retail premises in Willis Street.[25]

A jubilee of night-soil

In the summer of 1889, Inspector of Nuisances Alfred Johnson checked the plumbing of 5,697 dwellings across the city. Finding most of them sanitarily 'good', his report concluded that 'the backyards of the city are not nearly in so bad a condition to the eye as have been frequently depicted'. But with 117 houses classified as 'bad' (64 of them in Te Aro Ward) and 364 as 'untidy', he urged the municipality to do more:

Children wading in Wellington harbour in the 1880s. Reports that many kids skylarked around the mouths of the town sewers forced niggardly councillors to invest in a proper sewerage scheme.

WCA, 00138:0:2867

> Spots outside of premises, and, in some cases, inside yards and under houses, of open, filthy drains, over which the residents have no control at all … cannot be properly and efficiently removed till a thorough drainage of the city takes place and the localities freed from the daily fear of typhoid and other highly dangerous diseases.[26]

Johnson's report included an indelible image of children frolicking at the city's beaches amid water-borne sewage:

> One of the causes, perhaps, of the death rate in the city being large is that numbers of children are to be seen — particularly on the sunny days — congregated about the mouths of the main sewers of the city, just where the contents empty into the bay, amusing themselves by fishing etc, and seated in many cases right in the midst of the odours that arise from the drains.[27]

By 1889, John Plimmer's theories on sanitation were looking increasingly flimsy.

Johnson's revelations stirred councillors into debating the problem, but the prospect of spending tens of thousands of pounds on a solution remained unthinkable to many ratepayers. Then came a bombshell. Lord Cranley, the young son and heir of the newly arrived Governor, Lord Onslow, contracted typhoid fever in Wellington and nearly died. The family later fled Thorndon, finding sanctuary in Nelson. Lord Cranley's illness overshadowed the opening of Parliament in August 1889: parliamentarians were mortified, and the state of the capital's drains became a national laughing stock.

The government engineer who examined the plumbing at Government House on the eve of the vice-regal family's arrival had been aware of the risks:

> The government were very desirous that all possible precautions should be taken, especially as children were coming to the House, and neither trouble nor expense was spared in endeavouring to ensure reliable sanitation … [A]ll was done to guard against any ill effects from the unfortunately well known defective condition of the general city drainage system.[28]

The saga of the vice-regal drains took on the quality of a late Victorian melodrama. The *Evening Post* reported that shipping companies were being asked by tourists in transit how they could avoid landing in the city. Stories spread about the 'loathsome state' of the timber taken from the Thorndon drains: 'It was a sniff from one of these dreadful boards close to the Museum that gave typhoid fever to the child of one of the caretakers.'[29]

Young Cranley survived, but his nervous parents thereafter avoided the capital. In 1890 Mayor Charles Johnston was appointed godfather of the second Onslow son, a sign of improving relationships between the municipality and the Crown. The new borough formed that year in Wellington's northern suburbs was named Onslow, in honour of the family. But Lord Onslow's return to England half-way through his vice-regal term spoke volumes. In the absence of adequate sanitation in the capital, the Governor clearly feared for his young family's safety.[30]

Far worse was to come. During 1890, 77 residents of the city died from infectious diseases such as typhoid and cholera.[31] Bylaws were passed abolishing cesspits and outlawing the burial of night-soil, but the deaths continued. Desperate councillors called on the vice-regal engineer, H. P. Higginson, to draw up a sanitation plan for the city. He returned with an adaptation of an 1878 scheme, based on new routes for existing sewers, new storm-water drains, and open watercourses from the inner harbour out to the south coast. Higginson proposed a hydraulic drainage system starting at an intercepting sewer at the junction of Willis and Dixon Streets. From there it would head south-south-east, passing the north side of Wellington Hospital, through a mile-long tunnel to Kilbirnie, and ending up to the east of Lyall Bay. Engineers Ferguson and Cuthbert endorsed the scheme in their 1890 report to the municipality, making a flippant reference to the Colony's 50th birthday celebrations:

A muddler's story

City councillors nearly stripped Waring Taylor's name from the eponymous street in 1885, after this prominent Wellingtonian fell from grace.

After arriving in Wellington in 1842, William Waring Taylor went into business as a Te Aro merchant. As he acquired rural

Becky Masters

properties through the bullish 1870s, he grew rich and respectable. He became Member of the House of Representatives (MHR) for Wellington City in 1860 and Deputy Superintendent of Wellington Province in the same year, serving as its speaker for a decade from 1865.

His former schoolmate, the English novelist Charlotte Brontë, noted that he was 'destined to grow up an original … [A] unique stamp will mark him always.'[32] He was also described as 'a kindly, well-meaning muddler whose business failure and

misappropriation of trust funds led to his conviction in 1885'.[33]

The economic depression of the 1880s proved Taylor's undoing. Early in the decade he was in financial trouble over a Wairarapa property. In 1884 he appeared before the local bankruptcy court in a blaze of publicity, later facing fraud charges in the Supreme Court. In July 1885, as the 66-year-old Taylor was sentenced to five years' gaol, *the New Zealand Times* described him as holding the 'undisputed championship amongst New Zealand defaulters and scoundrels'.[34]

An outraged Councillor Petherick later moved that the name Waring Taylor 'be struck off the plans of the city', and that in future the street be called Britannia Street.[35] His fellow councillors were more forgiving, and the name Waring Taylor lives on in the city.

'It has … been very aptly expressed that the recent prevalence of zymotic [bacterial] disease in the city is merely Nature's celebration of a Jubilee of night soil.'[36]

Midway through 1890, councillors accepted the engineer's proposal. Incoming Mayor Francis Dillon Bell, mindful of continuing ratepayer support for Plimmer's views on sanitation, promoted a City of Wellington Loan Empowering Act to Parliament. The legislation ensured that drainage loans could be approved with a simple majority of votes, making it harder for stingy, short-sighted ratepayers to seek a loan poll to overturn them. The £165,000 loan (worth more than $26 million in today's terms) was debated at a public meeting in September 1892 at the Opera House and passed by 2,355 votes to 660. Medical officer Dr W. A. Chapple pointed out that local families shared the Onslows' concerns.

Many of the public are panic-stricken. Some are fleeing the district, while others are sending their families to more healthy situations while they themselves attend to their businesses … [N]othing short of a complete system of modern sewerage will make the city free as it ought to be from preventable disease.[37]

The city's typhoid epidemic peaked in 1892, as Wellington Hospital recorded 193 cases and 16 deaths.[38] The spectre of typhoid drove more people out of the inner city. Advertisements for the fast-growing suburbs on the city's perimeter played to these fears.

> Melrose has a clear, beautiful atmosphere being said by medical men and practical chemists to be exceedingly pure, and largely impregnated with ozone, that life-giving factor. The necessity that exists for fathers seeking residence sites where their children may be reared without the doctor's constant presence is felt by every family man in Wellington.[39]

Work began on the drainage scheme in 1892, just as the incidence of disease began to decline. Mayor Alfred De Bathe Brandon reported in 1894 that typhoid had shown 'a very considerable decrease during the past two years'.[40] The immense and complex project dragged on until the end of the century, amid cost over-runs of £30,000. When British intellectuals Beatrice and Sidney Webb visited Wellington in 1898, they learned that the municipality had consciously used its own workmen to dig the great sewer tunnels, 'having found it impossible to prevent scamping [skimping] by the contractor'.[41] According to a later Mayor, John Blair, the Council 'had been hustled into the drainage scheme at a cost to the ratepayer of hundreds and thousands of pounds more than the works should have cost; and it was likely that it would yet cost many more thousands'.[42]

More delays and cost over-runs lay ahead. A budget shortfall necessitated further legislation in 1898, with the city finally taking charge of the completed scheme in 1899. The first sewage poured from an outfall pipe at Moa Point, a rocky outcrop on the south coast. Although the last drain was not in fact finished until 1904, adequate sanitation had finally arrived in the capital. Wellington found itself the first main centre to install a city-wide sewerage scheme, beating Dunedin by nine years and Auckland by fifteen. The new sewers would meet the city's needs for a century.

Other infrastructural problems persisted. In the 1880s Wellington experienced a prolonged drought, with rainfall in the capital at its lowest in 30 years.[43] The dry spell peaked with a wind-fuelled fire in 1886 which destroyed a dozen buildings on Lambton Quay, near Woodward Street. The city's fire brigade trained nine hoses on the blaze, but the high pressure expected from the Wainuiomata waterworks failed to eventuate.[44] As flames consumed a music shop, a picture-framer's shop, and other business premises, water to other parts of the city was cut off to help boost the pressure in the hydrants to 150 pounds per square inch. A gauge in the municipal offices later showed a water pressure of just 60 psi. The early-morning shambles in Lambton Quay made a mockery of long-running efforts to fireproof central-city buildings, set up a viable fire brigade, and secure a water supply capable of meeting fire-fighters' needs.

For the next few years, borough engineers pondered how to maintain the pressure needed to force water up to houses built on the city's many hills. One blamed the low pressure on a leaking cement water race carrying part of the flow from the Wainuiomata reservoir. The diminishing size of the water pipes as they reached the outskirts of the city was cited as another problem. Poor workmanship didn't help: 'The damage to the bottom of the [water] race has, I am confident, been principally caused … by the men making a highway of it with hobnailed boots before it was properly set.'[45]

In the late 1880s, waterworks engineer Nicholas Marchant took the matter in hand. After trekking the mile-and-a-quarter length of the harbour-side water race, he concluded that what became known as 'the Great Leak' was only part of the problem. He pointed instead to the vast quantities of water used by a private company to generate hydro-electric power for street lighting in the city (see below): 'Water must cease to be distributed for [electric] power in Wellington all the year round, unless the gathering grounds are largely extended or storage works of large capacity constructed.'[46]

In 1889, Wellington had basked in the glory of being the first city in the Colony to be lit by electricity. On 29 June, Mayor Sam Brown flicked the switch, prompting poet Alan Mulgan to write: 'Tonight a thousand suns resplendent shine, from Lambton's curve to Newtown's far confine'.[47] The move followed years of campaigning by angry citizens, scornful of the feeble gas lamps provided by the municipality and worried about the risk of injury in darkened streets:

> Surely they have had enough experience to know that too much illumination
> cannot be given us on such wet and dirty nights as last night. There will, I fear,
> be some serious accidents originating from no other [cause] than neglect on
> their part and then they will perceive the necessity of lighting our darkness.[48]

Generating hydro-electric power for the street lights brought on an immediate headache. In 1888 the Gulcher Electric Light and Power Company installed

480 Swan Edison incandescent lamps, each of 20 candlepower, along the main thoroughfare. Water was passed through 30-horsepower turbines located in a generating plant on what is now Te Aro Park, in lower Manners Street. The noise was so loud that residents could not sleep. By 1890, the problems had compounded:

> There has been some misconception between the parties arranging the lighting contract … [A]lthough ample in volume, the [water] pressure from Wainui supply is insufficient, alone, to give the lighting power contracted for, and the extra pressure required for this has to be obtained from the Karori supply, which also by itself cannot work the engines … This is under any circumstances a serious defect.[49]

Variable water pressure saw street lighting regularly turned off after midnight. From 1892, further generation was required as electric lighting spread to private homes and offices, including the municipality's Featherston Street building. To cope with the additional demand, Gulcher's successor, the Electric Light and Power Company, built a steam-powered generating unit in Harris Street, on the current site of the City Art Gallery. In 1895, councillors were told that 'the dullness of the lamps in the council chambers was owing to the fact that the pressure of the water supply had been very low lately'.[50] The Council later bought the company, and expanded it into the Electric Lighting Department.

Clean and decent

As economic depression continued, Mayor John Duthie and a team of four councillors investigated municipal spending to find possible 'alterations or improvements'. Their report revealed an organisation in a state of paralysis, unable to embark on important civic works because of a lack of funds, and with the authority of an overburdened Town Clerk ignored by the Inspector of Nuisances and the Collector of Rates. With the salaries of thirteen executive staff costing a total of £3,544 a year, the Council was spending far more than equivalent local bodies in Dunedin (£2,670) and Christchurch (£1,301). The report painted a damning picture: 'The Committee had been struck by the want of organization and cohesion in the Corporation staff, as well as the absence of proper subordination of its several members to the recognized head of the staff'.[51]

A City Solicitor was later appointed to relieve the Town Clerk. Duthie meanwhile recommended sacking 40 day-labour staff, including five 'scavengers', six drivers, two carpenters and a night-watchman, preferring 'the adoption of the contract system for works of all kinds'. In language foreshadowing the corporate restructurings of a century later, the report argued that 'a considerable reduction can be made in the cost of the Wellington Corporation staff, and that by improved organization its efficiency can be increased'. The City Surveyor, however, soon complained that 'under the contract system a very much closer and more consistent supervision is required'.[52] Within a year, the municipality had reverted to the day-labour system.[53]

Alarm over the spread of typhoid made refuse disposal a priority. Teams of 'scavengers' in horse-drawn carts gathered the city's rubbish from iron boxes on the pavement. It was then carried to the municipal yards, located on reclaimed land at Clyde Quay, near the present site of the Chaffers Street supermarket. Disposal problems led to a decision to collect and burn the rubbish in the council tip, on the edge of the yards. By 1888, the mountains of accumulated waste had hastened the arrival of a refuse 'destructor' or incinerator. Mayor Sam Brown officially opened the great brick building with its imposing chimney. The flame was lit on 1 May 1889 and kept alight around the clock. In its first eleven months, 15,500 cubic yards of refuse was burned.[54] Famously, the furnace was used to burn so-called 'fever linen' during the worst outbreaks of typhoid.[55] Its presence seemed to reassure the populace. The *Evening Post* even suggested that the chimney was part of a larger cleansing process:

> It is just possible, we think, that the outbreak of typhoid at the present time may be due in some measure to the improved sanitary systems introduced in connection with the Destructor. The free removal of rubbish has led to a general clearing up of back yards, and it is quite possible that the process has disturbed many buried sources of infection and liberated the germs of disease for atmospheric distribution. If so, the evil will probably only be a temporary one.[57]

Smoke from the destructor's chimney lessened its popularity. Disposal practices at the Clyde Quay yards failed to impress local businesswoman Matilda Meech, whose salt-water baths in Oriental Bay were a popular public bathing facility in an era when most people did not have access to a private bath. The pool was large and tidal, and enclosed by wooden palings. 'Sporty young men rowed over from the town if it was not too choppy, or walked around to Meech's baths. A red flag was hoisted during gentlemen's hours and a blue flag during ladies' hours.'[57]

An appetite for destruction

For just under 60 years, the two chimneys of the municipal destructor (incinerator) scarred the city skyline. Rubbish was collected in horse-drawn carts, taken up a ramp, tipped onto a storage floor, then fed through a door into the furnace below. Three shifts of 'destructor hands' kept the fires fed.

By the early 1900s, the city's new sewerage scheme needed power for the Shone 'ejectors', which helped to pump waste out to the south coast. In an early example of co-generation, a second destructor was designed to supply heat to generate steam for the system's air-compressor plants. Its furnaces, with their own chimney, were completed in 1908, at a cost of £20,000.

In 1911, an eight-hour shift earned a 'hand' the princely sum of ten shillings ($67 in today's terms). Burns and other injuries were commonplace, as firemen and 'greasers' toiled in cramped conditions and scorching

The smoking chimneys of the Council destructor dominated the Chaffers Street skyline for more than half a century.

WCA, 00138:0:12487

temperatures. Summary walk-outs, and even fights, occurred as men refused to handle the often wet and rotting rubbish. In 1913, the City Engineer agreed with the union that too many hapuka heads were being sent for burning.[58] By the 1930s, coal had to be added to household refuse to ensure a regular steam pressure.

In her 1974 book *Tooth and Nail: The Story of a Daughter of the Depression*, Mary Findlay writes of visiting her foreman father at the yard:

As I entered the Council yard, the old night-watchman greeted me. He was a friend of my childhood and many was the sixpence he had given me. 'Your father's on watch. Go in through the stokehold, I saw him there a minute ago.' The stokehold was to me a place of wonder. The walls had many small windows, most of them broken, and the roof was high and black. At the great doorway stood a mountain of coal and beyond it lay

In 1891, Meech complained about detritus from neighbouring furnaces. Members of the sanitation committee investigated, and found 'several dead dogs and a quantity of offensive refuse consisting of rotten meat and other decaying matter'.[60] Meech took the case to court and won £200 in compensation for loss of business.[61] Eight years later, the Council terminated her tenancy to make room for municipal salt-water baths that had become a craze in other parts of the world.

The city's dead were a far more sensitive disposal issue. After serving for half a century as the town cemetery, the Bolton Street graveyard was readied for closure, except for burials in existing family plots. The Cemeteries Act 1882 delayed the move: under the law, a site for a new cemetery had to be established before an existing facility could be closed. The difficulty of finding a new location meant the furnaces. Each furnace had four doors which swung at a bang from a long-handled shovel and revealed huge coal fires. There were two stokers or firemen, as they were called, on duty. During their watch they would shovel the entire mountain into the furnaces. One was a giant blonde Swede called Alex Pederson and the other a stocky, powerfully built Italian known as Garibaldi. They shovelled alternately. 'Bang' would go the furnace door, then one man would put in ten shovels and 'clomp', the door would shut. Then the other man would repeat the process on the next door. They were stripped to the waist, their faces streaked with coal and sweat. Each had a rag tied around his neck and at the end of each stint he would glance at a pressure gauge on the wall, lean momentarily on his shovel and wipe his neck with the rag.[59]

By the late 1930s, the destructor could not generate enough steam to keep the sewers moving. Increasing operating costs, the electrification of the sewerage plant, and the burial of rubbish saw operations scaled back from 1939, and cease altogether from 1946.

A line-up of destructor 'hands', photographed around the turn of the century.

ATL, S. C. Smith Collection, G-20047-1/1

that Bolton Street continued to be used for burials into 1890, a practice that constituted a public health danger, according to the *Evening Post*.[62] After looking at sites in Island Bay and Khandallah, the Council decided on Karori, which involved buying 95 acres of land at a cost of £4,000. The new cemetery was nearly not established at all. Under the 1882 Act, a new facility couldn't be built within the boundary of an existing city or borough. With Karori Borough due to be established in 1891, the land was still deemed 'rural' and the site was secured with weeks to spare.

Street repair remained the most visible — and audible — of all Council functions, especially the machinery associated with it. One day in August 1887, horses took fright as the steam-powered road-roller lumbered out of the municipal yards and along Courtenay Place, a roadman with a red flag walking 30 yards in front to warn other traffic.

> But for this precaution the consequences this morning would probably have been serious, and there would have been an incontinent flight on the part of horses attached to heavy drays, light expresses, and tramcars. Despite the care of the jehus [drivers], one of the tramcar horses was startled, and pulled its car about 12 ft off the line as it pranced about.[63]

The noisy steamroller was initially restricted to night-time use in areas such as Thorndon Quay. But demand for its services grew, as bus and tram wheels shredded the road surfaces. Municipal workmen regularly coated the main streets with metal (gravel), and built wooden crossings at busy intersections.

As Wellington approached its first half-century, councillors turned their thoughts from roads and rubbish to 'civilising' institutions such as a free public library and botanic garden: 'Perhaps, before very long, we shall learn really to enjoy our "splendid leisure" and follow the example of our European Continental brethren and establish public gardens in which we may take our pleasure in a rational manner.'[64]

The botanical gardens were popular with genteel strollers from Thorndon, but the Te Aro 'riff-raff' also favoured them as a quiet spot for love-making and illegal games of two-up.

Terence Hodgson collection

The Colonial Garden on Tinakori Road, set up by statute in 1869, started life as a glorified nursery for the Town Belt. By the late 1880s, as the gardens fell into neglect, the municipality reluctantly assumed responsibility for them. The Wellington Botanic Garden Vesting Bill of 1891 set aside land for an observatory, and stipulated that the original thirteen acres be kept as a botanic garden in perpetuity. According to the *Cyclopedia of New Zealand*, the garden was the city's 'one really pretty part'. It described the reserve as 'not suited to the rushing, thoughtless, multitude; but for the overwrought man of business who likes to admire Nature in all her rugged beauty, or for the poet or preacher who wishes to catch "an inspiration from the fountain pure"'.[65]

The municipal garden came to be more than just 'lungs' (clean air) for the genteel strollers of Thorndon; the riff-raff of Te Aro Flat regularly took the tram to Tinakori Road to gamble in its leafy shade. By 1894 special constables were stationed in the garden during daylight to crack down on games of 'two-up', and to prevent damage to the plants.[66] The behaviour of respectable visitors could also irritate staff. One Sunday in March 1895, a Miss Lingard was spotted 'thoughtlessly walking' on the grass. The custodian was reprimanded after he 'shook his stick in Miss Lingard's face and rudely ordered her to clear out of the gardens'.[67]

If a municipal garden was a desirable civic acquisition, a public library represented a hallmark of Victorian civilisation. A letter circulated by the Free Public Library Fund in 1889 argued that a 'free public library is essential to a city of this size, and it is submitted that its establishment during [Wellington's] coming Jubilee year would be an appropriate monument of the position to which the city has attained at this stage in its history'.[68]

Wellington had always been a bookish place. Half a century had passed since settlers, barely off the ship, held a meeting to set up a public library and adjacent reading room. The Pickwick Club attempted to raise funds for a library building, but failed. Local representatives of the Mechanics' Institute, the best known of the Victorian civic associations working to educate the English masses, enjoyed more success. Committee member Tommy McKenzie later turned the Port Nicholson Mechanics' Institute, Public School and Library into the more populist Athenaeum, housed in a distinctive building on Lambton Quay.[69] A municipal library was then mooted, with businessman W. H. Levin donating £1,000 and a further £2,000 raised by public subscription. The library was seen as a stepping-stone towards a town hall: 'The Public Library ought to be an architectural ornament to the city. The design ought to be capable of enlargement to contain a Town Hall and Art Gallery, and ultimately, if not in the first instance, municipal offices'.[70]

In 1893, with 5,000 volumes from the Athenaeum's tatty collection, a municipal library opened on the present site of the civic administration building. The library committee included such notables as James Hector, Charles Pharazyn, and scholar and civil servant Edward Tregear. The book selection committee was besieged with offers of collections, including works on natural science and theosophy. Residents flocked to the library, its newspaper room proving most popular. By the start of 1895 the number of subscribers topped 500.

A yacht glides over a pond-like Wellington harbour in 1890.

ATL, G-24705-1/2

Fifty glorious years

In January 1890, the Colony — and Wellington City — celebrated their first half-century. A great upsurge of civic pride helped to push infrastructural difficulties to one side. The *Evening Post*, musing on the achievements of the Colony's founders, commented: 'It would be particularly appropriate that in the Jubilee Year the Mayoral chair of the capital and senior city of the colony should be occupied either by one of the early settlers or by the descendent [*sic*] of one'.[71]

The ubiquitous Thomas McKenzie, who had been just thirteen years old in 1840, now served as secretary for Mayor Johnston's Jubilee Celebrations committee. His commemoration plans, centred on a street parade, were soon mired in controversy. Governor Onslow had proclaimed 29 January the fiftieth anniversary of the Colony's founding, commemorating the day of Captain Hobson's arrival in the Bay of Islands. McKenzie, however, decided to mark the arrival of the first settlers at Petone, on 22 January 1840. Auckland newspapers attacked the capital's decision to jump the gun, prompting the *Evening Post* to describe 22 January as 'a flesh and blood human jubilee':

> The one day, a de facto actual birthday, when the first actual living bona fide colonists arrived … and the other a parchment or sheepskin ceremonial birthday, a thing of red tape and of much sealing wax, with firing of salutes and waving of cocked hats.[72]

McKenzie's lifelong personal and business links with Maori ensured that representatives of the tangata whenua joined the commemorations. Included in a chiefly group of 30 were grandsons of the late Te Puni — Nopera and Honiara — plus a nephew, Te Teira. Wi Hapi Pakau represented the late Wi Tako from the Hutt District. From Petone came Mawhini Hohua. By this time, however, Maori were virtually absent from the city. Te Atiawa had left Pipitea to join their kin at Waiwhetu, in Lower Hutt. Ngati Tama had also moved away. The people remaining belonged largely to the Te Atiawa sub-tribes of Ngati Te Whiti, Te Matehou,

A dressed-up Willis Street hosts Queen Victoria's Diamond Jubilee parade, 1897. That year also saw the founding of Victoria College (later University). For the first few years, lectures were held in rental accommodation downtown. Around 1900, the decision was made to build on 'six verticle acres' in Kelburn.

WCA, 00138:0:10177

Ngati Tawhirikura and Ngati Puketapu. Pa sites at both Te Aro and Pipitea were unoccupied; Pito-one (Petone) Pa was abandoned soon afterwards.

The huge Jubilee parade passed through the city on a dusty January morning, with ten thousand people marching and another twenty thousand watching. Banner-waving schoolchildren, fife-and-drum bands, and a team of maypole dancers marched at the front. Then came the survivors from 1840, some on foot, others seated in a carriage draped with the New Zealand Company flag. Behind them came carriages full of municipal dignitaries and former Mayors, followed by fire brigades, and volunteer and professional soldiers. Like so many occasions in the colony, it was a celebration of what the colonists liked to call 'progress'. The procession took 50 minutes to pass.

The parade wound its way from Lambton Quay to the Basin Reserve, where speeches of self-congratulation were followed by children's sports events. As at Queen Victoria's Golden Jubilee celebrations, the climax was a torchlight procession and illuminations. A giant transparency graced the municipal buildings, carrying the city arms and motto, 'Suprema a Situ' (Supreme by Place), above the numerals '1840'. The next day, the *Evening Post* commented: 'Our first five decades have been those of real hard work, but after viewing yesterday's proceedings it needs no seer's eye to predict that our children will abundantly reap the liberal harvest sown by their progenitors.'[73]

As affectionate toasts were raised to the settlers during Jubilee Year, the political landscape was about to undergo dramatic and lasting change. After January 1891, John Ballance's reforming Liberal government ushered in a new era of populist urban politics, as the electorate edged aside the colonial gentry who had dominated the scene for half a century. The road to colonial democracy had been signalled as early as 1879, with the introduction of manhood suffrage. Increasing numbers of working- and middle-class parliamentarians came to the capital to fill the benches of the House of Representatives. At the local body level, however, rent-paying working men and women were still denied the vote.

Ballance's successor Richard Seddon, a West Coast publican and seasoned local body politician, exemplified the new breed of working-class politician who distrusted the soft-handed Wellington elites. He saw the capital as a shuttered enclave, out of touch with what was happening in the rest of the Colony. He distrusted the powerful and privileged civil service mandarins who, he believed, had become a law unto themselves by the 1880s. He reserved particular bile, however, for the gentleman sons of the pioneers, men such as Francis Bell, who disliked populism and opposed most of the Liberals' programme. Seddon gained

Premier Richard Seddon and family members, circa 1900. His seventh daughter, Elizabeth May (centre rear), born in 1880, became active in patriotic and social work and was elected a city councillor in 1941. Later Dame Elizabeth Gilmer, she served for eleven years, and was chairman of the Libraries and Parks and Reserves Committee.

ATL, Edward Child Collection, G-16535-1/4

a reputation as a scourge of the capital, a man who 'never lost an opportunity of taunting Wellington on the poor public spirit of its citizens'.[74] They returned the compliment: for years the Liberals polled poorly in Wellington. For Seddon, the reluctance of its councillors to widen streets and demolish overcrowded slums proved their immorality, and their capture by 'fat man' speculators.

> I say that in the hands of the members of the Borough Council are the lives of the citizens; that with no lungs, with unsanitary conditions, with overcrowding comes death; and you will find the mortality in the overcrowded parts of the cities — in the slums, where these unsanitary conditions exist — the percentage of deaths as compared with other portions of the city is very large ...[75]

Seddon's dislike of the Wellington municipality was due in part to the months he had spent in the capital since 1879 as an MHR, when he saw its handiwork as he cantered home on horseback. The Premier and his Treasurer, Joseph Ward, set up their own social 'court'. Theirs centred around 47 Molesworth Street (Seddon's home) and Premier House (or Awarua House, as Ward called it) in Tinakori Road. Seddon and Ward actively excluded people such as Francis Dillon Bell and other prominent conservatives who criticised the way the Liberals pumped up the civil service between 1890 and 1912.[76]

The practice of rotating the Wellington mayoralty around the city's gentry was lampooned by fellow parliamentarian, former Mayor and maverick George Fisher:

> When the time for the election of mayor comes around we go through this stereotyped process … [T]here are the usual heartrending scenes. The person waited upon, bathed in blushes, declines irrevocably, but asks for time to consider the awful suddenness of the request and finally resigns himself into the hands of his committee whom he requests to do with him just as they may deem meet and fitting. This childish performance is generally confined to Mr H. D. Bell, Mr John Duthie and one or two others of the coterie. Mr Bell says he does not want to be mayor and begs Mr Duthie to take the office. Mr Duthie says he does not want it and begs Mr Bell to take it. They almost fall on each other's necks in their painful solicitude for the welfare of the city — and the welfare of each other … [T]his performance goes on every year. The office is regarded as their personal property to be handed from one to another at their pleasure. There never would be an election if this coterie had its way … [77]

As Mayor, Francis Henry Dillon Bell worked hard to secure a sewerage scheme for Wellington. A prominent lawyer, he became a parliamentarian in 1893, after serving two terms as Mayor (and returned for a third term in 1897). When the Reform Party came to power in 1912, Bell became a minister and was later appointed Attorney-General. After William Massey's death in May 1925, he became the first New Zealand-born Prime Minister, filling the role for just sixteen days.

WCA, 00510:0:13

Such barbs were well-aimed. Too often, councillors were diverted by trivial matters such as preventing auctioneers from ringing bells to advertise sales, banning boxing exhibitions in a Manners Street hall, and ensuring that shooting galleries were closed by 10 p.m. Time was spent debating a bylaw to stop the citizenry throwing fruit peelings on the pavement.[78] In 1896, the *Evening Post* was still damning the Council as a sleepy hollow of narrow privilege, out of touch with the needs of the populace:

> Until the best and the ablest of our citizens as well as the humblest ratepayers become imbued with some at least of the spirit they express, the capital city of this country cannot arise from the slough of despond in which it now sinks with such seeming indifference.[79]

Votes for all

The 1890s began with the first outbreak of national industrial unrest, and ended with the emergence of a strong Wellington-based union movement. A trans-Tasman maritime strike drew Wellington Harbour Board labourers into an unsuccessful two-month stand-off in late 1890. Days before the strike ended, the first Labour Day was declared for 28 October 1890, as a march of unionists celebrating the eight-hour day filled city streets. By 1892, the Eight Hour Day Demonstration Committee was hiring Newtown Park for an annual Labour Day rally and lobbying the Council to declare it a public holiday. Councillors opposed the idea, but gave Corporation employees a half-day off and agreed to close the streets to vehicular traffic from 9.30 a.m.[80] Desiring to gain a better understanding of industrial matters, the municipality ordered a copy of the report of the Australian Royal Commission on Strikes.[81]

Although the Long Depression was lifting by the mid 1890s, unemployment remained an ugly fact of national life. In the absence of formal assistance for the jobless and their families, Wellington mayors raised 'subscriptions' to fund prominent local charities such as the Benevolent Institute, and created work for the city's unemployed in areas such as road-building, tree-planting and gorse-cutting. In 1895, Mayor Charles Luke told a Council meeting that 22 men had applied that day for gorse-cutting work, compared with 50 a fortnight earlier.[82] A delegation in 1896 reported that 160 local men were without work, and attending union representatives urged councillors to pay no man on relief less than six shillings a day.[83]

'Municipal socialism' was a liberal collectivist philosophy adopted in the nineteenth century by major British local authorities such as Glasgow and

Birmingham. By the mid 1890s, it was gaining currency among progressive elements in Wellington, including its union movement. Preached by the influential British intellectuals Beatrice and Sidney Webb, its central idea was returning cities to their residents through public ownership of key services such as water, gas and tramways. Municipal socialism was strongly advocated by the Wellington Progressive Municipal Association (WPMA), set up in the 1890s to represent the thousands of working men and women in the city who were still denied a vote in local body elections. Groups such as the WPMA emerged as the inner city reached bursting point and major decisions loomed on enlarging city boundaries and expanding municipal services. Meanwhile, property-owners and a few councillors formed the rival Ratepayers' Association, a conservative body that would later become the dominant Wellington Citizens Association. Fledgling civic parties initially without any formal links to national politics, they provided rallying points for the left and right of the political spectrum.

Local body electoral reform was an issue dear to the heart of Richard Seddon, who became New Zealand's longest serving Prime Minister. In debate on the Municipal Corporations Bill in 1898, he argued that such reform was necessary to bring the Colony into line with parliamentary voting, where the residential qualification was only three months and no-one could vote more than once. He singled out Wellington City Council as a particular offender, pointing to the disproportionate power wielded by 138 ratepayers holding five votes each, within a burgess (borough) roll of 4,000 votes, in a population more than ten times that number. He dismissed the argument that giving the vote to a host of workers without property would plunge the city into debt.

> I say here, with a due sense of responsibility, that those who live in the tenements — those who inhabit and pay rents for the houses in the cities — pay the rates. The contention that it is only the owner who pays the rates, and that [only] he is entitled to representation, is simply nonsensical.[84]

Sidney and Beatrice Webb agreed, describing the local franchise as 'even more antiquated than we thought':

> Only occupiers having six months' tenancy unexpired when the roll is made up can be put on the burgess' roll (or pay rates directly; in all other cases the owner is rated); they have from one to five votes each according to their rateable value; in the election of councillors a man may vote (from one to

five) in every ward in which he is rated for property, though for Mayors and on referendum issues he can only vote once in the borough … [W]e find that the registered burgesses usually amount to only half of the number of separate houses; to half the number of adult men in the town; and to about a quarter of the parliamentary electorate. In nearly every ward the holders of two to five votes could outvote those having one only.[85]

Seddon was also keen to remove the ability of niggardly ratepayers to sabotage polls on civic loans. In Wellington, and similarly elsewhere, the tactic forced the municipality to abandon plans for a city abattoir, a crematorium, the completion of Kelburn Park, and a recreation ground at Thorndon. Seddon duly introduced legislation to change the rules surrounding such polls, allowing a loan proposal to be carried with a bare majority of votes. The *Evening Post* approved:

Nothing has been more marked in the local government of this colony than the careless indifference of ratepayers and citizens to the great questions of collective activity. If for no other reason we should support the Premier's bill because it promises to put an end to this selfish negligence, to awaken our people to a more vivid sense of their responsibilities to their neighbours and the district in which they live … it says that ratepayers who take an interest in public affairs shall rule and not those who are callous and apathetic.[86]

Democracy reached the tenements of Te Aro in 1898, as Seddon's legislation extended the vote to rent-paying tenants and sub-tenants throughout the Colony. The spouses of qualified electors were also franchised. Plural voting was abolished. By 1910, all resident citizens in Wellington and other New Zealand towns and cities would be able to vote.

The 1898 election to the mayoralty of John Blair, a free-thinking publisher and educationalist, reflected a change in the civic mood. Echoing many of the ideas put forward by Seddon's Liberals and the Webbs, Blair believed that the state should help safeguard the interests of the working man, and that public bodies should therefore take over control of vital local services such as tramways. He stated that the Council, to a man, 'did not desire to see the tramways a day longer in the hands of a syndicate than could be avoided'.[87] Within a few years, the city owned its tramways, as did Auckland. Such a radical move might have put Blair offside with the city's more conservative elements. But he won their support in 1899 with calls for expanded city boundaries to take in the boroughs of Melrose, Karori, Onslow

John Blair, Mayor of Wellington 1898–99. A publisher and businessman, Blair embodied the enlightened and reforming spirit on Council as the century ended.

WCA, 00510:0:7

and Miramar, which had developed on the fringes of the city (see Chapter 4).

Like Seddon, Blair tempered his radicalism with fervent loyalty to the Empire. On Trafalgar Day, 21 October 1899, there was dancing in the street as an estimated forty thousand people (equivalent to the entire population of the city) voiced their patriotic support for the First New Zealand Contingent departing for the South African War. Eight brass and pipe bands greeted the 200 soldiers as they marched into the central city from their camp at Karori. At Jervois Quay wharf, the contingent halted in front of a platform on which were seated the Governor, Lord Ranfurly, Premier Seddon, and other dignitaries. The ceremony, however, was led by the Mayor, reflecting his standing in the capital's pecking order.

The big question at the end of 1899 was whether Seddon's newly enfranchised tenement army would rush to the ballot box and vote for revolutionary change. It didn't happen in Wellington, but enough new voters, both men and women, enrolled to make the *Evening Post* compare the activity on polling day with that of a general election. Seddon's ground-breaking reforms soon brought ratepayers and progressive municipalists head to head. Political competition and 'ticket' voting were about to transform local body politics in Wellington and elsewhere.

City of Wellington
and Surrounding Boroughs
circa 1900

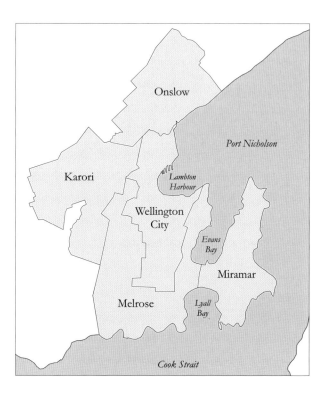

A People's Municipality

1900–1918

We are slowly rebuilding our city, and the cry is everywhere for more room for our increasing staff of workers, more room for development of trade, more room for expansion of business; and this is a centre where it is increasingly difficult to find room for the homes of the people within reasonable radius of their occupation.[1]

A family group poses at the entrance to the newly built Karori tunnel in early 1900.

ATL, W. H. Field Collection, F-115936-1/2

Boxing Day 1899 brought a belated Christmas present to the ratepayers of Karori Borough, as the tunnel through Baker's Hill opened to traffic. Since assurances in 1897 that the new main road and the excavation would take six months and cost no more than £4,000, two years had passed, two sets of contractors had decamped, and Karori ratepayers had twice been polled for loans totalling £6,000.[2] Tunnellers struck what was described as 'greasy-backed country, and a lining had to be put in to hold the hill up'.[3] The rock proved so treacherous that the 'blanket' of hand-made bricks had to be trebled in thickness. Landslides left the road above unstable, and it eventually collapsed, leaving a 30-foot gap across Raroa Road.

As construction came to an end, it emerged that the tunnel wasn't wide enough. The tiny Borough managed to complete the job late in 1899, with the tunnel and approaches opening just in time for the symbolic turn of the century. But without a further injection of capital, the works were not expected to last the winter. The

The little village in the hills

Good access to Karori was seen as the key to its future prosperity. Settled in the 1840s, it had become part of Hutt County when the provinces were abolished in 1876. The County was an unwieldy construct, stretching from the shores of Cook Strait to the mouth of the Waikanae River, and east to the Rimutaka Ranges, excluding only Wellington City and a few adjacent road and town districts.

As the city fringes were transformed from scrubby farmland and bush-tangled valleys to suburban settlements, Karori residents complained about the County Council's reluctance to fund much-needed infrastructure such as roading. It was a phenomenon experienced on the periphery of most of New Zealand's cities. The three-mile road from Lambton Quay was steep and narrow, with Baker's Hill such an obstacle that there was talk of a cable-tram from Aro Valley.[4] Some thought the solution was to establish a separate borough which would be eligible for government subsidies, but opponents feared that this would disadvantage established landowners. The separatists had the numbers, however. Karori broke away from Hutt County, and the inaugural meeting of the Karori Borough Council took place on 21 October 1891.

By 1912, no fewer than 113 boroughs had been established nationwide,[5] including Karori, Melrose, Onslow and Miramar. Melrose Borough encircled the city in a horseshoe shape, from the Botanic Garden to Oriental Bay, over the Hataitai Hill and out to the south coast. The distances between its scattered villages made the task of providing water, sewerage and transport both expensive and impractical for one small local body. By the turn of the century, the logic of a single authority absorbing the growing suburbs on the city's fringes was becoming obvious, setting the scene for a 'Greater Wellington'.

distressed Borough councillors, fearing the wrath of ratepayers, twice asked the Wellington City Council for help, but received a 'positive refusal'.[6] The decision was made to approach a higher authority, namely Premier Richard Seddon.

On 29 January 1900, Karori Mayor R.C. Bulkley and his fellow councillors got their audience with Seddon in his private office in the Government Buildings. The so-called 'One Man Cabinet' was a busy man. At the time, he was grappling with the South African War, and deciding what to do about bubonic plague, as a global pandemic currently affecting Australia was poised to cross the Tasman. However, the Premier's open dislike of the Wellington City Council saw him happily distracted by the tunnel crisis on Baker's Hill. He urged the Karori deputation to use the Municipal Corporations Act to prise money out of the city. As a former borough councillor himself, he could tell them 'that the City Council could be made to contribute … [I]f he were Mayor of Karori he should not hesitate to take a course that would settle that question.'[7]

Beyond solidarity with their plight, the Premier could offer them little more than a handshake, a three percent loan, and the comment that 'the necessity for more money was obviously due to bungling on the part of somebody'.[8] But rather than face another brush-off from Wellington City, Karori ratepayers voted to raise a £2,000 loan to pay for the additional works, lifting the final cost of their tunnel to £8,000. Seddon may not have known of the outcome, but he showed himself willing to exact revenge on the larger local authority.

Wellington City entered the twentieth century with a flurry of construction and public works, enjoying an economic and population boom that lasted until the First World War. This chapter describes how the municipality, in its most progressive period of governance, rebuilt and extended the city. Wellington stood supreme as the country's commercial, financial, administrative and transport centre. The combined population of the city and its suburbs was nearly 50,000 in the 1901 census, and would more than double by 1921.[9] The civil service was booming. Between 1896 and 1912 the number of permanent departmental jobs more than doubled, from 2,105 to 5,351.[10] Such was the level of commercial confidence in this period that one commentator even suggested that moving the seat of government elsewhere would be 'no crushing disaster' for the city.[11]

The end of an era

The death of Tommy McKenzie in 1911, at the age of 84, was another reminder of the passing of the settlement era. By the end of his long and rich life, he was seen by many as the authentic 'father of wellington'.

On the morning of the funeral, Ruhia's cloak was taken to the family home to cover his coffin. The story of his escape at Pipitea was told once more:

Seventy one years ago, a Maori mat was thrown over the late Mr McKenzie, when he was a boy of 13, to save his life from the chief Porutu; today the same mat (over a century old) is upon him. Between those two placings, the city has grown from a wilderness to Greater Wellington.[12]

Tommy McKenzie's coffin, seen here outside St John's Church in Dixon Street.

ATL, PAColl-5345-2

McKenzie Terrace, below Victoria University, commemorates his life.

Wellington was *the* maritime hub.[13] It was the port that never slept: open by day and floodlit by night for fleets of steamers, and worked by watersiders discharging goods or filling holds with frozen meat, wool and other exports bound for Europe. By 1900, the value of exports passing through Wellington approached £3 million, and would exceed £5 million by 1913.[14] Much of it was greasy wool bound for European markets, brought from the provinces by train or steamer to the port, where it was squeezed into bales by great hydraulic presses. During 1914 and 1915, the port handled three million bales of wool and 867,000 tons of frozen meat and butter. As the volume of frozen cargo grew, so did the

Revolution on wheels

In April 1898, businessman William McLean approached the Wellington City Council for a licence to run his imported Daimler Benz motorcars.[15] The city fathers voted to await the passage of an Act of Parliament setting the maximum speed for motor vehicles at 12 miles per hour.

Meanwhile, McLean gained permission to exhibit his cars in a procession, 'on condition they are placed in charge of competent drivers'. His own competency was questioned when he crashed into the Basin Reserve fence while taking the Mayor for a drive: 'Hislop received a bloody nose (no seatbelts in those days) and he and McLean almost came to blows over the incident.'[16]

A Hutt Road traffic jam, circa 1930: motorists stream from their cars to observe an unrecorded event in the harbour.

WCA, 00138:0:167

The private motorcar was soon a fixture on the city's streets. Diarist Pat Lawlor recalled in 1903 that vehicles slowed down from 10 to 5 mph as they turned into Cuba Street, allowing youngsters like him to keep pace as they ran alongside.[17]

As early as 1910, the Council alerted motorists to the 'danger for children of fast motoring on Queens Drive, Miramar and Cliff Road, Roseneath'.[18] The upgrading of the Hutt Road in 1911 boosted the demand for cars. During 1914, the Council was looking at imposing a petrol tax 'for extra revenue … to maintain the city roads owing to the damaging effect of motor traffic'.[19]

In 1916, councillors heard that only 498 of the people driving the 1,000 cars registered in Wellington had certificates of competency. They urged that offenders be prosecuted.[20] Parking began to be allowed in 1917 in half a dozen streets, including Bowen Street. Cars had to be at least five feet apart, and parked parallel to the curb. Headlights became compulsory following police reports of cars driving in darkness along the Hutt Road.

demand for new facilities. Connected by railhead and surrounded by icy cargo sheds and towering cranes, the new Glasgow Wharf became the headquarters of the meat trade by 1901.[21] Wellington's waterfront, as gateway to the city, was also seen as contributing to its unique character:

Queen's Wharf bustles with activity at the turn of the twentieth century.

Perhaps it is this constant contribution of outside commercial activity, together with the special advantage the city derives from being the port of first arrival and final departure of so many mail steamers and ocean going vessels generally, that helps invest Wellington with a certain air of cosmopolitanism which is often noticed and commented upon by tourists as being absent from other centres of the Dominion.[22]

The city fathers celebrated the capital's pre-eminence in the building of an 'exuberant' Town Hall and Council Chamber (see below). The growing status of the Mayor of Wellington also led councillors to decide it was time for His Worship to be 'appropriately robed'.[23] Mayor John Aitken, elected in 1900, was given approval to get his personal tailor to run up an ermine gown.[24] A wealthy Wadestown hostess, Mrs Sarah Anne Rhodes, later presented the municipality with its jewel-encrusted mayoral chain, each link marking a former mayor. Over time, a ritual was established for meetings of the full Council, reflecting the emerging presence of party politics and ticket voting:

> Promptly at 7.30 pm the officer in charge of the town hall announces, 'Ladies, gentlemen, and councillors, please be upstanding for His Worship the Mayor', and preceded by the macebearer the Mayor enters the chamber in scarlet and ermine robe and cocked hat. Having reached the mayoral chair, he asks those present to be seated. The councillors sit in a horseshoe shaped table. Labour members on the left (looking towards the mayoral dais) and Citizens on the right, each councillor normally occupying the same place for the whole term of a council. On the dais to the Mayor's left are the Deputy Town Clerk and a vacant chair kept for special guests. On the Mayor's right sits the Town Clerk, readily accessible for such consultations with the Mayor as may be necessary. To his right again, beyond the dais, are the tables for the press. Behind the councillors, in two horseshoe rows, sit most of the officers, with the committee clerk and other officers responsible to a specific committee sitting as close as possible to its chairman, to be ready with advice, files, or such information as he might call for during the meeting.[25]

By now, representatives of working-class voters in the tenements had their feet under the Council table. In 1901 Dave McLaren, the Glasgow-born leader of the Wellington Wharf Labourers' Union, was elected to Council as an independent. At that election, 8,870 men and women voted for the Ratepayers' Association or

Empire City: this ornate triple-arched entrance to the General Post Office on Featherston Street spoke of Wellington's opulence and ambition in the early twentieth century. In Alfred Drury's work, *Girdled Earth*, two figures seated in repose support a globe beribboned with the signs of the Zodiac. The 1942 earthquake weakened the bell tower, and the bells and the statuary were later removed. The GPO building was demolished in 1972.

Terence Hodgson collection

WPMA tickets — between four and five times more than the average poll during the 1890s.[26] Between 1901 and 1913, full adoption of the residential franchise saw the number of eligible voters ballooning from 13,360 to 34,179.[27] Many were the young single men filling the dingy boarding houses and cheap eateries of Te Aro. Some belonged to the local wing of a militant urban proletariat, advocates of revolutionary socialism. For many workers, the Liberals had lost their reforming edge after a decade in office. The strike, not polite laws dealing with arbitration, would increasingly become the answer to industrial disputes after 1907.

The men sitting on the left of the Council Chamber reflected these new preoccupations. Cr McLaren was returned in 1903 with a New Zealand Socialist Party platform, and at the following election as part of an Independent Political Labour League ticket. Support for workers' representation came to be accepted by a conservative press, buttressed by the *Dominion* after 1907, its title a tribute to the colony's new status. The *New Zealand Times* summarised the changing status quo:

> Three elements need to be fairly blended … the commercial, the employing and the employed … [T]he third is not represented in the Council and never has been. Elsewhere modern progress has placed the worker in the representative positions of municipal life and the worker has always justified the confidence reposed in him by his shrewdness, honesty, devotion to business, knowledge of practical detail and familiarity with the wants and needs of a very large section of the ratepayers.[28]

Mayor John Blair's move to 'municipalise' the tramways in 1899 led to continuing agitation for Council ownership of gas and electricity and the establishment of a fairer rating system. Enterprises undertaken by 'the people's municipality' would eventually embrace electric lighting, a milk supply, an abattoir, a zoo, and even an orchestra.

The new century also brought with it a series of infrastructural and public health hangovers. Rapidly falling water levels at Karori reservoir led to the construction of new concrete dams both there and at Wainuiomata. Crises over sanitation still lingered, with fears of plague in 1900 replacing typhoid as the new public health nightmare. Faced with a frightened electorate, Seddon again made a scapegoat of the Wellington municipality as councillors dithered over spending money to cleanse the city. The Premier even threatened to 'square off' (punch) an alarmed Council deputation.[29] His colleague Joseph Ward joined the attacks on Wellington City, accusing it of failing to clean up accumulated filth near the Government Buildings.[30] Seddon ordered the councillors to 'purify the city'.

These lads may not look too 'bolshie', but Queen Victoria's statue, originally located in front of Queen's Wharf, fast became a notorious gathering place for socialist orators. In 1911, six years after it was erected, the statue was coated with black varnish and ferried to the quieter pastures of Kent Terrace.

ATL, J. N. Taylor Collection, F-104836-1/2

In the first years of the twentieth century, Wellington City embraced 'municipalisation', the public ownership of services. This abattoir, built at Ngauranga in 1910, joined a long list of council enterprises that included electricity and lighting, tramways, a milk supply, and even an orchestra.

WCA, 00157:1:90

Te Aro's Chinatown

At the turn of the century, Haining Street, squeezed between Taranaki and Tory Streets in the heart of Te Aro, was Wellington's street of shame: home to Chinese opium-smokers, gamblers and white slave traders. Writer Pat Lawlor recalled the lurid reputation of the Chinese quarter, in the centre of the city's poorest slum area:

To many children, it was forbidden territory. We were told that even if we went near that drab, narrow, little street with its congestion of tumbledown houses, we might be kidnapped, boiled in a copper and made into preserved ginger … we were fascinated by the stories of opium smoking. Bonishee had told us that the smell of it as you went past the houses was so thick you could not only 'cut it with a knife', but go into wonderful dreams.[31]

Some of the residents were, however, respectable Chinese, a number of whom had come to the capital from the depleted goldfields of the South Island to open laundries, set up fruit-barrow businesses and, in many cases, grow vegetables. For them, Haining Street was 'Ton Yang Gaai' or Chinese People's Street.[32]

By the late nineteenth century, growing discrimination against the Chinese was reflected in laws and policies such as the infamous £10 poll tax. In 1887, the *Evening Post* caricatured the 'celestial' owners of fruit barrows as 'gibbering like monkeys'.[33] Opposition to Chinese involvement in market-gardening in the region was taken up by the Anti-Chinese League in 1896. Initially the City Council supported moves by local vegetable growers and the league to establish a 'European' market.[34] Councillors subsequently changed their

mind, and the idea was abandoned.[35] Brothels, and legal gambling and opium dens did, however, operate in Haining Street. In January 1900, Mayor Aitken received a petition from fifteen concerned residents of Taranaki Street, who were outraged at the immoral activity in the street:

Many of the buildings there are common bawdy houses, frequented by both Chinamen and Europeans, while others are used as gambling and opium dens … [M]en and women of drunken habits and of notoriously bad character continually visit the adjacent hotels and prove a source of annoyance to people living in the neighbourhood. On Sundays especially the street is the scene of open vice.[36]

The 'open vice' complained of mostly occurred in buildings owned by absentee landlords, who did little to maintain their properties and overlooked anti-social behaviour, as long as the rents kept coming in.

In 1903, members of the Council's housing of the poor committee, led by socialist David McLaren, inspected Haining Street. It was one of 54 streets on their list, mostly in over-crowded Te Aro, but also in rundown parts of Newtown and Thorndon.

Haining Street in particular would have seemed alien territory to most of the committee members. Nonetheless, they knocked on the door of every house in the street, finding the 'boss of a gang' at number 26, prostitution at number 27, a 'rotten and dilapidated' opium den at number 23, and a house specially fitted up for Fan Tan (a form of gambling) at number 37. Committee members expressed alarm that the people at number 30 were 'all in bed' when they called, and that 'no-one was up at 11.30 am' at numbers 8 and 10.[37] They concluded that most of the houses inspected were unfit for habitation, and recommended that 'the facts as tabulated should receive the serious consideration of the incoming council with a view of improving the housing condition of the working classes'.[38]

Two years later, as the municipality continued to anguish over inner-city slums, Haining Street gained lasting infamy when a racist murdered a lame Chinese man outside number 13. English migrant Lionel Terry shot and killed Joe Kum Young to draw attention to his extreme anti-Asian views. A death sentence was later commuted to life imprisonment.

Police scrutiny of the area continued well into the twentieth century, with regular midnight raids on opium and gambling dens. Pakapoo, an illegal game of chance similar to Lotto, drew many non-European gamblers. The street meanwhile continued as a mini Chinatown, home to the first Chinese restaurant in the city, and shops selling Chinese groceries and other goods. Today the demonised dwellings of Haining Street are long gone, replaced by office buildings and a few bland apartments. Barely a sign of the Chinese presence remains.

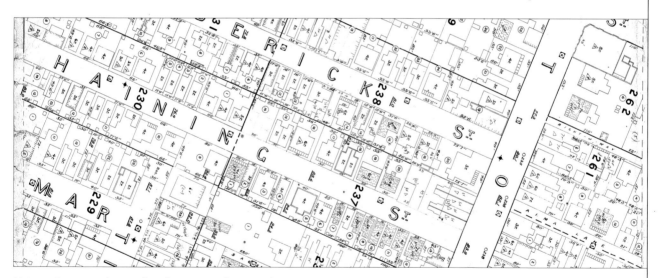

Haining Street, as depicted in Thomas Ward's meticulous 1892 survey map. Dwellings are drawn in outline, with verandahs and out-houses clearly visible. Ward's map also detailed the number of rooms, measurements of sections, whether the walls were made of brick, wood or iron, and the roof of slate, shingles or iron, and even indicated streetlights and hydrants.

WCA, 00514:7:1

He said it was a wonder the pestilence had not been here long ago when he reflected upon what had been brought under his notice in regard to the filthy condition of places immediately surrounding Wellington … [A]s for slums, he would have a way of dealing with them put before Parliament next session.[39]

The Premier was no doubt aware that, as the spectre of plague hung over the city, councillors had voted to spend £50,000 on a palatial Town Hall. As the panic reached its peak in April 1900, the Council moved 'that the Union Steamship Company be asked to moor their Inter-Colonial Steamers away from the wharves after five o'clock in the evening, so as to prevent rats leaving from them'.[40] A threepenny bounty was paid on every rat taken to the Council's destructor. The municipality hired additional sanitary inspectors, and demolished rundown dwellings in Haining and Tasman Streets.[41] Notorious harbour-side slums, in lanes between Courtenay Place and Cuba Street, were cleared.

None of this was enough to placate Seddon. A Bubonic Plague Bill was the first piece of legislation on the Order Paper when the 1900 parliamentary session began. It was soon replaced by a Public Health Act, a sweeping reform that gave birth to a Department of Public Health. Municipalities were stripped of their existing and under-used powers to act as local boards of health. Central government agencies could now compel local bodies to clean up refuse and demolish slums where rats could breed. It was a major step in the direction of the centralisation of public authority and resented by many local authorities around the country which valued their historical autonomy. By August 1900 the plague scare had passed, and the bounty paid for rats brought to the destructor dropped to a penny.[42] But the relationship between the state and local bodies had changed. For politicians such as Seddon and Ward, it meant that tight-fisted municipalities would never again be allowed to threaten the wider body politic. It was a sign of things to come.

Overhead electric wires for trams required regular maintenance. Council crews operated from the upper level of this horse-drawn device, seen working in Oriental Bay around 1905.

WCA, 00138:0:3185

The man who planned the settlement in a raupo hut by candlelight, William Mein Smith, sketched this view of Wellington harbour midway through 1842. It is a detail taken from a full panorama.

Charles Gold's painting shows one of the harbour-side landslips, possibly along the Hutt Road, caused by the 1855 earthquake.

ATL, B-103-016

When Samuel Brees painted this Te Aro beach scene in 1847, the modern day intersection of Taranaki and Manners Streets was the sandy shallows in the foreground. The bay stretched along Willis Street to the prominent Clay or Windy Point, where Stewart Dawson's jewellers was later established.

ATL, A-109-037

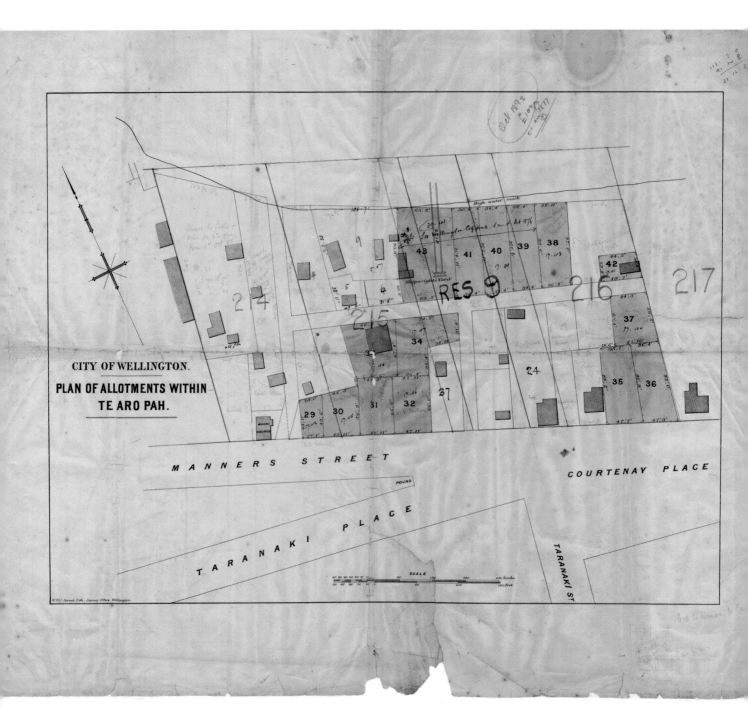

CITY OF WELLINGTON.

PLAN OF ALLOTMENTS WITHIN TE ARO PAH.

A road runs through it: in 1870 the Council used this government survey map showing allotments in the Te Aro pa area to plot the proposed extension of Taranaki Street to the foreshore.

WCA, 00248:2:6

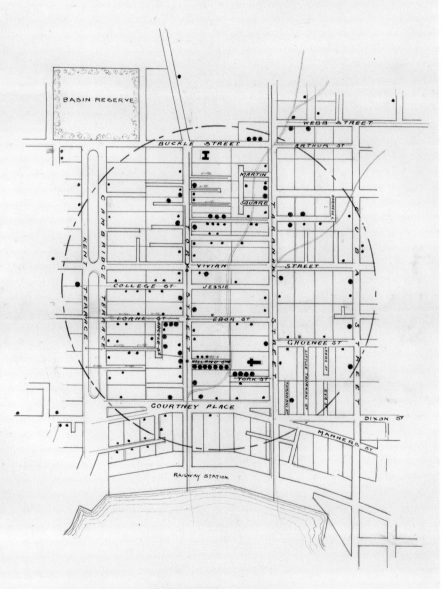

Fever mapping: an investigation of Te Aro in 1892 linked the outbreak of typhoid to the condition of stormwater and sewer drains. Outbreaks prevailed along certain sewer lines, and almost exactly matched periods of heavy rainfall. When it poured with rain, the outfalls were blocked, and sewer vapours that could not escape seeped back up through water closets and drains into people's homes.

WCA, 002333:34:1892/740

— TYPHOID AREA —

● DENOTES TYPHOID CASES 1892.
 ″   ″   ″   1890-1.

In 1905 the prominent architect Frederick de Jersey Clere designed these plans for a Chinese Mission room in the heart of Te Aro.

ATL, Plans 80-0866

WELL DONE, WELLINGTON!

New Zealand Federation of Labor.

MANIFESTO

TO THE

Members of the Wellington Tramway Union

Fellow Workers,—

Your magnificent vote against the tyranny and high-handedness of the City Council is a credit to your solidarity. The demand that your members be freed from the baseless charges and suspicions brought forward by ignorant or misguided officials is most encouraging indeed.

In taking up the stand you have, you will meet with the unanimous support of all unionists worthy the name. To swing into line behind you will be the action of all workers with a spark of manliness and self-respect.

Your determination to put an end to creatures who would not hesitate to blast the character of your fellow-unionists is deserving of the highest praise.

During the next two weeks STAND SOLID. The united press will howl at you! The combined forces of Capital-

thoughtless and oftimes brutal body

called the Public will hurl denunciations at you.

Amid it all, STAND SOLID. Men of the Wellington Tramways Union, your one weakness is the fact of your isolation from the militant body of organised workers in New Zealand, the Federation of Labor. If you were but associated with that body, as are the Auckland Tramway Union, very soon would the City Council be brought to its knees.

Although not connected with the Federation, **the Federation will be with you** in this fight. It will encourage you and assist you as far as it can. Later it may ask you to join it and fight with it, but to-day it is prepared to do its duty towards the organised workers of the Wellington Tramwaymen's Union.

Again we greet you, comrades, and bid you fight the injustices and insults

We are with you to the last.

J. GLOVER, Sec. N.Z.F.L.

Printed at the "Maoriland Worker" Printery, 290, Wakefield Street, Wellington.

In 1912 the New Zealand Federation of Labour issued its manifesto to the members of the Wellington Tramway Union on crimson paper. The conservative *Evening Post* then famously described the unionists as the 'Red' Federation of Labour, or 'Red Feds'.

ATL, Eph-B-Labour-1912-01

A Dreary Day
in Windy Wellington

Wellington's weather has always shaped views of the city, as this postcard from the 1920s shows.

Redmer Yska

A touched-up photograph of the Wellington Town Hall, complete with romantic moon.

Redmer Yska

Walter Leslie painted this view of Wellington from across Oriental Bay on a calm day in 1909. At the time, the low-rise city skyline was dominated by the (somewhat exaggerated) chimneys of the destructor on the left and, to the right, the smokestack of the coal-fired electric plant on Jervois Quay (used to power the city trams).

The electric horse

> Slowly and steadily the car came down the track from the Newtown shed, brilliantly lighted inside with eight 16-candle-power lights, having a 32-candle-power headlight, and the destination lights (showing the words Wellington and Newtown at each end) were of 16 candle-power. Besides this lighting, frequent flashes of electricity were thrown off from the works beneath the car and the point of contact of the connecting arm with the trolley wire overhead showed a vivid blue light. The whole spectacle as the car proceeded along the track was unique and brilliant.[43]

The midnight debut of the first electric tram in June 1904 followed years of chaos, disruption, and the sacking of a top city official. Public ownership of the tramways was a long-held dream, part of a grand Wellington City Betterment Scheme that included widening and paving streets, and constructing a Town Hall. The electric tram hastened the end of the horse-drawn age and opened up land for housing by providing cheap transport for workers.

Celebrations for the 1907 opening of the Seatoun tram line included Miss Molly Fabian's presentation of a bouquet to the Lady Mayoress.

WCA, 00138:0:03161

On 14 May 1900, the municipal ownership of tramways cleared its first hurdle as councillors agreed to pay its private owners £19,382. Ratepayers later endorsed the loan. To celebrate, the Mayor and councillors attended a ceremony at the Newtown tram-sheds, returning to town in a special car for lunch at the Café Victoria in Brandon Street. For Mayor Aitken, municipal ownership would help to guarantee a better service:

> With the city as owners, the service could be kept abreast of the times. No one could deny that our city and our population were congested, and open air spaces were limited. With a good and cheap system, people could get further afield, and this would improve health and prove a great benefit to inhabitants as a whole.[44]

The municipality reopened an existing horse-tram line, a profitable service between Thorndon and Newtown, with cars that seated up to 58 people. The city engineer, working on plans for an electric tram service, proposed an overhead trolley system.[45] Detailed plans to run trams to the edges of the city won ratepayers' support in 1901, with a massive £225,000 loan later approved. The first stage involved rebuilding the existing route between Thorndon and Newtown, followed by extensions out to Island Bay, Brooklyn and Kilbirnie. A deputation nearly persuaded the Council to lay tram-tracks through the middle of the Basin Reserve, to avoid awkward cornering.[46] A London-based firm later received £110,000 to lay the tracks and three million wooden blocks, and to erect poles and overhead wires for a fleet of 33 tramcars. The City of Wellington Electric Light and Power Company was commissioned to run a £25,000 coal-fired steam plant on Jervois Quay, with a 30 ton boiler and 130 foot high smokestack, built to supply 'white coal' (electricity) to power the fleet.

The government watched events from the sidelines. Shortly before construction work started on the new tracks, Acting Premier Sir Joseph Ward alarmed many by suggesting during a parliamentary debate that central government, and not councils, should own tramways in the main centres, with municipalities receiving a share of the profits. Under state ownership, he argued, tram fares would drop.[47] Believing that public transport would be a cash cow, Mayor Aitken was sceptical:

Staff toiled in dirty conditions in all weathers to keep the city's fleet of trams running. This 1908 group portrait shows some of the workers who helped maintain the tracks and overhead equipment.

WCA, 00138:0:08696

The position is very simple … [T]he citizens who use the trams are the owners, and rightly so. They should control them and have full benefit of the profits. Are we to have our tramways in Wellington interfered with, say, by members from Auckland or from some place in the South Island, and have profits which rightly belong to the people of Wellington scattered as it were all over the country?[48]

On 29 October 1902, the first lump of road metal was turned in a ceremony opposite the government railway station at the end of Lambton Quay, one of the two stations in the area. Aitken predicted that tramways would help create a new city.[49] Within weeks, an army of up to 300 unskilled 'navvies' or labourers on a shilling an hour were tearing up central city streets and laying rails, between which squares of jarrah were placed to create a solid surface. Despite the resulting dust clouds, fanned by equinoctial gales, the men made good progress. Schoolboy Pat Lawlor watched the blocks being laid, one by one:

The blocks of Australian hardwood went through a huge tar-soaking machine. They would be assembled at one end, shortly to disappear into the tar reservoir. They would emerge dripping, to be 'cemented' with pug before joining the immense pattern on the street surface. Except for the conveyor belt, all was done by hand.[50]

The work was hard, with long hours. To avoid interrupting traffic, the men 'pegging' the tracks started before dawn. Assistant Engineer R. A. Hamerton was too early to ride to work on the private cable tram to Kelburn, which opened in 1902. He based his subsequent application for a pay increase on these early starts:

It was customary for me to start work at daylight, Sundays included, month after month. To state that I started work at 3 o'clock in the morning and finished at midnight — the odd three hours including walking to and from Kelburn — would be to state an exceptional case. On an average day however work began at 4am and ended at 11pm … [T]his continued until I worked myself on to a bed of sickness, where I remained for over a fortnight, narrowly escaping a serious lingering illness.[51]

The stress showed. On 9 December, work stopped as a result of what was later called 'municipal muddling'.[52] Working to plans supplied by the municipality, navvies broke into a forgotten storm-water drain running the length of Kent Terrace, with spectacular results. The accident was a very public embarrassment. The City Engineer, Richard Rounthwaite, was suspended for his 'deplorable mistake'.[53] Few tears were shed. Joining the Corporation in 1898 after a career in a small English municipality, Rounthwaite soon made himself unpopular. In 1902, the Ratepayers' Association questioned his high salary and the need for twenty departmental staff.[54] The city's construction fraternity also disliked Rounthwaite's officious manner:

> in our unavoidable and frequent contact with the City Engineer, there is a
> marked want of proper courtesy and consideration, such as should be shown
> by a Public Officer, to enable a better and more harmonious feeling to exist
> in the conduct of business.[55]

Rounthwaite resigned, and work recommenced. But the Kent Terrace fiasco reinforced public doubts about the municipality's ability to manage projects on this scale. The *New Zealand Times* also raised questions about accountability: 'A government whose departmental officials had blundered so badly as those of the City Council would have found itself promptly turned out of office.'[56]

In January 1904, the first ten tramcars arrived from England. From the Newtown

---

Away with the fairies

The popularity of new leisure activities on the cusp of the twentieth century saw the Council eyeing the Town Belt once again.

In 1907, an amusement park known as 'Wonderland', based on the pick of the sideshows from the recent Christchurch Exhibition, opened in Miramar. Envious of its financial success, the Council planned to allocate 3 acres of the Town Belt for an equivalent facility in Oriental Bay, to be known as 'Fairyland'.

The decision to rent the land to a local business syndicate for just £10 a year slipped through on 14 March 1907, with councillors predicting that Fairyland could be at the centre of a major promotion for the municipal tramways.[57] Vigilant local businessman William Tonks then stepped in, cautioning against any interference with Town Belt land.[58] In a stiff letter, he warned: 'A lease as proposed of the Town Belt is illegal, and would be resisted by an injunction if necessary.' The proposal quietly disappeared.

end of the express route, tracks were laid along Adelaide Road to connect with the line at Kent Terrace. By June, the first trams were running to the city from Newtown. The people of Melrose Borough soon enjoyed the benefits of collaboration, as electric trams pushed out the city boundaries. Where the trams went, tracts of undeveloped land became desirable locations for suburban bungalows. The municipality pensioned off its horse-tram service weeks after the electric trams began operating. Early in 1905, Mayor Thomas William Hislop and his councillors took a night-time victory lap through the city: 'With much civic pride, the [tram] car traversed all routes adorned with flowers and greenery, and outlined in electric lamps of red, white and blue with a line of lamps being carried up the trolley pole to complete the decorations.'[59]

Everyone wanted a ride on the glamorous trams — preferably not paying the regulation fare of a penny a section. Travelling *gratis* on the trams became the ultimate perk. Councillors voted themselves free travel. Passes 'made of gold' were later designed and handed out to all councillors, the Town Clerk, and the City Engineer.[60] Other recipients included the government gaoler and Suzanne Aubert, founder of the Sisters of Compassion.[61] A culture of being generous with the people's assets began to develop.

Such was the demand for tram travel that there was talk of people being 'hurried off' cars, and conductors were instructed that only well-dressed people were allowed on board. Manual workers had special cars set aside for them, with those taking their seat before 8 a.m. (later 7.30 a.m.) being entitled to a return ticket for the price of a single fare. Evidence that their ranks included women appears in a 1907 Council rejoinder to the Chamber of Commerce: 'the statement made in their letter that work women are not allowed to ride on workmen's cars is incorrect. Work women are and have been allowed in these cars which are not called workmen's cars but workers' cars.'[62]

Women's presence on the trams created a particular hazard — hatpins. In a confined space, these jewel-tipped pins, some up to a foot long, became potentially deadly weapons, and minor stabbings were common. Councillors later passed a bylaw aimed at any woman who in 'any street, carriage or public place in the city wears an unprotected hatpin so as to cause risk of injury to any other person'. One conductor reported that 'he never knew the minute when the fate of one of his eyes would be sealed by a sharp point as a woman leaned over to pay her fare or rushed up to get out'.[63]

By 1910, the tram-tracks stretched for 22 miles, nearly a third of it in double tracks, with new routes to Lyall Bay and up the hill to Wadestown. A total of 42 cars crisscrossed the city throughout the day, with 74 operating during the evening rush-hour. Running the tramways was a massive undertaking, involving 83 cars carrying 22 million passengers a year, and providing jobs for nearly 500 staff.[64]

At this point, Premier Sir Joseph Ward, who took over as head of the Liberal government in August 1906, resurrected his earlier suggestion that municipal tramways be nationalised. He argued that safety and employment issues necessitated the Tramways Amendment Bill in 1910. Regulation was proposed after Parliament heard that a tram licensed to carry 45 passengers had left Athletic Park with 145 crammed on board, and that another had travelled from Newtown to Thorndon without its essential king bolt.[65] Former Wellington Mayor and Hutt MP Thomas Wilford called a national conference of tramways authorities to review the draft legislation. Ward agreed to redraft the law after his supporter, Wilford, emphasised that 'the tramway concerns undertaken by the municipalities give good service, cheap rates and are well run'.[66]

For the greater good

In a moment laden with symbolism, the Mayor of Wellington stood up in the Council Chamber and brandished the mayoral chain of Melrose Borough. He moved that it be melted down and hammered into a pendant, to be attached to the chain of Wellington City.[67] The date was 13 April 1903, a fortnight after Wellington's 3,620 acres merged with Melrose's 3,840 acres, the two briefly becoming wards of the 'greater' city. It was an early manoeuvre in the elaborate dance of amalgamations, reorganisations and reforms that would continue for half a century, as the city's independent-minded 'outlying districts' struggled with the economics of providing water reticulation, sewerage and transport.

Abolition of the long-standing ward system in March 1901 gave the city the status of an 'undivided borough', thus helping to prepare the ground for a 'greater' Wellington. A merger with Melrose Borough, or parts of it, had been talked about for years. North Kilbirnie and Roseneath were expected to be the first areas of Melrose to join. Nothing happened until the 1901 release of the Greater Wellington Scheme, which spelled out the mutual advantages to Wellington City and its adjacent boroughs of a merger. Melrose ratepayers wanted to share the amenities enjoyed by their city neighbours, especially the promise of electric tramways. But, like similar areas around the country, they were also cautious about the financial implications of merging with a larger authority that was facing mounting debt. Wellington's promise to connect Melrose to its tramways network helped, as did a commitment to construct better roads to populated parts of Brooklyn. After months of public debate, leaked documents and rowdy public meetings, the merger still seemed elusive. The *Evening Post* despaired:

> The Melrose Council has long been one of the most disorderly local bodies in the neighbourhood. Local vested interests are apparently given undue weight by its members … faction fights run high at Council meetings, and the borough parliament is an excellent example of petty parochialism run mad. We cannot believe that the great body of ratepayers approves the unseemly proceedings to which we have again and again drawn attention.[68]

Eventually, Melrose ratepayers approved the merger. From June 1902, public meetings were held throughout the Borough, at which the proposal was explained and debated. Then followed months of petitioning for and against the proposal, with lengthy discussions over who should be polled. On 13 March 1903 a referendum was finally held, with most voters favouring the proposal. A month later Melrose Borough Council held its last meeting. The Greater Wellington Agreement was forwarded to the Governor, Lord Ranfurly, for validation. The former Mayor and councillors of Melrose became part of the United Borough of the City of Wellington, gazetted on 1 April 1903. The marriage with Melrose saw a brief return to the ward system, until this was once again abolished in 1905.

The amalgamation hastened the growth of new subdivisions in the eastern suburbs, with hundreds of houses springing up along transport routes. By the end of 1905, the trams were winding their way right out to Island Bay. The service to Brooklyn opened midway through 1906, and the important Kilbirnie route, connecting up the eastern suburbs, started in April 1907 and reached all the way to Seatoun by Christmas. Getting a tram through to the isolated township of Kilbirnie (much of it now Hataitai) involved carving a single-track tunnel through Mt Victoria, at a cost of £70,000. The work, which took well over a year, was done by a hundred miners working in three shifts, 25 bricklayers and apprentices, and teams of drivers and truckers to cart away the spoil.[69] As with the Karori tunnel, the scheme was locally contentious, took months longer than expected, and cost far more than the ratepayers in the new Melrose Ward were happy with. Once again Seddon, whose health was starting to cause trouble, played a cameo role, this time by praising the excavations. Karori Borough, meanwhile, had to wait until 1907 before trams ran through its tunnel.

Helping to drive the building boom was a change in the rating system. In 1902, the regime changed from 'annual value', or a levy based on the amount of rent a property would yield in a year, to 'unimproved' or land value as it is now known. By encouraging landowners to build or sell rather than sit on idle land, the new rating system acted as a spur to the building trade. From the time the rent-based system was introduced in 1870, it was seen as giving land speculators no incentive to build, thus holding back the city's development. Wellington's growth from the late 1880s had coincided with continuing rises in the rates collected from a relatively small pool of households, as the Council dug deeper to fund complex and expensive infrastructure. By 1901/02, the total rates levied were £36,454, and the Council had taken out more than £700,000 in loans. In 1897 the *Cyclopedia of New Zealand* parroted the official line that 'no community enjoying the privileges provided by the City Fathers for the inhabitants of Wellington, could reasonably expect to escape the burden of fairly heavy rates'.[70]

Between 1878/79 and 1900/01, the rate levied by the Council more than trebled from 1s in the pound to 3s 3½d. Basing a rate on rents received made sense in the British setting, dominated by big landowners with many tenants. But in the Colony, debate raged over which form of rating best suited its local bodies. Rating on annual value tended to penalise smaller homeowners who were striving to improve their property. On the other hand, unimproved land held back by speculators had no rental value, even though it had a market value which grew as other properties in the neighborhood were developed. The passage of the Rating on Unimproved Value Act 1896 provided municipalities with an option and reflected Seddon's preference. As the numbers of ratepaying households increased, the municipality came under pressure to adopt the new option. The working-class WPMA successfully campaigned on the issue in the 1901 election, with a Trade and Labour Council petition in support carrying 1,203 signatures. Rating on the Unimproved Value was on the agenda.

The number of new dwellings in Greater Wellington was increasing annually: 814 were erected in 1905 alone, 200 more than in the previous year. Construction slowed after 1907, but picked up again in the pre-war years. The Town Clerk was elated: 'no better index to the continued prosperity of the city could possibly be afforded, and the result largely accounts for the very great increases in land values in and around the city'.[71] Taxation and rating on land values helped fuel the suburban housing boom. The new rating system did not fully succeed in discouraging speculators, however, as a report to councillors noted:

The introduction of unimproved value rating did not have the effect expected of forcing land onto the market. Persons holding large areas which adjoined Wellington and which were used for farm purposes were unable to pay increased rates and had no means of roading the land and preparing it for subdivision. The result was that they were forced into the hands of syndicates.[72]

The problem of how to rate rural land on the periphery of cities would remain a vexed question for many years to come and result in many pieces of increasingly complex legislation relating to differential rating.

Tram-power also transformed the social life of the city. A new emphasis on leisure for the urban worker could be seen out at Lyall Bay, which became a popular destination for swimmers, sunbathers, and picnickers on their day off. They stepped off the tram at the end of Onepu Road, had a cup of tea at the Silver Slipper, and enjoyed a healthy seaside promenade. Donkey rides and beach photographers completed the tableau. Advertising material from 1913 shows that beaches were becoming part of the popular consciousness:

Delivery staff of the Phoenix Aerated Water company outside their Thorndon offices. The Thistle Inn is visible (left) behind a passing council tram.

Terence Hodgson collection

> There is a magnificent sweep of sandy beach and the healthy pastime of mixed surf bathing is freely indulged in. Good fishing may be had in the bay and from the rocks. There are bathing sheds on the beach, and tea and luncheon rooms on the promenade. Hot water is provided free on holidays to picnickers. The sand hills, clad with gold-brown tufted grass, add to the scenic charm of this locality and the breezes from the blue straits are most invigorating.[73]

Despite the reference to mixed bathing, councillors were determined that residents of the new suburbs should comply with the city's stringent bylaws on public bathing. Complaints about men bathing only half-clothed led to new regulations in 1905, which decreed that:

> No person over the age of ten years shall bathe on any beach within the view of persons passing along the streets of the City of Wellington or within the view of persons in any dwelling house in the said city unless such person so bathing shall be properly clad in a bathing garment reaching from the shoulder to the knee.[74]

In 1909, the municipality erected notice boards 'calling the attention of bathers to the necessity of wearing costumes of the neck to knee type and of suitable material'.[75] At Lyall Bay, swimmer Ernest Clay was arrested in 1913 for 'exposing about three inches of his manly bosom'.[76] The case was thrown out of court, as sunbathing and physical culture grew in popularity. Such breaches of the bylaw failed to deter the rapid development of seaside suburbs such as Lyall Bay, where the population grew from 455 in 1911 to 2,235 a decade later.[77]

The desire of suburbia to quarantine itself from inner-city temptations was apparent in the 1908 general election, when the people of Wellington South and Wellington Suburbs voted in the liquor poll to keep their areas 'dry'. Organised sport was also seen as building moral fibre. The Wellington Town Belt Reserves Leasing Bill of 1908 allowed the Council to lease 100 acres of Town Belt land to athletic clubs and similar bodies.

Melrose was the first borough to be absorbed by Greater Wellington, but not the last. The dissatisfaction of the people of Kaiwharawhara, Ngaio, Khandallah and Wadestown with Hutt County had led to the formation of Onslow Borough in 1890. A toll gate erected by the County Council at Kaiwharawhara in the 1870s had become their symbol of resistance, with residents opposed to revenue from the gate being spent in other parts of the County. A petition was raised, seeking the formation of a borough that could levy rates and spend the revenue locally. The petitioners were successful, and the first meeting of the Onslow Borough Council was held on 19 April 1890. By 1907, Onslow Borough was regularly criticised for neglecting its section of the Hutt Road, from Tinakori Road to Ngauranga, and in 1911 the government stepped in to widen the road and fill in the pot-holes.[78]

A municipal palace

A Town Hall does not make a city, and a city may thrive and do good work without one, but it is beyond question that a city is seriously handicapped if it lacks a place where the citizens may meet in adequate numbers and discuss its public affairs, and it is equally unquestionable that there is no city which has suffered more seriously from this defect than the City of Wellington ...[79]

From minstrel to mayor

The most memorable of Onslow's mayors was Robert Bradford Williams, an African-American tenor who first visited Wellington in 1886 as a member of the touring Fisk Jubilee Singers, a group of performers of Negro spirituals.

Williams was born in Georgia in 1861, the year the American Civil War began. After graduating with a Bachelor of Arts degree from Yale University, he became a professional singer. He met his future wife, Kate Burke, in Melbourne while touring and later moved to Wellington, where the couple raised three children.

In the capital, he is believed to have worked on his law degree in Sir Robert Stout's office. He then practised as a barrister from an office in

ATL, 164671-1/2

Featherston Street. A prohibitionist and Methodist, he later became choirmaster of the Wesleyan Church in Taranaki Street.

After an unsuccessful bid for a parliamentary career in 1902, Williams served five terms as the respected Mayor of Onslow.[80] He died at Otaki in 1942.

During 1907, the residents of Wadestown elected to leave Onslow Borough and join Wellington City. In 1908 and 1909, various parts of Karori and Onslow also came on board. Another decade passed before the boroughs of Onslow and Greater Karori formally joined the city, in 1919 and 1920 respectively.

In 1904, the city gained its long-awaited Town Hall, an imposing monument to civic self-confidence. The building exceeded the budget, and took nearly twice as long as planned; and on the eve of construction, the vain municipality increased the proportions to make it look even more splendid.[81] As soon as it was opened on 7 December the classical-style building, with its Roman portico and 177-foot-high clock tower, was praised as 'well planned, commodious and beautiful'.[82]

The move from Featherston Street was seen as long overdue. Calls for a city hall dated back to 1873.[83] In 1886, as a committee baulked at the probable cost, the *New Zealand Mail* grumbled that 'the want of a town hall has been badly felt in this city'.[84] A site was set aside on reclaimed land at the bottom of Cuba Street in 1889, but the demands of basic infrastructure made building on it unaffordable.

The late Victorian era was a sociable one. Pressure grew for a central auditorium in the city to host musical performances, lectures, political meetings, bazaars and other functions. Churches and theatres such as the Opera House helped to fill the gap, but a skating rink in Vivian Street was the main indoor gathering place at the turn of the century. In 1897, the *Cyclopedia of New Zealand* announced that Wellington could now afford civic 'luxuries' such as a Town Hall:

> The very large sums borrowed for … waterworks, reclamation, drainage, street formation, and other useful and needful undertakings, make such heavy demands for interest that a very large proportion of the City's income is sent away to the British moneylenders. In this way the Corporation coffers are kept unpleasantly low. Councillors and ratepayers are therefore agreed that there is at present very little money available for luxuries. 'There's a good time coming,' however. The income of the Corporation in both rates and rents is increasing rapidly, and the citizens are hopeful that in a few years' time, important additions to the fine buildings of Wellington will be made in … the erection of a splendid Town Hall.[85]

The Wellington City Empowering Act 1897 enabled the municipality to raise a series of loans, including £25,000 for a hall and spacious corporation offices. The issue dragged on as councillors prevaricated about their existing accommodation in Featherston Street. In April 1900 they resolved to spend £50,000 on the hall, with ratepayers later giving almost universal blessing to the loan. Architects were invited to submit their designs, based on a concert hall (complete with organ), seating 3,000 people, the Council Chamber, departmental and public offices, and a reception room for up to 700 people. In 1901, Joshua Charlesworth won the

In 1901 a visit by the Duke and Duchess of Cornwall and York excited the loyal citizenry. Here, staff on the roof of the Union Steam Ship Company building on the corner of Customhouse Quay and Johnston Street crane to get a good view of the civic procession. The domed towers of the harbour board office can be seen behind.

ATL, Malcolm Ross Collection, G-6660-1/1

competition with a design for a building in the neo-classical Renaissance style, with imposing front and a high tower.

Later that year, the visiting Duke and Duchess of Cornwall and York laid the Town Hall foundation stone as part of a civic pageant. Concerns about escalating costs were apparent by the time tenders were called, with work beginning in May 1902. It was a long slow process. Finishing the ornate 'patent zinc' ceiling, in pale pink, blue and brown, took months and a large squad of sub-contractors. Late in 1903, Charlesworth assured the Town Clerk that progress was being made: 'the carpenters, plumbers and plasterers are pushing ahead, but the bricklayers are frequently stopped on account of the shortage of bricks'.[86] A *New Zealand Mail* editorial reflected the growing public impatience:

> The never ending town hall is the next bone we shall have to pick with [the councillors]. Soon, everywhere, experts may arise who will get them out of the deep rut they have got into with that, and again peace will reign. The inconvenience … has made us rage against the unheard of slowness of this building of our town hall.[87]

In March 1904, Wellingtonians had their first glimpse of the interior, with its 'fine plaster work, with its many friezes and ornamental frescoes'.[88] By June, smoke billowing from the nearby tramways power-house was said to be discolouring the exterior, and alarmed councillors talked about 'an injury being caused to the Town Hall'.[89] But all was well, and construction was completed in the last months of the year in time for the pre-Christmas opening. Ratepayers would have to dig deep. The final bill came to £79,268, including the organ (installed early in 1906) and furnishings.[90] Auckland City paid a similar price for its town hall seven years later.

Encased in flags, the building was unveiled in December 1904, launching a gala week of celebrations and concerts beneath the glow of electric lights. Mayor Aitken led a robed procession into the building for the opening ceremony. A grand concert that evening featured soloists, a male chorus, and instrumentalists. The hall's acoustic properties came in for particular praise, the *New Zealand Times* hailing it as 'one of the finest concert halls in Australasia'.[91]

The municipality's new investment soon became the hub of the city's social and cultural life. In 1905, councillors voted to spend £30 to prepare the floor for dancing purposes.[92] Pat Lawlor records the reaction to a vigorous dancing display at a Town Hall bazaar:

> I can see them now, also the shocked faces of the older people. To the tune of some musical creation a score of young men and women cakewalked around the town hall with heads thrown back, hips swaying and eyes alight. Of course it was as innocent as the ballet dancing of the juveniles but as a preliminary departure from Victorian rigidities it was reckoned as startling.[93]

The city fathers had more serious matters to attend to. An overloaded electricity system was slowing the trams during the peak half-hour after 5 p.m. In 1904, street-lighting circuits were bought from the Electric Light and Power Company, as a prelude to municipal ownership of the business. A loan of £150,000 was raised three years later to compulsorily purchase and modernise the company's assets, including the Jervois Quay and Harris Street steam-power plants. As part of the deal, the municipality took on 58 of the company's employees. The Electric Lighting Department, later to become the municipal Electricity Department, was born. By 1905, the success of the city-owned tramways had turned conservative sceptics such as Cr John Luke into true believers. Luke now saw city ownership of the power company as a logical step:

> The example of the tramways justified the ratepayers in authorizing the city
> council to carry on this new branch of municipal enterprise. He was no party
> to burdening the rates, but he felt that even if the rates were not relieved, the
> public would be given a much better light than at present.[94]

'Municipal enterprise' expanded, with a zoological garden being established at
Newtown Park in 1905. A Council crematorium, built at Karori Cemetery in 1909,
was the first in the Southern Hemisphere. This alternative to burial took time to
gain acceptance in the city, but won support on public health grounds.[95] The Karori
facility, with its coke-fired incinerating chamber, cost £1,433, two-thirds of which
was publicly subscribed. In 1911, the cost of cremation was £2 12s 6d for citizens,
and £4 4s for non-residents.[96]

Further municipal investments included £20,000 for a replacement rubbish
destructor at the Clyde Quay yards in 1908, and £15,000 for a city abattoir at
Ngauranga a year later. A municipal fish market opened on Jervois Quay in 1911,
with the Council providing accommodation and a salesman. A Council-funded
fishing trawler business, purportedly to bring supplies of fresh fish cheaply to
locals, folded after four years.

A ratepayer-funded orchestra became the icing on the municipal cake. For the
first decade of the new century, citizens heard orchestral music *al fresco*, from band
rotundas in public parks, gardens, and at the seaside. The municipality subsidised
four local orchestras and a pipe band by as much as £250 a year. In 1910, councillors
voted to underwrite a 45-strong municipal orchestra — another Australasian first.
The orchestra rehearsed and performed at the Town Hall, under the City Organist,
until its demise in 1913.

Off the rails

In 1912, Wellington's whole-hearted embrace of municipal enterprise was tested
when industrial action stopped the trams. The result was six days of anger, public
recrimination — and a lot of walking. The Waihi miners' strike from May to
November 1912 is usually recalled as the event that ignited the union movement.
But it was the Wellington tramwaymen's success in getting the municipality to
remove an employee whom they saw as an informer in February that started off
a militant two years. The headline in the Federation of Labour's *Maoriland Worker*
newspaper proclaimed: 'Men Win — Council Surrenders'.[97] The events in Wellington
had dramatic and lasting consequences — polarising councillors, harming worker-

In 1912 union leader and sometime socialist David McLaren was elected Wellington's first Labour Mayor. His squabbles with militant union factions saw him lose the mayoralty after a year.

WCA, 00510:0:12

employer relations, and forcing the municipality to overhaul its business and management systems.

By 1910, the Corporation's 400 'trammies' — the oil-streaked motormen, the tweed-clad conductors, and the firemen and greasers in the power-house — were a microcosm of the local working class. Their elected champions on Council and in Parliament helped to ensure that tramwaymen no longer worked 73 hours a week for 4½d an hour.[98] In 1905, David McLaren campaigned for the city's trams to be adapted to give workers greater protection from rough weather.[99] Under public ownership, tramwaymen in the capital had lost their traditional status as among the most exploited of workers.[100] They enjoyed better pay and conditions than their Auckland counterparts, initially employed by a private company. Nonetheless, any attack on the union's integrity was bound to lead to conflict.

Initially, the trams were a cash cow for the municipality. By 1911, the estimated 22 million passenger rides a year produced weekly revenues of £3,000 (more than $400,000 in today's terms) much of which passed through the hands of the 130 conductors.[101] A squad of ticket inspectors monitored their activity, but management privately believed that pilfering was widespread. A week before Christmas 1911, Cr Shirtcliffe leaked an internal report that pointed to 'a considerable amount of malpractice with regard to ticket sales', and claimed that conductors had 'thievery down to a fine art'.[102] The Tramways Union was outraged, and immediately singled out George Fuller, a zealous ticket inspector, as the source of the accusation. The municipality in turn was accused of exalting 'the spy and the informer', as unionists vowed to give 'no quarter to the councillors who would establish a huge municipal scabbery'.[103] They gave an ultimatum that the union would strike unless Fuller was removed from contact with the men.[104] A seven-page list of his alleged misdemeanours was produced.

By the last week of January 1912, direct action was looking inevitable as an exhausted and divided Council squabbled over Fuller's future. Mayor Wilford meanwhile had left for England for surgery. Tramways management drew up plans for a non-union service, but councillors ruled it out on the grounds that it would have dire consequences.[105] As the union readied to strike, seamen, labourers, drivers, and other local unions expressed their support. The militant socialists of the Federation of Labour, fresh from campaigning on the Auckland trams, also rallied to the cause. Its manifesto, written on crimson paper, congratulated the Wellington union on 'its magnificent vote against the tyranny of the City Council'.[106] After receiving its copy, the *Evening Post* coined the memorable phrase, the 'Red Federation', and the name stuck.[107]

The zealousness of ticket inspector George Fuller enraged tramway unions and helped trigger a six-day strike in 1912. He was later assigned to a desk job, and is pictured here (back row, fourth from the right) with head office staff of the Electrical Tramways Department.

WCA, 00138:0:8698

The strike began on 31 January, amid the kind of settled weather that Wellingtonians fantasise about. Union members — 120 motormen, 130 conductors, 90 car-shed hands, and 40 power-house hands and overhead staff — marched to the Trades Hall in Lower Cuba Street to hear speeches by 'Red Fed' organisers. As the strike continued, commuters walked and cycled to work in the February heat. Meanwhile, councillors huddled in the Council Chamber, as the pressure mounted. 'Strike Sunday' (4 February) drew 3,000 supporters to the Basin Reserve, where speakers suggested that the current action was the precursor to a General Strike to be called the next day.

The government then intervened. On Monday morning Sir Joseph Ward, in the dying days of his premiership, drove his motorcar from the Council Chamber to the Trades Hall to break the deadlock, later telling a crowd of 2,000 that the trams would soon be running. Fuller was given a desk job, and the union was assured that no striker would be victimised. Management of the tramways was immediately restructured, as councillors voted for a board of officials to run the business. Figures released at the end of March revealed an enterprise struggling with huge debt repayments.[108] By the middle of the year, the new board of management was ordering calculating machines, and proposing a combination of cost-cutting measures and commercial advertising to make the tramways more 'self-supporting'.[109]

Socialist thinker and former public servant Edward Tregear carried a streak of radicalism to the council chamber when he was elected in 1912. As part of his municipal socialist beliefs, he proposed a people's farm and public laundromat. Concerned about creeping commercialism, Cr Tregear later alarmed motormen when he ripped down advertising boards from a tram outside Kirkcaldie & Stains.

ATL, F-30365-1/2

The political fault-lines exposed by the strike lingered. On the right were the employer-friendly Citizens, promising to uphold the 'city's rights' against industrial militancy. On the left was a slightly over-cocky union movement. The labour movement looked unstoppable after 1912 when the full adoption of the residential franchise in that year's local body elections saw the number of eligible voters swell to nearly three times the size of a decade earlier. The United Labour Party mobilised worker support from Trades Hall in a campaign that successfully elected David McLaren as Wellington's first Labour mayor in 1912. McLaren, however, squabbled with militant union factions and lost the mayoralty after a year.

Radical ideas resounded in the Council Chamber, as Edward Tregear, a prominent socialist intellectual who had been a reforming Secretary of Labour, was elected in 1912. At this time, national politics was in a state of flux. The Liberals lost office in July 1912. Reform's William Massey formed a government that was hostile to unions and would remain in power until 1928. Tregear kept the workers' dream alive, proposing a municipal farm and even a people's laundromat, 'where clothes could be washed and dried by their owner at almost a nominal cost'.[110] Tregear was also concerned about creeping commercialisation and what he portrayed as a dilution of socialistic values. He alarmed motormen in 1913 by tearing newly installed advertising boards for such products as Creamoata and Radium Boot Polish from their tramcars:

> I beg to report that on the 2.27 trip from Oriental Bay when the car was stopped at Kirkcaldies stop, Councillor Tregear pulled the advertising board off front of the car and placed it on front platform remarking that if they wanted to know who did it I could refer to him.[111]

In 1913 John Luke took over the mayoralty on an anti-Labour ticket. Cr Tregear spent much of that year out of the Chamber, working with Federation of Labour stalwart Peter Fraser, a recent arrival to Wellington. As the pair worked to form an embryonic Labour Party, militant workers prepared for an industrial showdown. Action by 1,600 Wellington watersiders triggered what some called 'The Great Strike' of 1913 — three weeks of clashes between police and strikers, in the worst outbreak of civil unrest ever seen in the country. On 29 October, more than a thousand strikers blocked work on the wharves before storming the gates of the Basin Reserve to hold a protest meeting. The Council refused the strike committee's request to hire the Town Hall for a public meeting chaired by Mayor Luke.[112] Justices of the Peace, however, were free to use the Town Hall to swear in hundreds of civilian police, known as 'special constables', and to issue them with long batons. Some unionists dubbed them Massey's Cossacks, especially when they were augmented by farmers on horseback from outlying areas. One recalled ugly scenes on 5 November as a mounted column of specials made its way from Taranaki Street to the wharves. At Cuba Street the violence reached its peak, with trams being used as weapons. One of the 'specials' recalled:

> There were two trams waiting there, one on each side of the road, as though they wished to let us pass safely through. Our leading horses at once proceeded, with the next horses following as closely as possible. The trams then rushed together at great speed. At least one horse was knocked down, and others were hit with great force, the riders escaping injury by smartly shifting their legs. Two of our men then jumped on a tram each and when the trams reached their terminus they arrested the drivers. They were both found guilty.[113]

Feelings continued to run high. Wellington did not return to normal until Christmas.[114] The Tramways Board chairman assured councillors that 'some motormen were being kept under close supervision'.[115] Mayor Luke placed on record his Council's thanks to the special constables, 'who so readily responded to the call and at great sacrifice assisted in promoting and maintaining the public peace and true interests of the Dominion'.[116] Cr Tregear, on the other hand, described the specials as 'outcast scum from the country, brought down to bludgeon citizens into submission to the Government'.[117] The defeat of the unions and the arrest of Peter Fraser and other strike leaders brought pressure for Tregear to resign, but he remained a councillor until 1915.

The Home Front

As the industrial upheaval receded, leisure became a municipal preoccupation. Councillors approved the purchase of 650 acres in Days Bay as a sanctuary for daytrippers from the city, the government and private donors providing the bulk of the funds. A golf course was established at Berhampore. Close to 54,000 trees and shrubs were planted out in parks across the city, including the new Central Park. A Council-subsidised 'ocean wave' machine installed at Lyall Bay proved very popular; later, a bylaw was passed stipulating the size of surf-boards. Writer Robin Hyde evoked the new trend for sun-bathing, describing how 'most people prefer

Down the hall on Saturday night. Socialistic ideas swirled around the city in the early twentieth century. Former miner Michael Joseph Savage, one of many Australian unionists to cross the Tasman at this time, landed in Wellington on Labour Day, 1907. Hours after arriving, the future New Zealand Prime Minister attended a political meeting addressed by Ben Tillett, visiting British labour leader and unionist. Left-wingers of both sexes also gathered here at the Socialist Hall, 80 Manners Street.

to lie on the beach, turning on the gramophones and slowly cooking themselves the colour of raw steak'.[118]

When war broke out in Europe in August 1914, Mayor Luke, fresh from a briefing in William Massey's office, urged citizens to support the British flag. Councillors rose and sang the national anthem, 'God Save The King'. The Mayor vowed to keep open the jobs of staff who volunteered to join the Expeditionary Force. The city's role as the main departure point for troops saw the Council regularly involved in farewell ceremonies at the Basin Reserve.

By September 1915 the Town Hall had been turned into a recruiting station, and Mayor Luke reported that 1,200 men had enrolled there. Free use of the hall was granted 'for patriotic purposes'. The Municipal Officers' Association gained permission to turn part of the basement into a rifle range. So many Corporation staff were joining up that by February 1916 the Fire Brigade was asking the government to exempt the urban-based fire services: 'Up to the present, 20 men have gone to the front, four are in camp and two are going — a total of 26 from the permanent staff of 38'.[119]

The capital became the administrative heart of the war effort, with departing troops trained in surrounding camps and equipped from bulging government stores. Conflict in Europe failed to suppress the city's commercial and residential expansion. The war years also saw the number of tramway passengers jumping from 25 million in 1914 to 32 million two years later.[120] Labour shortages, especially of motormen, persisted. Of the 232 Corporation staff who went to war, 103 had worked on the trams.[121] So great was the general manpower problem that councillors took the unprecedented step of training women as gardeners. The aim was to give them 'the privilege of being taught such gardening work as the Superintendent of Reserves deems suitable', although the Council was 'not to be placed under any obligation, moral or otherwise, to give them employment after the expiration of their training period'.[122] A grumpy committee chairman later reported 'that the women now requested payment for their work'.[123]

With the contentious introduction of conscription in 1916, the Council resolved 'to do everything possible to forward the objects of the Recruiting Board'.[124] It refused to let the Anti-Conscription League hire the Town Hall. At the same time, Lady Stout, wife of the Chief Justice, gained permission to use the Concert Chamber for her lecture to the Anti-German League. Former staff members, whether enlisted or balloted, continued to receive full wages, but as the war dragged on there was growing reluctance to subsidise single men.[125]

The wharves were under military control from the first day of war, with routines disrupted as vessels were requisitioned as troopships to transport soldiers to Europe. The export trade flourished as Britain snapped up all the butter, cheese, wool and frozen meat that New Zealand could produce. Wellington's milk supply proved an unlikely victim of the boom. Early in 1917, the district's dairy farmers, long unhappy with revenues and problems caused by middlemen, now threatened to divert the city's milk to the butter factories.

Calls for the Council to take charge of the city's milk supply dated back to the early 1890s. In 1906, one supporter claimed that municipalisation would 'obviate a great deal of infant mortality'.[126] Concerns about private vendors watering down milk and selling it in a filthy condition had led to the Wellington City Milk-supply Act 1914. This gave the Corporation powers to establish milk stations and to run the milk business, but beyond a role in inspecting dairies the milk supply was left to the marketplace. The government then set the scene for a municipal milk supply by passing the Cost of Living Act 1915. In 1916, a deputation from the Plunket

Society, led by community activist Annie McVicar, reported that milk quality and rising prices was forcing mothers to resort to artificial milk. Asked if she had evidence that the poor milk supply had caused the death of any infants, McVicar replied: 'Oh yes, I am sorry to say we have.'[127]

During 1917, councillors hosted meetings with dairy farmers and milk vendors, most of whom resisted the idea of a municipal takeover. A £1,500 milk depot was constructed on Thorndon Quay where milk, mostly coming in by rail, could be tested and its sales co-ordinated. The new facility, hastily built and poorly equipped, opened early in 1918, but closed within hours amid chaotic scenes and intransigent vendors. Cr Charles Norwood, whose name became synonymous with city milk as well as Morris motorcars, concluded that 'the Vendors' general conduct was in itself sufficient, even if all other conditions had been right, to wreck the scheme'.[128] Undeterred, councillors decided, in April 1918, to establish a Municipal Milk Department, believing themselves the first local authority in the world to do so.

The Council's first move was to build a £12,000 depot in Dixon Street to collect and treat the milk. A dairy factory at Otaki was purchased. By 1919, milk was being bought in bulk from dairy farmers, treated at the depot, and collected by private deliverymen who then went door-to-door, using the old 'can and dipper' method to fill household billies. Continuing hygiene risks led to the buying, bottling and selling all being done 'in house'. Within a few years, Wellington's municipal milk supply was gathering national and international acclaim.

As the war came to an end, a captured Turkish machine-gun was mounted on the first-floor landing of the Town Hall. In September 1918 Mayor Luke, now an MP in the Massey government, led the councillors in three cheers to express 'thankfulness and joy at the glorious part taken by the New Zealand soldiers in this Great War'. By this time, a total of 22 Council staff had died, and a further 24 had been wounded or gassed.[129] As news filtered through that Germany was about to capitulate, Luke outlined plans for bells, bunting and civic festivities to mark 'a unique historical [occasion] that would not be repeated in the lifetime of anyone now living'.[130] History would, of course, prove him wrong. More immediately, Armistice Week would bring a devastating influenza epidemic which would kill thousands and plunge the country into a national emergency.

Convulsions

Chapter 5

1918–1939

I stood in the middle of Wellington City at 2 pm on a weekday afternoon, and there was not a soul to be seen — no trams running, no shops open, and the only traffic was a van with a white sheet tied to the side, with a big red cross painted on it, serving as an ambulance or hearse. It was really a City of the Dead.

Medical orderly Alfred Hollows[1]

The great skin-bound minute books of the Wellington City Council detail all of its mutterings and procedural motions, sitting by endless sitting, year by year, all the way back to the days of the Town Board. But for the month of November 1918, the municipal record is blank: nothing is recorded. Like many others in the capital — and elsewhere in the Dominion — the city fathers avoided any form of gathering, fearing the influenza epidemic scything through the city would reach inside the chamber and kill them all. By the time councillors reconvened on 2 December, the worst of the panic had passed: the city's dozen makeshift hospitals were running out of patients, and most of the 757 local victims had been buried at Karori cemetery. The minutes record a list of Council dead, and a general tribute to tram conductors 'who had succumbed to the disease'.[2]

More of the story can be found in the evidence of the Influenza Epidemic Commission, which was assembled early in 1919 to analyse the country's worst recorded natural disaster, and to advise on how a repetition could be avoided. From the typed testimony of over a hundred witnesses, a dark picture emerges of the chaos and confusion in Wellington as those charged with responding to the outbreak fell ill themselves. By mid 1918, fears were growing that the influenza pandemic ravaging the Northern Hemisphere could reach the capital, with rumours of sick soldiers in camps outside the city. Prime Minister Massey was more preoccupied with winding up a long war and getting the troops home. Following a serious outbreak in Auckland in October, Health Minister George Russell talked of inoculating southbound rail and ferry passengers. The *Dominion* noted that 'flu carriers had been arriving from Auckland every day for over a week without any hindrance from officialdom'.[3] In a cruel twist, the desire of citizens to gather together to celebrate the Armistice helped fuel the contagion.

Ambulances like this were used to carry victims of the 1918 'flu epidemic. The Wellington Town Hall, visible in the background, was the headquarters of the voluntary relief effort.

ATL, NZ Free Lance Collection, C-16206-1/2

Mayor Luke picked up the relief effort in the capital, as the central government response crumbled. In his deposition, Luke recalled the condescending attitude of the health bureaucracy: 'The district health officer told me that our duties as a city council were confined to the cleansing of the city, to the cleansing of the backyards, and the drainage of the city in a general way'.[4] Unruffled, Luke ordered in quantities of disinfectant. Inhalation chambers, which sprayed the occupant with zinc, opened in the Town Hall, and public servants were ordered to make a daily visit. As Armistice Week began in the second week of November, an orderly lunchtime queue outside the Town Hall erupted in chaos.[5] Downtown government offices emptied, and tramways services were cut as a third of the staff came down with 'flu. Makeshift hospitals and convalescent homes opened in public halls. Organisations created during the war and run mainly by women provided a framework for the volunteer effort. The exhausting and risky work saw the number of volunteers plummet as people started dying.

When the epidemic reached its peak in mid November, most of the medical top brass — the hospital superintendent, the matron, and the district health officer — were in the fever ward at Wellington Hospital, along with 40 members of the nursing staff. With those in charge either dead or incapacitated, the official relief effort in the capital lay in tatters. The Mayor and others were left to co-ordinate activities as best they could. In an era before antibiotics and complex vaccines, people relied on proprietary products to kill germs. Many died. Men in their twenties and thirties faced the greatest risk. Maori were seven times more likely than Europeans to die from the disease — sixteen are known to have perished in greater Wellington and the Hutt Valley, out of a Maori population of about 500, although one estimate puts the figure higher.[6]

The Town Hall 'bar'

One of the heated debates during the 1918 influenza epidemic was whether alcohol was a help or a hindrance to sufferers. District health officers soon settled the argument by ordering the closure of all city hotel bars to stop the spread of infection.

Some Wellington doctors, however, insisted that 'alcoholic stimulants' were a vital nostrum (patent remedy) for their patients, and it was agreed that the Town Hall should be the distribution point for prescribed quantities of spirits. In one of the lighter moments of the epidemic, Mayor Luke, a prominent abstainer, personally took charge of what became known as 'the Town Hall bar':

Most people presented signed orders for a measured quantity of whisky or brandy, but one hopeful tried his luck and asked the mayor for a bottle of brandy. 'Have you got an order?' 'No, but I can get one.' 'Who is your doctor?' 'Dr ---.' 'Just a moment, he's here in my room now. I'll bring him out.' By the time the mayor and doctor reappeared, the applicant had fled — all that could be heard was the clatter of his boots disappearing down the corridor.[7]

Mayor John Luke pulled the Wellington relief effort together during the 1918 'flu epidemic, showing leadership and courage. In 1920, during happier times, he hosted a lavish Town Hall reception for the visiting Prince of Wales (standing next to the mayor).

ATL, F-151354-1/2

Midway through November, the inter-island ferries and coastal shipping trade ceased. Factories, shops, theatres, dance halls, billiard saloons and hairdressing salons all closed. Hotels followed suit. Luke and fellow Wellington MPs Peter Fraser and Harry Holland called a citizens' meeting. The city was divided into sixteen blocks, each with its own 'captain', with the relief effort co-ordinated from the Town Hall. As chairman of the Citizens' Vigilance Committee, Luke was blunt in his advice to captains: 'I told them ... that they were just as responsible in their positions as captains of the groups for fighting the disease as I was responsible for the city as a whole. I said, "Do not come to me with small trivial things, but act".'[8]

Luke and scores of fellow volunteers worked around the clock, organising hospital admissions and issuing food and medicine. He ordered seats to be removed from the Town Hall auditorium to make way for a temporary hospital with 60 beds.[9] Fraser and Holland were appointed captains of the Central and Brooklyn blocks respectively. Both men subsequently caught influenza. Fraser famously went house-to-house in Te Aro Flat's overcrowded dwellings and boarding houses, where almost half of the capital's influenza deaths occurred.[10] He signed forms authorising costs involved in fighting the epidemic to be sent to the municipality.[11] His efforts ensured his subsequent election as a city councillor. No less energetic, Luke enrolled 25 volunteer sanitary inspectors and joined them in entering houses 'to do cleaning'.[12]

On 21 November alone, 58 deaths were recorded. At Karori, cemetery staff needed help to dig trenches. Many of the corpses turned purple or black, thus adding to the sense of horror and disbelief. Four mail trucks transported the dead. The mayoral car got so much use that the Council minutes referred to the 'considerable amount of damage done to the vehicle'.[13]

Overall, between a third and a half of all New Zealanders caught the infection during 1918. The initial difficulties in the capital made it the city with the highest per-capita death-rate.[14] The recriminations began. In Parliament, Health Minister Russell attacked Mayor Luke, who was also the MP for Wellington North, claiming that councillors had delayed slum clearances in the city because of 'the influence of landlords and moneyed interests':

> When I came to Wellington I went to the Mayor and said 'What is wanted here is a thorough inspection and cleaning up of your city'. His Worship said 'But we have no slums here'. I said 'Have you not Haining Street?' 'No' he said 'Haining Street is clean'. I ask the honourable member for Wellington North what he thinks of Wellington now.[15]

Luke had only recently familiarised himself with the decaying areas of Te Aro Flat. But he knew that demolishing inner-city slums brought the perennial problem of re-housing those evicted. The Epidemic Commission, which included former mayor McLaren, concluded that 'old, dilapidated, worm-eaten, vermin-infested' structures had been a factor in the spread of the disease. The commissioners urged an overhaul of public health administration and the imposition of minimum housing standards. The Health Act 1920 enhanced and clarified the powers of local bodies, adding safeguards to ensure that councils acted. The new shared responsibility for public health between local and central government was likened 'to the relation of junior to senior partner in a commercial firm'.[16] Local government in New Zealand, traditionally left to its own devices, was about to get a lot of attention from the senior partner:

> Within a decade a revolution had occurred, with central government installing itself as overseer of roading, planning, borrowing and expenditure … partly it sprang from a recognition of local body inadequacy, and partly from a belated realisation that local government activities were not self-contained but impinged on the well-being of the entire body politic.[17]

The 1920s began on a high note, as Wellingtonians determined to put war and epidemic behind them. In September 1921, Council employees got the afternoon off to watch the deciding rugby test against the Springboks, who were touring for the first time. The match was played in bucketing rain, and ended in a scoreless draw. Weekend crowds also flocked to the new Kilbirnie speedway to watch dirt-track motorcycle racing. There was a relaxed, almost carnival atmosphere in the city, with civil servants leaving work early. This annoyed the government mandarins presiding over a public service that had swelled by 1,500 to 6,000 during the busy war years.[18]

The opening of eating places such as the Quicklunch establishment in Featherston Street reflected growing American influences in the city. Prime Minister Gordon Coates, with his ever-present cigarette and mastery of the dance floor, came to symbolise a more cosmopolitan era when he was dubbed the 'Jazz Premier' in 1925. A whiff of sophistication could be detected in the city as early as 1920, when a 'most exclusive' cabaret opened in a quiet Thorndon Street, opposite the residence of former councillor Edward Tregear. Proprietor Miss Borlase taught dance moves to schoolgirls, among them Iris Wilkinson (better known by her subsequent pen-name, Robin Hyde). Late-night jazz and taxi traffic in the no-

By the 1920s Athletic Park had established itself as the mecca for local rugby. Its legend was born during the first tour by the South African Springboks in 1921, when the deciding test was played in pouring rain (the game famously ended in a 0-0 draw). This picture, taken in 1930, shows the litter-strewn Western Bank after a big game, with soap boxes, benzine tins, and 'remnants of lunch' among the detritus.

ATL, Dominion Post Collection, EP-Municipal-Athletic Park-03

exit street drove the sleep-deprived Tregear, now aged 73, to petition his former colleagues on the Council, to little avail. The sensationalist Wellington-based *New Zealand Truth* newspaper took up the cause, running headlines about the 'Gay Goings-on in Goring Street', 'Householders Hot over High-born Hullabaloo', and 'Mirth, Motors and Maledictions'. Reporter Pat Lawlor wrote of 'the new order of things, the beginnings of the era of jazz bands, the grinding orchestration of motor gears and motor horns on nightly joy rides — a new age of ungodly noises'.[19]

Tense schoolgirls salute the Prince of Wales in 1920, as the object of their attention tries to keep his hat on.

ATL, K. A. Stewart Collection, F-57604-1/2

'An innovation full of promise'

The Scottish-born Annie McVicar was the first woman elected to the Wellington City Council, arriving in the capital in 1901. A trained nurse, she involved herself in social activism, gaining headlines in 1916 when, as a spokeswoman for the Plunket Society, she linked infant mortality to contaminated milk.[20]

McVicar entered politics to further her work for the health and education of women and children. In 1915 she became one of the first women on the Wellington Hospital Board, and remained on the board until 1938. In 1919, she was elected to the Miramar Borough Council. When the borough merged with Wellington in 1921, she became one of the city's nineteen councillors.

The *Evening Post* was delighted: 'Never before has Wellington had a lady city councillor, and the innovation is full of promise.'[21] McVicar helped lead the city's relief effort during the economic slump of the early 1920s. She held her Miramar seat in 1923, but was defeated in 1925.

McVicar became a Justice of the Peace in 1926, and in 1938 was awarded an MBE in recognition of her years of hard work for the community. She died in 1954, aged 92.

Annie McVicar, Wellington City's first woman councillor.

ATL, Evening Post Collection, C-17877-1/2

Civic housekeeping

In August 1920, Miss N. McNair was appointed inaugural 'Lady Sanitary Inspector' as the municipality employed additional staff to meet its new public health obligations. Local women's groups championed the appointment of lady inspectors, 'not to pry into other women's housekeeping, but … to have a kindly and observant eye generally for the many discomforts of the sort that militate against health'.[22] During 1921, seven sanitary inspectors visited 3,061 buildings, and served 175 demolition notices and 142 orders to exterminate rats.[23] Many of Wellington's worst slums were inspected and condemned.

The decision to appoint a woman to a job higher in rank than the usual female position of 'typiste' indicated that the municipality sensed the changing social mood. Part of it stemmed from women's prominence in the wartime fundraising and relief effort, for which they were called 'our amazons'. However, less was written about militant groups such as the Wellington Housewives' Union or the Women's Anti-Conscription League, formed in the capital in 1916.

The first women candidates stood for the Wellington municipality in 1919. Female property-owners and ratepayers had been able both to vote and to stand for Council since 1876 — a full seventeen years before women's suffrage was won. In 1893 Onehunga elected Elizabeth Yates its 'lady mayor', the first woman to hold such a position in the British Empire, and Ellen Melville was elected to the Auckland City Council in 1913.

Women's groups urged good 'civic housekeeping', as health, housing and community issues were increasingly seen as synonymous. Kindergartens, parks and restrooms were identified as practical solutions to urban problems. In 1919, a delegation of 51 women attended a high-profile town-planning conference at the Town Hall. Town-planning was the issue of the day — a local manifestation of a British movement stemming from concerns about the ills of Victorian cities. The influenza pandemic added a sense of urgency to the conference. Political activist Jessie Aitken, a member of the Wellington Hospital and Charitable Aid Board, added her voice to calls for women to be at the centre of all decision-making to do with housing and town planning. Mayor Luke, however, had other priorities, and his presence at the conference ensured that the first of many municipal playgrounds, known as 'play stations', was built. Jessie Aitken believed that housing for working families was a more important issue for local and central government than children's swings. As a member of the Housewives' Union, she lobbied the Council to 'erect houses to supply the very pressing needs of the community'.[24] The municipality built a few homes for its employees in Lyall Bay and Northland in the early 1920s, but avoided involvement in public housing until after the Second World War.

The influenza epidemic had rattled the state health bureaucracy. Despite the Council's appointment of additional sanitary inspectors, central government kept a watchful eye on activities. The Director-General of Health intervened in 1921 when municipal sanitation staff hired Murphy's Gang, a team of professional rat-catchers, to clean up vermin-infested buildings in the city. His offer to detail a senior inspector to reorganise the sanitary inspection staff and to supervise Murphy's activities was rejected by the Council's public health committee: 'this is a matter which the council would prefer to deal with itself, and … as it is reported that the operations of the rat catchers employed have been satisfactory, no additional assistance in this connection is at present required.'[25]

In 1925 the municipality donated £500 to Health Week, which became one of the high points of Wellington's winter calendar. The inaugural event featured a Health and Hygiene Rally in the Town Hall, attended by 1,200 people, with stalls, demonstrations, lectures, and entertainments. Health Week in 1926 coincided with

Murphy's terrible hand

In the years before the First World War, Murphy the rat-catcher was a fixture on the Wellington waterfront. The little Irishman's fox terriers helped to create the legend, but it was 'Murphy's terrible hand', reaching into crevices in the wharf sheds, that yielded two or three wriggling rodents at a time.

To help prevent further public health crises in the city, the Council offered a generous bounty for every rat brought to the destructor. It was not enough. In 1921, Murphy and three associates were called upon to lead the crusade into the city's rat-infested slums.

During the first months of 1922, Murphy's gang killed 730 rats.[26] But the charge per rodent of 3s 7d made his 'terrible hand' a costly proposition. The Council soon turned from rat-catching to public education. In 1925, a staff member inadvertently told a newspaper reporter that the city was 'over-run with rats'. The Council made a £500 donation to Health Week rather than recall Murphy.[27]

a Clean Up campaign in the city. Councillors heard that the sanitary inspectors were successfully limiting that winter's recurrence of mild influenza: 'Special attention is being paid to ventilation of theatres and halls and instructions have been issued to proprietors to disinfect daily.'[28]

Parliamentary scrutiny continued, as evidenced by the passage in 1926 of an ambitious Town-planning Bill, and greater central oversight of local body borrowing and roading. The municipality formed a town planning committee and established a two-man department, but staff were floundering by 1930. The new planning regime obliged bigger cities such as Wellington to introduce zoning and to provide details of all future building to a government town planning board. Wellington, like most other councils, ignored the deadline for these changes as economic conditions worsened.

Public health remained a civic preoccupation in the aftermath of the 1918 'flu epidemic. Here, a new street cleaning device is being trialled.

ATL, Evening Post Collection, C-24392-1/2

Pigeon Park, a narrow wedge squeezed between Manners and Dixon Streets, became a popular meeting place for city workers and visitors between the wars.

Wellington City Libraries

Turning up the volume

After 1920, the clanking of the milk department lorries meant that city residents could no longer be guaranteed a good night's sleep. By then the petrol engine was well entrenched, with 3,740 vehicles (including 140 of the offending trucks) registered in Wellington City.[29] With the new post-war technologies came new urban sounds, among them the movies, the radio, and the gramophone. In 1923, the city's first parking places, known as 'theatre parks', were set aside in Courtenay Place between the hours of 7 p.m. and 11 p.m., as the street became an entertainment and transport hub. This was the era of the great picture palaces, and the De Luxe cinema (later renamed the Embassy), which opened at the end of the street in 1924, could seat 1,749. Live performances were also popular. In July 1928, Te Puea's pioneering Te Pou O Mangatawhiri (TPM) concert party from Waikato gave a fortnight of performances there, at the invitation of Prime Minister Coates.[30] On 16 July 1927, radio station 2YA was first beamed from a 5,000-watt transmitter on top of Mt Victoria, its powerful signal establishing it as the national radio station. In 1929, as the volume of city noise grew, councillors voted to ban shopkeepers from playing phonographs and radios in their doorways.[31]

Despite a brief but severe economic recession in 1921, Wellington continued to thrive, as large sections of the population settled into modern, consumer-driven domesticity. The economic roller-coaster ride of the post-war years was on the upswing. Solid years of prosperity and the growth in service-oriented jobs helped to transform Wellington, as the financial and commercial sector clustered in the vicinity of Featherston Street, and the Te Aro slums made way for factories and warehouses. Eight-storey towers of reinforced concrete and steel rose above the central city, replacing the squat wooden tin-roofed buildings of the Victorian era. The new high-rise buildings also attracted lower fire insurance premiums than their wooden predecessors.[32] Sleek new towers, such as the T. & G. Mutual Life Assurance Building in Grey Street and the AMP Building on Customhouse Quay, confirmed Wellington's new status as a seat of financial power. Concern that tall buildings would literally overshadow the inner city saw the municipality restrict their height to nine storeys.

The suburban dream had become reality for many citizens by the mid 1920s, especially as returning soldiers were rewarded with generous housing loans. Roads of concrete and asphalt, tunnels, and a viaduct were constructed to connect the city with its suburbs. Limited state funding was available for public housing, but the government preferred to advance millions of pounds for private home-ownership. By 1926, half of all working families were said to own their own homes. The state also championed electric power for domestic lighting, heating, and cooking, thus fuelling a consumer revolution, aided by municipal authorities marketing home appliances from their downtown showrooms. Demand soared for labour-saving 'mod cons' and the electricity to run them. More than 20,000 local consumers were affected when the municipality reconfigured its electrical system in 1925 to link up with the state-owned grid. No fewer than 1,831 electric irons had to be rewired around the city.[33] The following year, the Electricity Department

Council workmen busy sealing Victoria Street in the 1920s.

WCA, 00132:0:4

introduced a district domestic tariff. Business boomed. Through the 1920s numbers of households connecting to electricity for cooking and heating grew by around 2,000 a year.

After an absence of half a century, Maori began to trickle back into Wellington, many of them from the Hutt Valley. Though some took manual or factory jobs, others joined the civil service or enrolled at university and training college. Official figures put the Maori population above 300 by the mid 1930s, although one new arrival recalled that 'you could count the number of families on your two hands'.[34] In 1928, Ngati Toa hired the Town Hall for a fundraising 'Joy Night' to rebuild its meeting house in Porirua.[35] Groups such as the Ngati Poneke Young Maori Club, set up in Wellington to support young Maori arrivals to the city, began performing before European audiences that had never been exposed to Maori culture. Headlines such as 'Maoris at Play' were probably inevitable, but in 1930 the capacity crowd attracted to a concert party at the Town Hall took the Council by surprise: 'To prevent a recurrence of the congestion in the vestibule such as existed at the Maori entertainment, it will be necessary to provide ticket-selling boxes'.[36]

Motor vehicles too had changed the face of the city. The Motor Omnibus Act 1926 gave local bodies controversial powers to license private bus operators. Municipalities such as Wellington, with a huge investment in trams, were seen to have a vested interest in keeping out competition. As the noisy trams increasingly fell out of favour, the financial losses began to worry councillors. Levels of municipal borrowing troubled both the government and ratepayers. From the 1870s, municipalities were legally obliged to publish their often complicated accounts and make them available to ratepayers — and to central government.

In the very early days of the municipality, the City Auditor had been appointed alongside other Council officials; but after 1886, the Office of the Controller and Auditor-General assumed oversight of the city's finances. In 1922, a Local Bodies Finance Bill was proposed to deal with excessive borrowing by local bodies, as loans totalling millions of pounds were raised on the London market, often to fund socialist municipal agendas. The move was widely condemned as central government meddling, thus raising the hackles of John Luke, MP and former Mayor:

> To stop our tramways undertaking, to prevent the people from obtaining electric power and electric light, to prevent the municipality from purchasing the Day's Bay property, or to prevent the building of houses for the people, would have been inimical to the true interests of the people ... It is often

most difficult to get suitable men to take up positions in the local bodies, and
it will be still more difficult if they are going to be subjected to the censure
of the public, as indicated in this instance, when Parliament is being asked
to put a wall around such men so they cannot launch out on a progressive
policy for the good of the citizens.[37]

The Local Government Loans Board Act 1926, setting up a gate-keeping body
for municipal loans, further consolidated central government control over local
body borrowing. Nonetheless, Mayor George Troup managed to persuade the
government to approve at least a dozen loans to deal with unemployment, as
economic conditions worsened after 1927.

A railways engineer and architect, Troup was prepared to trample over
governments and ratepayers to achieve his vision for the city. He secured the
National Art Gallery and Museum, the Carillon, and the imposing brick Railway
Station. He operated as a kind of Town-Planner-in-Chief, plucking money from
the ether to realise his dreams. One of his many ambitions was to secure modern,
streamlined transport corridors to the east and west of the city. To open up the
west, he envisaged a road from Bowen Street, around Bolton Street Cemetery to
Tinakori Road, via Sydney Street. The plan included tramlines, as part of a new
route to Karori and Northland; the projected cost was close to £80,000. Supporters
of the 'Western Access Scheme' claimed that avoiding the long route to the western
suburbs via Molesworth Street would save time and £2,000 a year.

The Wellington Ratepayers' Association pointed to declining revenues from the
tramways and petitioned for more nimble motor-powered buses. Parliamentarians,
however, were opposed to the streets in their quiet Thorndon domain being dug
up. A 1928 Commission of Inquiry later recommended the proposed Bowen
Street route, a replacement for the Kelburn Viaduct, and even a tunnel connecting
the horseshoe bend on Glenmore Street with Norway Street. It also favoured a
traffic tunnel through Mt Victoria. Wellington's unemployed would help bring
such schemes to fruition. Ironically, it was during the grim years of economic
depression that much of modern Wellington was built.

The fiasco surrounding the construction of the Northland tunnel helped to
ensure that the Aro Valley and Glenmore Street were never joined. Designed and
built by Council engineers and tradesmen with little knowledge of tunnelling,
the project was a saga of accidents, poor systems, and shoddy workmanship:
'Handicapped in all directions', thundered the *Dominion*.[38] Once again, the
municipality was made to look incompetent. It emerged that no records were kept

On 10 January 1928, Mayor
George Troup joined Laura
Hood and Dorothy Moncrieff at
Trentham Racecourse, as the
women waited for their pilot
husbands to arrive from Sydney.
The airmen disappeared en
route, and their widows' vigil
seized the imagination of the
country.

ATL, Evening Post Collection, G-5960-1/4-EP

MAN ORIGINALLY
RESPONSIBLE FOR
NORTHLAND
TUNNEL

The 1926 construction of the
Northland tunnel was a chapter
of accidents, poor systems and
shoddy Council workmanship.
The engineer's design flopped,
the carpenter making the
wrongly shaped timber ribs died,
and in the end the tunnel caved
in. Alan Reeve's cartoon, under
the heading 'people we'd like to
meet', ridicules the Council's
tunnelling effort.

Alan Reeve, *Lions and Lambs of Wellington*
(1932)

nor instructions written down; the surveyor conveyed information 'on small pieces of paper with measurements marked out in pencil'.[39] Construction engineer Walter Aked's oval design proved impractical; the carpenter making the wrongly shaped timber ribs died; the concrete cracked apart. In the end, the tunnel caved in, and had to be strengthened at a cost estimated at £50,000. A subsequent Commission of Inquiry lambasted the City Council.

Construction of a six-foot-wide tunnel to carry water from the Orongorongo River proved more successful. Dynamited from valleys at each end through two miles of solid rock, the tunnel enabled water to be carried to the Wainuiomata reservoir, and thence through a 21-inch steel main to Karori reservoir. The tunnel helped secure a water supply to meet the city's future needs, and prepared the ground for a regional supply. Completed in 1926 at a cost of £500,000, the 'Rongo Rongo' scheme was the largest of its kind in Australasia, breaking world speed records along the way. At its helm was Robert Semple, coalminer, trade union organiser, wit and firebrand, who is remembered for leading 'Red Fed' (Federation of Labour) support for striking 'trammies' in 1912. After the tunnel was completed, Semple embarked on a ten-year career as a city councillor, becoming an MP and, eventually, a Cabinet Minister.

Shaping the city to fit municipal ambitions had its problems. The blasting and digging for Semple's great tunnel had occurred in the remote valleys of the Orongorongos, far from public eyes and ears. It was harder to conceal the impact of major works in the central city. Sydney Street residents such as Miss Glyde demanded compensation when work on the Western Access Scheme began. Her letter of complaint reads like a dispatch from a war zone:

> some 400 shots gelignite fired (exact record kept on calendar) jumping house off foundations, under continual bombardment, knocking off jars and photographs, showers of stones and earth on roof, bits of brick tumbling down chimneys, electric lights blown out several times, not only fused but even stops blown out. No notification given of impending blasts, everyone got nervous breakdowns … glaring headlights turned on house during night and loud crackling noises rounding bend, disturb continually during sleep, thinking place on fire.[40]

A blessing in disguise?

Although the capital prospered for much of the 1920s, unemployment lingered. In 1921, the economy contracted in the worst downturn since the early 1890s.

Destitute men, women, and children queued for soup ingredients at the Town Hall, as casual wharf and labouring work dried up. In an era before the unemployment benefit, the unskilled and their families were at the mercy of local charity agencies. In June 1922, chocolate-makers Cadbury & Fry presented half a ton of cocoa for distribution 'to the poor of the city'.[41] Cr Annie McVicar joined the Society for the Protection of Women and Children in the relief effort. In August 1922, a delegation of unemployed men asked the Council to set up work schemes.[42]

The response was a return to the outdoor relief schemes of the late nineteenth century. Municipal activities to alleviate local unemployment can be grouped into three distinct phases. The first spanned the brief economic slump of 1921. The government responded by passing a law allowing councils to borrow for unemployment schemes without the need to poll ratepayers. Conservative politicians of the time viewed unemployment as the responsibility of local authorities or employers, not of government. In Wellington, 300 jobless men were assigned to plant trees for 10s a day, while unemployed returned soldiers levelled sand-dunes in Lyall Bay. A £12,000 loan covered the cost of jobless men excavating the hills of Khandallah for new housing estates. Roads on Mt Victoria and at Lyall Bay were improved. Loans were sought to extend Anderson Park, form new inner-city recreational grounds such as Prince of Wales Park, and clear gorse on Town Belt land.

The second phase was overseen by Mayor Troup. Although the Great Depression is usually dated from the Wall Street Crash of 1929, unemployment in Wellington began to rise in 1926, as export revenues began a slide that would reduce their value by 40 percent. The municipality moved to take advantage of more generous state assistance, in the form of a £1 for £1 subsidy on wages. Troup's humble Scottish origins helped to ensure that the city's unemployed were treated fairly and humanely. Although elected on the right-leaning Civic League ticket, Troup had a socialist heart. At the 1928 Municipal Conference, he proposed a system of unemployment insurance — an issue dear to Peter Fraser and the Labour Party. The 'unemployment' loans continued, with tens of thousands of pounds borrowed for civic works, including street construction in Island Bay and Melrose. Municipal overseers divided 600 relief workers into 'A' and 'B' teams, the former building Grafton Road, the latter levelling sand-dunes in Lyall Bay. Further loans helped to fund the construction of Nairnville and Western parks, the road around Point Halswell, the widening of Glenmore Street and Tinakori Road, and Magpie Lawn in the Botanic Garden. The City Engineer felt the 'tremendous strain' of supervising so

Tunneller, unionist and later Labour Cabinet Minister Bob Semple, with his wife Margaret. Both served terms as city councillors.

ATL, Evening Post Collection, C-21189-1/2

many workers: 'during last winter the staff had to cope with extra work in connection with relief works of an extent never before experienced by the City Council'.[43]

This was just the beginning. Additional loans paid the workers enough 'to enable them to maintain themselves and their families in a reasonable condition of comfort'.[44] In all, Troup borrowed nearly £210,000 (more than $16 million in today's terms) without having to consult ratepayers. Karori's lengthy Campbell and Donald Streets, and adjacent roads, were widened. Large sections of Brooklyn Hill were excavated and roads built. More than 77,000 trees were planted on the city side of Mt Victoria. A £21,000 loan raised in 1929 funded a network of roads between Brooklyn and Aro Valley. Relief gangs joined up Hataitai and Roseneath, and carved out the Pass of Branda. Another £30,000 loan funded the building of the Winter Show Grounds, including a racetrack over the 'Jam Tin Gully' rubbish tip. In 1930, the state doubled its wage subsidy, allowing Troup to pay his unemployed army 14s a day.[45] The Mt Victoria road tunnel was dug, a scenic drive to the summit was built, and Hataitai Park and Pirie Street Reserve were constructed.

Hangar offences

In the 1920s, aviation was the essence of glamour. Crowds turned out when daredevil pilot and flying instructor George Bolt landed his flying-boat on Wellington Harbour late in 1921. The first flight from Auckland to Wellington took five hours and six minutes.

After the municipal aerodrome opened in 1929, Bolt became a regular user. So did two of his pupils, Geoffrey Goodwin and Francis Chichester, who established the Goodwin–Chichester Aviation Company to provide charter flights and pleasure rides.

Chichester later became world-famous for his yachting achievements, but in the late 1920s he was in trouble with the City Council for failing to

Mayor Thomas Hislop welcomes Jean Batten to the city in 1934.

WCA, 00155:0:123

pay rent on aircraft housed in the municipal hangar.[46]

The most famous aviator of the 1930s, Jean Batten, known as the 'Garbo of the Skies', also ended up in debt to the Council. Her plane was housed at the aerodrome during her triumphant visit to the capital in 1934, after her record-breaking flight from Britain to Darwin. She came as a guest of the government, and stayed with the Governor-General, Viscount Bledisloe.

In 1936, councillors wrote off the 5s 10d she owed in hangar fees, noting that she was 'not now in New Zealand'.[47] Batten would soon undertake her greatest journey of all — the first-ever direct flight from England to New Zealand.[48] A street near Wellington airport is named after her.

One of Troup's greatest achievements was a municipal aerodrome. A budding aviator himself, Troup was keen for Wellington to join this new era of transport. In November 1929, a promotional pageant was held at Rongotai Aerodrome to mark the official opening. Troup himself donned a flying helmet and went up in a Gypsy Moth biplane as pilot. From there, the Mayor could survey the 46 acre airfield and runway, all built by the city's unemployed. Its construction had spanned much of the decade, with vast expanses of Lyall Bay sand-dunes flattened, covered with six inches of weathered rock and soil, and sown with grass.

When Troup stepped down from the mayoralty in 1931, for health reasons, his departure marked the end of the most successful phase of municipal assistance for the unemployed. Between 1926 and 1931 the Mayor's pick-and-shovel army had transformed the capital.[49] It could be said that Wellington was built by the sweat of its unemployed. No wonder Cr Semple departed from the party line in 1932, when he privately suggested that unemployment was 'a blessing in disguise':

> We have been able to take advantage of the Government's assistance and carry out works which otherwise would not have been touched for many years to come. Through that channel we have been able to do a lot of work which will be of value to the City in years to come.[50]

'Frenzied finances'

As worsening economic conditions plunged the country into the Great Depression, ratepayers' associations protested against 'extravagant' Council borrowing and spending. Thomas Charles Hislop — war hero, aviator, and son of a previous mayor — took over the mayoralty. A member of the ultra-conservative New Zealand Legion, Hislop would later lead a right-wing political movement opposing the Coalition government of George Forbes. Hislop's first year as Mayor proved eventful. On the morning of 3 February 1931, the country experienced its greatest natural disaster on record when a powerful earthquake hit the Hawke's Bay region, leaving 256 people dead. Wellington councillors expressed their 'sincere sympathy', dispatched a petrol-powered shovel and driver to Napier for a month, and ordered a report on the safety of the Town Hall's clock-tower.[51] Rosa Coory, a pupil at St Anne's School in Newtown, recalled the quake: 'We felt it quite strongly, as we were upstairs in a rather shaky wooden building, and I remember Sister telling us to get under our desks.'[52]

In June 1931, councillors resolved that the wages and salaries of Corporation staff earning more than £5 a week should be reduced.[53] Then in October came revelations of the worst financial scandal since William Bannister made off with the rates money in 1865. A. W. Richardson, a temporary clerk in the Rate Collector's Office, was accused of pocketing more than £96. His fellow rates officers were said to have known of earlier thefts in the office.[54] The timing of the 'defalcations' was unfortunate, as ratepayers were having to watch every penny. Rating levies had risen by £85,000 between 1928 and 1930, and Troup's unchecked borrowing for unemployment relief still rankled in some quarters. Richardson was sacked, and the colleagues who had looked the other way had their salaries cut.

Hislop announced a commission, led by Australian engineer H. E. Morton and local accountant H.D. Vickery, 'to enquire into and report upon' all aspects of municipal administration and operations. The *Evening Post* talked of a 'civic overhaul'.[55] In January 1932, hearings began behind closed doors in the Town Hall, as commissioners interviewed dozens of officials, councillors, ratepayers' groups and members of the public. Confidential background papers indicate the effort that went into collating and presenting the municipality's financial position — including the total number of staff, which had never appeared in Council minutes. Documents show that, at the end of 1931, there were 2,342 people on the payroll, including 717 in the City Engineer's department. It emerged that 32 departmental employees were aged over 65, including an 86-year-old 'diligent worker' employed in one of the yards.[56] The Wellington Ratepayers' Association was outraged. Cr Semple agreed, in typically colourful language, that the department was over-staffed, using too many 'pannikin bosses' to supervise labour gangs: 'I have many times seen these men on cold mornings done up as though they were going to visit the North Pole, watching two or three men work.'[57]

Council workers pouring tar on newly laid tram lines in Customhouse Quay, 1930.

WCA, 00146:0:065

Commissioners heard rates collector Mr Goodber outline an archaic and unwieldy system of cheque and cash collection, multiple rate books, and handwritten accounts. Lax practices by the wages clerk contributed to the likelihood of theft. Tramways losses came under close scrutiny. The municipality's £1.3 million investment in tramways (more than $100 million in today's terms) made it a sensitive issue. Officials reported that revenues were falling by more than £20,000 a year, and that half of the 159 trams were used only during the weekday rush hours. Ratepayers called for 'trackless trams' or buses, with one group describing the tramways finances as a 'hovering danger'.[58]

Town planning was revealed to be in a chaotic state. During Troup's term, the Mayor and his officials had stopped talking to each other.[59] Zoning was yet to be introduced, and plans for street-widening and transport improvements had been neglected. The Director of Town Planning said that internal problems were affecting relationships between the Council and government: 'One of the difficulties here is that all are not pulling together … we find difficulty co-operating even with the Government.'[60]

The inquiry became a referendum on the Troup era, and what ratepayers' groups described as its 'frenzied finances'. As economic conditions deteriorated in 1931 and New Zealand banks raised the exchange rate, Hislop warned that the financial outlook for 1932 was 'extremely obscure':

> We do not know what this exchange business is going to do with us, nor quite what money we are going to have available this coming year. We had £220,000 this last year but we are £50,000 back in the rates now and I suppose we will end the year with about £40,000 behind in rates and we will have to budget accordingly.[61]

Figures provided by ratepayers showed that one property owner had rate increases totalling 141 percent over four years, while others had increases averaging 60 percent.[62] The Ratepayers' Association condemned Troup for exploiting his ability to raise loans by 'the mere passing of a resolution by the Council and no questions asked by Councillors'.[63]

> One thing is certain: No more loans must be raised unless first sanctioned by ratepayers. It is nothing short of a scandal … a municipality is the servant of its citizens. Anything it can do to increase the prosperity of the city it should do. To burden citizens is, so to speak, to kill the goose that lays the golden egg.[64]

The great civic shake-up turned out to be a minor tremor. Most of the 2,300-odd staff kept their jobs. Hundreds of pages of frank testimony were shelved. Minor recommendations in the commission's 154-page report were acted on. The Rate Collector's Office was merged with that of the City Treasurer. Rates demands were now typed. The City Engineer's Department was tweaked, with the number of district engineers cut from four to two.[65] But the 'civic overhaul' never came. The *Evening Post* was philosophical:

> Altogether it is difficult to see what the council has achieved by its Commission investigations ... some think that a differently constituted Commission would have done better. But at least they cannot propose another such inquiry for some years.[66]

The big slide

At the time that Cr Semple commented on the 'blessing' of unemployment, 100 men a week were signing on for relief work in the capital.[67] The national total of men without work had been rising for five years, ballooning to more than 50,000 over the summer of 1932.[68] Faced with falling export prices, the Forbes government abandoned public works and major railway schemes. Local authorities were left to mop up. The third and most gruelling phase of the municipality's efforts on behalf of the city's unemployed was about to unfold.

The government was in serious trouble. As in the 1918 influenza epidemic, the Mayor of Wellington was forced to pick up the relief effort. In the 1920s, George Troup had been unable to resist borrowing to fund an army of unemployed workers, especially when generous state subsidies were on offer. But the cash-strapped government now funded only the wages of relief workers, leaving local bodies to carry the high additional costs of supervision, materials, insurance and transport. In Wellington, the same free public transport available to men on relief was extended to unemployed women. An Unemployment Board co-ordinated the national relief effort. Hislop agreed to its request to set up a voluntary local committee to run relief works in Wellington. Such committees worked alongside Labour Department bureaux, where the jobless signed on before becoming eligible for relief. The local unemployment bureau was located in the army barracks on the corner of Buckle and Taranaki Streets.

Gordon Coates was Minister of Public Works in a Cabinet opposed to state welfare, one that believed in 'no dole without work'.[69] A range of programmes,

During the Depression the Wellington City Council employed thousands of men on relief schemes around the city. Here, relief workers clear and flatten sand dunes at Lyall Bay.

WCA, 00157:1:37

including the basic relief scheme (No. 5), was therefore established to provide work for the unemployed in urban centres. Under the scheme, local bodies employed men on a rationed basis according to family status. Scheme 5 became the backbone of relief in Wellington. It allowed two days' work per week for single men, three for married men with one dependent child, and four for married men with two or more children. There was a controversial requirement for men to 'stand down' one week in every four. During that time, they and their families depended on hospital boards and other charities for basic rations. In the height of the Depression years, Wellington Hospital Board was said to be spending £1,250 a week on charitable aid.[70]

Scheme 5 was immediately over-subscribed, as 36,000 of the 50,000 registered unemployed signed on.[71] During 1931 alone, 1,600 of Wellington's unemployed joined the scheme. The daily wage paid by the state fell from 14s to 9s, then became 10s for married men and 7s 6d for singles.[72] Hislop decided 'to fall in line with the Government' and pay an additional 1,000 men the lower rate.[73] The sheer weight of numbers forced the Unemployment Board to stop making payments, causing the available work to be further rationed. The municipality agreed to let part of its new £150,000 milk depot in Tory Street be used as a distribution point for donated foodstuffs. Meanwhile, the financial and administrative burden of organising 1,600 relief workers was being felt:

> approximately 17 percent of the cost of these works is being borne by the Council by way of wages for foremen and gangers as well as supervision by the Engineering Staff ... practically 50 percent of the time of the District Engineers and Overseers is spent on these works.[74]

Rationing out the work was a complicated process:

> The men are paid at the Corporation yard after finishing the work … [A]bout 1000 relief workers are paid each day … [R]elief workers work Monday, Tuesday, Wednesdays for married men. Thursdays and Fridays for single men and the foreman cannot leave the job to come in to identify the relief workers before signing. Work is paid for by the hour.[75]

Unemployed men line up at a Wellington soup kitchen during the early 1930s.

ATL, Evening Post Collection, G-8646-1/2-EP

As the administration costs soared, councillors voted to raid the brimming coffers of the Municipal Electricity Department (MED). During 1931, at least £20,000 was taken from electricity profits, pointedly not from falling rates revenues.[76] The MED was soon known to councillors as the 'Jersey milking cow', and visits became regular.[77] Following developments in the civil service, the municipality cut staff salaries by 10 percent.

By 1932, more than 4,000 men were signing on every day at Buckle Street, where municipal clerks were protected by wire-netting. More than 650 of those who lined up on 8 January were not placed in work.[78] Jobs were said to be 'left in the air' as the weight of numbers overwhelmed administrators. Fights broke out as work was rationed and the number of paid hours curtailed. Relief worker P. J. Flanagan was assaulted and severely injured by a fellow worker.[79] Men at Rongotai were stood down 'on account of unsatisfactory conduct'. Political groups on the left mobilised, ranging in affiliation from the Labour Party to the rival Communists. Street meetings had been outlawed since 1929. Permission was granted, however, for a dozen relief workers to cultivate turnips, carrots and parsnips on a 2½-acre plot in the Town Belt, near Newtown. Unemployed women, too, were stirred to action. Labour activist Elsie Locke recalled the actions of one women's committee: 'I remember on one occasion we walked to the Council Chambers behind a red flag which we'd made ourselves, and we draped it over the Mayor's chair before the Mayor came in. We had to remove it when he came.'[80]

In May 1932, police scattered a crowd of 2,000 striking relief workers in the Cuba Street area. Many strikers were batoned, and one witness described the entrance of the Trades Hall in Vivian Street as looking like a battlefield dressing station.

ATL, NZ Free Lance Collection, G-101110-1/2.

By mid 1932, work had dried up for single unemployed men. Dunedin's jobless took to the streets at the start of the year, and serious disturbances and looting later occurred in Auckland. Scheme 5 was collapsing under the weight of numbers, and the pressure was showing. Petone Borough Council stopped employing 500 men under the scheme, forcing the Mayor of Lower Hutt to step in to avoid a crisis.[81] Coates prepared to send up to 1,000 single men to what were called 'concentration camps' in nearby farming districts, each camp comprising about 100 men.[82] Those refusing to go would be ineligible for relief. A group of 700 men in Wellington met and decided to refuse camp work.[83] On 10 May, the city's entire relief workforce went on strike. Their march on Parliament ended in arrests and hundreds of smashed windows in the inner city. The following day in Cuba Street, police charged a gathering of 2,000 strikers, injuring many of them. Labour activist Margaret Thorn described the scene:

Men and women, particularly heavy, slow-moving women, were terribly knocked about. The vestibule of the Trades Hall was like a battlefield dressing station when I arrived. There were three women in their late 50s on the floor. Fred Cornwell was holding one. Her legs and buttocks were showing through her torn dress and were a purple, swollen mashed mess. Men were standing around bleeding from the mouth and head.[84]

Mayor Hislop instructed Council staff to join a temporary force of 500 special constables, making premises in Victoria Street available to house them:

Members of the Corporation should be called upon for service in protecting Corporation and City property … [and] to enrol as special constables … authority to be granted for payment of tea money to members of the staff engaged on these special duties when occasion demanded.[85]

Some staff resented the Mayor's edict, with its echoes of the 1913 strike:

They recruited special constables and they were of two sorts. Those who went in voluntarily … [and] then there were some of the business people, and above all the City Council [who] put the young men on the mat and told them their jobs were on the line and either they recruited as special constabulary or their jobs were gone … [I]t was a very bad show and of course that increased radicalism.[86]

Facing a 10 percent drop in rates revenue, councillors looked desperately for possible economies. Cr Semple unsuccessfully campaigned to close the municipal zoo. The city organist was sacked. The Council grumbled about people seeking free cemetery plots at Karori, and called for tighter procedures.[87] Coates then abolished the stand-down period in Scheme 5, and called on mayors to expand the scheme. As the city's unemployed rose above 4,000, greater numbers of men were sent to the same job. This helped to entrench a view (which lingers to this day) that many of the public works carried out during this era were pointless.

The more people that could be put to work the better. So the fewer tools they had, the better. You might have a job say in Anderson Park where you might have one shovel for three men, or one grubber to two men and these people would scratch around in this clay and load it into a wagon and instead of

having a horse … the men would push it and tip it into the gully because you
could use more men in that way.[88]

Nonetheless, miles of grass verges, several parks and play areas, and an extended
airport all emerged from local relief efforts. But the cost of administering Scheme
5 was bankrupting the municipality. In September 1932, Hislop threatened to
pull out altogether, arguing that with 4,033 men employed, Wellington carried a
disproportionate burden. He contrasted the capital's position with the numbers
employed in Auckland (1,664), Christchurch (1,087) and Dunedin (1,842).
Calling the financial situation 'exceedingly grave', he argued that the government
should increase its contribution.[89] He estimated the cost of supervising 4,000 men
to be £23,000 a year.[90] The government agreed to pay up to £10,000 to cover the
supervision costs of 2,000 men, and to fund all the insurance costs associated with
Scheme 5, with the Council covering the remainder. Councillors took a further
£10,000 from the MED coffers, but the crisis continued. Hislop again made ready
to pull out of the scheme, 'in view of the present financial position of the city'.[91] A
despairing government agreed to shoulder a greater share of the burden.[92]

In an era before serious news photography, and with television cameras a
generation away, it was all too easy to banish the human story of the unemployed
to a handful of paragraphs in the newspapers. Even during the darkest days of
the Depression, the *Dominion* and *Evening Post* kept their focus on the continuing
parade of social and community events. While thousands of jobless men and
their families suffered greatly, life for the majority of citizens who kept their jobs
continued much as normal. Wages dropped, but so did prices, allowing many
residents of the leafier suburbs to buy more of the fashion garments that dominated
the display advertisements. Despite the Depression, new electricity connections in
Wellington grew from 29,200 in 1932 to 36,151 in 1934. At the height of Hislop's
negotiations with the Unemployment Board, the city's socialites kicked up their
heels at a lavish and overcrowded 'Cinderella Ball' at the Town Hall. Cherubs in
paper costumes frolicked amid the elaborate scenery. Trestle tables were laden
with refreshments, including 'a large ice cream chest'.[93]

Unemployment peaked midway through 1933, with 57,352 men nationally
registered as out of work. The true figure was said to be closer to 80,000.[94]
Auckland, with more than 11,000 unemployed in 1933, had the highest number
of the four main centres. Even in that peak year, however, its City Council engaged
only 1,705 men on Scheme 5.[95] The high number of unemployed in the capital is
partly explained by a shortage of work in surrounding districts. Local employers

also used Scheme 5 as a convenient way to lay off surplus workers. We can only speculate as to whether the Wellington City Council's readiness to expand Scheme 5 also stemmed from a desire to complete the great Troup enterprise.

Hislop put on a brave face for the National Confidence Carnival at the end of 1933, which featured a night bombing display at Rongotai airport. But many were cynical about what became known as 'cheer up' week:

> Oh, it was a *sad* affair. The fire brigade went around to Oriental Bay at night and played their hoses on the water, and the Electricity Department shone coloured search-lights on the water. Then they had dancing in Oriental Parade. They used to have community singing in the Town Hall at lunchtime too. The idea was if you could get people to forget their troubles and regain their confidence, then the Depression would just disappear. I don't think it worked.[96]

During 1934, the number of local workers on Scheme 5 fell to 2,516,[97] sixteen of whom headed families with more than seven children. As the number of jobless dropped, the government agreed to pay a prototype dole, known as 'sustenance'. By 1935, most of the men on relief had opted for the dole. Scheme 5 was on its way out. Hislop asked the government to increase the dole 'by at least ten shillings weekly', and the Council began employing men at standard rates.[98] A group of 300 of the best relief workers were taken on for six months. Some of them transferred to the Reserves Department to build a sports ground on Brooklyn's Ridgeway. For many New Zealanders, the Labour Party landslide at the end of the year symbolised the end of the Depression years. The unemployed received a Christmas bonus and a week's holiday.

It's a lovely day tomorrow

Labour's stunning election victory on 27 November 1935 heralded a new era, one that would see the birth of the welfare state. An expectant crowd of 3,000 gathered at Wellington Railway Station on 2 December to greet a triumphant Michael Joseph Savage, who arrived to the sound of locomotive whistles and loud cheers.

Yet financial hardship lingered. In July 1936, a junior Corporation solicitor and future politician named Jack Marshall evaluated 110 applications for remission from a 10 percent penalty for late payment of rates. That year, money owed to Council by prominent debtors had to be written off. Bob Semple, by then a Cabinet Minister, had a debt of 9s for a load of sand.[99] Another prominent former councillor, Annie McVicar, owed £18 5s 10d for unpaid water accounts on her home in Miramar. The Solicitor's Office complained that 'all efforts to obtain payment had been unsuccessful'.[100]

Labour moved to implement such policies as a five-day, 40-hour week. The cost to the municipality was put at £80,500, more than half of which went on extra payments for Sunday and holiday shifts in the Tramways Department.[101] Early in 1936, compulsory unionism was introduced. Young Jack Marshall was kept busy helping to form the Wellington Local Body Officers' Union, of which he became a reluctant foundation member. In 1937, as Labour began constructing state houses in Miramar, the Council agreed to waive the fees for building permits.[102]

In April 1936, Peter Fraser resigned from the Council, as his government set about repairing the battered economy. He was typical of a breed of Labour MPs who reinforced their standing as politicians by showing their mettle at local government level. Labour was passing laws it had waited a generation to implement, showing a steely resolve that local authorities would come to fear. During their time on Council, Fraser and Semple saw for themselves the profound impact that local government activities had on national affairs. This, and continuing shortcomings in the performance of councils, may explain their readiness to take many local body powers with them as they moved into central government. With Labour occupying the Treasury benches, local authorities would get used to centralisation.

As the misery of the Great Depression lifted, the jobs and the confidence trickled back. One sign of a rise in disposable income was the appearance in 1936

The Tip Top milk bar, on the corner of Cuba and Manners Streets, in the mid 1930s.

ATL, Gordon Burt Collection, F-15556-1/1

of Wellington's first milk bar. Located at 64 Willis Street, the Black and White led the way for a host of imitators, including the Milky Way and the Tip Top. The Corporation's stranglehold on the city's milk supply later saw it taking legal action against the owners of the Sunshine Milk Bar in Manners Street. The Sunshine was later found guilty of selling milk without a licence.[103]

From the mid 1930s, another European war looked increasingly likely. In March 1938, less than a decade after the gala opening of Wellington Aerodrome, people living nearby lodged their first complaints about early-morning disturbances from commercial and especially military aircraft. The defence forces readied themselves for possible armed conflict, the Council agreeing to grant leave of absence on full pay to staff attending military camp. As the nation prepared to celebrate its first century, attention in the capital turned to the Centennial Exhibition it was to host. The outbreak of the Second World War would cast a shadow over festivities.

Centennial to Crusade

Chapter 6

1939–1960

Captain Smith, our first town planner, working by candle in a Maori hut, had given birth
to a problem child that had grown more burdensome with the years.

Robert Macalister, Deputy Mayor of Wellington, 1948[1]

It was a moment of reflection that became a solemn wartime ritual. After New
Zealand, following Britain, declared war on Germany on 3 September 1939,
the same scene was played out on evenings when councillors met in the Council
Chamber. At nine o'clock, a large valve radio was switched on for the nightly bulletin
of news from the BBC, crackling through on Station 2YA. As the pre-recorded
chimes of Big Ben rang out, those present bowed their heads. Sombre organ music
sustained the mood. Like many of their fellow countrymen, councillors used the
so-called Minute of Silent Prayer to reflect on the events unfolding in Europe —
and later in the Pacific — and the sacrifices of local servicemen and women. Mayor
Hislop said his thoughts during the 'God Minute' were for those who had died.
The practice continued for more than a year after the war ended.[2]

Wellington had a big stake in the timetable for war. Many in the capital appealed
to a higher authority as war with Nazi Germany threatened the centennial fair, due
to open in November 1939. It was a decade since Mayor Troup first suggested
that Wellington host a national exhibition to celebrate the nation's centenary,
with Hislop gaining government approval for the idea in 1936. Planning began

William Trethewey's statue of Kupe dominated the Maori Court at the Centennial Exhibition.

WCA, 00119:0:23

immediately. For the city fathers, it was also an opportunity to make lasting improvements to the capital. Te Aro Flat was an early favourite for the exhibition site, where modern buildings could replace slums. The £750,000 cost of clearing a residential area and re-housing affected families, however, ruled out the idea.[3] In June 1937, the Council's giant grader began levelling 55 acres of wind-swept sand-dunes in Lyall Bay, bounded by a dirt-track speedway, a rubbish tip, a dozen sports fields, and Rongotai aerodrome.

Over 29 frantic months Wellington was made ready, in a process that helped free the city from a century of geographical isolation, even confinement. The Main Highways Board rebuilt the Ngauranga Gorge road as a four-lane highway, with the municipality adding an overhead ramp to give access from the Hutt Road to Aotea Quay. The inner city was tidied up. Walls were erected around the Council's destructor on Chaffers Street; for the first time in 30 years, the 24-hour furnaces were extinguished, and the men allocated new jobs. The destructor's proximity to the 'Exhibition routes' sealed its fate. The roads around Oriental and Evans Bays were widened and illuminated. A new route, Alexandra Road, linked the eastern portion of Mt Victoria to Wellington Road, via the Town Belt. Lyall Bay Parade was improved to cater for cars, which were expected in their thousands. Tramlines were extended so that passengers could alight by the exhibition gates. Corporation staff created a Centennial Park and municipal motor camp at the north end of Miramar's Darlington Road.

For the Labour government, the exhibition was an affirmation of national unity and pride. The accent was on 'progress' — in agriculture, industry, democracy, racial harmony and culture. As November approached, a glimpse of a bold new future sprang from wasteland on the Rongotai site. With a 170-foot Art Deco tower at their heart, the cluster of fine-boned modernist buildings would look, as one newspaper noted, like a movie set.[4] The decision to enclose the sprawling buildings under one roof was a cunning move to avoid the winds that blew mercilessly that summer. Around the great tower stood sculptures of 'dauntless' pioneering men and women, picked out by night in blue lights. Three main exhibit courts lay among three acres of buildings, reflecting pools and fountains. William Trethewey's statue of Kupe, with its romantic view of his discovery of New Zealand, dominated the Maori Court, with handicraft stalls and daily concerts by the Ngati Poneke Young Maori Association. Like many of the exhibits, the carved whare runanga or meeting house was finally assembled just as the gates opened.[5] The massive Government Court featured displays from 26 government departments. A battery of 37,000 electric and neon lights, burning up more than a million watts of electricity, were ready to be switched on after dark. The aim was to 'give the buildings an appearance of glass palaces and stain the smooth waters of the lagoons with exotic hues'.[6]

For three years, the exhibition had dominated the life of the municipality, as thousands of pounds were spent preparing the city for an influx of four million visitors. Having invested nearly £24,800 ($2 million in today's terms) in the New Zealand Centennial Exhibition Company Ltd, the municipality was also its biggest single shareholder. As chairman of its board of directors, Hislop presided over seventeen committees responsible for such areas as accommodation, transport and publicity. As months went by, construction costs kept rising. When low-flying aircraft from the aerodrome were identified as a potential risk, civil aviation officials ordered the exhibition architect, Edmund Anscombe, to restrict the height of his buildings. The City Council was to be held responsible for any accidents.[7]

Early in September 1939, as Germany invaded Poland, the Cabinet decided to press ahead with the exhibition. As the opening date approached, and demand for floor space dried up, Finance Minister Walter Nash guaranteed the exhibition company's overdraft. And so on a sunny Wednesday, 8 November 1939, some 20,000 guests watched the Governor General, Lord Galway, open the Centennial Exhibition. A relieved Hislop spoke of his 'profound happiness' that the event was under way. He entreated the audience to recall the pioneers of 1840, all but comparing their travails in voyaging to the new colony with those of getting Wellington's fair off the ground.

The Ngati Poneke Young Maori Association performed daily concerts at the exhibition. The shows were popular with the throngs of local fair-goers, many of whom had never been exposed to Maori culture.

ATL, Eileen Deste Collection, F-36226-1/2

> Almost every conceivable difficulty has had to be faced, but those difficulties have been faced in a spirit of confidence and I believe with courage; and I confidently believe that when these doors open, the people of New Zealand will agree that the difficulties have been overcome …[8]

But frivolity, rather than paeans to the pioneers, would be the drawcard for most visitors. Rongotai College surrendered its sports fields to Playland, an amusement park that sprawled over ten acres. On offer was a host of rides and attractions, many direct from the recent Glasgow Empire Exhibition. The 3,000-foot-long Cyclone roller-coaster, with its three-car trains and 2,000 lights, was the star turn. Also popular were the Crazy House, Speedway, Ghost Train, Octopus and dodgems. 'Kiwi trains' ferried fare-paying passengers around the grounds. Presiding over the action was the Laughing Sailor, a mechanical barker (showground tout) whose robotic chortles rang out for up to thirteen hours a day. Despite the sailor's jollity, visitor numbers never approached the promised four million. The final gate of two and a half million exceeded the total New Zealand population, but it still wasn't enough. On 14 February 1940, the municipality discontinued the bus service from Roseneath, 'owing to the lack of patronage'.[9] Public hall licences were extended without cost to businesses that had hoped to do better with their exhibits. On 26 February, the government took over the assets and liabilities of the exhibition company, paying out £70,000 to cover an overdraft. A deficit of £36,000 was recorded, leaving shareholders with nothing.[10] In June, the government took over the exhibition buildings for air force barracks, with the 'temples of progress' gradually being dismantled for a new airport:

> When the wind blows at Rongotai, more than 200,000 square feet of building rocks. The once grand and glittering construction that housed the Centennial Exhibition is creaking and groaning to its end, twisted in arthritic warps and shivering like a stage orphan in a storm.[11]

The statuary and other props were dismantled, and sold by auction at Kilbirnie's Centennial Guest House. Kupe ended up in a prominent corner of Wellington Railway Station. Decades passed before he was rescued, in a damaged state, cast in bronze, and given a permanent home on the waterfront. The municipality paid £1,000 for the centennial fountain; its mechanism eventually ended up in Kelburn Park, where it still powers the fountain. The Laughing Sailor was sold for £60 and dispatched to Hastings.[12]

Hunkering down

War was always going to take the shine off Wellington's party. Six days after the state fair opened, the military authorities sealed off Alexandra Road, near the top of Mt Victoria.[13] The aim was to keep prying eyes away from the mobile anti-aircraft guns that bristled south of the summit. For the rest of the war, only the occasional Council tour bus got through. A searchlight and sound detection equipment were

In anticipation of four million visitors to the 1940 Centennial Exhibition, the Council made frantic efforts to spruce up the city, including the construction of an overhead ramp on Aotea Quay to give access from the Hutt Road. The government's Main Highways Board meanwhile rebuilt the Ngauranga Gorge road as a four-lane highway.

ATL, S. C. Smith Collection, G-45295-1/2

placed near the 2YA transmitter, with operators spending the summer in tents. Barracks were then built for up to 176 personnel, as the area was designated a Prohibited Place under the Defence Emergency Regulations. In 1940, sentries fired on burglars fleeing the camp.[14] Rumours grew of a Nazi 'Fifth Column' in the city, made up of aliens, immigrants, and other sympathisers. Hislop told his fellow councillors in February that 'recent explosions on tram lines' had been referred to police.[15] Councillors discussed precautions against enemy spies lighting fires and sabotaging water and electricity supplies.[16] Cr L.W. McKenzie was told that police had been handed lists 'of all those persons in the Corporation service who might conceivably be regarded as coming under suspicion'.[17] In the aftermath of a police swoop on the Island Bay fishing community, a list of Council staff with Italian names was prepared.[18] Not even English composer and actor Noel Coward, on a visit as a roving ambassador, was safe. At a civic reception in 1940, his gently ironic parody of the British upper classes was challenged by the Mayoress:

> She said to me in ringing tones that I was never to dare to sing 'The Stately Homes of England' again as it was an insult to the homeland and that neither she nor anybody else liked it. I replied coldly that for many years it had been one of my greatest successes, whereupon she announced triumphantly

to everyone in earshot: 'You see — he can't take criticism'. Irritated beyond endurance I replied that I was perfectly prepared to take intelligent criticism at any time, but I was not prepared to tolerate bad manners. With this I bowed austerely and left the party.[19]

Not all citizens shared Mrs Hislop's sentiments. Birthplace of the New Zealand Christian Pacifist Society (CPS) in 1936, Wellington had a strong pacifist tradition. From 1939, CPS members and other dissenters were a regular presence in New Zealand towns and cities, despite emergency regulations making the practice illegal. On the day war was declared, CPS founder Ormond Burton, a veteran of the First World War and a Methodist clergyman, preached an anti-war message outside Parliament Buildings.[20] The fact that five members of the Cabinet, now preoccupied with raising an army, had been gaoled for opposing conscription in the First World War made the issue particularly sensitive. Hislop became an unlikely government ally. His contempt for 'shirkers and emissaries of Russia' was well known. In February 1940, the Mayor forced a showdown with the 'conchies' (conscientious objectors) when he joined a crowd of several thousand in Pigeon (now Te Aro) Park, where the CPS was due to hold a protest gathering. Three days earlier, Hislop had issued a challenge at a recruiting meeting:

> I believe these people talk of holding a meeting on a piece of Corporation land by the Royal Oak Hotel on Friday. I am going to do my best to see that the meeting is not held. I don't mind what they do in other parts of New Zealand, but if they want a fight in Wellington they can have it.[21]

Expectations rose as Friday night approached. Ormond Burton feared he would be torn apart. It was a volatile mix: placard-carrying dissenters and communists thrown together with returned and current servicemen, some of them singing patriotic songs. As Burton mounted a soapbox, he was rushed by police, and he and another man were arrested. Mayor Hislop made a grand entrance from Dixon Street, flanked by police and his escort from the Wellington Regiment. As he moved to address the crowd, a few raised their hands in mock Nazi salutes, chanting 'Heil Hislop'.[22] Several people fainted in the crush. Ormond and his co-offender were sentenced to a month's hard labour.

The Mayor's views affected the way the municipality treated its staff. Conscientious objectors who refused to perform community service

Mayor Tom Hislop was seen as a remote, even erratic figure, and his right-wing views regularly brought him into conflict with the wartime Labour government.

Alan Reeve, *Lions and Lambs of Wellington* (1932)

THE OUTSIDER

HIS WORSHIP THE MAYOR — MR. T. C. A. HISLOP

as an alternative were marginalised. J. H. Prentice, a member of the Electricity and Tramways staff, was dismissed during 1941. He was then gaoled for a month for 'failing to report for military service'. The experience of W. S. Parker showed that many Council workers shared Hislop's views. His fellow employees in the Milk Department told the Dairy Superintendent that 'they will refuse to work if Parker is retained in the dairy'.[23]

For Hislop and other conservatives on the Council, the Labour Party's traditional union base was giving it too much political power. Over 30 years, Labour had consolidated its presence on Wellington's local bodies, with six members elected to the City Council in 1938, including Margaret Semple, wife of the Cabinet Minister. A Labour caucus met regularly. The *Evening Post* and *Dominion* routinely accused Labour councillors of engaging in party politics and mouthing propaganda. The fact that the rival and dominant Citizens ticket was the National Party in all but name was overlooked. During 1941 Hislop and his right-wing deputy, Ernest Toop, sniped at the 'socialists' as they struggled to impose economic and security controls. During the local body elections of 1941, Labour councillors' links to the unions became a key issue in a scandal involving a Citizens candidate for the Harbour Board.

It was an affair that quickly turned ugly. Exactly what happened in the office of prominent Jewish stockbroker Hubert Nathan on Friday 9 May was soon lost in claim and counter-claim. Only the beginning was clear. At an election meeting in Wadestown the previous evening, Nathan criticised the number of past and present union secretaries on the Labour tickets for local bodies in the capital, including eight who were standing in the municipality. He asked: could such candidates serve ratepayers *and* the city when they were forced to bow to union authority to keep their jobs? No one disputed the fact that a union official had telephoned Nathan late on Friday morning to ask if he and an associate could drop by for a chat; nor that five men subsequently entered Nathan's office at 2.30 p.m. It was the stockbroker's account of what happened next that caused all the ructions:

In 1941 the Jewish stockbroker, racehorse owner and Citizens Harbour Board candidate Hubert Nathan found himself at the centre of a political firestorm. His accusation of 'Gestapo' intimidation by a group of union leaders was so skilfully played by Mayor Hislop that Labour was destroyed at that year's local body elections.

ATL, S. P. Andrew Collection, F-18674-1/2

> They shut the door behind them and immediately began to abuse me. They called me the scum of the earth, reviled me because I am a Jew, told me no Jew should hold any public position in the country; also I was a money-grabber, that I was not a producer like them, and that I ought to be at the war … [A]nother threatened that if I did not withdraw and apologise in writing, he would take steps to stop my travelling on the steamers, in the trains, and on the trams, and that he would stop the delivery of meat, bread and milk to my house.[24]

Four days passed. On the Wednesday before polling day, Nathan's account of the incident was splashed over the newspapers, giving the unions little time to respond. The Labour Representation Committee described Nathan's allegations as 'hardly credible'. Hislop, on the other hand, referred to 'Nazi' tactics. The word 'Gestapo' was heard at public meetings. On the eve of the Saturday elections, newspaper editorials condemned 'the use of union power to victimise opponents'.[25] The result was a devastating loss for Labour, with not a single candidate elected to Council and its 1938 votes halved. Hislop finished 9,000 votes ahead of his Labour rival, Wellington South MP Bob McKeen. For the first time in 30 years, no Labour candidate was returned to any of the three elective local authorities. Nine years passed before a Labour candidate was returned to Council. The Citizens-friendly *Dominion* gloated:

> The result of the elections should have a wholesome and invigorating effect
> in the check which has been administered to the pretensions of those extreme
> elements in the Labour movement which arrogated to themselves the right to
> impose their opinions and their will on others.[26]

Labour was in the dog box. The Citizens' clean sweep brought Elizabeth Gilmer, an active conservationist and the daughter of Richard Seddon, into Council. The Nathan affair highlighted general discontent with the management of a war that seemed a world away from Lambton Quay. The terror engendered by the Japanese attack on Pearl Harbor in December 1941 would change all that.

Preparing for the worst

In November 1941, the capital had its first blackout, a month after Auckland. The wardens of the municipal Emergency Precaution Service (EPS) rated the effort as good. An embryonic EPS set up after the Napier earthquake highlighted the need to prepare for acute local disaster. After the outbreak of war, the Wellington civil defence model was adopted nationally, with a manual issued to all towns and cities. Thousands of volunteers flocked to the EPS, or enrolled in the rival Home Guard and Women's War Service Auxiliary. Under the EPS scheme, Wellington was divided into 25 districts, staffed by ten service units. As in other centres, the Mayor was in command, working alongside the Police and Post and Telegraph departments. Maintaining water and electricity supplies was the principal responsibility of the EPS. Days after the attack on Pearl Harbor, nearly 11,000 Wellingtonians were signed up to the EPS, including 1,618 women and 199 Boy Scouts.[27] Compulsory membership of the Home Guard for all men between the ages of 35 and 50 led to the demise of the EPS, which was later revived and renamed Civil Defence.

Harbour-facing homes and buildings were blacked out. As Christmas 1941 approached, one shop sold five tons of heavy cardboard, more than 100,000 yards of black building paper, and gallons of black paint.[28] Bolts of cloth were dyed to make curtains to cover the great windows of the new Central Library on Mercer Street, where lights blazed late into the night. Hislop warned citizens not to relax the blackout.[29] By New Year the emphasis had shifted to air-raid shelters and tunnels. More than 100 buildings, from Kirkcaldie & Stains to the AMP building on Customhouse Quay, provided basement shelters. The government agreed to pay half the cost.[30]

The Council worked to calm a frightened city. Cr William Appleton, an advocate of Moral Rearmament, helped to create a message based on 'moral and spiritual renewal'.[31] 'Morale cards', inscribed with teachings from this international movement, were widely distributed. The Rationalists' Association complained about the use of public money 'to publish religious propaganda which is very offensive to a large section of the population'.[32] Three timber-lined tunnels, each with room for as many as 5,000 people, were dug under the Carillon and in Hospital Road, Newtown. Concrete-block shelters appeared in the city as Singapore fell to the Japanese. The grounds of Parliament, bulldozed for public shelters, were compared to 'Gallipoli or a relief map of New Guinea'.[33] Under the pohutukawa trees lay a bomb-proof bunker, where the War Cabinet and armed service chiefs deliberated. Plans were made to evacuate the city's wartime population of 123,000

Wellington Public Library bindery staff (from left, Jay Bennett, Merle Kerr, Ngaire Robinson and Sophie Stewart) donned tin helmets and armbands in 1941 for fire watch duty on the central library roof.

WCA, 00138:0:10928

'Conductorettes'

During the war, women helped to fill acute labour shortages in Wellington and other main centres. In 1941 the busy Tramways Department hired its first 'tram girls' or 'conductorettes', dressing them in a uniform of dark blue trousers and so-called 'battledress' tops. By 1944, there were 175 women conductors — nearly a third of the total Tramways staff — clipping tickets.[34]

Women were also brought in to 'man' the civil service and banks. Competition among such offices saw many women staff poached

Three 'conductorettes' in their uniform of dark blue trousers and 'battledress tops'.

ATL, S. P. Andrew Collection, F-43970-1/2

from the trams. Women also performed the night-time cleaning of trams in the depots, but the government overruled a municipal attempt to hire women to work as track maintenance gangers.[35]

Local women served at the benches of the Ford factory at Seaview, where the manufacture of munitions replaced car assembly. By 1945, a squad of 700 women had famously produced nearly seven million hand grenades, more than a million mortar bombs, and other weaponry and war equipment.[36]

in the event of an invasion. Municipal parks and reserves were to be commandeered for civilian camps. Launch-owners were assigned to carry thousands of citizens from Island Bay to Eastbourne if the Hutt Road were put out of action.[37]

Policies were drawn up to deny invaders access to the city's resources. Documents reveal that local EPS personnel had orders to destroy anything that might be useful to the enemy. The harbour entrance would be blocked by five ships sunk with depth charges. Cars, buses, trucks, tractors, fire engines, locomotives and even bicycles and wheelbarrows were to be 'ruthlessly destroyed and permanently immobilised' to avoid their falling into enemy hands. Sawmills, dairy factories, tanneries and canneries were to be burned down, blown up, ruined with gas cutting torches or smashed with sledge-hammers. In order to succeed, the approach had to be selective, ruthless, carefully planned and rigorously applied. Secrecy was paramount:

Inflammable stores, such as tar, bitumen, oils etc, if available, should be distributed round to suitable points to ensure a good conflagration, easily started. For instance, timber yards, coal dumps, timber stores and cargo etc could well be set alight by these means. A great deal of useful destruction can be done by floating cranes, tugs, or other suitable floating craft pulling wharf cranes, heavy machinery, railway trucks, locomotives etc over the side of the berths before they themselves are in turn scuttled.[38]

'Liquor and lust'

The 'invasion' of American troops calmed the city's nerves, ensuring that no locomotive was ever slung off King's Wharf. Marines in their immaculate uniforms were appearing around town by May 1942; several thousand more came off the USS *Wakefield* in June. Over the following eighteen months, tens of thousands passed through camps around the Wellington region, with smaller numbers based in Anderson and Central Parks. The wharf precinct became a staging post. In July 1943 a fire on board a heavily laden munitions ship, *John Davenport*, nearly resulted in the waterfront being blown up.[39] Marines took over the boat harbour at Clyde Quay, with the clubrooms of the Port Nicholson Yacht Club being expanded into a malaria hospital and administration block. The American charm offensive began with a US naval officer presenting Mayor Hislop with a sketch of General MacArthur.[40] The need to entertain the visitors on 'dead' Sundays saw councillors lifting the ban on certain activities, such as the evening screening of films. An American Red Cross facility was erected on Council land near the Central Library.[41] In 1943, a Wakefield Street building owned by the Electricity Department became a miniature all-services sports stadium, where Marines could box and play basketball.

Suspicion and resentment still lingered. The eagerness with which young local women embraced the sophisticated and affluent visitors led to the sullen epithet 'bedroom commandoes'. Racist abuse by Marines from America's southern states was said to be behind the infamous Battle of Manners Street. On Saturday 3 April 1943, outside the Allied Services Club, belts and knives were wielded during four hours of fighting in which a thousand American and New Zealand troops, plus hundreds of civilians, are said to have been involved.[42] A few weeks later, local servicemen scuffled with their American counterparts during a boxing match at the Basin Reserve.

'Liquor and lust' became the new catch-cry as concerns mounted, and fingers were pointed at the Americans. In May 1943, a fourteen-year-old girl vanished near Anderson Park. A child welfare officer described juvenile prostitution as an 'ugly and increasing trend'.[43] A deputation from the Inter-Church Council on Public Affairs urged Hislop 'to call a conference to discuss methods of combating the present moral laxity which … is prevalent in the city'.[44] The Mayor himself led a deputation to the government to discuss ways to combat prostitution and venereal disease. The *Woman's Weekly* described alcohol as 'the most dangerous ally of the scourge'.[45] Maori women, drawn to the 'good times' of the big city, were seen as especially vulnerable. F. B. Katene, chairman of the Ngati Poneke Tribal Committee, urged the government to restrict sales of alcohol in lounge bars and private bars to young Maori women.[46] Anti-vice squads were later formed in Wellington and Auckland, targeting 'sly grog' liquor sales as much as 'disorderly women'.

The war years dragged on. The rationing of everything from petrol to pencils continued. The Council got behind a national 'Dig for Victory' campaign which promoted communal vegetable-growing as a way to relieve boredom and boost the patriotic effort. Land was provided for 550 allotments, including two giant 'display plots' in front of the Central Library.[47] Meanwhile, a severe earthquake in June 1942 toppled more than 7,000 chimneys and damaged buildings.[48] The cement had barely dried on replacement chimneys when another quake struck. The old public library building was judged unsafe and demolished. Bookings were suspended while the Town Hall was strengthened. Councillors prepared a deputation to Prime Minister Fraser, seeking a state subsidy for the city's damaged chimney-pots. Fraser, busy running a war on several fronts and preparing for an imminent general election, declined the request.

Former city councillor and Labour parliamentarian Peter Fraser (front left) and Mayor Hislop (front centre) held profoundly different views of the world. Hislop and his conservative allies on council, such as William Appleton (rear, extreme right), never stopped needling the wartime Labour Cabinet over its one-time opposition to conscription. Fraser got his own back in 1942 when, as Prime Minister, he refused to see a Council deputation seeking a state subsidy for thousands of quake-damaged chimney pots.

WCA, 00155:0:006

In April 1944, Hislop stood down from the mayoralty. Over fourteen years he had steered the city through the lows of depression and the highs of centennial celebration. Much of his war years had been devoted to needling the government. Powerful enemies such as Peter Fraser helped to ensure that Hislop never achieved his goal of a parliamentary career, but his conservative legacy lived on in successors such as William Appleton.

As early as October 1944, councillors made ready for the war's end. The waterfront, closed since 1939, now reopened. The Wellington Rugby Football Union praised the municipality for getting 'city reserves back from the Army Authorities for recreation purposes'.[49] An air-raid shelter in Marion Street became a soap storage depot. The government too had been preparing for the return of the troops. The Department of Housing Construction built blocks of flats, in Auckland

and Wellington, in reinforced concrete. The first in a series of showpiece state-housing blocks for single people went up in Berhampore. Further blocks were built on The Terrace, in Hanson Street, and notably in Dixon Street. The ten-storey Dixon Street flats, towering over Willis Street, were seen as the centrepiece of Labour's 1943 election manifesto. Bizarrely, these constructions were justified as essential defence works, at a time when the building industry was harnessed to the war effort.[50] No building permit could be issued without government consent, a practice that lingered after the war. Labour's heart, however, was in family-based communities in outlying areas such as the Hutt Valley. Before the war, the municipality had assisted in the massive state housing rental scheme, providing hundreds of sites for detached homes in Wilton, Northland and Karori.

Nearly six years of war came to an end. On 8 May 1945, Wellingtonians poured into the streets to celebrate the Allied victory in Europe. Many flocked to so-called Liberty Corner, a wooden band rotunda on land bounded by Featherston and Hunter Streets, where patriotic Liberty Loans were promoted. Its proximity to the wharves had made it a social hub in wartime, with charity wheelbarrow races run from there to Stewart Dawson's Corner. By the time victory over Japan was declared in August, it was known as Victory Corner.[51] Young and old sang and danced there until the band played 'Auld Lang Syne' at 10 p.m. and everyone went home.[52] A choral thanksgiving service was later held in the Town Hall, culminating in the singing of 'Land of Hope and Glory'. A total of 770 Council staff had served in the armed forces: 37 had been killed, and 32 wounded. Councillors named a street in a Karori subdivision Victory Avenue.[53]

On VE Day, these women joined the crowds thronging confetti-strewn city streets to celebrate victory in Europe.

ATL, John Pascoe Collection, F-1508-1/4

A stable aftermath?

Planning the peace was well under way before victory was declared. Early in 1945, the government revisited its plans to overhaul local government, resurrecting a parliamentary committee to draw up proposals. Labour favoured amalgamation as a way to strengthen governance at the local level and, importantly, to reduce the surfeit of ad hoc and territorial authorities. From 1946, a Local Government Commission encouraged areas run by tiny town boards, such as Johnsonville, to merge with bigger neighbours such as Wellington City. Nascent regional planning councils were established as a further challenge to local body parochialism. In 1946, the Wellington municipality contributed £1,288 to its local planning council.[54] The massive Hutt River scheme, completed in 1957, exemplified an emerging regional outlook, as the government agreed in 1943 to fund a massive pipeline to distribute water from Kaitoke to Greater Wellington.

The municipality welcomed the string of state-funded improvements to the city's infrastructure, initiated on national economic grounds. Councillors were flattered in 1950 when the capital was chosen for the site of the country's inaugural motorway, tacked on to the end of the highway between Tawa and Johnsonville. In 1949, the municipality endorsed plans by the Main Highways Board for a six-lane highway along the Hutt Road. Control of the airport, too, was slipping out of the Council's hands. The inadequacy of Rongotai aerodrome for peacetime aircraft led Cabinet to announce a ban on passenger operations there in 1947, thus reducing air traffic by two-thirds. Together, the Council and the government mapped out a massive redevelopment of the site, with a flying-boat base being constructed at Evans Bay in the interim.

Wellington City was long overdue for urban renewal. In 1944 the City Engineer called for slum clearance laws 'to provide adequate areas for the growth of industry and housing'.[55] The Housing Improvement Act 1945 shifted responsibility for demolishing rundown housing from central to local government. The legislation also established a new approach to public housing, with the state providing for suburban families and local authorities looking after the elderly and the poor in the inner city.[56] In 1945, the municipality hosted a conference to discuss the 'reclaiming' of the Te Aro slums, as part of its first formal planning scheme. The widening of Taranaki Street followed.

Fresh and bold ideas for the city emerged. In 1946, a group of progressive architects and architectural students formed the Architecture Centre, to promote social concerns through 'modern' buildings and town planning. An emphasis on education led to a series of Summer Schools of Design, in conjunction with town planners in the Public Works Department. In 1948, students attending the school produced a series of ambitious plans for reshaping the inner city. *Te Aro Replanned* included an entertainment zone along Courtenay Place, a civic centre by the existing Town Hall, and a vibrant waterfront based on public promenades and apartments. The ideas attracted considerable publicity. Opening an exhibition of the designs in the Central Library, Deputy Mayor Macalister praised the work, blaming the early settlers — not recent policies — for the city's current planning woes. Some of the students behind *Te Aro Replanned* would later make their mark on the city.

The municipality focused on building homes for ex-servicemen and their families in suburban areas, often using materials from demolished military buildings. Temporary transit housing was also established in Miramar. Special effort went into providing for the many hundreds of former Council employees who had returned from the war, among them former City Solicitor Jack Marshall.

City transport, too, was in transition. For the trams, the war years had been the busiest ever, with commuting American servicemen and petrol rationing pushing passenger numbers close to 63 million in 1944.[57] Centre seats had been removed from trams to squeeze in more bodies. Repairs and upgrading had been deferred, because of wartime shortages. Early in 1945, the municipality announced that one of the tram routes would be changed over to single-operator trolley-buses. Ten trolley-bus chassis and overhead equipment were ordered from Britain. In 1949, the first trolley-buses rolled between the Railway Station and Oriental Bay, with extensions to Roseneath and Hataitai. Later that year, trolley-buses replaced the Tinakori Road and Wadestown trams. Tram-lines along the Northland, Karori, Brooklyn and Aro Street, and Miramar routes were torn up.

Manpower shortages lingered, as wages remained frozen. In 1947, the City Engineer estimated there were 2,000 vacant positions for skilled and semi-skilled labour in the city.[58] The Corporation denied rumours of 'chaotic' conditions in the Tramways Department.[59] Its milk committee was more frank:

> The position has now become so desperate with the loss or the threatened loss of experienced workers to more remunerative positions, and the difficulty of recruiting satisfactory workers from the transient and indifferent labour offering in the city, that unless some action is taken a partial or complete breakdown in the [Milk] Department's processing and distribution services is not only likely but probable.[60]

Stability had become Labour's post-war mantra. A wage rise for the Council's milk roundsmen and dairy-hands lay with an all-powerful Director of Stabilisation. He declined.[61] Tight controls on wages, prices and costs continued after the war ended, along with the rationing of petrol and steel. Dairy products, too, were rationed until 1950, with most of the nation's cream being turned into butter and exported as part of a massive 'Aid to Britain' campaign. Cream remained in such short supply that a Rationing Control Office permit was needed to buy a quarter of a pint. In 1949, a four-year-old Wellington boy suffering from asthma and malnutrition was refused a cream ration, despite a doctor's letter.[62]

Councillors complained that town planning was impossible under the stabilisation regime.[63] In 1948 they had to beg the government for a permit to build a four-storey civic administration block. Prime Minister Fraser agreed, on condition that the Council 'did not press too hard for steel'.[64] The building was not completed until 1956. At the end of 1949, a National administration replaced the 'Shortage Government'. The opposition National Party had found a receptive audience for its platform of personal freedom and private enterprise. With rationing lifted, sales of municipal cream rose from 17,889 pints in 1949 to 63,196 pints a year later.[65]

Despite talk of 'making the pound go further', Prime Minister Sidney Holland retained much of the state apparatus. Inflation returned. Fresh enemies, however, were identified as the Cold War developed abroad. The electricity restrictions of the 'socialistic' 1940s worsened as the 1950s arrived. A shivering Cr Galloway complained that water-heaters in the Council building were turned off on winter evenings.[66] The municipality was short of 400 staff, including 100 on the trams.[67] Immigrants were targeted as possible employees. When an exhausted Peter Fraser died in December 1950, many staff attended the funeral of the Council's most famous son. Councillors now debated tamer issues: whether children should be allowed to carry bows and arrows on trams; a soap-box derby in a gully near Karori Park.

Labour's bruising defeat in the 1941 local body elections in Wellington led to pressure within the party for a strategic withdrawal from local body politics. In 1950 Frank Kitts, a civil servant and Labour Party stalwart, defied the party machine and stood at the election. He was elected to Council and to the Hospital and Harbour Boards. Former parliamentarian and councillor Gerald O'Brien recalled the events:

> I was chairman of Peter Fraser's electoral committee and Frank Kitts was a member. We were both opposed to concession of the field of municipal politics believing them important to the general good. By chance I met with Frank as we were heading across Dixon Street to Ferendinos' fish and chip shop. He was pessimistic because the party had no obvious mayoral candidate, around which the election would turn. Frank at the time was a public servant with the Government Stores Board. My response was that we did have a candidate and it was he — Frank Kitts. I still recall his expression of dismay at my suggestion, but it was rapidly resolved by Frank accepting

the obligation. To our astonishment we won the vote and the decision was made to contest the municipal election with a full ticket headed by Frank Kitts. In the event Frank topped the poll for the council and Labour won 6 seats out of fifteen, although he did not make the mayoralty until 1956, after which he never looked back.[68]

Kitts came from Waimate, birthplace of another Labour icon, Norman Kirk. Like Kirk, he was a big man, using his imposing six foot two inch, 17 stone frame to overshadow his opponents. Kitts had joined the Labour Party at the age of sixteen, sharing its fundamental philosophy that 'man's labour was not a commodity to be bought and sold and exploited for the purpose of accumulating wealth for a few'.[69] But mostly he kept his political views to himself.

On 5 March 1951, Kitts and his fellow councillors listened as a grave Mayor Macalister described 'the state of emergency that had arisen from a waterfront strike':

> The government had requested that he should act as chairman of the Emergency Supplies Committee which had been set up to ensure the provision of supplies for Wellington and adjoining districts. This committee was performing a most essential and useful function.[70]

A showdown with what National called the 'wrecker' unions was underway. In February 1951, members of the militant New Zealand Waterside Workers' Union, which was seeking a wage increase, banned all overtime on the wharves. Employers then locked the watersiders out and the ports came to a standstill. The government told the unions to get back to work, but the ultimatum was rejected. At the end of February, air force personnel unloaded ships as the capital faced shortages of bread and meat. Holland declared a state of emergency and deregistered the watersiders' union. Like his mayoral counterparts in the other main centres, Mayor Macalister was dragooned to help the government hold the line against what it termed 'communist' subversion. The Mayor's controversial powers included helping to set up replacement unions to run the port. Midway through 1951, councillors declined an application from strikers and their families for their electricity not to be disconnected for non-payment.[71] The dispute ended on 15 July, the costliest in New Zealand's history in financial terms, with the waterfront unions broken up.

The Council faced a minor union showdown of its own in 1951. The local Trades Council complained about the Wellington Municipal Officers Association, a

Council 'union'. The powerful and feared right-wing unionist Fintan Patrick Walsh claimed that the association was being used as a 'stopper' to stall negotiations with recognised unions.[72] Macalister replied that the association was entitled to deal with the municipality. Councillors, sensing that an era of union militancy was passing, ignored the delegation.

Royal gales

At the end of 1950 came news that a reigning monarch might finally visit New Zealand. The war had ruled out a centennial visit by King George VI a decade earlier. Elaborate plans had been drawn up for a month-long tour in 1948, but cancelled after the King took ill. His recovery saw a third attempt pencilled in for May 1952. Councillors greeted the announcement with joy. The King's busy itinerary in the capital led the Council to convene a Royal Visit committee at the end of 1951, and to appoint a caterer. Additional glasshouses were built at the Council's nurseries in Berhampore for the cultivation of begonias.

The event was preceded by visits from various British dignitaries. In August 1951 the Lord Mayor of London, Rt Hon. Alderman Sir Denys Lowson, inspected the Council Chamber, accompanied by a First Esquire and Swordbearer. The Council's new ceremonial mace was not yet on hand for their visit. The lack of a municipal mace had been noted in 1950 by a visiting Harrogate Borough Council Alderman, Sir Bernard Lomas-Walker, KBE, JP, and his own council had decided to make the gift of a silver-gilt mace to Wellington City, 'to commemorate the 1951 Festival of Britain and as a token of appreciation of the generous help that New Zealand has given to the Mother Country during and since the war.'[73]

The King's sudden death in February 1952 threw plans into chaos. An announcement followed that Britain's new Queen, the former Princess Elizabeth, would visit New Zealand at the end of 1953. The attractive young Queen's coronation in June of that year was a glittering and joyous occasion, made even more special for New Zealanders by the announcement that Edmund Hillary had climbed Mt Everest. The royal party was due to visit the capital in January 1954. Arrangements were made to shift the date of the 1953 municipal elections to fit in with the visit. Ceremonial trappings were put in place, and 'light-weight' mayoral robes approved. Excitement mounted as the month-long visit to New Zealand drew near. Cr Stevens asked Mayor Macalister 'to ensure that councillors be given their rightful place in the ceremonies in connection with the Royal Visit'.[74]

This was a chance to spruce up the post-war city. Suburban progressive

On 11 January 1954, Mayor McAlister hosted the young Queen Elizabeth II at a glittering civic reception in the Town Hall. Gusty summer rain forced the Queen to wear a coat.

ATL, F-19851-1/4 (ANZ, AAQT 6538 18/E/2)

associations organised mass 'clean-ups'. Khandallah and Ngaio residents fought unsuccessfully to have the royal arrival rerouted from Ngauranga Gorge to their suburbs.[75] Controversy surrounded the banning of the Royal Crest from municipal milk bottle tops. Councillors agreed to pay for Union Jacks for every primary school pupil in the region. Electric 'Crown' signs used in London for the Coronation were imported, despite the cost of £500.

Then it all came true. 'The capital gleams as never before', crowed the *Evening Post*. On the morning of 11 January, half a million Berhampore begonias carpeted the city centre. The trolley-arms of trams fluttered with pennants, with 'Welcome to Wellington' signs at either end of the tramcars. The verandah of Kirkcaldie & Stains on Lambton Quay groaned beneath 14 tons of flowers. For the 30-minute civic reception, the Town Hall was a riot of gladioli: purple blooms filled white grecian vases atop tall white pillars, and massive bunches decked the walls in the gallery. Red begonias hung in baskets around the organ loft. Wellington's civic reception was the only one on the Royal itinerary scheduled to be held indoors. The bureaucrats' decision proved wise, as fickle summer weather closed in. The hope that Her Majesty might be spared the January gales inspired one local poet to importune the forces of Nature:

Young and old watch as the royal entourage drives by.

ATL, F-42949-1/2 (ANZ, AAQT 6538 20/B/5)

O vagrant winds keep peace

This is the evening when a garden spills

Its summer incense for a Sovereign's case

Disturb this city not: for proud, apart

It wears the Rose of Windsor on its heart.[76]

Gusty rain forced the Queen into a coat of oatmeal-cream silk, trimmed with a black velvet collar, worn over a black dress. Councillors won their 'rightful place' at the civic ceremonies, and nearly all the curtseying women were the wives of councillors or politicians.[77] The hoi polloi had to be content with lining the streets to see the royal limousine, with some using Council-approved periscopes to get a glimpse above the crowd. At Athletic Park, 9,000 cheering schoolchildren, watched by 20,000 parents, waved their flags as the Queen drove by. The *Evening Post* was overcome:

> As the mother of two young children 12,000 miles away, the Queen today assumed the role of mother to her wider family, and it was this maternal aspect that so caught the imagination and love of the New Zealand citizens of the future.[78]

The royal timing was perfect. The city was settling into an era of peace and prosperity that would last for two decades. Macalister sensed the unifying power of the Royal Visit, describing it as 'one in which there has never been better co-ordination and co-operation between the council and all sections of the community'.[79]

Ironically, it was Macalister's personality clash with his fellow Citizens councillor, tea and coffee merchant Ernest Toop, that split the anti-Labour vote in 1956. In an upset result, the mayoralty went to the high-profile Labour candidate, Frank Kitts, who had been elected MP for Wellington Central in 1954. Kitts devoted a large part of his working life to the mayoralty, in contrast to predecessors who took a few hours a day from their busy professions to attend to municipal business. Without a Labour majority on the Council, Kitts could never afford to alienate himself from the dominant Citizens block. Instead he talked of 'teamwork', preferring to stand above the fray, thus creating a leadership vacuum which allowed the City Engineer and committee chairmen to dominate. His approach to the job reflected the consensus ethos of the 1950s, which became less workable as the power shifts of the 1960s emerged.

Better economic times saw the Corporation embrace public housing. City pensioners were the first group to be targeted, with the first of dozens of pensioner

A royal korero

Wellington's civic reception for its royal visitors stopped in its well-oiled tracks as the Duke of Edinburgh, Prince Philip, paused to chat to the two 'representatives of the Maori race', hidden among the dozens of local body politicians and their wives.

In addition to the formal Maori welcomes at Waitangi, Rotorua and Ngaruawahia, tour organisers had decided to provide a token Maori representation at local receptions such as the one in the Wellington Town Hall.[80]

On 11 January, a crowd of 2,300 watched as every city councillor and his wife was presented to Her Majesty, along with all local mayors and other dignitaries. Even the niece of the Makara County Council chairman got to curtsey.

Under the watchful eye of Mayor Macalister, the 30-minute reception went like clockwork. The only hitch came when Prince Philip stopped to chat with Lady Miria Pomare and her son, Te Rakaherea. A co-founder of the Ngati Poneke Maori Association, she was the widow of the late Sir Maui Pomare, the famous Ngati Mutunga and Ngati Toa leader, medical reformer and politician.

There was a moment of laughter when the Mayor, who was announcing the names of those to be presented, failed to notice that the Duke had kept Mr Pomare for a few minutes' chat, with the result that the waiting line started to grow longer.[81]

Lady Mildred Amelia (Miria) Tapapa Woodbine Pomare, photographed in her early thirties.

ATL, S. P. Andrew Collection, G-14582-1/1

flats constructed in 1953. An end to wartime shortages hastened developments in infrastructure. The Hutt River regional water scheme was implemented after steel for the pipes became available. When completed in 1957, the 21 mile pipeline connected a weir on the Hutt River at Kaitoke with the Lower Karori Reservoir, carrying water to supply Greater Wellington. The inhabitants of Johnsonville and Newlands, recently amalgamated with Wellington, celebrated the arrival of more drinkable water.

A new generation had more frivolous things on its mind. Adolescent boys and girls, recently dubbed 'teenagers' by American advertisers, flocked to suburban swimming pools to swim and sunbathe. From 1948, poolside males could slick back their locks with hair oil from vending machines.[82] The term 'Cuba Street Yank' was coined to describe local youths sporting wartime American crew-cuts and the latest 'stovepipe' trousers.[83]

The 'tea party' Mayor: Frank Kitts left a clerical job at the Government Stores Board to embark on a political career that spanned three decades. As Mayor, he gained a reputation for accepting every invitation, attending dozens of school fetes, rugby club openings and other ceremonial occasions every year. Kitts' food consumption at such functions became legendary: he was said to swallow sausage rolls 'like he was posting a letter' and famously devoured two cooked chickens at a single sitting. Mayoress Iris Kitts was well-liked, but attracted pity as rumours circulated about her husband's philandering.

WCA, 00010:2:1

In July 1954, the *Dominion* broke the news of a scandal involving teenagers frequenting an American-style milk bar on Lower Hutt's High Street. Police rounded up nearly 60 schoolgirls, most aged under fifteen and pupils at Hutt Valley Memorial Technical College. Six older male youths, variously labelled 'bodgies', 'teddy boys' or 'milkbar cowboys', also appeared in court on charges of 'carnal knowledge'. A Children's Court magistrate put some of the girls on probation and gave most of the others a severe ticking off. A government in election mode immediately convened a Special Committee on Moral Delinquency in Children and Young People. Its upright members began two months of hearings in Parliament Buildings on 5 August, and its 78-page report, which linked 'moral chaos' to American popular culture influences, was later distributed to every New Zealand family.

By the end of 1954, trolley-buses were carrying advertisements for Coca Cola, soon to become the municipality's biggest sponsor.[84] Johnny Cooper, a young country singer from the East Coast, was typical of rural Maori who flooded into the capital after the war. He hoped to become a professional singer, but stuck with a Council job as a grave-digger at Karori cemetery:

> I used to dig the graves and practise my songs down the hole. I was actually in it, no guitar, but singing while I was digging, practising my songs, and people would look in and wonder what was going on. Mad, eh, when you come to think about it. But it was a good place to practise and nobody complained.[85]

In 1955, Cooper recorded 'Rock Around the Clock', the first version of the Bill Haley hit to be recorded outside the United States, and performed at rock 'n' roll dances in the Town Hall. Followers of the brash American sounds remained a subversive minority. Performances at the new Sound Shell in the Botanic Garden were restricted to more respectable 'string and swing' orchestras. When the venue was suggested to the Council for a live broadcast of the popular radio show *It's in the Bag*, the response was: 'only cultural performances should be given at the Sound Shell'.[86] Young people disagreed:

A large portion of Wellington's teenage population danced on the lawn in front of the sound shell at the Botanical Gardens last night. Highlight of the evening was a spontaneous jiving exhibition by a young lady in yellow jeans and black and white blouse. Her partner's dress was equally colourful. In most dances the more modern minded youths formed small groups and jived. Nobody was hurt.[87]

The city's intellectuals gathered at coffee houses such as the French Maid in Lambton Quay. Percolated coffee, at 6d a cup, had proved a surprise hit at the Centennial Exhibition, where it was served with cream and biscuits.[88] Many of the regulars at the French Maid were members of an informal community of educated refugees who had arrived from Germany, Austria and Czechoslovakia in the mid 1930s. The presence of the 'reffos' was noted during the war:

A steady influx of European migrants in the past two or three years has made Wellington the most cosmopolitan city of New Zealand. Once an event to attract attention, the sound of alien speech in train or street is today a commonplace. Already aliens are beginning to disseminate continental habits and notions of food, drink, clothing, art, medicine and education … [T]he migrants go where the food is unusual and good coffee is to be had.[89]

Viennese architect Ernst Plischke had arrived in Wellington in May 1939. His design for the Dixon Street flats and a series of private commissions enhanced his reputation as an urbane modernist. In 1957, the clean lines of Massey House on Lambton Quay made Plischke's 'crystal block' an instant temple of modernity. Roy Parsons' bookshop in the building featured a 'reffo' coffee bar on its mezzanine floor, a cosy place where customers enjoyed such delicacies as real yoghurt and Hungarian goulash. The *Listener* spotted a trend:

With their concealed or subdued lighting, pot-plants and foam rubber or cane upholstery, [coffee bars] create on this otherwise rugged frontier an atmosphere of continental-style luxury happily independent of the overseas exchange situation … [N]ooks and corners in the capital disclose the Buttery, La Scala, the Sans Souci, the Mexicali, Coconut Grove, Man Friday and Picasso.[90]

But rugby — not coffee — remained the preferred opiate of the people. Every available bus and tram was brought into service on 23 June 1956, when a touring

The Lambton Quay entrance to the Cable Car in the mid 1950s.

ATL, Dominion Post Collection, EP/1956/1200

Springbok side beat Wellington. Six weeks later, Wellingtonians turned out once again in the stiffest of winter southerlies to watch the All Blacks lose to South Africa.

Inner-city streets were crowded with traffic. By the early 1950s, trams, trolley-buses and diesel buses were battling for territory with growing numbers of private cars. In 1953, the municipality called for tenders for 400 parking meters. Auckland's meters were said to be yielding its Council more than £3,000 a week, and the capital's meters paid for themselves in two years.[91] Lambton Quay soon sported more than a hundred meters. By 1954, the parking meter account was in surplus by £20,000.[92] Roading infrastructure became a Council priority. In 1956 the opening of Churchill Drive provided a link between Wadestown and Ngaio. An alternative vehicular access to the Hutt Road was finally available.

Safeguarding remnants of the city's past was not a priority for a municipality dominated by engineers. Skirmishes over what could and should be preserved began to undermine the consensus of the 1950s. Little evidence remained of the settlement's origins, with one remarkable exception. Tucked away at the end of Bond Street, still known to many as Old Customhouse Street, sat the city's oldest buildings, still in commercial use after close to 120 years. In 1958 the Customhouse, the smaller of the low, slate-roofed structures, housed a car lubrication business, while an engineering firm leased George Hunter's original Exchange Building, where settlers and Maori once queued for hoes, turpentine, and velvet waistcoats. The Exchange had also served as the first Town Hall and Reading Room. In 1938, the Provincial Historical Society asked the Council to acquire the building and re-erect it on a new site.[93] The proposal to relocate the building in the Botanic Garden was knocked back after the cost was estimated at £800.[94]

In 1945, ownership of the land switched to the municipality. A series of reclamations had already pushed the waterfront a long way out from the two weathered buildings. By the mid 1950s they lay marooned like a couple of old wrecks, beneath their tall modern neighbours. In 1957, the newly created National Historic Places Trust hailed their significance. Initially, Kitts agreed to preserve them; he then announced that demolition was imminent.[95] Trust secretary John Pascoe concurred — then changed his mind, after calls from furious members of the Early Settlers and Historical Association, backed by an *Evening Post* editorial.[96]

Borer experts and architects concluded that the buildings could be restored. The campaign to save the buildings dragged on into the winter of 1958. On 11 August, Kitts and his engineers received a deputation:

After a further discussion, postponement of the demolition was virtually agreed to by the Mayor, who asked Councillors Arcus and Archibald, as chairmen of the Electricity Committee and the Town Planning Committee respectively, to support this suggestion at the next meeting. Mr Pascoe asked for two months' postponement, to which the Mayor agreed.[97]

Four days later, the Exchange was bulldozed at dawn. The first that most citizens knew of the demolition was a photograph in that afternoon's *Evening Post*. Trust chairman Ormond Wilson said that future generations would deplore the action.[98] The Council announced that a car park would be built on the site (where the Lombard Street parking building now stands). Trust supporter H. B. Wylde saw parallels with the outbreaks of moral chaos recently identified in the Hutt Valley:

Marooned in the heart of the city: the Bethune and Hunter Exchange building, on the corner of Cornhill and Bond streets, in the 1950s. This remaining fragment of the settlement area was summarily bulldozed in 1958 to make way for the Lombard Street parking building.

WCA, 00138:0:10186

The whole country is being wiped raw of anything not screaming newness like a land slide, builder's bulldozing or bodgie's britches … we must realize at the outset and in all material projections that we deal with the spirits of a once real scene peopled by our own Forebears, both Maori and British … [N]o doubt they have now become reconciled to our addictions to motor cars and visionary car-park buildings and our sort of pubs but God forbid that we build either on this parental ground … [L]ike our planners, our teddy boys are lonely and lost before being indecent. This is fertile soil for trouble in the widest civic senses.[99]

If the Exchange was a metaphor for the city's untidy past, then the new airport at Rongotai symbolised its shining future. Over the seven years of its construction, it too would be mired in controversy. A decade earlier, Prime Minister Peter Fraser and the municipality had agreed on the need for a new city airport. Getting it built proved more difficult. A proposal based on removing Rongotai College was rejected. An alternative scheme, which involved removing a hill with 180 houses on it, was approved. In July 1952, Council and Ministry of Works staff began work on the site. Hillsides were pushed into the sea; 3 million cubic feet of spoil added 135 acres to Evans Bay and Lyall Bay, including 80 acres of sealed runway. The main sewer outfall was rerouted, and four miles of new road was laid.

The final cost of the new airport was £5 million, of which £1.5 million came from the city's coffers. A Council-endorsed brochure had a slightly embattled tone: '[The airport's] precision-patterned airfield, hangars and buildings are the final answer to prejudice, fear, frustration and misunderstanding. It is an exciting memorial to men who refused to lose faith, the pride of everyone who worked for it and on it.'[100]

On 24 October 1959 the airport was officially opened, a highlight being the crowning of 'Miss Wellington Airport'. Gales postponed the scheduled aerobatic display by the air forces of New Zealand, Australia, Britain, and the United States. On the Sunday, celebrations nearly ended in tragedy when an RAF Vulcan bomber hit the embankment during landing, smashing its undercarriage. Rongotai would go on to become the country's busiest domestic airport.

Curbing the chaos

Wellington ended the decade with an inaugural summer festival, featuring a procession of floats, a flyover of Vulcan bombers, and an appearance by basketball showmen the Harlem Globetrotters. Ballet was performed in the parks, as the

Disappointed umbrella-wielding crowds were turned away when bad weather disrupted the airport's opening in October 1959.

ATL, NZ Free Lance Collection, PAColl-8602-17

municipality relaxed its control of social and cultural activities. On 12 February 1958, the long-running practice of issuing individual permits for screening films on Sundays ceased.

The thaw was slow in coming. Religious messages were inscribed on milk bottles during 1955.[101] Members of the Open Air Campaigners movement preached on the beaches at Lyall and Island Bays. Authority was granted for an open-air church service in Newtown Park, followed by a pets' parade. When Billy Graham's evangelical road-show stopped off in the capital in April 1959, 40,000 people, including Cabinet ministers and deputy Opposition leader Jack Marshall, gathered at Athletic Park to hear him; more than 2,000 pledged themselves to Jesus. Kitts had sent teenage idol Johnny Devlin a telegram, inviting him to the crusade.[102] In a famous photograph known as 'The Three Leaders', Billy Graham posed with Johnny Devlin ('the Wanganui Elvis') and Labour Prime Minister Walter Nash.

Other young people, rebelling perhaps against this public probity, indulged in delinquent behaviour usually identified with the times. In October 1958, the Town Hall custodian complained of toilets and fixtures being damaged during rock 'n' roll dances, 'notwithstanding the presence of the police'.[103] The Town Clerk noted that it was the third time this had happened. Councillors were warned to be wary of rock 'n' rollers masquerading as normal youths. Suspicion fell on organisers of a proposed Sunday club for young people: 'One of the applicants has conducted the rock 'n' roll dances in the Town Hall in the past, and there is some reason to believe that the present application may be a subterfuge to circumvent the law governing Sunday entertainments.'[104]

Meanwhile, many citizens were more preoccupied with traffic jams than with rebellious teenagers. In 1959 a retailer complained of having to wait eight minutes to cross Willis Street.[105] A group of businessmen, architects and advocates of public transport formed a Wellington Independent United Action Group to investigate the 'traffic chaos' caused by poor planning. Saul Goldsmith broke away to form a 'Save the Trams' group. George Porter, an architect and town planner, saw a chance to implement the post-war vision of *Te Aro Replanned*. He and two others joined the Citizens ticket, and all three were elected to Council in November 1959. The ground was prepared for a battle between the engineers and the planners.

Tar and Cement

Chapter 7

1960–1975

Your engineers lack aesthetic training. Their roads are not designed to assist the landscape but to desecrate it.

American industrial designer, J. O. Sinel[1]

On a mild Saturday morning in May 1964, Mayor Kitts squeezed himself into the driver's platform to pilot Wellington's — and New Zealand's — last tram on its final journey, from Thorndon to the Newtown tram-barns. The 10.30 car edged through the city, leading the procession at a funereal pace, the mayoral foot hovering over the brake pedal to avoid the Onslow Silver Band (formerly the Municipal Tramways Band). Thousands crowded the footpaths in silence to catch a farewell glimpse of what had become a Wellington institution. The previous evening, late-night shoppers with souvenir tickets had packed out the 'last trams' in their red, white and blue bunting, and inscriptions such as 'We've had a fair innings' and 'We bow to progress'. Now the Very Last Tram, crammed with civic dignitaries and draped in the city's colours of black and gold, clanged through the Saturday streets, carrying the message 'End of Line'.

Many saw the demise of the tram as a victory for the motor car. Older people in particular sensed that a chapter in the city's history was coming to an end, and recorded it on film. Others preferred to look ahead. Cr Manthel, a car dealer and chairman of the transport committee, waved the last tram off, a cigar between his teeth; for the man driving the changeover from trams to trolley-buses, it

A souvenir ticket issued for the last ever municipal tram ride, Saturday 2 May 1964.

Redmer Yska

The last tram makes its final run,
with Mayor Kitts at the wheel.

WCA, 00340:0:993

was a happy ending. Tram enthusiast Saul Goldsmith disagreed: his referendum of ratepayers opposing a £1.5 million loan to complete the conversion had failed. Kitts himself confessed to a secret desire to keep the trams, describing the decision to replace them as 'a retrograde step'.[2] But the die was cast: at the start of 1964, the first of twenty English-built trolley-buses was swung ashore by the floating crane *Hikitia*.

Eighty-six years after the first steam-powered trams made their appearance on Wellington streets, their successors had been made redundant by the motor car and such emblems of modernity as motels, parking buildings, and mini-skirted meter maids. The *Dominion*, in covering the final 'journey for sentiment', revealed its impatience with the antiquated tram, describing the 'familiar, unsuccessful attempt to squeeze the scrawny, throbbing vehicle past parked obstacles in the chaos of Manners Street, [which is] not much wider than the double tracks'.[3]

The capital looked to a happy, petroleum-dependent future. The 1960s had opened with a government statistician's calculation that the country now had half a million cars.[4] More than 75,000 vehicles were registered in the Wellington region alone. Elegant new overpasses across the motorway at Johnsonville symbolised the glamour and freedom of the automobile. The 'motor age' was also portrayed as a shortcut to economic prosperity. For the city's traffic superintendent, the businessman's car was more important than his telephone.[5] The city struggled to cope, however, with the 29,000 commuter vehicles pouring in daily from the Hutt Valley, Porirua, and outlying areas.[6] At peak hours, the congestion in narrow inner-city streets caused long delays. The municipality came under pressure to solve an acute traffic and parking crisis. In his capacity as MP for Wellington Central, Kitts supported a 1959 National Roads Amendment Bill, allowing the government to build free-flowing state highways into urban centres. Millions of pounds collected from petrol taxes were made available to pay for them. For Kitts the Mayor, the possibilities were tantalising.

In 1961, the municipal traffic
department paraded its
impressive fleet of motorcycles
outside the Town Hall.

ATL, Dominion Post Collection, EP-Transport-
Traffic Officers-01

By now the old heart of the city was giving out. As mobility increased, the population of the rundown inner-city suburbs had fallen steadily: in 1959, the proportion of the regional labour force living in the city was 50 percent, compared with 65 percent in 1945.[7] By 1961, the population of Greater Wellington was 249,532, with less than half (123,969) living in the city itself.[8] Housing shortages persisted, however, with many pensioners, single people, and childless couples struggling to find accommodation. The construction of high-density housing was identified as a way to rejuvenate decaying inner-city areas, lift rateable values, and shelter the needier members of the populace. Urban renewal, the subject of a Council-run conference in 1962, became the catch-phrase of the day.

The curved roof lines of the new Freyberg Pool spoke of a bolder future, while commemorating a war hero and swimming champion from another era. The opening in 1960 of Shell House, a fourteen-storey box of glass and steel, led the transformation of The Terrace from residential street to business centre. Office workers donned sunhats and sunglasses to cope with the glare and heat. Tradition was still evident on Lambton Quay, however, in the starched table-cloths and solid silver cutlery of the Midland Hotel's dining room. Across the road, teashops such as The Buttery still served scones and delicate sandwiches to the growing army of civil servants, housed in high-rise boxes such as the Bowen State Building. Within a decade, the shortage of government office space became acute, as public service numbers nationwide topped 50,000.[9]

"LOOK, MATE, IF YOU PATRONISED THE THINGS YOU WANT TO SAVE INSTEAD OF BLOCKING THE STREETS WITH THAT RUDDY GREAT HEAP, THE THINGS YOU WANT TO SAVE MIGHT GET SOMEWHERE!"

No cartoonist has ever caught the kindly but jaundiced mood of Wellingtonians as well as the *Evening Post*'s Nevile Lodge.

ATL, Courtesy Debby Edwards, B-133-091

In July 1961, Wellington received its first television broadcasts via WNTV Channel 1. The New Zealand Broadcasting Service sought the Council's permission to build a road to a TV relay station, later buying 30 acres on top of Mt Kaukau for a TV transmitter.[10] The opening in 1962 of the Commonwealth Pacific telephone cable (Compac) finally allowed New Zealanders to make overseas phone calls from home. Kitts took advantage of the ceremony to lobby his Melbourne counterpart for a direct Melbourne-to-Wellington air service. Meanwhile, Wellington's harbour, once a source of civic pride and prosperity, was accused of being a decaying port. In two decades, the capital's share of the import

'Digging' groovy sounds at the public library's music room in the 1960s.

WCA, 00340:0:1446

trade had fallen from 24 to 8 percent; its share of the export trade from 34 to 12 percent.[11] Pressure mounted to replace the current waterfront system, dependent on troublesome 'wharfies', with containerised shipping.

The new airport at Rongotai was made ready for the coming of the jet age. A duty-free shop was opened in 1962 to cater for the 50,000 domestic and 35,000 international passengers passing through the terminal that year.[12] Pre-recorded 'mood' music tinkled over the public address system. Four passengers in particular would come to symbolise the new era. On Sunday 21 June 1964, only weeks after the last tram rattled off to the Newtown depot, a TEAL Electra touched down at Rongotai with the Beatles on board. A crowd of mainly female fans, estimated at 6,000, had massed since dawn to greet their heroes. One gashed her thigh trying to climb the wire fence; pressure from behind forced two others through the fence. When the quartet emerged from the aircraft, the screams drowned out the noise of the turbo-prop engines. Members of the Ngati Poneke concert party performed a haka as the Beatles disembarked, then hongied and presented them with tiki. Feigning alarm, Ringo Starr commented to a nearby policeman: 'Hey fook! We come in peace!'[13]

The capital had not witnessed such adulation since the 'Royal Summer' of 1954. And the relatively muted reaction to the Queen's 1963 visit showed that she, too, played second fiddle to the emerging 'pop royalty'. The behaviour of the young fans, products of the post-war 'baby boom', had not been anticipated. A week before the Beatles arrived, Police Chief Superintendent W.S. Craigie said he had no intention of treating their tour as a royal visit, pointing out that New Zealand teenagers were rather more balanced than their overseas counterparts.[14] The fans soon proved him wrong. The crowd of around 3,000 outside the St George Hotel forced the Beatles to enter the hotel via the bottle shop. Undeterred, the fans maintained a vigil on the Church Street steps behind the hotel. One group was intercepted in the small hours climbing up the fire escape on a mission to 'cut the Beatles' hair'. The following day, the *Evening Post* caught the puzzled mood of its more mature readers: 'The Beatles are not royalty, or war heroes, or even triumphant All Blacks … [F]our young men who look and talk like stewards off an English ship were responsible for a scene never experienced at Wellington airport.'[15]

On the Monday evening, the Beatles played two identical concerts at the Town Hall. Their eleven-song sets, almost inaudible above the screaming of ecstatic fans, lasted less than 30 minutes. The sound system so annoyed John Lennon during the 6 p.m. show that he stormed offstage. It was all a bit much for a sedate city more accustomed to the music of Llew Arnold's Accordion Ensemble, which was issued with a Council permit in 1963 to play at the band rotunda in Oriental Bay. The Beatles were not what the city fathers had in mind when a 1962 Festival of Wellington brochure promised 'dancing in the street'. In August 1964, yet another travelling pop 'spectacular' in the Town Hall drowned out a classical recital upstairs in the Concert Chamber: 'Patrons of the latter function were greatly inconvenienced by noise from amplified musical instruments and also the young persons in the corridors and the light wells between the two halls.'[16]

Armed with disposable income, the baby-boomers went in search of late-night entertainment in a city traditionally closed down by 9.30 p.m. As early as 1961, the City Health Inspector reported that overcrowded, badly lit and poorly ventilated coffee bars were becoming hubs of entertainment for the city's young people. He did, however, concede that such venues were 'providing a needed social life essential to a city such as Wellington, especially those in the younger age group living in rooming establishments and members of crews of ships at port'.[17]

A mini-skirted Walker Brothers fan makes a crash landing on stage at The Big Show at the Town Hall in January 1967. Also on the bill were Roy Orbison and the Yardbirds.

Don Roy, *Dominion*

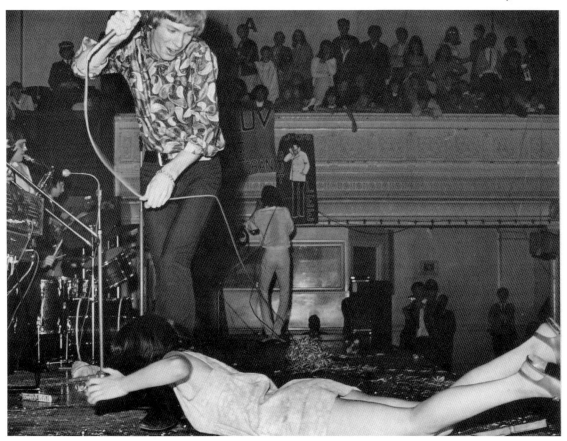

The Citizens-dominated Council was sympathetic. In 1961, the old Municipal Corporations Act was amended to allow patrons of coffee bars such as the Downtown Club on Jervois Quay to dance until 2 a.m. The Council, inadvertently, thus helped to create a 1960s 'beat boom' in the capital, where dozens of local Beatles and Rolling Stones imitators bought guitars, grew their hair, and performed live. Across the city, as many as twenty venues with names such as Teenarama, Warm Leg and the Psychedelic Id hosted a 'mod', later 'hippie', clientele.

It was all a colourful distraction from other, more pressing issues. Wellington was slow to enter the era of the planned city, and the lack of a proper district scheme — or town plan — was becoming an embarrassment. Town planning ideas had first become influential in the 1920s, then dropped from sight as the world economy collapsed. In the post-war years, town planning again became a powerful international movement, as engineers, architects, and planners worked to rebuild Western cities to 'modern' requirements. In Europe, wartime bombing had provided them with a clean slate; but in the United Sates, which had been spared this fate, they sent in the bulldozers instead — all in the name of progress. New Zealand joined the movement via the Town and Country Planning Act 1953, which required local bodies to produce 'master plans'. Aimed at containing urban sprawl, this was an approach based on the allocation and control of land use, with community feedback invited in a formal but limited process.

Excited devotees unfurl a Union Jack during a 1967 Town Hall pop show featuring the Animals, the twins Paul and Barry Ryan, and that '60s mouthful, Dave, Dee, Dozy, Beaky, Mick and Tich.

Don Roy, *Dominion*

Wellington City Council, however, continued to operate an 'undisclosed scheme', basically allowing it to operate in secret, through an informal, non-notified process. The approach suited a closed organisation — one dominated by engineers, not town planners. The City Engineer's Department alone employed up to a third of total Council staff. The men who had always got on with building things saw planning as starry-eyed and utopian. For others, however, proper planning was democracy in action — the way to achieve good decisions on vital issues such as transport and housing.

The municipality, too, was changing. In 1962, the Te Atiawa elder and Labour stalwart Ralph Love was elected to Council, thus bringing a Maori voice to its deliberations for the first time. The once unthinkable practice began of paying councillors for attending meetings. In 1963 they received 30s per meeting, up to a maximum of £76 a year.[18] With the advent of decimal currency in July 1967, the payment was converted to $3.[19] The number of councillors meanwhile increased, from fifteen to eighteen. One of the additions came as a result of the city's decision in 1973 to take over Ohariu Riding from Hutt County.

A Maori voice

In 1962, Makere Rangiatea (Ralph) Love, Te Atiawa elder and public servant, became the first Maori to be elected to the Wellington City Council.

Born in 1907, he was a direct descendant of Wi Tako and the other chiefs who controlled Petone, Ngauranga, and Pipitea at the time of the Treaty of Waitangi. He was educated in Petone, and after leaving school joined the Native (later Maori Affairs) Department, with stints as Assistant Controller of Social Welfare, and Deputy Registrar of the Maori Land Court. He had a strong interest in sport, especially rugby, and was instrumental in the development of Maori rugby.

During his time on the Council, he championed high-density inner-city housing, to allow people to

Ralph Love chats with Springbok forward Chris de Wilzem during the legendary 1956 rugby tour.

ATL, NZ Free Lance Collection, C-24593-1/2

walk to work. In 1965 he left the Council and was elected Mayor of Petone on a Labour ticket.

In his retirement, Love emerged as a national figure, and as a senior kaumatua to his people. As deputy chairman of the Wellington Tenths Trust, he 'lost no opportunity to bring the grievances of his people to public attention'.[20]

A focus of protest on many land issues in Wellington and Taranaki, Love instigated a number of claims to the Waitangi Tribunal on these matters. At the time of his death in 1994, he was still pursuing claims on behalf of his people.

Routed in secrecy

In 1960, the Bolton Street cemetery — resting place of the city's founders — was a pleasant oasis of greenery, popular with lunchtime strollers from nearby government offices. Its central location, on the foothills just west of the inner city, also attracted Ministry of Works (MOW) engineers as they contemplated a suitable route for a motorway through Thorndon to the Basin Reserve. During the 1959 parliamentary session, Kitts rehearsed the arguments for bringing a new highway into the very heart of the city:

> Commercial and industrial concerns have spread into what were originally residential areas, forcing the population out of the city into what are called dormitory suburbs on the outskirts. The result has been an increase in the number of commuters into the city. At present something like 20,000 people come in each day, and the yearly increase in that figure is likely to be 500 a day.[21]

The engineers concluded that the highway should skirt one side of the central city or the other. In 1955, City Engineer F. B. C. Jeffreys had called for an elevated 'expressway' to be constructed along the waterfront to the bottom of Taranaki Street. Councillors warmed to the idea but the cost, estimated at £6 million ($220 million in today's terms), ruled it out.[22] In 1959, an urban motorway for the capital suddenly became a real possibility. In October, Jeffreys had a private briefing by MOW engineers on their final choice — the western foothills option.[23] When he told the Mayor and leading councillors, Kitts offered full co-operation.[24] In June 1960, the Ministry submitted plans to the National Roads Board, based on the western foothills route. A blurry photograph placing the cemetery near the path of the proposed motorway accompanied the documents, but was overlooked. The parties involved kept everything to themselves:

> The extent of National Roads Board/Ministry of Works intentions as to details of a future Wellington motorway facility was at this stage a secret reserved only for those agencies and a few selected Wellington City Council and Corporation individuals.[25]

It was the archetypal planning dilemma: the state with the power and the funds to build a motorway, but still needing the blessing of the local authority. For

Wellington City, it was a matter of not looking a gift horse in the mouth. Faced with a transport crisis, the Council had to strike a difficult balance between a car-infatuated city and a public transport system that was falling out of favour. The omens were bad: when twenty retailers lobbied for shuttle trams on Lambton Quay in 1959, only three of them said they had taken public transport that day.[26] Worse, Council engineers seemed unable or unwilling to address urgent and complex transport issues, such as the need for parking buildings and one-way systems. Cr Gordon Morrison, an engineer who was transport committee chairman, summed up the problem: 'Wellington's narrow streets determine the ability of traffic to move. It has taken 30 years to widen Taranaki Street. Clearly the widening of streets is not a solution to traffic problems.'[27]

The municipality decided to bring in outside consultants — a rare move in the 1960s, but accepted practice within a decade or two. A big firm of American consulting engineers was asked to prepare a transport 'master plan' for Wellington City. Kitts pointed to the Council's lack of in-house planning capacity, and talked of giving the consultants an open brief. It seems clear, however, that for Kitts and his inner circle the western foothills route had been decided on as early as 1960. The stratagem was simple. Consultants De Leuw, Cather and Company were to rubberstamp the Ministry's motorway proposal, and the municipality would approve it. The City Engineer, back from a fact-finding trip to the United States, made this clear to councillors in October 1960.[28] A meeting of municipal and government officials confirmed the decision to bring in the consultants on that basis:

Cr W.G. (Gordon) Morrison, engineer and Council committee 'baron'.

WCA, 00010:2:1

> The Ministry of Works proposals for an urban motorway from Thorndon to Te Aro along a route west of the business area of the city appears to be the only feasible and practical one for the immediate development of the motorway system into Wellington City. The National Roads Board has agreed in principle to the investigation of such a route, which will *be an adopted one* [emphasis added] in any investigation and preparation of a Master Transportation Plan.[29]

In November 1960, a representative of De Leuw, Cather was summoned to Wellington. A fee of US$220,000 (nearly US$3 million in today's terms) was negotiated.[30] The municipality zoned a strip of land from Thorndon Quay to the Basin Reserve as 'motorway' under the Town and Country Planning Act. The western foothills route was thus covertly added to the 'undisclosed' town plan.

Part of Bolton Street cemetery in 1976, with the new motorway flyover under construction. A headstone marking the graves of Mary Ann Noakes and Mary Ann Nye can be seen in the foreground.

ATL, Dominion Post Collection, EP/1976/2436/28

The Roads Board, meanwhile, agreed to pay the full cost of motorway construction and of purchasing properties along the route.[31]

Three years passed. On 21 August 1963, the De Leuw, Cather report was released. Included in the 'master transportation plan' was a street improvement scheme, a one-way street system, off-street car parking, and an ambitious underground extension of the railway system. A 'north west connector' along one side of Aro Valley would provide residents of Karori and Ngaio with a direct route to the city, via a long-discussed tunnel under Raroa Road. One in eight houses in Aro Valley would be demolished to make way for the new highway.

As expected, the consultants recommended a motorway route along the western foothills to the Basin Reserve, although their report avoided any mention of the likely impact on the Bolton Street cemetery. The waterfront route was suggested as a second option. Newspapers were sceptical. The *Dominion* accused the master plan of lacking ideas. A proposed concrete flyover above the Basin Reserve infuriated the Wellington Cricket Association. The Wellington Open Spaces Association referred to an 'acquisitive clique, warranting the forebodings of

On sacred ground

Opponents of the motorway through the Bolton Street cemetery in the 1960s might have learned from the energetic Selwyn King, a Wellington land agent. His 1928 campaign against 'the wholesale knocking down of tombstones' stopped the western access route from slicing through the historic graveyard.[32]

An indistinct newspaper drawing of a proposed tramline route from Lambton Quay to Tinakori Road first aroused King's curiosity. When he studied the Western Access Commission's report at the Town Hall, he discovered that the long-anticipated road to the western suburbs would affect at least a hundred early settlers' graves. He wrote to the Town Clerk, stating that councillors and citizens had been misled by the illustration. It was the beginning of a relentless letter-writing campaign to local newspapers and the municipality.

In a flurry of backroom activity that foreshadowed the events of the 1960s, Mayor Troup worked hard to win the support of historical and community groups such as the Karori Progressive Association, promising an elaborate memorial to replace the affected graves.

As the city anguished over the issue, Troup claimed that an alternative route would cost £50,000 and involve twelve sections. King used his professional knowledge to challenge the figures, estimating the true cost at no more than £20,000: 'and what is £20,000 to a city like Wellington to retain its honour?'[33] A modified route to Tinakori Road was later built, involving far fewer graves.[34]

an earlier generation which had set aside these breathing spaces in an expanding metropolis'. It claimed that the plan was 'inspired by a "vandalism in high places" complex to which Wellingtonians had become too adjusted'.[35]

Kitts made ready to adopt the recommendation for the motorway, as the Roads Board issued its formal blessing. The outstanding problem was the Basin Reserve. A new consultant was hired, British town planner Professor Gordon Stephenson, who concluded that the sports ground could be saved.[36] De Leuw, Cather later produced alternative plans enabling this to happen.[37]

Another year passed. Half a decade after decisions affecting the cemetery were made, nothing had yet been said publicly. Kitts remained confident, however, that in an era of growth and expansion, most ratepayers would still support the planned route. In an address to the Wellington Beautifying Society in 1964, Kitts proposed a memorial park, 'with no question of desecration'.[38] People attending a commemoration service beside the Wakefield family graves were therefore startled later that year when Kitts remarked that settlers' graves and monuments *would* be affected. Nor would they mind, added the Mayor. 'The way I look at it, is that these men of great stature would not want to stand in the way of progress.'[39]

The penny dropped. In October 1964, the Bolton Street Preservation Society emerged from among the city's intellectual and professional elite. Its membership exemplified the media-savvy pressure groups of the 1960s, with some already involved in the Campaign for Nuclear Disarmament (CND) and other 'progressive' causes. Using the typewritten press release, the handbill, and the telephone, such groups cultivated sympathetic journalists and mobilised mass support. The preservation society was formed after a meeting between public servant Dennis Rose and barrister Shirley Smith. Zoology professor John Salmon was elected chairman. Hundreds of copies of a circular letter inviting interested parties to join the struggle were mailed out. The primary aim was to preserve the historic cemetery 'within its present boundaries, free from the encroachment of any motorway or other public work as an open space for public enjoyment and relaxation, and as a memorial to the early settlers of Wellington'.[40]

Newspapers took up the cause. Society members put their energies into supporting an alternative scheme which architect and town planner James Beard had conceived for local retailers. Instead of a motorway extending to Mt Victoria, Beard proposed an improved public transport system, parking buildings, and extensive pedestrian malls. He suggested a route along Grant Road, with a tunnel entering the cemetery under the Seddon Memorial by Anderson Park, and emerging in Shell Gully on The Terrace.

The urban motorway cuts a great swathe through the heart of historic Thorndon.

ATL, Dominion Post Collection, EP/1969/3580/33

It is fundamental that in the growth of our city, and in the interests of economy and amenity, that the preservation of the essential characteristics of Wellington be retained. Our problems of traffic and transport are tending to destroy these characteristics but attempting to solve these problems with wide scale redevelopment is superficial.[41]

For the Ministry of Works, the inability of this route to carry traffic volumes made it expensive and unviable. Dennis Rose now describes the Beard scheme as 'not that convincing an alternative'.[42] Undeterred, society members drafted press statements and submissions, and arranged deputations to local and central authorities, including Prime Minister Keith Holyoake. Powerful supporters of the cause, including retired heads of government departments, became actively involved. The Council's change of heart over the Basin Reserve gave cause for optimism. But it soon became clear that with a state-funded motorway at stake, the Council was less flexible.

The mood soured. Society members had assumed that the motorway proposals had been dreamed up by ugly Americans, not true Wellingtonians. But as it emerged that the Council had been hatching the scheme since 1959, the Mayor's reputation as a consensus builder began to unravel. The *Evening Post* commented:

Early failure to publish details of the proposals restricted the possibility of informed comment at the time when changes could most easily have been made … [T]he failure of the city to publish its plan is denying the citizen his right to participate fully in the planning process.[43]

Cr Olive Smuts-Kennedy, elected in 1965.

WCA, 00010:2:1

Economist William Sutch (Shirley Smith's husband) urged a delay: 'The absence of a proper town plan means that any decision to proceed with the motorway scheme must be premature. Any motorway must be fitted to the city's future expansion and not the other way round.'[44] Outraged articles and 'letters to the editor' filled the local and national press. In December 1964, a *Dominion* feature was headlined: 'Bolton Street Cemetery is our Westminster Abbey'. In similar vein, Olive Smuts-Kennedy, later a city councillor, wrote: 'what a sacrilege it would be if [the city] were all to be made so municipally trim as to take away its soul … [W]e have no ancient buildings and few early relics of a lasting character — the more reason to preserve what we have'.[45]

Others were not convinced. One correspondent criticised the run-down state of the cemetery:

Most of it is overgrown and untidy; it is wet underfoot; most of the paths are not safe when damp; ivy has taken over many graves; others are receptacles for dead leaves or grow weeds; headstones have been damaged and knocked over, and the chapel in the grounds appears to be rotting away ... [W]hy didn't the moaners do something when they had it? This would justify their noise now. As it is, the sooner the MOW put their bulldozers into it, the better.[46]

Kitts ducked for cover. Instead, society members sought answers from Hugh Fullarton, the MOW's District Commissioner of Works and chief architect of the motorway project. He explained that, for economic, engineering and safety reasons, the western foothills route was the logical choice. All that the society could realistically expect was a government commitment that damage to the cemetery would be minimised. Minister of Works Percy Allen asked his officials to explore ways to reduce the likely adverse effects. Among the new proposals was a piazza spanning the motorway, and a park to commemorate those whose graves were displaced. The Ministry channelled effort and considerable resources into its design. Initially, the society welcomed these ideas, then changed its mind. As it became clear that preservation of the cemetery was unlikely, Professor Salmon warned that 'bulldozers and giant earthmoving equipment would rip through settlers' graves'.[47]

As the 1965 local body elections drew near, the decision hung in the balance. The issue of civic participation, highlighted by the motorway controversy, dominated the campaign. Huge public interest in a draft town plan, released in May, indicated a growing mood of civic activism. Eight of the fifteen members of the new Council publicly endorsed a fresh approach to government on the motorway issue. As tenders for constructing the Thorndon overbridge closed in October 1965, the Roads Board refused to be the public scapegoat. One headline read: 'Roads Board Slams Fist On Table Over City Dithering'. The National Roads Board had warned:

> Criticism of the motorway plans had received a lot of publicity and several
> members of the incoming city council seem to have doubts. Should the
> council not confirm its desire to have a motorway past the congested city area,
> then the Board must consider whether or not the construction of the bridge
> and paving of the foreshore motorway to full width should continue.[48]

The Board called on the Mayor to reaffirm his long-standing support for the motorway. No longer was it prepared 'to ride roughshod' over any local authority.

The pressure on Kitts intensified, as it became clear that as many as 2,000 people, mainly in Thorndon, stood to lose their homes. At a meeting with angry residents at the foot of Glenbervie Terrace in October 1965, Kitts blustered that his Council was 'not responsible' for the motorway and therefore had no powers to stop it: 'The only thing the council could do was to ask the National Roads Board and the Ministry of Works to halt the plan. It did not have the authority to compel any Government Department to do anything.'[49]

Yet another consultant was summoned. Professor R. T. Kennedy of Auckland University, reporting in December 1965, confirmed that the western foothills route was sound, with a few reservations. This allowed newly elected councillors to refuse a deputation from the Bolton Street Preservation Society seeking a reappraisal of the scheme and a deferment of construction. Councillors finally — and unanimously — approved the western foothills route.

The opposing forces battled on. Over the next two years, submissions were churned out, mostly focusing on the Beard scheme. But the preservation society had limited powers and resources. On 6 April 1967, following a government edict, the Council closed the cemetery. Although the cause appeared lost, the society sniped on. When a Bill authorising work to start on the cemetery went to Cabinet, Salmon made a comment about 'parliamentary grave-digging in the dark'.[50] The Minister of Works hit back:

Government was carrying out this work at the request of the National Roads Board which was the agent for the Wellington City Council. It was not the government's wish to have a motorway routed through the cemetery, but the wish of the local government of the area.[51]

In 1970, a new one-way system was introduced in the inner city in an attempt to overcome traffic congestion. In this view of Featherston Street, a van in the foreground traverses Grey Street, while a trolley bus crosses on Panama Street.

ATL, Dominion Post Collection, EP/1970/0362/33

At a public meeting in Thorndon, Cr Morrison finally conceded that the Council was responsible for the decision. His reference to the temptations facing every cash-starved local authority could serve as an epitaph for the whole motorway fiasco: 'In effect, although some other transport system might be technically preferable, the important consideration was that the [National Roads] Board had the money and was prepared to spend it.'[52]

Motorway construction began. The Council investigated ways to dismantle the cemetery and move its occupants, as the Ministry insisted this was not its responsibility. Council officers, including the City Sexton, P.J.E. Shotter, were appointed to the task. In 1966 they visited Auckland to see how its council was shifting graves at Symonds Street cemetery to make way for an urban motorway. They learned that the Auckland City Council was leaving the whole grisly process to the Ministry of Works. At Bolton Street, efforts were made to record all of the graves due to be disturbed, using photographs and film. A history of the cemetery was commissioned. Next of kin were approached, and a number of funeral ceremonies were performed before a common grave, known as the memorial grave, could be prepared.

The motorway emerged from the rubble of Thorndon houses and their leafy surrounds. In 1969, the first stage was opened. Work then began on moving the residents of Bolton Street cemetery. The area was closed off, with the work of the bulldozers screened from public view. Human remains were moved to the memorial grave in cardboard containers. Work proceeded slowly, as it became clear that many more than the expected 700 graves were involved. More than a thousand 'unknown' burials came to light; by 1972, the total number of disinterments had reached 3,693. Dennis Rose, secretary of the preservation society, pointed out that the campaign had put a stop to some of the more destructive proposals: 'We succeeded in preventing a northbound off ramp dropping down onto Bowen Street. This would have swept away an extra block of the cemetery. I always feel good about it as I drive past.'[53]

Housing the people

On 26 August 1965, as the local body elections approached, Kitts found a welcome distraction from the motorway debacle in the opening of the first stage of Hanson Court flats. The 30 low-rental units, on the fringes of Newtown, were the Council's first tentative foray into public housing — a civic endeavour that would eventually produce affordable high-density homes for thousands of citizens, in such iconic structures as the Te Ara Hou flats in Newtown, the Arlington Flats, and the Central Park flats. The resulting 2,300 units would make the Council one of the country's biggest residential landlords.

The decision to venture into rental housing was largely due to the efforts of George Porter, the energetic chairman of the Council's housing committee. A former architect with the housing division of the Public Works Department, he shared the Modernist belief of many post-war planners that most people didn't know what was good for them. Porter's

Parking meters first appeared on city streets in 1953, and 'meter maids' made their debut a decade later. The first intake wore a military-style uniform of navy blue skirts, white shirts and black ties, but by the 1970s the Wool Board had designed this sky blue outfit, complete with cap and knee-high boots.

ATL, Dominion Post Collection, EP-Transport-Parking-01

campaign to make public housing a major local body function stirred up long-banished ghosts of municipal socialism, and suspicions that the Corporation was heading towards a new role as a provider of social services. But as a planner, Porter also believed that the city needed to rejuvenate its limited land base and lift rateable values. It proved a difficult task. Porter was forced to do battle with his committee colleagues, his Citizens caucus, an often resistant Council, and Corporation officers with other responsibilities and agendas. But along the way, he single-handedly pulled together the administrative infrastructure for both housing and town planning.

Porter's mission had begun in 1962 as the municipality hosted a conference on urban renewal and councillors set up a separate housing committee. He put together a programme covering pensioner flats, public rental housing, housing for sale to the public, and housing for corporation staff. Porter capitalised on the government's desire to move away from a quarter-century of directly providing state houses. The state was happy to pass the baton to local authorities, with their detailed knowledge of local housing needs, especially among groups such as pensioners. The scene was set for local bodies to embark on often elaborate

Demolition of 'decadent' nineteenth-century dwellings accelerated through the 1960s, as urban renewal and public housing became the new preoccupation. Here, Mayor Frank Kitts poses in front of a Nairn Street house being torn down to make way for Council multi-storey flats.

WCA, 00340:0:496

housing programmes funded by cheap government loans, with planning carried out at local level. Above all, Porter believed that tackling a long-standing housing shortage would safeguard Wellington's economic viability:

> Since private and public efforts have been unable to meet the problem, it follows that special efforts are essential if the city is to reach its full potential in the future. There is now evidence of an awareness in local government and civic organizations and a growing impetus towards effective action.[54]

Porter became a legend for his readiness to badger successive Housing Ministers by mobilising regular deputations to their parliamentary offices. Representatives of the Auckland, Christchurch and Dunedin city councils joined him. The interest rate for loans under the Housing Corporation's urban renewal redevelopment scheme was pegged at a modest 3.5 percent. In 1962, the Local Authorities Loans Board approved Cr Porter's application for the Council to borrow £230,000 for the Hanson Court project. The flats were later opened in style, with the Minister of Housing, John Rae, among the invited dignitaries.

In 1963, the Corporation turned its attention to the 'cabbage patch', an ugly collection of corrugated iron and wooden shacks sprawling over several acres at

The Wellington City Council's foray into public housing began here, in Hanson Street, Newtown, in 1965. This great civic endeavour eventually created some 2,300 units, producing affordable high-density homes for thousands and making the WCC one of the country's biggest residential landlords.

WCA, 00508:0:01074

the intersection of Nairn Street and Brooklyn Road. The properties were bought up, tenants re-housed, buildings demolished, and land cleared to make way for high-rise blocks of flats. Porter was happy to bring like-minded visionaries into his team: the flats were designed by Warwick Keen, an associate from the *Te Aro Replanned* days of the 1940s. Mayor Kitts, who saw Cr Porter as a fellow socialist in Citizens' clothing, was content to let him establish his fiefdom. Yet Porter still battled to get individual schemes implemented. One useful vehicle was a housing development subcommittee, where he cracked the whip over his Council colleagues and Corporation officers. Yet he was also willing to delegate, once others had proved their worth:

> [It was] a joint committee of councillors and officers chaired by Cr Porter himself, to review regularly the progress made in implementing each housing construction proposal from initial investigation to completion. As soon as the chairman was satisfied that this sub-committee would work smoothly if left to the officers, he resigned from it.[55]

Porter also worked behind the scenes to ensure that the municipality produced its town plan. The furore over the Bolton Street cemetery sent a clear message that citizens expected to be informed about and involved in their city's future. Besides, a published plan was years overdue. Auckland City Council's provisional district scheme reached the objection stage as early as 1958, becoming operative in 1961. Wellington City planners, meanwhile, occupied a sleepy corner of the City Engineer's Department. In 1964, British town planning consultant Professor Gordon Stephenson called for the establishment of a separate town planning department, with a staff of nineteen. Describing the existing planning office as 'sadly undermanned', he advocated a strong group of qualified planners.[56]

By July 1964, no decision had yet been taken. Cr Porter and his committee colleagues remained at loggerheads on the issue. Porter threatened to resign unless Stephenson's recommendations were implemented; he described town planning as the 'most vital' of the Council's functions, and one that needed to be recognised as such, and not treated as a 'departmental sideline'.[57] Some within Council argued that the proposed move was premature. Meanwhile, the municipal scrap attracted wider interest. Referring to Porter's threat to resign, the *Dominion* commented that Wellington could 'ill-afford his going'. It went on to condemn the Council for its continuing failure to publish a town plan:

[Wellington] is a city dying at the centre. This is no good for retailers, for industry or the capital's future. The almost dead heart of Wellington can be rejuvenated only by promoting urgent redevelopment that brings new citizens into the central area, not drives existing ones out into the increasingly distant and expensive dormitory suburbs.[58]

Porter and Labour sympathisers resorted to political subterfuge. Working with Labour councillor Gerald O'Brien, an experienced political operator, Porter introduced a written proposal for a stand-alone planning division. He took the action late in a Council meeting as officers were getting ready to go home. Councillors were then visited to gauge their support. O'Brien recalled his meeting with prominent Citizens councillor Dennis McGrath: 'He was a powerful intellectual force on council and might have been dangerous to our cause. He said "I know why you're here — you have the numbers. For the sake of the city, I will make it unanimous"'.[59]

Their manoeuvrings had the desired effect. After his superior resigned midway through 1964, Ken Clark, a mid-ranked member of staff, was asked if he could produce a District Scheme in a year:

> When I said I could, somehow a Town Planning department was established and I was appointed City Planner with Professor Kennedy our consultant. I was too young to be allowed to go it alone. I was lucky to have a good staff and we duly produced a scheme. We went through all the legal hoops and eventually had an 'Operative District Scheme'. The Town Plan controlled the direction of the city's land use and of its growth. The new department comprised not only town planning but also housing development and survey. Other functions were added later as I was accepted as a suitable Head. I was on the same standing as the CE [City Engineer] and all the other Heads of Department. Some were surprised I had done so well.[60]

Clark completed his draft scheme in May 1965, and it was officially released at a meeting in the Town Hall attended by 700 citizens. Detailed street-by-street, building-by-building maps, specifying how every square inch of the city should be used, were unveiled. Under the new planning regime, citizens who disagreed with any aspect of the plan could object in a formal and public process. Wellington's new town plan was even celebrated in a television special. The local branch of the New Zealand Institute of Architects called the plan 'the most important civic event since the war'.[61]

At the end of 1966, the Council finalised the massive document, which covered zoning, traffic and development proposals for the next twenty years. The plan also reflected the current assumption that the population of the Wellington region would double in the final decades of the century. One popular recommendation was to turn Cuba Street into a pedestrian mall. While the focus on town planning ushered in a new era of 'people power', it also created heavier workloads for standing committees. Members of the town planning committee, for example, were relieved of all other assignments. One member recalled a meeting which began at 11 a.m. and continued, with meal breaks, until 11 p.m.

As the impact of the motorway construction was felt, Cr Porter turned his attention back to housing, forming a 'motorway re-housing' committee to help those displaced from their homes. It was 'morally wrong', he argued, to evict older people, and he pledged to secure a guarantee that alternative homes would be found.[62] This resulted in a flurry of deputations to the Works and Housing ministers, both of whom welcomed Porter's suggestion of a joint process for re-housing people affected by the motorway. Works Minister Percy Allen went further, suggesting a 'top level liaison', based on regular meetings to discuss 'joint planning in a capital city'.[63] In 1966, a century after the seat of government moved to Wellington, a 'capital commission' of parliamentarians and city councillors was formed. Beyond housing, agreement was needed on the development of the so-called Government Centre to house the growing ranks of public servants. The master plan encompassed the Bowen, Vogel, Rutherford, Fergusson and Freyberg buildings, with open spaces and linking roadways between them, sprawling across 30 acres of Thorndon.

Two committees shaped the new city/state consensus, covering its technical and political dimensions. The first, the capital city planning technical committee, was made up of officials from the Ministry of Works, New Zealand Railways, the Harbour Board and the City Council. The second, the capital city planning policy committee, chaired by Allen, was composed of city councillors and Housing Minister Rae. The technical committee met every six weeks, with the politicians getting together at least twice a year. Porter, however, soon became disillusioned with the stately pace of progress.

In 1967, councillors agreed to a ministerial request to close off part of Sydney Street West for the construction of the Charles Fergusson building. The City Engineer, however, lamented the lack of a policy-making or approving body within government to deal specifically with the planning of the Government Centre.[64] Agreement on the construction of Rutherford House dragged, especially as the

Council wanted to locate a transport centre there, and four suburban transport authorities already used the site. The *Dominion* quoted an unnamed councillor who claimed that Wellington City was 'playing host to a greedy and unappreciative child'.[65] Cr Morrison blamed the Ministers involved:

> As soon as we raise an objection to Government activities which interfere materially with our [town] plan, the committee of Ministers and Councillors ceases to function. This is not the fault of Government officers, who work under extremely trying conditions. Whenever a conflict of interest, or a difference of opinion arises, they are immediately subjected to extreme pressures by the Ministers concerned. These Ministers are interested only in the matter affecting their own particular department. If they want a building within the centre, and the Government Architect has looked one out, they will insist on having it — whatever effect such a decision may have on the overall Town Plan.[66]

The relationship soon reverted to traditional levels of testiness and suspicion. In 1970, after press reports that the government had bullied the municipality to close a road by the Cenotaph, Allen expressed his displeasure in a letter to Council:

> The closing of this section of the street was not a ministerial requirement. I am informed that the proposal was initiated by the city engineer … I have endeavoured at all times to ensure the highest degree of co-operation between government and local authorities. To this end I proposed the establishment of a capital city planning committee to co-ordinate government and city planning, and I think you will agree that this has helped iron out a lot of problems where there could have been conflicts. It is disturbing to me as it must be to you to have ill-formed statements which could upset the harmonious relations which I believe now exist.[67]

The citizenry strike back

1968 has been called 'the year of the barricades'. It has come to symbolise an era of social and political upheaval across the world, much of it galvanised by opposition to American military involvement in Vietnam. Prime Minister Keith Holyoake's decision in 1965 to dispatch a small number of New Zealand troops to the conflict sparked widespread protest, much of it co-ordinated locally by the Committee on Vietnam. Its members sought permission to hold lunchtime forums in front of the Central Library, and were instead offered the small grassy island around Queen Victoria's statue on Cambridge Terrace.[68] Later, they got their way. When US president Lyndon Johnson passed through the capital in 1966, he was stalked by protestors, although most citizens were happy to greet 'LBJ'.

The formal opening of Parliament in June 1968 was abandoned as a result of mass demonstrations, with Governor-General Sir Arthur Porritt being forced to enter by a side door. Anti-war demonstrations became a routine part of city life, along with lunchtime 'teach-ins' outside the Central Library, which were said to disturb library staff.[69] A 'Peace, Power and Politics' conference at the Town Hall in 1968 gave the local anti-war movement a taste of the tumultuous events in Chicago, Paris and Saigon. A crowd of 1,400 heard speeches from such prominent campaigners as the former Indian Defence Minister, V. K. Krishna Menon, Professor Conor Cruise O'Brien, and British-American film-maker Felix Greene.

Many middle-class 'baby boomers' channelled the passions unleashed by anti-war protests into social movements which embraced women's rights, civil rights, the environment, and gay and lesbian rights. In 1970, members of the newly formed Wellington Women's Liberation Front engaged in 'feminist pub liberations', demanding to be served in the public bar of the New City hotel on Majoribanks Street. Other local women battled for the Council to provide childcare facilities, a cause that dated back half a century to the town planning conference of 1919. One woman recalled:

> Approaches to the City Council didn't have much effect and I grew quite monomaniac about child care centres. Whenever I walked through town I saw potential playgrounds and crèches, but I knew there was little I could do as long as I did not commit myself ... [T]he answer of the 'local body' was the offer of a house in Adelaide Road which could be used until it was demolished in a few years' time. Cost of bringing it up to bylaw standards — $5000.[70]

Young Maori activists, emulating the Black Power movements in the US, coalesced in groups such as Nga Tamatoa. Protests were mounted at Waitangi, and a 33,000-strong petition was presented to Parliament in 1972 calling for Maori to be taught in schools. Other groups worked to build an alternative society based on notions of revolutionary liberation. A left-wing activist group, Progressive Youth Movement, turned its attention to Wellington's housing, conducting a survey in a depressed area which revealed exorbitant rents and poor living conditions.[71] Some alternative thinkers left the city to establish rural communes. Others sought out old houses at low rents for urban communal living and, in some cases, for a crèche. One squatter group, the self-styled Slum Stormers, claimed it was 'a crime to leave these houses empty when there are people who need a home'.[72]

Another housing activist was poet James K. Baxter, who at the end of 1971 asked the Council for a house to accommodate 30 members of his 'tribe' of bare-footed, long-haired followers. Cr Porter, seeing Baxter as 'attempting to cater for a definite social need', asked the Housing Minister for 'an old house in the path of the motorway which could be rented temporarily to Mr Baxter and his community'.[73] But the poet couldn't wait, and soon moved his tribe into a mansion at 26 MacDonald Crescent 'with no lighting and no water and three smashed grots'. They stayed on, free of rates and rent, for six weeks until municipal sanitary inspectors declared the building unfit for human habitation.[74] In his poem 'Firetrap Castle Song', Baxter recalled his exchange with the Council:

> I said maybe I'd have to grab a house
> If the City Council couldn't come up
> With something better than thirty dollars a week
> For a ramshackle derelict hovel.
> The council got worried, they told me to cool it,
> I talked to Mrs Campbell and Mr Porter,
> They had no houses, they said, but Mr Carlin
> Would write to the Ministry of Works about it.[75]

In 1971 Cr Porter was at the height of his powers — leader of the Citizens group on Council, and often described as the de facto Mayor.[76] The arch-planner now turned his attention to 'renewing' the historic Aro Valley, with its crumbling wooden cottages and transient population of Maori, Pacific Islanders and students, many of whom resembled Baxter's followers. The valley was singled out to be the prototype for the Council's first Comprehensive Urban Redevelopment Area (CURA), under the terms of the Urban Renewal and Housing Improvement Amendment Act 1969. The government would meet the cost of planning, land acquisition and clearance, and subsequent construction.

It was a planner's dream. The valley was to be geographically divided into five-year 'development zones' spanning two decades, during which time the existing population of 1,200 was expected to nearly treble. The aim of the $10 million scheme was to replace one hundred houses with multi-storey concrete blocks of flats aimed at pensioners and single people; four-bedroom 'communal flats'

Known as the 'de facto Mayor', Cr George Porter, architect, planner and visionary, was a determined individual who single-handedly drove the Council's public housing policy.

WCA, 00010:2:1

and shops were also to be included. During 1972 two Council planners worked full-time on the scheme. A decision was made not to consult formally with affected residents, on the grounds that this would slow progress.[77] However, the Council's first community services officer was sent to brief local residents on the CURA, and a planning officer was based at a community house at 48 Aro Street.

Community unease grew. On 20 July 1973, ministerial approval of the scheme was granted. Five days later the visiting Australian Federal Minister of Housing, Les Johnson, questioned the Council's approach. In front of a *Dominion* journalist, he put Cr Porter on the spot:

> Do you have some sort of privileged position whereby you can tell people what they will have and what they should like? Back home they wouldn't trust me to say how a place will be developed. There are too many organizations, pressure groups, minority groups of all descriptions, the labour movement, environmental organizations, town planners — you name them — they all want a say in what happens.[78]

It should have served as a warning. Six weeks later, Crs Porter and David Shand, flanked by three Council officials, faced a hostile crowd of 150 people in the Matauranga School hall on Aro Street. For two and a half hours they were quizzed on whether houses would be 'acquired' by Council, as had been proposed. Porter, taken aback by their angry reception, told the chairperson: 'I am quite prepared to stay at home and watch television … I don't need to be here.' Cr Shand was more conciliatory, telling the packed hall: 'You seem to think that this is all a *fait accompli*. I want to emphasise that it is not.'[79]

The Council backtracked, offering free legal advice to residents wishing to make objections by a revised deadline, and appointing a full-time community worker to the area. Meanwhile, an Aro Valley Action Committee emerged from among owner-occupiers, tenants and landlords, and met with Porter. The committee displayed formidable skills, negotiating alternatives to the proposed CURA scheme, and later helping to persuade the Council to abandon the proposed 'North West connector' highway through the valley (the town planning committee conceded that this road would have a 'stultifying effect on the development and aspirations in the Aro Street area').[80] The action committee was later acknowledged as a prototype for the community councils recommended in Labour's Local Government Act 1974.

To the Upland Road

In 1973, a serious accident on the Wellington Cable Car changed the face of one of the city's most famous tourist attractions. State-of-the-art Swiss technology later replaced what was essentially a brace of Edwardian-era trams and trailers, counterbalanced on a 2 km long wire rope.

The service was first proposed in the late 1890s by the Upland Estate Company to transport people from the city to its planned subdivision in Kelburn. In 1902, the service was launched by the Kelburn and Karori Tramway Company: 'The experience of being wafted effortlessly into the regions above is an exhilarating one,' reported the *New Zealand Times*.[81]

The immediate success of the service led to an attempt by the municipality to take it over in 1910, but ratepayers objected. By 1912, as the new Kelburn Park gained a reputation as the 'favourite playground of the city', passenger numbers on the Cable Car had topped a million a year.[82]

In 1933, the Tramway Company was compelled to change its winding mechanism from steam-power to electricity. The City Council finally succeeded in buying the service in 1946, following accusations that it was running a competitive bus service to undercut the Cable Car.

Deregulation of the transport industry has seen the Cable Car remain in Council hands, with increasing emphasis being placed on the tourist potential of the service.

By 1974, as petrol trebled in price, long-term planning ventures like the Aro Valley CURA were falling out of favour. The rules governing state-funded works tightened, with local bodies being asked for a 'social and physical environmental audit on all major projects before they are approved'.[83] Cr Porter saw this as the last bureaucratic straw. In June, he asked his colleagues for 'leave of absence from all meetings'.[84] Without Porter there as catalyst, the Aro Valley scheme lost momentum. A modified form was later approved, but only a fraction of the proposed housing units were ever built. The Aro Valley community had shown itself to be a formidable opponent.

> If the council's proposals had been introduced in 1963, it is unlikely that they would have met with the level of resistance encountered, if any at all. Society had changed in a variety of ways. At the most general level, one can point to the critical role of television in reducing the apparent distance between ruler and the ruled.[85]

As the 1960s party ended, the economy stumbled and inflation began a steady rise. The WCC woke up with an infrastructural and financial hangover, as this 1973 Lodge cartoon illustrates.

ATL, courtesy Debby Edwards, B-134-451

Green shoots

By the 1960s, environmental awareness was seeping into the national consciousness. In 1966, the Council terminated its night-soil collection service, a hidden if necessary civic evil dating back to the Town Board days. Few mourned the passing of the 'night-men' and their unspeakable cargoes. When a £3 million addition to Palmer Head outfall was completed in 1965, the Corporation boasted that every building in Wellington was now connected to the sewers. This project, known as the Main Drainage Rehabilitation, was the first major overhaul of the sewerage system since it was laid down in the 1890s. In his 1966 annual report, the City Engineer claimed 'it has capacity for the anticipated development for many years ahead'.[86] His confidence was misplaced. In 1965, his own departmental laboratory again detected sewage pollution on the beaches of the inner and outer harbour.[87]

The quickening in ecological awareness was played out in Parliament. Regulations were passed in the early 1960s, defining water quality standards and prescribing permits for every waste outfall. The Water and Soil Conservation Act 1967 emphasised water quality and allocation, with the role of the Pollution Advisory Council broadened to include the classification of all rivers and coastal waters. Under these classifications, regional catchment authorities were obliged to maintain water quality standards. Anyone discharging pollutants into a natural body of water needed a permit to do so. Certain areas of coastline were designated for sewage discharge; others were kept sufficiently pure for swimming.

Expensive replacement works looked likely for the city's sewerage system. In 1969, the Pollution Advisory Council (PAC) recommended treatment plants 'to improve the quality of the effluent before discharge into the harbour precinct'.[88] Mayor Kitts subsequently supported the notion of a committee charged with pollution issues, 'as this is becoming a problem for Wellington'.[89] Meanwhile, the PAC issued a preliminary classification for the city's coastal waters. Councillors heard that the pollution of Wellington Harbour was increasing 'to an alarming degree'.[90] Midway through 1971, as the PAC prepared to release its final damning classification, the Council decided to seek expert advice on the seriousness of the problem. Professor Salmon, head of the Zoology Department at Victoria University (and former Bolton Street cemetery campaigner), was approached. At a seminar on conservation in the region in 1970, Salmon had expressed concern at the level of sewage pollution in the harbour:

> It is polluted to a stage where anything could happen to it. If pollution continues to go on, there could be a biological catastrophe such as happened at Boston, Massachusetts a few years ago. If the pollution is brought under control it seems likely that the harbour will gradually recover, but at present, large areas of Wellington harbour are sterile of marine life, and marine life elsewhere is rapidly disappearing.[91]

By now environmental groups were making their presence felt. In 1972, a deputation from Action for the Environment asked councillors to explore ways of retaining 'as much natural vegetation and bush as possible'.[92] A standing committee on the environment was established the following year. The move coincided with the election of an environmentally aware Labour government, which harnessed massive public opposition to the raising of Lake Manapouri for hydro-electricity generation. The incoming Prime Minister, Norman Kirk, was quick to appoint Joe Walding as an activist Minister for the Environment.[93] However, Walding's requests for environmental audits were not appreciated by Wellington councillors, who baulked at paying an additional $50,000 a year to treat the effluent discharged at Moa Point. Talk of 'biological catastrophe' was greeted with scepticism: 'the evidence to date is conflicting — possibly due to seasonal variations, and the results are by no means conclusive.' Councillors did, however, concede that 'there are indications that the present discharge from Moa Point may be a source of pollution'.[94]

At the start of 1974, an economy based on imported oil reeled with the impact of huge price increases. The government prohibited sales of petrol between noon on Saturdays and 7 a.m. on Mondays. Economic activity stalled as inflation increased and the long upward trend in unemployment continued. Conservationists saw the crisis as both highlighting the vulnerability of the 'motor age', and disproving the popular view that planning and poured concrete could solve all of society's problems. As the local body elections approached, councillors gave permission for the Values Party (the country's first 'Green' party) to hold a series of political meetings in the new Cuba Mall and on the lawn in front of the Central Library. As the middle-class face of the counterculture, the Values Party was gaining a following for its environmental and survivalist platform. Values mayoral candidate Tony Brunt, aged 27, spoke of zero economic and population growth, and the need for the Council to reach out to the dispossessed.

Mayor Kitts was expected to win another term. By 1969 he had worn the mayoral robes for thirteen years, beating Hislop's record. An *Evening Post* editorial from that year, calling for 'more positive Mayoral leadership on controversial issues', suggested that the city wanted more than a tea-party mayor.[95] A familiar sight on his daily strolls to the Town Hall from his Mt Victoria home, Kitts had become an institution. But by the 1970s his presidential approach seemed to belong to more certain times. This would show on polling day, November 1974, as a mayoral institution was voted out of office.

Friday night shopping on Willis Street in the early 1960s.

Painting by W.W. Stewart, courtesy Graham Stewart, Grantham House Publishing

Mayor Fran Wilde and councillors at work.

WCA, 5408:003

This sketch of mine is of our
cable car. Help me and my
Citizens candidates get this and
and our city really moving.
There is so much to do to make this
City grow in beauty, trade and
excitement, and we really want
you to be involved with us in the
challenge.

Michael Fowler

CITIZENS MAYORAL CANDIDATE

In the run-up to the 1974 local body elections, Wellingtonians opened their letterboxes to find this distinctive calling card from mayoral candidate Michael Fowler. The gimmick helped propel him into office.

Redmer Yska

The municipal vehicle fleet in the Council's distinctive yellow livery, late 1980s.

Julia Brooke-White

The Michael Fowler Centre, with the City to Sea Bridge and lagoon in the foreground.

Julia Brooke-White

The harbour from the City to Sea Bridge.

Café society emerges along
1990s Cuba Street.

WCA, 45294:0026

The bright lights of
Courtenay Place, which
during the 1990s emerged
as the heart of the city's
entertainment district.

WCA, 2002-05-01

Crowds line the red carpet in Courtenay Place for the world premiere of Peter Jackson's *The Lord of the Rings: The Return of the King.*

WCA, 2003-12-01

Elijah Wood (Frodo) pauses to sign autographs at the *Lord of the Rings* premiere.

WCA, 2003-12-19

One of Peter Jackson's fell-beasts glowers over Courtenay Place from its eyrie atop the Embassy Theatre, while Queen Victoria looks on indulgently from her Kent Terrace pedestal.

Kevin Stent

New Year's Eve crowds in Civic
Square.

Sea Change

Chapter 8

Chapter 8

1975–1990

I am a descendant of Tara who came to this area and founded its settlement six hundred years ago … [T]hose of us descended from Tara through Tuteremoana could consider the Moa Point area our turangawaewae [spiritual home].[1]

Ray Ahipene-Mercer, 21 July 1986

On Monday 13 October 1975, Trevor Rupe, better known as Carmen, stood on the steps of Parliament in the rain to greet the Maori Land March. The historic walk from Te Hapua in the Far North had begun a month earlier with a trickle of marchers; now more than 7,000 thronged Lambton Quay, 15 abreast. At their head was 79-year-old Whina Cooper, carrying the flag of Te Roopu o te Matakite. Prime Minister Bill Rowling, his suit dripping, later accepted her 'Memorial of Rights' signed by 60,000 people, including tribal elders from across the nation. Their mission: that 'not one more acre' of land be lost to Pakeha or Crown ownership.

It was a big day for the city. The *Dominion* reported that many of the Council's Maori workmen took the day off to look after Te Matakite elders and their families, some of whom were housed at the old Central Park hospital.[2] Mayor Michael Fowler hosted a midday reception for the marchers at Pigeon Park, and even carried hot coffee to Nathan Dun Mihaka and other militants after they pitched a breakaway 'tent embassy' in Parliament grounds. The Town Clerk, Ian McCutcheon, took a sterner line, turning down a request for a $50 donation from Council 'to keep the Maori marchers marching'.[3]

209

In the early 1970s, Carmen's International Coffee Lounge at 86 Vivian Street heralded a new spirit of civic hedonism; its $1 cover charge included a free coffee.

Ans Westra

At 39, Carmen's political views were probably more aligned with Te Matakite than with the youthful firebrands of Nga Tamatoa.[4] She had been raised with six brothers and sisters on a tribal block outside Taumarunui, in a farmhouse without electricity. Her father had Maniapoto links; her mother was descended from Ngati Haua. As a transsexual, prostitute and businesswoman, Carmen seemed an unlikely spearhead for the great urban migration of Maori in the 1950s and 1960s. She had returned to the capital in 1967, via Mt Crawford Prison, Auckland and Sydney, and opened her infamous International Coffee Lounge at 86 Vivian Street. Encrusted with jewels, her hair stacked high, and her ample body encased in floor-length gowns, Carmen wafted around the tables, chatting with her colourful clientele, supplying illegal alcohol and arranging sexual assignations. She became a gate-keeper for the city's secret life: her claims to know about gay and bisexual MPs even saw her hauled before an outraged Parliamentary Privileges Committee.

The election of Norman Kirk's Labour government in 1972 had been a coming-out ball of sorts for the post-war baby-boomers, a generation that valued tolerance and alternative lifestyles as much as an independent foreign policy. Carmen symbolised a new spirit of civic hedonism, her Vivian Street establishment becoming a refuge from the stalled economy, rising prices and unemployment of the latter 1970s. This chapter explores the city's evolution over fifteen years, from sensible public service town to the colourful and sophisticated metropolis envisaged by Carmen.

Hurricane Michael

Michael Fowler's narrow victory in the 1974 mayoral election was another sign that a restrained age was passing. His *joie de vivre* was an infectious contrast to the worthy but grey Kitts. When a reporter told Fowler that Newtown zoo lacked any lions, he quipped that the last ones had died of boredom. It was a good joke: typical of the personality, flair and iconoclasm this working architect and unashamed Modernist brought to the mayoral table.

Fowler is perhaps best known for tackling the seismic vulnerability of inner-city buildings, described by a prominent earthquake engineer as a 'terrible risk'.[5] At the same time, he helped create a development frenzy which ripped off the brick-and-plaster face of the old city, replacing it with shining glass and steel. During Fowler's term, half of the 187 at-risk buildings along the city's Golden Mile were bowled, including the ornate Victorian 'wedding cake' structures on the west side of Lambton Quay. The 'Empire City' of Seddon and Massey was no more. Towering cranes were

Nevile Lodge's view of the 1974 mayoral contest between Kitts and Fowler.

ATL, courtesy Debby Edwards, B-134-518

to crowd the city skyline as structures like the 30-storey BNZ building, with its impenetrable black exterior, rose above a devastated central business district.[6] Few owners took up the costly option of strengthening their buildings, although a few treasures such as the Public Trust Office and the State Insurance Building survived. Some hail Fowler's courage in tackling a long-neglected problem. Critics say that his legacy is, in heritage terms, an impoverished city.

Fowler's ambition was always plain. Born in Feilding in 1930, he attended Christ's College as a boarder, and later became an architect. In 1968 he was elected to the Wellington City Council, having told the astonished chairman of the Citizens team in a preliminary interview that he wanted to be Mayor. In 1972, Fowler stood for the National Party in the Hutt electorate, but lost in the Labour landslide. He turned back to the Wellington mayoralty. In the run-up to the 1974 local body elections, thousands of people opened their letterboxes to find a calling card printed on textured paper, with an iconic sketch in best 1970s sepia of the Wellington cable car. The card urged voters to get the city moving, to help it 'grow in beauty, trade and excitement'. This campaign strategy had worked for Fowler in 1968:

After the plodding Kitts mayoralty, Michael Fowler's youthfulness and vitality seemed palpable.

WCA, 00340:173

> Nobody knew me in the council or in the city. I got on [the Council] because I had a Gestetner copier in the office. I churned out 40,000 copies of a pamphlet which my family and our friends put into almost every letterbox in Wellington. I said my name is Michael Fowler, ten times. I said what I was going to do, which was pretty brief, and then I signed it.[7]

By 1974 he had refined his approach. Using a technique that would become his trademark, he raised a campaign budget of $10,000 by asking 50 people to contribute $200 each. Public relations swallowed up $1,800 of this amount, with consultant Dai Hayward grooming a largely unknown candidate and using the slogan 'tea party mayor' to attack Kitts.[8] Privately, Fowler never expected to win, and he only secured the mayoralty by several hundred special votes after weeks of waiting.

The Fowler mayoralty was to be about openness, informality and consultation: a deliberate contrast with that of his predecessor. Another hallmark of the new regime was Fowler's boundless sociability. Former committee clerk Graeme Peterson recalls being summoned to the Mayor's office early one working day, where a briefing to the boss was capped off by several large gins. When he blearily returned to his desk at around 10 a.m., his colleagues asked what had happened to him.[9] Fowler took part in a weekly late-night talkback programme on Radio Windy. Council and committee meetings were opened up to the public. In another departure from tradition, the Mayor no longer donned 'plumage' for such meetings. Fowler also engineered a series of public forums where citizens were invited to air their views on the city's problems, and hear about the solutions the Council was planning.

We used to meet outside the library on the lawn. Councillors like Betty Campbell always came. The first time there were about 40 people there. We were saying, 'What shall we do with the city?' We talked about housing, public as well as private, and about densities. We talked about the harbour, the Town Belt and transport. We had seven or eight of these things, but by the time we got to the last meeting we needed six buses and tore up to the top of Mt Victoria, looked down and talked about the buildings below.[10]

On the carts

From the days of horse-drawn rubbish carts, the men responsible for Wellington's backdoor rubbish collection gave its City Council a human face.

At the start of the twentieth century, 'scavengers' loaded household rubbish into cast-iron receptacles and carted it to the Corporation Destructor for burning. Motorised trucks and the burial of rubbish had become the norm by the late 1930s, part of the 'controlled tipping' system that began at the Chaytor Street tip in Karori (now Appleton Park).

By the 1960s, the 'dusties' had become a Wellington institution as they scaled flights of steps in search of backdoor rubbish bins, a canvas sack over their shoulder. The early start and finish made a job 'on the carts' popular with university students (including the author) and with sportsmen keen to keep fit. All dusties dreaded the 'wet bin', where filthy water accompanied the rubbish that was emptied from bin to sack. Dogs and broken glass were other hazards.

Calls to terminate or contract out the service grew louder in the 1970s, as industrial problems increased and other cities axed similar services. But councillors were mindful that for ratepayers in the hillier suburbs, the 'dusties' were a boon, as the quantities of beer and other treats left out for them at Christmas could testify.

By the end of the deregulating 1980s, claims that the backdoor service was inefficient and expensive were finally being heeded. Environmental issues, such as rubbish recycling, were also seen as relevant. A few councillors held out, claiming that no single proposal had ever evoked as many protests. In 1993 a kerbside collection was introduced, bringing a chapter in the city's history to an end.

Fowler's dream

Consultation, however, would soon get in the way of Fowler's greater mission: to create a new cultural centre to lift Wellington 'out of the doldrums' and enhance its economic prospects. He envisaged a venue 'for orchestra, pop, soloist and choir performances, for conferences, for wrestling and boxing shows, for dances, exhibitions, assemblies'. The idea found favour with a Labour government keen to patch up its differences with the municipality. Fowler had been furious when the government decided to call a halt 'indefinitely' to the expensive extension of the urban motorway to Taranaki Street, and the decision was later reversed.[11] At a reconvened meeting of the Capital Commission, Finance Minister Bob Tizard made it sound as though government approval for a $5.5 million loan for the proposed cultural centre would be a formality. An ecstatic Fowler returned to his office and drank a toast to the project. Working drawings were commissioned from architects Warren and Mahoney with a six-week deadline, and Fowler was delighted with the result: 'I remember writing to Miles [Warren], and saying, "As far as I am concerned there's an orgasm on every page"'.[12]

Council rubbishmen at work in the Khandallah hills, early 1970s.

Ans Westra

The Federation of Wellington Progressive Societies (FWPS) was less excited. It estimated that continuing inflation would make Fowler's projected $6.8 million project balloon out to $20 million, a prediction that proved frighteningly close to the mark. In June 1975, the city's rates soared by an average of 29.7 percent, with Fowler insisting that the proposed cultural centre had nothing to do with the increase.[13] Since 1949, rates had risen by an average of 8 percent a year.[14] FWPS criticised 'the apparent nonchalance with which ratepayers are being committed to this project without any real say in its form or function, and without being asked if they are agreeable to meeting the cost', and threatened a poll of ratepayers on the proposed loan.[15] To Fowler's consternation, the Government Loans Board refused the loan. As larger urban councils became enterprises handling millions of dollars in rates, rents and government grants, government scrutiny was increasing. Under the National government elected in 1975, that scrutiny would intensify. The municipality of Wellington had assets on its books worth tens of millions of dollars and employed more than 2,000 staff, yet produced no annual financial report.

The Mayor decided that the city should raise the money for his cultural centre, controversially using ratepayers' money to facilitate the process. He enlisted the advertising agency Lintas to develop a fundraising campaign, later unveiled as Operation Waterloo, after the Duke of Wellington's famous military victory. The $6.8 million was to be raised by a series of 'regiments' representing business, sporting and professional interests, as well as women's and Maori groups, each led by a 'colonel'. The campaign was launched with a fanfare on 23 October 1975. A $100-a-double dinner and variety show raised $18,000, with the entertainers including Max Cryer, Johnny Farnham and Suzanne Prentice. The Lintas-designed symbol for Operation Waterloo — a flowing black 'W' with a red dot — proved controversial, with Nigel Cook of the Architecture Centre claiming it was open to vulgar interpretation: 'Is it a waterbed with someone lost on top?'[16] In the final three months of 1975, Lintas charged over $21,000 for its services.[17]

As Operation Waterloo got under way, Air New Zealand donated half a dozen round-the-world tickets.[18] Early in 1977, Mayor Fowler and a party including his deputy Ian Lawrence, Cr Brian O'Brien and a Lintas executive left for a five-week fundraising tour of Europe and the US. In their luggage were the Warren and Mahoney plans. Using diplomatic channels, the delegation gained access to the boardrooms of IBM, Lloyds Bank and Helena Rubenstein, meeting executives

Fowler and colleagues (his deputy Ian Lawrence is on the right) arrive home in 1977 at the end of their whirlwind 'Operation Waterloo' fundraising tour of Europe and North America. The Mayor later estimated that his team had secured promises of $500,000 towards the 'cultural centre' that eventually became the $17 million Michael Fowler Centre. A year later, only $158,000 was in the kitty.

ATL, Evening Post Collection, F-28048-1/4

with often scant knowledge of or interest in their far-flung branch offices. Lawrence recalls:

> We had long days and long nights. We would break into teams during the day and go door knocking. We knocked on doors of significant commercial enterprises in the US and in the UK, mainly in New York and London. Some we had appointments with; many others we didn't. We just plucked up courage, if you like, and did it. In the evenings we would have a meal and analyse what we had achieved during the day. Then we would set out a programme for the following day. It was a very demanding experience, but very rewarding in terms of what we achieved, in understanding what you can do with energy and dedication.[19]

The team faced a number of knock-backs. Too often, luminaries such as US billionaire Nelson Rockefeller and Saudi arms dealer Adnan Khashoggi were not at home when they called. In Washington, a senior American diplomat cautioned them against upsetting inter-governmental relationships: 'New Zealand had never asked USA for aid; he did not want to start now'.[20] The British were more accommodating. In London the eighth Duke of Wellington, Arthur Valerian Wellesley, gave Fowler a list of companies with 'Wellington' in their name. On his return, the Mayor predicted that the mission would yield more than $500,000. A year later, there was $158,000 in the kitty. Operation Waterloo was later described as a flop.[21]

Fowler's attempt to solicit funds from controversial Saudi arms dealer Adnan Khashoggi (principal owner of Wellington's Travelodge) prompted this cartoon by Nevile Lodge.

ATL, courtesy Debby Edwards, B-135-136

Town halls, old and new, overshadowed the 1977 local body election. This was also the year when Fowler's accounting arrangements aroused the interest of the Muldoon government. The Audit Office described as 'very doubtful' the practice of charging Operation Waterloo expenditure to the Recreational, Cultural and Civic Amenities Account.[22] The news came as Muldoon imposed a freeze on local body loans. He followed this with a Public Finance Act containing stringent regulations over local body finances, with annual financial statements to be furnished to the Audit Office.

'A new beat and a brighter look'

In 1977, the triennial local body elections were shaping up to be another dull affair — another round of what the *Dominion* rudely called 'pothole politics'. Veteran Sir Frank Kitts prepared for his last poll. Values candidate Cr Tony Brunt spoke of the 'madness' of extending the urban motorway to the foot of Mt Victoria, while Mayor Fowler assured voters that the on-again, off-again road was just a decade away. Aware of growing middle-class sensitivity to environmental issues, Fowler promised a $21.2 million sewage treatment facility at Moa Point.

Then Carmen announced she was standing for the mayoralty. Her aim was to give Wellington 'a new beat and a brighter look', to lighten up municipal politics, and to promote a café society. Supporting her candidacy was a squad of socialites led by millionaire property developer Bob Jones. Carmen's manifesto — quite shocking by 1977 standards — called for hotel bars to be open until 2 a.m., the drinking age to be lowered to eighteen, and prostitution, abortion and homosexuality to be decriminalised; she even supported nude bathing on Wellington beaches. Candidates' meetings were transformed from the dull affairs of the past, as Carmen herself recalled:

The local halls were packed. Never before had an aspiring candidate, male or female, appeared night after night in a stunning ball gown. I was, at the one time, a candidate, a curiosity, and a *cause célèbre*. My arrivals and departures, by limousine, were accompanied by rousing cheers and audiences responded vocally and enthusiastically to my (Jonesian) eloquence.[23]

Jones played the Svengali, ghost-writing his protégée's speeches and press statements. It was a capital prank, and not even the Prime Minister was able to talk him out of it:

Rob [Muldoon] raised it with me at my home. 'This is the capital city,' he barked. 'The Queen comes here. So do heads of state and other dignitaries, and convention requires a mayoral welcome and reception. You'll make us the laughing stock of the world' ... I refused to withdraw. Far from making us the laughing stock, I argued, we would set an example to the world. Carmen, who was virtually illiterate, was the perfect political leader. She could be guaranteed to do nothing at all in office; the ideal outcome.[24]

As polling day approached, Labour councillors accused Fowler of waving a 'begging bowl in Piccadilly Circus'. It emerged that only $78,750 had been raised for the cultural centre in the past five months — far less than had been predicted. Labour demanded an investigation into Operation Waterloo.[27] Others questioned Fowler's eagerness to demolish most of the existing Town Hall, arguing that strengthening it would cost only $2 million, not the $6 million quoted by the Mayor. Meanwhile a visiting Israeli conductor compared the Town Hall's auditorium to 'the best halls in Europe'. Lady Blundell, wife of the outgoing Governor-General, agreed. A final reprieve was, however, seven years away.

The campaign soon descended into chaos and tackiness, but the candidate herself became more earnest as polls showed she might be a contender. In addition to the mayoralty, she decided to try for a seat on Council. Ian Lawrence recalled: 'I had a concern as the election approached that Carmen wouldn't win but would take enough votes from Fowler to put Kitts back and therefore a lot of the good work that had been done might be put on hold or set back.'[25]

On polling day Carmen attracted 1,686 votes, thus confirming that the capital was not yet ready for her. Fowler was returned with 17,041 votes, outpolling a spectral Kitts, who still managed to garner 14,022 votes. Brunt's green pedigree gained him 7,996 votes. In another sign of the times, a record six women were elected to Council. Despite the colourful campaign, only 43 percent of the electorate bothered to vote, down from 44.3 percent in 1974. The *Dominion* grumbled about political anarchy more closely resembling the recent antics of Auckland punk rock visitors, the Scavengers, than a local body election campaign: 'Such humour can be too sophisticated for the citizen who takes his potholes so seriously that he can't believe council election time is just an off season for national affairs pranksters.'[26]

Thanks to Bob Jones, her deep-pocketed Svengali, Carmen's mayoral campaign budget was able to fund daily advertisements of this kind. She lost, but garnered more votes than expected — and from unexpected quarters. Jones records that Lady Holyoake, the wife of the Governor-General, went out on polling day with her daughter and son-in-law (Wellington Central MP Ken Comber) to vote for Carmen.

Gabor Toth

The Mayor's enthusiasm for his pet project was undiminished. As his second term began, Fowler urged a re-awakening of public interest as the estimated cost approached $10 million.[28] Cynicism grew as the Mayor appeared to be abandoning the fundraising effort, and prepared to go back to the government for a $5 million loan. The FWPS, claiming that the cultural centre could cost as much as $67 million, gathered 7,000 signatures to force a ratepayers' poll. When Fowler's officials invalidated many of the signatures, there was public outrage. The Ombudsman, whose jurisdiction had been extended to cover local bodies in 1976, stepped in. The loan was eventually granted, as Fowler's attention turned to civic lotteries as a further source of revenue.

By the early 1980s the cost of the cultural centre had blown out to $14.25 million, as Muldoon's wages and prices freeze battled 15 percent inflation.[29] Fundraising from civic lotteries continued, but government restrictions kept the tickets out of tobacconists and other outlets. Fowler later described the second lottery as 'an absolute disaster'.[30] His beloved cultural centre had become an albatross around his neck.[31] Meanwhile, the shoddy state of the Council's accounting systems was confirmed as the Audit Office pointedly queried aspects of its annual accounts for 1979/80, the first required under the Public Finance Act regulations. Public concern over rate rises and the state of the municipal books led to the formation of a Rates Reform pressure group. In 1981 its spokesman, Michael Gibson, claimed that the Council had delayed publication of the 1979/80 accounts until after the local body elections. In 1982 rates rose by a mere 12.8 percent, about half of the previous year's increase.

Construction work on the new cultural centre began in 1982. Industrial disputes, alterations to the contract and wind problems slowed progress, delaying completion by more than a year and pushing the final bill to $17.5 million. An on-again, off-again opening date in September 1983 became a mayoral nightmare, making it difficult to secure guests for the official ceremonies. During the global fundraising tour of 1977, the Duke of Wellington had agreed to officiate. In 1982 Fowler booked first-class travel, worth $10,000, for the Duke and Duchess and organised free accommodation for them at the James Cook Hotel. Letters flew back and forth between the Mayor's office and the Duke's home in Reading. When it eventually became clear that the opening date was fluid, the Duke pulled out. In his reply, Fowler all but begged him to reconsider, saying he was 'shattered' by his decision.[32]

More problems arose. Danish plate-makers Bing and Grondhall were ready to ship 500 commemorative plates, worth $8,700, with the wording 'Wellington Town Hall, New Zealand, opened by His Grace the Duke of Wellington, 1983'. In the end, the Duke took pity on his namesake city. But the grand opening still lacked a 'superstar' guest speaker. Months before the opening, the town hall committee began the search for a suitable celebrity. The list included such disparate figures as Jane Fonda, astronaut Neil Armstrong, former head of the UN Kurt Waldheim, Orson Welles, US economist J. K. Galbraith, and even Mother Teresa.[33] With Television New Zealand due to film the opening ceremonies, its Head of Entertainment, Malcolm Kemp, suggested crooner Tony Bennett or 'Wonderwoman' actress Linda Carter. He advised against J. K. Galbraith, who was due to attend that year's Labour

Party conference, describing him as 'a very socialistically minded economist who intensely dislikes the Reagan/Thatcher/Muldoon type administrations and their currency policies'.[34]

Time was short. Fowler wanted another aristocrat, the Earl of Snowdon, celebrity photographer and brother-in-law to the Queen. When he proved unavailable, the committee was forced to turn to another British dignitary, former Prime Minister Edward Heath, who asked for a $10,000 fee and first-class air travel. Work began on the musical component of the opening festivities. The two international acts chosen were the minor US band Hues Corporation, and the re-formed Australian folk group The Seekers. A series of local musicians were lined up as the second-string 'homegrown' component. The emphasis on international 'stars' drew scathing criticism from arts broadcaster Simon Morris in a letter published in the *Dominion*:

> Which would the public prefer to see: one member of a defunct sixties folk-group accompanied by three nobodies, a one hit wonder cabaret act, and an English ex-Prime Minister subsequently trundled out of office after reducing the Brits to a three day week; or Sharon O'Neill, Fred Dagg, Midge Marsden, the Roger Fox Big Band and the [New Zealand] Symphony Orchestra?[35]

As the official opening on 16 September approached, the attractions of the chosen 'superstar' palled. Barely 100 of the 2,600 tickets were sold in advance of Heath's lecture on 'The outlook for global economic recovery and East–West relations'. The Council decided to discount the tickets, with Deputy Mayor Lawrence explaining that the real aim of the event was 'a chance for a lot of people to experience a performance of some kind in the auditorium for $10'.[36] A crowd of 700 — less than a third of the hall's capacity — attended the hour-long address.

The cynics bit their tongues as the building was officially opened in perfect spring weather. The Minister of Local Government, Allan Highet, told a crowd of 2,000 luminaries it was 'a sparkling Wellington day for a sparkling Wellington occasion'. Governor-General Sir David Beattie read a telegram from the Queen. The Duke of Wellington handed Fowler a great golden key on a red cushion. A fanfare of trumpets sounded. A jubilant Mayor looked around the auditorium and remarked, 'It's not bad, is it?' He had reportedly broken down and cried earlier in the year when councillors voted unanimously to name the building after him. All was forgiven. As the tributes flowed, one councillor rattled off a list of alternative names: Fowler's Folly, the Fletcher Challenge Lament Hall, the Warren and Mahoney Memorial Hall, the Squashed Top Hat, Tin Foil Alley, Jaws II and the Never Never Hall.[37] The *Dominion*, however, was effusive in its praise:

> This glittering glass and steel-framed testament to one man's enthusiasm has emerged from drab scaffolding to beauty with the startling immediacy of a piece of legerdemain. Eschewing the heavy conformity of traditional public architecture, the building seems poised to blast off into space, firing the imagination of the citizenry and hopefully serving their future needs and interests.[38]

By the late 1970s, Civic Square regularly hosted protests like this one calling for a nuclear-free Pacific. Within a few years the Fowler council would be split over the issue.

Ans Westra

The Fowler charm had prevailed. Earlier in the year, however, the Deputy Mayor had signalled the need to acknowledge tough economic times with a million dollar cut in wages and salaries. Nine months before the official opening, councillors had approved another $500,000 loan and a further $1 million raid on the Leasehold Property Account. Fowler had ducked a meeting called by Labour councillors 'to discuss the financing and building of the Michael Fowler Centre and its future operations'.[39] A week before the opening, additional 'variations to the contract' totalling $412,075 were slipped through a Council meeting.[40] Of the final bill of $17 million, Operation Waterloo had raised just $3 million, $5.5 million had been raised by government loan, and $8.5 million had come from the municipality's Leasehold Property Account.[41] Wellington had paid heavily for Fowler's dream.

A mayor for turbulent times

By 1976 the capital was proclaiming itself 'Scene City', with images of tourist attractions filling the windows of Kirkcaldie & Stains. That year's Festival of Wellington was bigger and brighter than ever. Fowler talked up the idea of a Grand Prix, and the Gear Meat Company sponsored an inaugural car race around the city streets. Jogging was the new fad, and Fowler called on the Parks Department to provide showers at Anderson Park for sweaty public servants after their circuit of the Botanic Garden.[42] But new municipal services came at a price. Rates kept rising through the mid 1970s amid changes in the assessment system, with rates now calculated on the capital value rather than the traditional unimproved value. Fowler also introduced differential rating, aimed at reducing the proportion of the general rates bill paid by the residential sector. Nonetheless, by 1977 some householders' rates had risen by 70 percent in six years.[43] Another cause for concern was that Wellington's population had grown by a mere 1.8 percent between 1971 and 1976, barely half the growth rate of the previous five-year period.[44] The national economic omens were equally bad. As unemployment approached its highest levels since the Depression of the 1930s, Muldoon's National government pursued a sharply deflationary policy.

In 1980 Fowler won a third mayoral term, and he was subsequently knighted. With controversy surrounding his new cultural centre, he preferred to talk about achievements in social housing, as further complexes opened that year at Central Park and Aro Street. Another of his pet issues was building a 'greater Wellington'. Fowler had long been convinced that the only way for Wellington to compete with Auckland was for all local bodies in the region to join forces. In 1968, as a new councillor, he had shocked seasoned members of the Citizens team by proposing the amalgamation of Wellington City, Lower Hutt, Upper Hutt and Porirua: 'It went down like a lead balloon. As an enthusiastic young councillor, I had unintentionally said to senior colleagues like Morrison, Archibald and Spry, "What the hell have you been doing?" I was sent to Coventry for six months.'[45]

In 1978, Fowler welcomed laws embodying Labour's long-desired regional approach to central and local government planning. Under Muldoon, embryonic regional councils gained responsibility for urban and rural development, major land and water use, and regional reserves. This confirmed a trend that had been apparent locally since 1945. Fowler convened a meeting of local mayors and chairs of territorial authorities to explore ways to co-operate with the new bodies. Publicly, the municipality laid out the welcome mat. Behind the scenes, however, the City Engineer was concerned about the loss of traditional Council functions.[46]

Local bodies such as Wellington City Council diversified, embracing a range of social and community projects. Renovation advice offices opened in Newtown, Berhampore, Mt Victoria and Te Aro, as the municipality rewrote its policies on urban renewal to help the baby-boomers to 'do up' old inner city houses. The capital followed Auckland's example in opening a citizens' advice bureau. Fowler agreed to a government request to establish special work schemes for the city's unemployed. By 1978, the municipality was involving itself 'to a substantial extent' in the new Temporary

After the mid 1970s, unemployed youth were a fixture of the Wellington landscape. By 1978, the council was helping to run special work schemes for the city's unemployed such as the Temporary Employment Programme (TEP). In the early 1980s it came up with a range of schemes, including tree planting, to meet the requirements of the Project Employment Programmes (PEP), which soaked up one in five of the nation's 72,000 unemployed.

Ans Westra

Employment Programme (TEP).[47] The Council's role in forming an unemployed taskforce saw councillors contemplating 'special incentives for the development of industry and employment opportunities'.[48] In the early 1980s, the municipality devised schemes, including tree planting, to meet the requirements of the Project Employment Programmes (PEP), which soaked up one in five of the nation's 72,000 unemployed. The Wellington Unemployed Workers Union was provided with a van — 'nothing flash, but mechanically sound' — but councillors drew the line at granting the unemployed free admission to municipal swimming pools.[49]

As the 1980s began, Television New Zealand moved its head office from Featherston Street to Auckland, taking its flagship six o'clock news bulletin with it. Wellington-based newspapers such as the *National Business Review* and *New Zealand Truth* soon followed. Gloom settled over councillors as they formed a special committee to investigate ways to stop the exodus. A report to the town

Age of protest: increasing disillusionment with Fowler's 'New Look' Council is evident from this carefully choreographed protest from 1976, opposing Council plans for a *Wahine* memorial.

ATL, Evening Post Collection, F-22007-1/4

planning committee confirmed that the city's population was no longer growing.[50] Cost-cutting became a priority, with the 1979/80 year expected to be a difficult one financially.[51] Councillors congratulated themselves for saving $2,400 by ordering additions to the mayoral chain in silver, not gold.[52]

Social turmoil was another blow to Council morale. In 1981, Muldoon famously 'refused to interfere' in a rugby tour of New Zealand by the South African Springboks. Outraged, Fowler swore not to make any Council-owned grounds or facilities available to the touring team, nor let them charter its buses.[53] Over 59 days, the country witnessed unprecedented scenes of civil disturbance. At dusk on 29 July 1981, a crowd of 2,000 protesters assembled in Parliament grounds, where the buildings were cordoned off by waist-high hurricane-wire fences. In lower Molesworth Street, people leading the march were clubbed by police in riot gear. Among the eight people hospitalised for head wounds was sixteen-year-old Karen Brough, daughter of Cr Jenny Brough.[54] Cr Helene Ritchie later moved, unsuccessfully, that the Council close the streets around Athletic Park for the second test match.[55] Police in riot gear and protesters wearing padding and cycle helmets later battled each other on the streets of Newtown.

As the tour was played out on the television news, New Zealanders saw themselves as a divided nation. Some recalled the 1977 New Zealand film *Sleeping Dogs*, with its eerily prophetic scenes of police clubbing protesters and armed government 'specials' hunting down members of a resistance movement. The film was commercially successful, and helped pave the way for a viable cinema industry, inspiring many local imitators. In 1979, Fowler met a group of Wellington film-makers seeking permission to use city streets as a backdrop for car chases in a film called *Goodbye Pork Pie*. For the scenes around the Basin Reserve, the film makers even wanted to erect a six foot high scaffold near the statue of Queen Victoria. It was no ordinary film: the Wellington sequence included scenes of a yellow Mini careering through the pedestrian underpass and concourse of the Railway Station, along platforms 8 and 9, and onto a moving freight train. Fowler sensed the likely economic benefit to the city. In his note to the Town Clerk, he gave his blessing: 'I'm keen to co-operate with these people — it could be good for Wellington.' [56] The film proved a runaway success, as local audiences recognised themselves and their country in the hilarious and anti-authoritarian fantasy. The Wellington sequences poked fun at the capital's notorious weather and stressed its darker bohemian underbelly, yet many Wellingtonians see *Goodbye Pork Pie* as a love letter to a city of mystery and enchantment.

On the beach

In the early 1980s, Fowler was struggling through his last term. He faced opposition from a witheringly effective Labour team, with its so-called 'troika' consisting of leader Helene Ritchie, Rosslyn Noonan and Hazel Bibby, former leader of the Federation of Wellington Progressive Societies. Tensions came to a head in 1982, when Ritchie proposed a motion declaring the capital a nuclear-free zone. Cr Bibby described it as 'perhaps the most important motion to be debated by this council'.[57] In the end, two members of the Citizens team crossed the floor to vote with the Labour minority. Going nuclear-free was a sign of the times, with the capital following the lead of Christchurch, Lyttelton and Devonport. Fowler was furious at this 'stupendous nonsense', and vowed not to stand again. In August 1983 he flaunted the fact that he was accepting an invitation to visit the US warship *Texas*, and even planned to invite the ship's officers to call on him in his mayoral office.[58]

At the 1983 local body elections, Fowler's protégé, Ian Lawrence, won the mayoralty with an 8,000-vote majority over Ritchie. The Australian-born lawyer had been a low-key presence on the Council for twelve years, nine of them as Fowler's deputy. Lawrence was always a backroom operator. Promising to keep the capital 'humming', he got off to a bad start with the Labour troika when he proposed that Council contribute $40,000 towards a government campaign to bring the 'Miss Universe' contest to Wellington.[59] The group Women Against Pornography picketed a Council meeting and circulated a 500-signature petition. Cr Ritchie talked scathingly of 'a lost cause and a stupid idea'.[60] Lawrence had more luck in securing the Nissan Mobil saloon car race around the waterfront, making this a popular if noisy fixture throughout the 1980s. But he was always a mayor with more highbrow tastes. In 1986 he worked hard to get the International Festival of the Arts off the ground, helping Wellington to cement its much-envied reputation as the nation's cultural capital.

In 1984, plans were hatched for a state-funded National Art Gallery in Molesworth Street, with the lower part of the street permanently closed and traffic redirected up a widened Murphy Street. Wellington Central MP Fran Wilde called Minister of Works Tony Friedlander 'ignorant and insensitive' for refusing to revive the Capital Commission to discuss the government's development plans with Council.[61] Friedlander had dared suggest that Wellington's needs were no different from those of Auckland and Christchurch. In an outraged memo to Lawrence, Cr Terry McDavitt called for Council 'to be as obstructive as reasonably

A debt of honour

Former Prime Minister Sir John (Jack) Marshall returned a kindness when he came out of retirement in the mid 1980s to help Mayor Ian Lawrence set up the inaugural International Festival of the Arts.

Marshall's close relationship with the Council dated back to 1936, when he joined the City Solicitor's Office as a 24-year-old barrister and solicitor. He was soon busy chasing the rates and rent arrears that lingered after the Depression years.[62]

After an active wartime career in the Pacific and Italy, Marshall was one of hundreds of former Council employees who were provided with housing and employment as part of their rehabilitation. After becoming the MP for Mount Victoria in 1946, he expressed his gratitude

Jack Marshall.

ATL, PAColl-3063-1-25 (ANZ, AAQT 6401 A35016)

to the Wellington municipality:

I am well aware that one of the main reasons for the council entering into the working arrangement was to assist in my rehabilitation. The accommodation provided and the work which I have received from the council were invaluable in that connection and I will always be grateful for the generous action of the council in helping me to catch up on the lost years of the war.[63]

After a long and distinguished political career, Marshall became Prime Minister in 1972, but his tenure ended with the Labour victory at the end of that year. He retired from politics in 1975 and died in 1988.

and legitimately possible … I for one don't think council should approve any Government building that goes outside our ordinances in any way'.[64] When the Commission resumed its meetings under a newly elected Labour government, discussion centred on a 'Pacific arts centre' — comprising the National Art Gallery and new National Museum — to be built on the waterfront.[65]

Lawrence looked like a man suited to less turbulent times. When David Lange led the Labour Party to victory in the snap election of 14 July 1984, the win injected new life into the eight Labour councillors. As the nuclear-free New Zealand policy passed into law and into legend, Cr Ritchie in particular felt that the Council's earlier stand had been vindicated. Domestically, too, the new Finance Ministers were plotting revolutionary change — nothing less than a dismantling of the interventionist economic structures of the previous 50 years. At giddy speed, the government launched a succession of public sector reforms, each based on free-

"IT'S ALL YOURS, IAN"

A BRIGHTER WELLINGTON BY MICHAEL FOWLER

Michael Fowler's loyal deputy Ian Lawrence might have deserved the mayoralty after twelve years of hard work, but he lacked the vitality and shameless self-confidence that had served Fowler so well. Lawrence's greatest contribution as mayor was helping to get the International Festival of the Arts off the ground.

ATL, courtesy Debby Edwards, B-136-446

market theory. Local bodies were not immune, as Labour vowed to reduce the size and role of government in order to achieve greater economic efficiency and public accountability. During Labour's first term, Local Government Minister Michael Bassett, a former Auckland city councillor and long-time supporter of amalgamation, set the new Local Government Commission to work at rationalising the plethora of local bodies.

Re-awakening the past

On a different front, Labour amended its 1975 Treaty of Waitangi Act, which had set up the Waitangi Tribunal to enquire into claimed grievances relating to the Crown's failure to provide protections guaranteed by the Treaty. At that stage, the Tribunal could respond only to claims relating to Crown actions or inaction since 1975. The 1985 amendment backdated the Tribunal's brief to 1840, thus opening the door for historical grievances to be brought before the Tribunal. It was a turning point for bodies such as the Wellington Tenths Trust, established in 1977 to represent the beneficiaries of the Wellington land reserves. These people were descendants of Te Atiawa and other Taranaki people living in the Wellington region at the time of the disputed 1839 purchase of land by the New Zealand Company (the Port Nicholson Purchase). As the administrator of mana whenua (local guardianship) interests in the city, the Trust was now able to lodge claims with the Tribunal relating to the land reserves, known as 'tenths' because one tenth of all land sold to the New Zealand Company was to be set aside as native reserves, most of which never eventuated. Ngati Toa also had a claim to land within the city.

The Tenths Trust was part of the Maori resurgence in the city since the Land March of 1975. Maori traditions and values in resource management, especially relating to the pollution of traditional fishing grounds by raw sewage, was emerging as a regional and national issue. In August 1977, Ngati Toa led a delegation of local tribes to a Planning Tribunal hearing to protest about the proposed municipal outfall south of Titahi Bay. Meanwhile, local newspapers were advertising public courses in Maori language and culture, to be held on local marae and taught by experts from the community.[66] These and other moves suggested that the city was ready to acknowledge and embrace its long-hidden Maori roots. After a hundred years, the municipality unearthed the ancient name 'Kumutoto' to signpost a sealed parking area under the motorway, halfway up the valley where the name once held sway. As well as being a major pa, Kumutoto was the name of one of the 'lost' streams and rivers that once flowed into Whanganui-a-Tara. The famously cold and healing waters of Kumutoto had been channelled into culverts and, like its name, hidden from view for generations.

Another harbour-side pa site was reawakened in 1982, when an urban marae was opened at Pipitea to cater for the growing Maori population in the region, with tribal affiliations stretching from Cape Reinga to Stewart Island. Ruhia's famous cloak, gifted to the Dominion Museum in 1947, was worn at the opening by one of her descendants. The establishment of the first kohanga reo (language nest, or Maori immersion pre-school) in Wainuiomata in 1982 reflected a rebirth of te reo (the Maori language); the first kura kaupapa Maori (Maori language school) opened its doors a year later. The Maori Language Act 1987 enshrined te reo as an official language of New Zealand.

Meanwhile, councillors debated a new sewage treatment plant at Moa Point. To some extent, it was the same old power play between political factions on Council, and yet another scrap about scarce ratepayer dollars. But in the end, it left the municipality with a major challenge. As a former chairman of the big-spending works committee, the new Mayor was aware of the need to address long-neglected issues relating to infrastructure. Midway through 1984, the Council resolved to build a $10 million milliscreen plant as the first stage of a sewage treatment and disposal scheme estimated to cost at least $100 million. The intention was to locate it on the south coast at Moa Point, where raw sewage had been dumped into the sea since 1899. Lawrence announced plans for a plant to sieve objectionable solids, and for a short outfall into Cook Strait. Cr Ritchie opposed the plan, calling for higher quality (and more expensive) land-based 'secondary' treatment. Her motion narrowly failed. Meanwhile, the Regional Council was asked to classify water quality on the south coast.

In September 1984, environmental and political activist John Blincoe set up a Wellington Clean Water Campaign (WC2). The aim was to persuade the municipality 'to commit itself to high-quality land-based treatment (to at least secondary standard) at a sensible alternative site'.[67] After councillors approved a $10 million loan for the sewerage scheme in 1985, Blincoe announced that his group would force a ratepayers' poll on the issue. Cr Ritchie's open support for the campaign led to accusations that the group was an arm of the parliamentary Labour Party. Lawrence, meanwhile, struggled to get across the message that milliscreening was just the first stage of work at Moa Point, with further treatment being added in affordable steps. The issue was politically charged, with Lawrence and his fellow Citizens portrayed as Machiavellian polluters. He recalls:

> I was always determined to clean up the discharge of sewage into the harbour. Accusations that I was never going to support or push for any further treatment were not a true statement of the position. Not being an engineer, I was relying significantly on the technical advice given.[68]

The fight turned nasty. In a further attempt to stop the loan being raised, Blincoe and an alliance of Maori and ratepayer groups sought an injunction in the High Court. They were unsuccessful, but the move was provocative. Lawrence announced that the municipality would accept only 1,552 of the 10,915 signatures on the campaign's petition. Blincoe called it a 'scandalous situation where thousands of demands made in good faith are disallowed on spurious technical grounds'.[69] The *Dominion* warned that 'in these matters of heat and controversy justice must be seen to be done and the verdict explained fully'.[70] Lawrence concedes that the issue could have been handled better, but insists he remained at arm's length from the decision-making:

> It was not for the mayor and the council as elected representatives to rule on the validity of signatures on a petition. The law was fairly clear, the verification or otherwise was done by officers of the council who were charged with that duty. I would never know what was going on in that administrative context and yet the political opposition alleged I was manipulating those issues.[71]

At a Council meeting on 15 May 1985, Cr Ritchie demanded to see the now disallowed petition, 'on the grounds that as a councillor, she was entitled to see all council reports and correspondence'.[72] Lawrence refused. Cr Noonan tried another tack, asking the Mayor how he reconciled the withholding of the petition with the recent extension of the Official Information Act to local authorities. At the next Council meeting, Ritchie accused Lawrence of being 'obstructive, undemocratic and frustrating the course of justice'.[73] Walkouts, verbal abuse and loud yawning while others were speaking became routine at Council meetings.[74] For the first time since the 1860s, Council minute books recorded councillors being absent from the chamber during meetings, often for a matter of minutes.[75] By the end of 1985, Lawrence was exhausted.[76]

In August 1985 the advertising agency Colenso published a full-page advertisement in local newspapers, featuring a toilet on the shores of Wellington

Harbour, above the words: 'How do you feel about going on the beach?'[77] Lawrence talked about 'a campaign full of errors', but he was losing ground. A $10,000 public relations budget was approved to 'explain the proposal to ratepayers'.[78] By then, Maori concerns were at the forefront of the debate. Ray Ahipene-Mercer, of Ngai Tara and Ngati Ira descent, and a formidable spokesman for the Wellington District Maori Council, was among the Clean Water campaigners who sought an injunction in the High Court. Cr Ritchie, sensing the Council's vulnerability on the issue, condemned a submission on water classification as 'racist' and 'a request to pollute', and accused councillors of failing to consider Maori values:

> Many of the bays around Wellington were traditionally gathering places for
> the Maori and nothing short of a water standard which would allow edible
> shellfish to grow was acceptable. To the Maori, the sea and the food in it was
> an important part of their life.[79]

Council officers joined the fray. In 1986, City Engineer Neil Fyfe attacked opponents of the scheme for arguing on emotive and ideological grounds, and not on the facts.[80] Ahipene-Mercer called his remarks 'an insult to the Maori people'.[81] Behind the scenes, Fyfe urged Lawrence to meet with local Maori. Documents show that Fyfe and others closely scrutinised the Waitangi Tribunal's 1984 decision on a landmark Manukau Harbour claim, which called for better policies and laws to honour the guarantees in the Treaty relating to fisheries. Advice on pre-European Maori history was sought from Steven (Tipene) O'Regan. Above all, the municipality feared that the Treaty of Waitangi Amendment Act 1985, soon to come into force, might overturn plans for Moa Point.

> [It] requires careful consideration to be given to the satisfaction of Maori
> perspectives during planning for major sewage treatment and disposal
> projects. The obligation stems from the Treaty of Waitangi, but it is only now
> reflected in legislation following increased awareness of Maori perspectives
> in the community.[82]

Lawrence met Maori representatives to explain his position. In 1986, for the first time in its 116-year history, the municipality established a schedule of regular meetings with tangata whenua to ensure that Maori traditions and values were formally acknowledged in planning processes.[83] A two-day marae-based course about Maoritanga was offered to councillors and senior managers, and staff signed up for free te reo courses at Wellington Polytechnic. An $8,000 series of workshops and seminars on the Treaty was organised, as the Council decided 'to embark on a process which examines Treaty politics and practices'.[84]

Meanwhile, the mud-slinging continued. Lawrence attacked Blincoe, suggesting that his group rename itself the Dirty Water Campaign. Ahipene-Mercer accused Lawrence and his supporters of 'monocultural attitudes' in their promotion of the capital and of the International Arts Festival:

> The city council can quickly find vast amounts of ratepayers' money to donate to the promotion of what are generally pakeha monocultural interests, but choose to ignore the cultural considerations and interests of Maori people with its plans to continue dumping sewage at Moa Point.[85]

The 1986 local body elections were approaching. Argument centred on the best location for a milliscreening plant, with the Karori Stream mouth and Gollans Valley, behind Eastbourne, being suggested as alternatives. Consulting engineers Beca Carter Hollings & Ferner published a report recommending a $66 million plant at Karori. Much had happened in the six years since the firm's 1980 study of Moa Point, in which Maori perspectives in the planning process barely rated a mention. The new report stated:

> The Wellington District Maori Council, which represents tribal and marae committees for the greater Wellington province, advises that the treatment and disposal of sewage in the Moa Point vicinity is unacceptable to it because of the historical and fishing significance of the area.[86]

As the 1986 local body campaign approached, Labour sensed Mayor Ian Lawrence was vulnerable on the Moa Point sewage issue. Its election campaign featured this infamous full-page advertisement.

ATL, N-P 1075-9

Public submissions later highlighted Maori cultural sensitivities relating to the Karori site as well.[87] As the local body elections approached, the Moa Point issue was fast slipping out of Lawrence's grasp. John Blincoe decided to stand for Council, but was passed over for the mayoral candidacy in favour of Jim Belich, a 59-year-old advertising executive. It later emerged that Belich's candidacy was the idea of Fran Wilde, Labour MP for Wellington Central.

Lawrence and Belich agreed to a nine-month truce on the outfall issue, but four days before the election things turned nasty again. In a devastating reprise of the Colenso effort, Labour's election campaign featured a full-page advertisement asking 'Where does Ian Lawrence sit?' beneath a photo of a toilet on the foreshore at Moa Point. Lawrence complained that it 'degraded the office of the mayor', but the damage was done. The ad became his political obituary.

> For years they have refused to listen. They still want to dump raw sewage off-shore at Moa Point. Now, suddenly, just before the election, they are trying to confuse the issue with two other options: Dumping raw sewage off Karori Stream mouth and still leaving a huge rogue sewer swirling around Cook Strait, at the mercy of our southerlies.[88]

Although less than half of the electorate bothered to vote, Belich won an election night majority of 2,354. With him came the first Labour ticket to hold a majority on the Wellington City Council. Belich's first action as Mayor was to abandon the Moa Point scheme, describing it as 'totally unacceptable' to Maori. At his first Council meeting, Belich looked back on the city's 146 years, paying tribute to the 'effort and sacrifice' of its founders. In a call for unity, he signalled the corporation's willingness to recognise and embrace the interests of the tangata whenua:

> This is your city, our city. Its future depends on our combined efforts. The Maori welcome we received when we entered the auditorium spoke of sacrifice, of people together shining rays of light on our problems and sharing in their solution. What a welcome and what a challenge.[89]

Ready for revolution

While his snowy-white hair and imposing stature made him appear a natural for the part, the new Mayor had not served the usual apprenticeship as a city councillor. This would prove an advantage — and a curse — for a civic leader with a reform agenda. Belich was the first Mayor of Wellington with little prior knowledge of the municipality's traditions and culture — and of the considerable limits of his new role: 'When I was elected in 1986, I sat at my desk, looked across at the Town Clerk, David Niven, and asked what power the mayor had. He stared back and said "None".'[90]

Belich was even less impressed when officials failed to provide him with the kind of budgetary information he might have expected from a business as large as the Wellington municipality. He blamed the lack of accountability on what he later called '100 years of ingrained attitudes':

> Within days of being elected I asked for a copy of any regular monthly
> financial overview of council operations. There wasn't one and I was referred
> to a metre high pile of that month's committee reports on my desk. The
> relevant figures from those reports couldn't be added up because the council
> was on cash not accrual accounting, and that was because legislation
> stipulated this was acceptable.[91]

The new Mayor set to work to reform the financial reporting systems, ordering
millions of dollars to be spent on new computers. He struggled to obtain
information from individual heads of the corporation's twelve departments about
their roles and current aims: 'Some were pleasingly prompt and clear; others
dragged or were inadequate.'[92] Cr and committee chair Sue Driver, a former Council
employee, described how the system worked:

> We take in $100m in rates but all the influence we had was on $2m. There
> was $98m in operations and maintenance money that we couldn't get hold
> of. Every time we said we wanted cutbacks, we couldn't see where the fat
> was. They'd come back and say they'd have to cut something like back-
> door rubbish collection, or they'd have to close the library if they had to
> economise. We didn't *believe* what we were being told.[93]

Concerned at the apparent immunity of city administrators to the Labour
government's *blitzkrieg* of economic reforms, Belich looked instead to his fellow
councillors. New standing committees were set up to help implement election
commitments: sewerage and drainage, city/community planning and services, and
economic development and city promotion. By late 1987, Belich had no fewer than
79 subcommittees operating, compared with an average of eighteen subcommittees
over the previous six years. Cr Blincoe, chair of the sewage and drainage committee,
was one of three councillors who quit their full-time jobs in order to get through their
Council workloads.[94] Deputy Mayor Ritchie shaped the rates reform programme,
another of Labour's election commitments. Decisions were needed on the future
development of Wellington Harbour, as ownership and responsibility passed into
Council hands as part of the local government reforms (see below).

Other items on the long agenda included a new domestic terminal for Wellington
Airport, and Belich's pet project, a new 'community-oriented' civic centre. Labour
councillors also revealed commercial ambitions. Despite an emerging philosophy
that local bodies should stick to providing core services, the municipality formed

a joint venture with Gracelands Export in 1988, spending millions of ratepayer dollars to upgrade the old municipal abattoir at Ngauranga. The scope of the works programme and the furious pace made Citizens councillors suspicious:

> Many meetings are taking place without those directly involved knowing the dates, times and venues, denying other councillors and members of the public the opportunity to sit in on matters in which they have an interest. This gives the impression that the Wellington City Council is conducting business in secret.[95]

Belich championed an 'active economic policy' to boost the faltering Wellington economy and stop the drift north. In May 1984, the *Evening Post* reported that the city had lost 4,857 people since 1976, and nearly 3,000 jobs since 1981.[96] State sector restructuring saw the number of public servants fall dramatically, from 89,105 in 1986 to 60,940 in 1988.[97] These trends helped to create an unprecedented role for Wellington as a centre of small businesses.[98] Hence Belich established a Capital Development Agency, with small business advisors and purpose-built commercial units. Planner Peter Healey was put in charge:

> The wheels had really fallen off the Wellington economy, with unemployment heading towards 15 percent. Our aim was to help people start new small businesses. The unemployed and the government money rolled in. People got a business plan, a government loan, and before they knew it a small shop in Cuba Street. Landlords hesitant about the likelihood of ever receiving their rent money came around to our view that supporting small business was 'the right thing to do'. Not all of our clients kept to the straight and narrow. One decided to make his money by extracting gold and silver from old computer parts. We set him up in a building in Marion Street and all was just dandy until he overcooked something, and in a colossal explosion, blew out every window in the complex.[99]

Belich worked to bring the municipality — a $280 million operation with 3,000 staff on its books — into line with imminent local government reforms.[100] Departments became efficient 'business units', each required to produce mission statements, business strategies and performance criteria. In 1987, for example, the 70-year-old milk department became a Local Authority Trading Enterprise (LATE), and was re-branded Capital Dairy Products Ltd. Trading departments became the local body equivalent of a state-owned enterprise, with managers expected to run their corporations along private sector lines.

Belich's known links to leading proponents of the government's New Right reforms, such as the combative Richard Prebble, started to show. At the start of 1988, David Lange's re-elected government was attacked for closing hundreds of post offices around the country. Belich came down heavily on Labour councillors who publicly criticised government actions.[101] Local Government Minister Michael Bassett announced a review of the boundaries, functions, structure and funding of local bodies. Councillors expressed 'dismay and deep concern' at the tight timetable.[102] Local government was just one of many areas coming under scrutiny, as resource management law, liquor licensing, ports, public hospitals, retail energy and transport were all readied for restructuring.

With the passage of the Local Government Act 1989, no fewer than 620 territorial and ad hoc bodies were rendered down to 86 local and regional units, including district or city councils such as Wellington City. The focus of these so-called territorial authorities was to be the provision of local services: water supply, control of land development, and recreational facilities, including parks and reserves. Their role extended to local roading and transport, sewerage and stormwater drainage and, importantly for Wellington, social and economic development. Beefed-up regional councils were charged with co-ordinating and setting policy for sustainably managed resources, including water and soil conservation and transport. Once proud institutions such as the Wellington Harbour Board vanished overnight, their commercial operations handed to publicly owned port companies.

After 119 years, the formal designation of the Wellington City Corporation changed to the Wellington City Council. Apart from absorbing the small borough of Tawa, however, Wellington City barely noticed the reforms affecting other urban centres. For Kerry Prendergast, one of two Tawa borough councillors to join the expanded Council, this was symptomatic of wider attitudes: 'The city never wanted Tawa and it was just tacked on. I think that was significant in not only the way they dealt with Tawa but part of the whole culture of where the management team was at that time.'[103]

In 1989 the municipality published a compulsory annual plan and report of results. In his introduction to the city's first formal statement of financial accounts in nearly 120 years, Belich paid a back-handed compliment to the municipality: 'Clearly, council has not been geared to the production of such reports, and it has taken a special effort on the part of officers to divert from other pressures to produce it.'[104]

Meanwhile, major fractures were appearing within Council. In 1988, Belich dumped his Deputy Mayor, Helene Ritchie, after it emerged that a contentious Council decision to change the rating system was invalid. Labour unity lay in tatters as Ritchie was stripped of her senior roles, including chair of the resources and airport committees. As Ritchie talked of 'a scandal of monumental proportions', the Mayor described her as 'not just difficult but virtually impossible to work with'.[105] A torrid Council meeting on 13 April 1988 was punctuated by constant points of order and angry exchanges between the Mayor and his former deputy. The raised voices in the chamber were regularly drowned out by a concert in the nearby auditorium by Australian rocker Jimmy Barnes. After returning to her room, Ritchie found two fans trying to enter the concert through her ground-floor window.[106]

In her capacity as chair of the resources committee, Ritchie had criticised central government for failing to pay full rates on its many properties across the city. The government had taken steps to address the capital's long-standing grievance on this issue when it agreed in 1968 to provide grants in lieu of rates. By 1987, Ritchie was claiming that the city would be $3 million a year richer if it could collect full rates from the Crown, including on schools and hospitals. The Railways Corporation, for example, paid a mere $81,987, whereas the full rates payable came to $320,848.[107] Bassett later promised that his new Rating Powers Bill would establish rating of Crown land. He also reluctantly chaired the Capital Commission in the late 1980s, but later refused to hold further meetings unless there was something of importance to discuss.

By 1990, Auckland had close to a million residents, with more than one in four New Zealanders living there. While the population of most New Zealand cities increased in the latter half of the decade,[108] that of Greater Wellington dropped from 325,697 in 1986 to 324,600 three years later.[109] A memo to Belich in May 1990 confirmed that the Auckland-centric Labour Cabinet no longer believed that the Wellington municipality should receive 'special treatment over Auckland for example'.[110]

In 1989, a restructured local government sector faced its first electoral test. Labour lost its majority on Council, and Ritchie, standing as an Independent, came within 932 votes of toppling Belich. The 21 councillors elected included nine women. What the *Evening Post* called Belich's 'big fright' was in part blamed on disaffection with the Labour government as a deep recession dragged on, and in part on continuing delays in implementing the sewage treatment scheme. Weeks before election day, the Council had resolved to proceed with a stand-alone, land-based secondary treatment plant, located near the south end of the Miramar golf course. By mid 1989, the scheme was inching forward, as the Council determined not to repeat the mistakes of the past: 'Once sufficient information is available, consultation begins with local kaumatua, the wider Maori community and other affected parties.'[111]

1990 was to be a year of birthdays. Wellington City prepared to celebrate the 150th anniversary of its founding, as the nation moved to commemorate the signing of the Treaty of Waitangi in 1840. As part of a year of national celebrations, the Commonwealth Games were to be held in Auckland, and the capital was to host the International Festival of the Arts. In the mid 1980s, Ian Lawrence had enthused about the tourist potential of a Wellington 'Expo', and Belich later set up a trust board to organise a programme of 'sesquicentennial' activities across the city. But as the landmark year approached and six years of social and economic turmoil took their toll, Wellington struggled to put on its party hat.

Sesqui City to Wellywood

Chapter 9

1990–2005

I wish I was in Wellington, the cafes and the bars
The music and the theatre, and the old Cable Car
And you can walk everywhere, 'cause nowhere's very far.

'Wellington', The Mutton Birds, 1995

Weeks before the 1990 Sesquicentennial carnival opened in the capital, jittery organisers warned that advance ticket sales were half a million dollars short of budget. Without an equivalent cash injection from ratepayers, the city's 150th birthday party was likely to be a flop. It was a harsh awakening for the new Council, distracted, like most New Zealanders, by the Commonwealth Games in Auckland, where Kiwis were striking gold.

The 1990 celebrations had begun on a high note, despite a depressed economy and a Labour government that was sinking after five and a half turbulent years. On Wellington's Anniversary Day, thousands flocked to Petone Beach to watch a re-enactment of the arrival of the settler ship *Aurora*, featuring two tall ships and carved waka. As 70 descendants of the original settlers, dressed in period costume, were rowed ashore, they were greeted by a 200-strong Maori welcoming party, and a speech by Te Atiawa elder Sir Ralph Love, a former Wellington city councillor. The themes of unity and reconciliation were repeated at the Commonwealth Games' opening ceremony on 24 January, where 'Mother of the Nation' Whina Cooper murmured: 'Let us live together as one nation in our aroha.'[1] The party mood reached the capital as a crowd of 65,000 braved summer showers to fill Trentham

Memorial Park for Kiri Te Kanawa's final homecoming concert on 28 January.

The six-week Sesqui carnival was due to open in late February, as part of the series of national festivities spanning the whole year. Sir Michael Fowler, chair of the Wellington 1990 Trust set up by Council to co-ordinate regional celebrations, was the man with the half-million-dollar headache. In a letter to Town Clerk David Niven on 29 January, he blamed his fellow New Zealanders for being 'inveterate late decision makers'. As ever, Fowler was bullish:

> Sesqui proceeds on target and there is every indication the show will be a roaring success. Even our bankers believe so, but they need some comfort at this stage in the form of a $500,000 underwriting to allow them to carry us through to the 24th February when the gate sales start. Without the support of the Wellington City Council, we are in deep trouble, though our creditors have been pretty reasonable.[2]

Nine months before the carnival opened its doors, Sesqui chief executive John Gittus unveiled what was in store. A floating casino, interactive scientific exhibits, wind sculptures and 'chundersome' rides promised to make it an event like Wellington had never seen before. None of this eventuated.

ATL, Dominion Post Collection, EP/1989/2576/11

Early in February, the full Council met in emergency session. Fowler's request for a cash injection was approved in a 'letter of comfort'.[3] Belich had been happy to let others take care of Sesqui, but now there was much at stake. After all, this was a double-headed celebration, marking both the founding of Wellington and the signing of the Treaty.

In 1988, the carnival had been conceived as a partnership between the 1990 Trust and the Wellington Show Association, chaired by Sports Foundation CEO Keith Hancox. A Sesqui board was then established, headed by Geoff Datson, a lawyer, economic consultant and former Deputy Secretary of the Department of Trade and Industry. Its high-powered members included Fowler and Hancox, but only one city councillor, Anna Weir. Belich sat back as the experienced Datson got to work. Australian John Gittus, fresh from marketing the successful Expo 88 in Melbourne, was appointed chief executive late in 1988. Board members marvelled as he unveiled budgets projecting a likely surplus of $1.2 million, with a best case scenario of $7.1 million. Predicting two million visits and an average of 54,000 visitors daily, Gittus promised to surpass the 1940 Centennial Fair, where 'attendances were achieved in wartime and when New Zealand's population was only 1.6 million. So my estimate for 1990 on the basis of New Zealand's current population is probably conservative.'[4]

Gittus took his sales patter to Council, outlining an event that would be 'conducted simultaneously' for twelve hours a day on two sites — the Wellington Showgrounds in Newtown and Taranaki wharf. More than 50 nations would present elaborate but unspecified displays. A floating casino, interactive scientific exhibits, an open-air Maori exhibit with giant hangi, wind sculptures and 'chundersome' rides would make it an event 'like Wellington has never seen before'. There would be, he promised, 'corporate and international exhibits; amusements; rides; entertainment; food of all nations; surprises; concerts; wine festivals; visual and audio treats; with an all pervading aura of fun'.[5]

Councillors nodded. The obvious question of why Sesqui would open *after* the school holidays was not asked. The requested $103,000 was approved, along with up to $500,000 of guaranteed funding.[6] Separately, the Regional Council guaranteed $400,000. By early 1989, the tightness of the sixteen-month timetable was showing. Ill feeling arose after the Council refused to spend a further $200,000 of ratepayers' money on running free shuttle buses between the sites. The Government then refused to allow a floating casino at the Overseas Terminal. The Department of Scientific and Industrial Research (DSIR), then in its death throes, pulled out of a high-tech walk-through tunnel telling the nation's story. The Maori village, Nga Paiaka, also broke away, setting itself up as a separate 'Maori Dimension' in the old Council works yard in Chaffers Street.

On 23 February 1990, Sesqui was officially opened with fireworks, singers and light shows. A week before, Gittus had admitted it would have been 'helpful' to have another year to prepare.[7] On opening day, just 18,500 punters showed up. Many were disappointed to find the Newtown site hosting little more than a regulation trade fair, with few of the thrilling sideshows that had clinched the success of the 1940 event. The main feature of the Taranaki wharf site was a brightly painted barn and a truckload of hay bales. An *Evening Post* editorial commented that the carnival 'deserved to succeed', as if it sensed that the city already had a dud on its hands.[8]

As March came and the crowds thinned, 150 staff were laid off. Cr Weir complained that board members had not been kept informed: 'Things are falling apart, and we are doing our best to contain it.'[9] The mood soured further as ticket prices were slashed, and the Council injected a further $50,000 to meet immediate costs, including wages. This came on top of the $1 million plus already committed. On 7 March, after only twelve days, Sesqui closed its doors, owing a total of $6.4 million. Recriminations began. An Audit Office

This advertising billboard for the ill-fated carnival remained on the outskirts of the city for months, attracting graffiti and much public outrage.

ATL, Dominion Post Collection, EP/1990/1122/31

review later concluded that neither the City Council nor the Regional Council had had enough information to commit ratepayers' money.

A chapter of accidents

Days after Sesqui folded, a local resident tried to run down John Gittus in the street: 'He was honking and shouting and drove straight at me. I had to jump out of his way.'[10] The Australian flew out a week later, leaving 148 creditors who were collectively owed several million dollars. It was all terribly messy. Many local businesses went into receivership, and were forced to accept 30 cents in the dollar compensation. The government-owned Works Corporation faced losses of $2.5 million for construction and other activity; its chief executive later accepted a final settlement of $320,000 of behalf of the taxpayer.[11] The municipality wrote off the $1.15 million it was owed. Hancox and Fowler later sent creditors a joint apology.[12] Datson called Sesqui the biggest flop of his career: 'I am reminded of the stockbroker during the share crash who said he was sleeping like a baby — he woke up every four hours and cried.'[13]

Behind the scenes, councillors and Trust members bickered, with Belich reluctantly agreeing to pick up the legal bills. Not all was lost, however: Nga Paiaka continued operating until late 1990. As if to taunt the city, a Sesqui billboard, covered in graffiti, lingered beside the motorway on the Kaiwharawhara reclamation for months, despite efforts to get rid of it. The carnival became synonymous with Council failure. Sesqui jokes abounded. To get 'a jolly good sesquiing' was 'to be duped, to lose heavily in a gambling situation, to become or take on the appearance or nature of a gittus'.[14] The cynical mood did not improve when Hancox was later jailed for four years for defrauding his employer, the Sports Foundation. Today, Belich concedes that Sesqui was the low point of his mayoralty. In the immediate aftermath, however, he sounded more detached:

> One of the things you have to do in business is you have to try and get some
> good people in place and then back them. You don't meddle. I thought we
> had some pretty good people in the persons of Sir Michael Fowler, the Show
> Association, Mr Datson and Cr Weir.[15]

The *Evening Post* could not disguise its fury: '"New Zealand's biggest event ever" boasts the sign outside the Sesqui carnival site in Newtown. What it should read is: New Zealand's biggest flop ever. This is the reality today as Wellington reflects on the shambles that Sesqui became.'[16]

The lingering Sesqui billboard was also portrayed in this Eric Heath cartoon.

WCA, 0001:1648:50:217

Belich by now had other things on his mind. In July 1990, he announced a major review by independent consultants of the Wellington municipality, pointing out that the city had been spared the major restructuring forced on many of its counterparts by the 1989 local body reforms and therefore needed a shake-up. An Independent Review Group (IRG) was set up, comprising economist Susan Snively, accountant Malcolm McCaw and former IBM chief executive Basil Logan. Meanwhile, an increasingly confident National Opposition, keen to make political capital out of a Labour mayor's discomfort, sniped from the sidelines. When National won the 1990 election, the new Local Government Minister, Warren Cooper, threatened to intervene in the capital, arguing that the Council should not 'hive off into doing things like the Sesqui … and building buildings that are unnecessary, that just serve their own image'.[17]

By Christmas 1990, staff were braced for the worst. Councillors noted that 'a number of staff appear to believe the review is likely to result in mass redundancies'.[18] Midway through 1991, the IRG reported back. The 170-page document was not the bland, consultant's report typical of the times. This one exuded a whiff of sulphur: the most savage and devastating criticism of the Wellington City Council in 121 years. Here, said the reviewers, was an 'introspective' organisation led by people only vaguely aware of an obligation to serve ratepayers. Here was the largest single business in the lower North Island, with a billion dollars of assets on its books and close to 3,000 staff (including its trading operations). Here was the second biggest municipal organisation in the Southern Hemisphere, after Brisbane. And at its helm were people making bad financial decisions and barely disguising their contempt for elected officials. Kerry Prendergast, then a new councillor, recalls the report's impact:

A robed Mayor Belich, looking every bit the part.

WCA, 00510:1:10

> It was incendiary. It identified that there were basically no systems or processes
> in place that you could rely on, that nothing was done in any particular order
> or any particular priority or to any form of strategy. I was young and naïve
> and I'd come into this huge body. Suddenly I was presented with a report
> saying, in effect, that the management board is a disaster.[19]

Financial tables confirmed the charges. The billion-dollar assets were not properly valued or accounted for. Poorly informed decision-making meant that the new Central Library in Civic Square would cost $10 million more than it should have.[20] Wellingtonians paid the second highest rates in the country, at $654 per capita, second only to Auckland's $731. Damning comparisons were made with North Shore City Council in Auckland, a body representing an equivalent population:

Wellington spent more than twice as much ($246 million versus $117 million), took more than half as much again in rates ($96 million versus $63 million), and had nearly two and a half times as many full-time staff on its payroll (1,869 versus 750).[21] Yet Wellington ratepayers' associations and groups representing commercial interests expressed high levels of disatisfaction.

The review prescribed 'fundamental rather than incremental' change, with stronger leadership the key to purging inefficient practices. Reflecting the dominant free-market ethos of the time, it urged that the Council's business activities be rationalised as a precursor to privatisation. Ratepayers were said to be subsidising the Council's rental housing stock — a $65 million investment that could be earning interest. Public housing assets, along with the Michael Fowler Centre, sports fields and swimming pools, should therefore be turned into profit-making LATES.[22] The report stopped short of recommending major asset sales.

Expecting the worst, staff packed a foyer of the Michael Fowler Centre to hear Town Clerk David Niven talk of reshufflings rather than sackings. Nonetheless, Belich now had a mandate for change, and the organisational shake-ups began. Jenny Fitzwater, then personal assistant to a senior manager, recalls events:

> The experience was unsettling and bewildering. When the IRG review was announced, morale was low. There was little consultation about what was happening. Staff were interviewed by a group of consultants they didn't know, and there was a lot of fear while waiting for the report. People were sure they were going to lose their jobs. Once the report was released, changes were implemented rapidly. Support staff in the main got new contracts, usually fixed term, with the end resulting in redundancy. Managers were now responsible for doing their own typing, diary management and administrative tasks. The staff who remained had loads more responsibility.[23]

May 1991 saw the release of the Independent Review Group's report, a document that savaged the Council and called for major restructuring. This humorous badge was produced as a way to lift plummeting staff morale.

Adrian Humphris, photographed by Becky Masters

As the dust settled, Belich insisted that the organisation 'could take the medicine', and refused to respond to criticism of senior staff. 'Council will proceed down the track fairly, reasonably, legally and I hope expeditiously'.[24] Former Mayor Ian Lawrence defended the Town Clerk, attributing the problems to the Labour-led Council getting too involved in community activities. The *Evening Post* compared the Council to the former Soviet Union, describing it as 'a cumbersome monolith, potentially strong but inefficient and lacking in tough leadership, accountability, new ideas and financial acumen'. The report, it said, was 'long overdue', and confirmed 'many of the suspicions ratepayers and others dealing with the council have had for years'.[25]

As the implications of the IRG review sank in, the municipality was back in the headlines. Long-serving City Solicitor Peter Rama had resigned in June 1990, following front-page newspaper disclosures that one of his many residential properties failed to meet safety codes. His senior colleagues, alerted to the practice, had turned a blind eye. Former Secretary of Internal Affairs Peter Boag, in his subsequent inquiry into the Rama affair, recommended a code of conduct for councillors and Council staff. The code was implemented at the end of 1991.

Staff resignations continued, however, and at the end of 1991 an acting CEO and 'change manager', Doug Matheson, briefly replaced the Town Clerk. A new era was ushered in with the arrival from the UK of the Council's new CEO, Angela Griffin, in 1991. Her appointment had been a response to the IRG's call for stronger leadership, which paved the way for the CEO to take a more active and powerful role in running the daily business of the municipality.

It then emerged in 1991 that the Council's investment in the Ngauranga Gorge meatworks had lost $33.5 million. The fact that the municipality had squandered millions of dollars to compete in the export meat market and to shore up jobs was not the huge public embarrassment that Sesqui had been, but the cost to ratepayers was far greater. In 1987 the Council had written a $7.5 million cheque for an upgrading that ballooned to $12.5 million. But the half million animals a year needed to make the works viable failed to eventuate, and the Council's business partner went into receivership, owing close to $4 million. It took years for the abattoir to be sold, to a meat slaughtering, processing and export business. In the second of three reports within two years into the Council's operations, the Auditor-General referred to 'inadequate evaluation of the risks' before, during and after the upgrade: 'Thus closes a most unfortunate chapter in the history of the Wellington City Council, which resulted in total losses to its ratepayers of $37.1m.'[26]

Calmer waters?

A year after the release of the IRG report, much had changed. The 60-plus subcommittees and fourteen standing committees had been reduced to a manageable dozen. The management structure had been revamped and slimmed down to eight new divisions. A new era of transparency dawned as the municipality opened itself and its books to public scrutiny.

With his restructuring mission launched, Belich eased into the remaining years of his mayoralty. But as expensive decisions loomed over the long-awaited motorway extension, Cr Stephen Rainbow of the Green Alternative Party proved a persistent irritant in raising environmental issues. Mud also flew from the sidelines, as former Citizens leader Rex Nicholls attacked Belich's leadership style:

> He doesn't exercise enough power. He has allowed himself to be manipulated into allowing the new civic centre with nice new offices to be built at enormous cost to the ratepayers and we don't need them ... [E]specially as different operations become corporatised, like the buses, and the office space to house all the staff is no longer necessary.[27]

A rare positive note was sounded with the November 1991 opening of Civic Square, a bold new space encircled by a disparate collection of old and new municipal buildings, each telling a piece of the city's story. The square provided a new heart for the city. Overnight, the silvery nikau palms encircling the new Central Library (opened a month later) became a symbol of a fresh civic identity. The refurbished town hall opened early in 1992. Belich, who chaired the subcommittee steering the project, calls the square the high point of his mayoralty:

Off the shelf: at the end of 1991 pupils from the Kelburn-based Children's Learning Group helped shift the first books from the old Wellington Public Library (later redeveloped as the City Gallery) to the new building next door.

ATL, Dominion Post Collection, EP/1991/3578/14

> It wasn't a new idea — but its time had come. The cost of the complete centre, including gutting of the town hall, was budgeted at $130m. This was frightening. But when we costed the individual elements, spread over time, it was obvious that if not tackled now as a whole, it would cost a lot more later ... [I]t was a tense period because if the town hall was not ready in time, the 1992 International Festival of the Arts would be seriously endangered. The project director, city architect Roger Shand, his staff, the architects [a selected panel led by Ian Athfield], the builders were put under extreme pressure. They all delivered on time, on quality — and under budget.[28]

The restoration of a Maori presence in the city, as part of a wider Maori resurgence, helped to shape this new identity. The Tenths Trust took its claim on the Port Nicholson Block to the Waitangi Tribunal in 1991, and waited more than a decade for its findings. They were seeking redress for the actions of past governments in taking the land, and compensation for losses suffered. The Council's increasing willingness to include Maori views in its planning procedures was shown in 1989, when it became the first local authority to establish a Maori committee with its own servicing unit. As the Resource Management Act ushered in a new era of consultation, the Council formalised relationships with mana whenua organisations, signing memoranda of understanding with the Tenths Trust and Ngati Toa rangatira (chiefs).

In the late 1980s, planning began on the redevelopment of the old Manners Street Reserve, latterly known as Pigeon Park. A lunchtime oasis for hundreds of office workers and the rallying point for protest marches to Parliament, this grassy island had deep historic significance. Located in the heart of a flax and toetoe fringed swamp, Te Aro Pa was home to Ngati Ruanui at the eastern end and Taranaki people on the western side. It was here that Wesleyan missionaries conducted the region's first service of Christian worship, in June 1839. In the 1870s, as the town encircled the pa, the land was carved up and bought by the Council. Such was the pressure on the land and its inhabitants that by 1881 only a few people remained. In 1910, a police station and Turkish baths on the site were demolished to make way for a park. During the early 1940s, Pigeon Park became a meeting place for pacifists who gathered on Friday nights to speak against the war. Unions often rallied there in the post-war years.

The return of Maori to the city was to be expressed symbolically in the creation of a new Te Aro Park. In 1988 the Council approved a concept by Dunedin artist Shona Rapira Davies for a new park as a waka-shaped sculpture, its prow jutting eastwards into Taranaki Street; tiled pools of water would form part of the new terracing, with patterns based on traditional Maori weaving. A contract with payment of $234,268 was later agreed with Davies, including the cost of 20,000 handmade tiles.[29] Funding came from an arts bonus levy paid by property developers. At the end of 1991, nearly a year after the agreed completion date, the *Evening Post* warned that costs on the unfinished project were likely to rise to a million dollars.[30] Cr Ruth Gotlieb, who helped approve the original contract, said she hated going near the park, and that the Council had become 'a laughing stock'.[31] Belich later agreed that the redevelopment was a 'botch up'.[32]

Te Aro Park opened with a dawn powhiri on a dripping day in May 1992. As part of the ceremony, a piece of greenstone was buried.
WCA, 54018:001

The park was opened in May 1992 with a dawn powhiri, and the ceremonial burial of a piece of greenstone beneath the waka's prow. Some Maori wondered if the artist's bad luck stemmed from the fact that work on waka was traditionally restricted to men.[33] The Audit Office fielded complaints from ratepayers who mistakenly believed that their rates were being squandered. Its subsequent report, which put the final cost of the redevelopment at $825,759, expressed concern about the way the project was managed:

> There was very little evidence of written communication between the Council
> and Ms Davies during the early stages of the contract … [S]tricter control may
> have led to an earlier detection of problems but there is no reason to believe
> that these would have been entirely eliminated.[34]

Meanwhile, the capital's reputation as a gritty and accessible urban location for film-makers was growing, helped by the success of *Goodbye Pork Pie*. City Public Relations Officer Gene Saunders approved: 'we get a degree of promotion we could never afford to pay for'. Accordingly, in the 1980s the Council gave permission for the makers of *Shaker Run* to let their Trans Am sports cars 'roll and crash' in Courtenay Place, followed by 'a stunt involving a car crashing through the Kirk Motors showroom window'; it also approved stunts such as cars jumping over the Cable Car, dropping off the motorway ramp, and hurtling over Gilmer Terrace from the top of one building to another during the filming of *Aces Go Places* by Hong Kong director Ringo Lam.[35]

In 1991, the Parks and Recreation Department gave local film-maker Peter Jackson permission to shoot his feature film *Braindead* at various city locations, including Brooklyn's Central Park, the Town Belt near Newtown, and Karori Cemetery. Jackson was then largely unknown, with two low-budget horror-comedy films to his credit. Council staff, however, knew his father, Bill Jackson, as their paymaster. A minor controversy surrounding the filming in the cemetery led Parks manager David Rowe to suggest that the approvals process for filming be tightened up.[36] Recognising the economic importance to the capital of the emerging film industry, the Council later established a separate organisation, Film Wellington, to work directly with film and production companies. By the late 1990s, Jackson was internationally acclaimed for films such as *Heavenly Creatures* and *The Frighteners.*

As his mayoralty drew to a close in late 1992, Belich's management team warned that the city was $130 million in the red.[37] Valuable municipal assets were prepared for sale to fund the shortfall. The Scottish bus company Stagecoach later paid less than $9 million for Wellington City Transport Ltd, which ran the city's loss-making fleet of trolley-buses with 386 staff.[38] As Wellington Electricity Management Ltd, now called Capital Power, was compulsorily corporatised under the Energy Companies Act, a debate began about its future. 'Re-engineered' corporate divisions progressively shed more than 200 jobs: 127 from Culture and Recreation, 93 from Cityworks, and twelve from Environment.[39] Hundreds more would follow. Getting rid of senior management was costly, as $1.2 million went on severance payments to long-term staff such as David Niven, Neil Fyfe and Richard Nanson.[40] The departure of Nanson, a capable head of Parks and Reserves, resulted from a personality clash with the new CEO, Angela Griffin.

Rabbits on the run

As the jobs-for-life era came to an end, secrets hidden deep within the Council were unearthed. On 10 April 1992, *Dominion* readers learned of the Order of the Rabbit, which had been in existence since the 1960s. Belich's claims that senior management actively conspired to keep power away from elected representatives seemed to be borne out. Here was a self-selecting brotherhood, bound by rituals and an oath of secrecy, working to protect the interests of its members. The oath, counter-signed by the Chief Rabbit, was revealing:

I (name of initiate) in the presence of this worthy and distinguished board of native and imported rabbits all slightly elevated, do hereby strenuously, plausibly and vehemently swear, undertake and promise that I will well and rabbitly play my part in the undertakings of the said board, that I will maintain the traditions of the founders, those worthy men who regarded all councillors as a pack of bastards, all officers as outstanding men and women, and every city undertaking as the happy hunting ground of the enterprising and devoted rabbit. I do further solemnly undertake that I will keep the secrets of the said board, cheerfully attend all conclaves and exercises, and make whatever payments may from time to time be due upon penalty of myxomatosis forcibly applied.[41]

Peter Rama, the disgraced City Solicitor and former rabbit, insisted that the 'Rabbit Board' was just a bit of fun. 'New officers would have a party and we'd keep them in suspense about their initiation. At the end of the night, after a few drinks, there would be a ceremony'.[42]

Former Town Clerk David Niven described the club as 'a team building exercise', where a dozen initiates met over dinner in the Council administration building: 'It is important to treat it lightheartedly. It would be a disaster if anyone took it seriously.'[43] But Belich was sceptical: 'I was concerned it was more sinister than that'.[44] The municipal rabbits scurried off, never to be seen again. Prendergast believes the disclosures confirmed the need for the IRG report:

Perhaps they all had too much to drink one night and someone dreamed up this thing and it was all very funny. But it's unbelievable that managers of an organisation responsible for so many staff and so many assets could be that immature and juvenile. We're talking about the very senior level.[45]

Three months before the 1992 local body elections, *North and South* magazine published a ten-page article headlined 'Capital Chaos: The Dubious Achievements of the Wellington City Council'. This catalogued, in excruciating detail, recent mistakes and failures:

> For the last 18 months, reporting of council activities has seemed like the obsessive documenting of a bad joke. As for the particular brand of humour involved — you'd laugh more heartily if you weren't a ratepayer … Mayor Sir James Belich bows out at the end of this term and, to date, there are eight contenders for the job at the October elections. Front-runner is expected to be Labour's Fran Wilde, currently MP for Wellington Central. Why would anyone want the job? Perhaps because nothing could surely be worse than the revelations of the last year and a half. Things have just got to get better.[46]

Fran Wilde and Belich at the new mayor's 1992 swearing-in. On the day of his last Council meeting, Belich said he felt like doing cartwheels.

WCA, 00517:7:1613

Absolutely positively Wilde

After the National Party under Jim Bolger won the October 1990 election, it showed itself ready to continue Labour's restructuring crusade, extending it into areas such as welfare benefits and state house rentals. In Wellington Central, Labour MP Fran Wilde retained her seat only after special votes were counted. A fifth-generation Wellingtonian and long-time supporter of the city, Wilde embodied the liberal values of urban baby-boomers, successfully championing homosexual law reform and Labour's anti-nuclear stance. After a short stint in Opposition, she decided to end her four-term parliamentary career and contest the Wellington mayoralty. Wilde's years in the House had honed her political skills, and her experience as a Cabinet minister in a reformist government made her well suited to lead an organisation in the midst of change.

On the day of his last Council meeting, Belich told a reporter he felt like doing cartwheels. Prendergast believes he has never been fully credited for spearheading the IRG review: 'Belich picked it up and ran with it, and I think that should be what he's remembered for.'[47] The way was clear for his successor to take over a reshaped organisation that was almost literally under new management. As the centenary of women's suffrage drew near, the prospect of Wellington electing its first woman mayor was tantalising. Wilde promised to 'breathe life' into the capital by attracting hotel investment and encouraging the development of inner-city apartments in vacant commercial buildings. As a founder of Tourism Wellington, Wilde was also keen to push the idea of 'Wellington Incorporated'. She ducked the question of the on-again, off-again urban motorway. On election day, she secured just a third of the mayoral votes. No group in the new Council held the balance of power: Labour, Citizens and independents each had six seats and the Greens four. Wilde announced that her first priority was to get the new councillors working as a team:

> We had an off-site meeting and all agreed we wouldn't vote in party blocs. I just didn't think it was appropriate for Council. I'd seen it not working. When you're mayor, you need to have a consensus style of leadership which is actually much harder. Or at least a majority agreement where the people who lose at least feel they've had a fair go. People always saw me as a bulldozer, but every time I had an issue I went round to all of the councillors and we just did lots of talking behind the scenes.[48]

Publicly, too, Wilde put her stamp on the job. The day after taking office, she rejected two mayoral institutions: the title 'Your Worship' and the black robes edged with ermine.[49] She wore these on only two occasions: for her swearing in, and for the James Smith's Christmas Parade: 'I sat in this car wearing the robes and chain, with a huge toy rabbit which I held by the ears. And as I was driving along, all the adults were laughing. They knew exactly what I was saying.'[50]

Wilde's appetite for work was evident on the night she was sworn in, as she ushered her new Council into a 75-minute, closed-door meeting. Her priority was the future development of the city — an aspect of the IRG report that had not yet been addressed. By the early 1990s the corporate exodus had gathered pace, a trend that would take nearly half of the capital's 60 head offices to Auckland or across the Tasman.[51] The city's claim to be the country's finance centre crumbled as three of the biggest banks and a major insurance company prepared to leave, taking hundreds of jobs with them. Just weeks after her election, Wilde persuaded councillors to participate in an inaugural two-day seminar to draw up a strategic plan and a future vision for the city. She envisaged Wellington becoming a 'city of excellence': 'We wanted our town to be dynamic, exciting, prosperous and healthy in every sense of the word; the sort of city which other people want to visit or want to move to permanently.'[52]

Early in 1993, Wilde unveiled a city branding campaign that embodied these ideals. At its heart was a promotional logo previously designed for Wellington Newspapers Ltd by the advertising agency Saatchi and Saatchi. The accompanying slogan, 'Absolutely Positively Wellington', caught on:

Wellingtonians always saw themselves as how other people described them, which was grey, boring and bureaucratic. So 'Absolutely Positively Wellington' was primarily aimed at them. It was giving them permission to feel okay about themselves and to talk about it and to go to Christchurch or Auckland or anywhere and say 'I'm from Wellington'. The response was just phenomenal. Then we thought, well, it's worked so well here we'll try it for promoting ourselves domestically — and it worked. It worked a treat. Previously, nobody would come here for leisure travel — it was all midweek visitations. But we had to start with Wellingtonians. But there was a leadership role for me and for the Council in saying 'it's okay to feel good about yourselves'.[53]

It was all a welcome respite from such solid business as bedding in the new 'integrated' regime for land-use planning. The 1991 Resource Management Act (RMA) enshrined Labour Prime Minister Geoffrey Palmer's noble but elusive principle of sustainable management. Wilde steered her Council through the introduction of a complex law enshrining community consultation with a view to 'avoiding or mitigating adverse environmental effects' rather than stopping the activities in question. Prendergast recalls how work began on the first district plan under the RMA:

Fran got in some phenomenal speakers, backed up by really good staff. She allowed the councillors to see a new vision for urbanisation. Owners of rural land on the edges of the city had anticipated it becoming residential. Under the new rules in the district plan, we turned it back to rural, limiting where developers could place green field development. We forced them to start thinking about infill housing in the suburbs and about apartment living in the city.[54]

A year into the job, Wilde was praised for her 'energy, purpose and optimism'.[55] Not all reviews were positive, however. Some ratepayers grumbled about the long-heralded shift to kerbside rubbish collection, and the cost of building Para Matchitt's distinctive city-to-sea bridge from Civic Square that opened in 1993. But Wilde's appeal to the Royal New Zealand Ballet not to move to Auckland tapped into a populist mood. She enthralled the city with the prospect of a multi-purpose sports stadium. After it became clear in 1994 that an earlier plan to revamp the Basin Reserve might cost up to $50 million, disused railways land was identified as a possible site.

The mayoralty proved a bigger job than Wilde had expected. Getting telephone calls from the *Evening Post* early on Saturday mornings soon palled. As she watched her Council divide over asset sales, she seemed to be pining for the closed-door certainties of Parliament:

> This council is a million times more transparent than any part of central
> government, which is conducted almost totally under a veil of secrecy where
> all the decisions are made within party caucuses or the Cabinet — there is no
> access there for media or the general public.[56]

Council jobs were cut, but Wilde played down the 'revolutionary' implications of Griffin's blueprint for continuing change, *Making Wellington the City of Excellence: Improving the Way We Work* (IW3). With her Thatcherite philosophy and 'can do' approach, Griffin embodied the IRG's call for a CEO with a 'strong leadership style'. She also carried the separation of the functions of regulation and service delivery — one of the central planks of the local government reforms — to new heights. On her watch, support even emerged for a user-pays sewerage system.[57] The motorway extension was redesigned as an inner-city bypass. The radical spirit of the Aro Valley lived on in the Campaign for a Better City (CBC), as green activists such as Roland Sapsford mobilised opposition to the proposed bypass through Te Aro. In 1998, CBC took an unsuccessful case to the Environment Court.

By the time Fran Wilde was elected Mayor in 1992, the long-running sewerage issue was still unresolved. In this cartoon she steps up to assist the outgoing Belich with a bottle of Harpic.

ATL, courtesy Eric Heath, H-100-002

Wilde changed her mind in favour of the sale of 49 percent of Capital Power Ltd to a Canadian company. 'We made a disaster of the meat works' became the standard justification for selling.[58] The issue resurfaced early in 1994, as the Bolger government continued to deregulate the energy industry. There was constant talk about 'selling off the family silver' at Council meetings and public forums. In March councillors voted eleven to six to sell the former Municipal Electricity Department, that old municipal 'milch cow'.[59] Wilde cleverly positioned the sale as a way to avoid rates increases for a further six years.[60] She justified the move in the 1994/95 annual plan:

> In the discussion on Capital Power, public concerns focused on the retention of control of this major asset and also on the need to deal with our debt so that we were in a position to proceed with the sewerage scheme without triggering off a financial calamity. I believe that the right decision — to sell a minority shareholding — addresses these major concerns.[61]

Wilde believes the decision to sell was appropriate: 'I just don't think the City Council should be electricity retailers. I would have sold the whole thing but I could not, I did not have the numbers to sell the whole thing, but I knew if we sold half of it, the other half would eventually be sold.' The sale helped her achieve a key ambition — sealing the deal on the long-awaited sewerage scheme:

> We went out for tender and we decided to go for a BOOT [build own operate transfer] scheme. Moa Point wasn't the best site, but all the drains in the city were moving towards it. We already had a resource consent for that site. With the other one, we would have had to start from scratch. There's huge redundancy in it, in that it's got tertiary land-based treatment plus a long outfall which we didn't need. People asked: 'Why don't you cut the outfall?' But the local iwi said: 'You'll have to go back to the Environment Court. We're not going to let you do it.' It was just one of those cases where you have to write out the cheque and move on. It was a case of getting councillors lined up and they all voted for it in the end. Getting them through the process was a miracle; it took a lot of behind-the-scenes work. You can't just bully them into it.[62]

Cr Peter Parussini was one of the few councillors prepared to question her approach:

> She's not averse to phoning you up and ranting and raving and swearing at you … She treats us [councillors] like children sometimes. I find it insulting. She sometimes forgets the council is a body of 21 elected councillors plus the Mayor.[63]

As she contemplated a second term, Wilde talked of cutting her ties with Labour and standing as an independent. She decided instead to stand down, saying she wanted to put her personal life first. In her final year, she looked ahead to the capital's strengths 'as the cultural capital and in knowledge and design-based industries'.[64] Anticipating the future importance of digital technology, Wilde backed an innovative InfoCity concept to provide the CBD with high-speed data transfer and Internet access. The Council joined a group of local investors who were paying $5,000 each to allow fibre-optic cabling to loop the city, using the electricity support cables for the trolley-buses.

A salesman for the city

Replacing Fran Wilde proved difficult. As the 1995 local body elections approached, Mark Blumsky, a shoe retailer, put himself forward. What the 38-year-old Nelson-born businessman lacked in political experience and formal education he made up for in social networks, an instinct for the popular mood, and boundless optimism. Standing as an independent, Blumsky identified his politics as 'slightly right of centre, with a social conscience'.[65] Like Belich, he had no previous Council experience. Free weekend parking in the central city became his main election platform. The city's educated middle classes tittered as the salesman from Mischief Shoes described Sky Sport as 'the best invention'. Blumsky recalls:

> I'd sold a lot of shoes in Wellington for a long time and I knew a lot of people. I also had Mischief Club — up to 10,000 people … a good supporters' base. We just pretended we were a can of baked beans and the aim was to have the public know we had more tomato sauce and more beans in our can. We just treated it like a marketing exercise.[66]

Matt Gauldie's official mayoral portrait of Mark Blumsky, with the lights of Courtenay Place behind him.

WCA, ART00546

The outsider surprised everyone by polling 26,372 votes, more than twice the number cast for his rival, Labour MP Liz Tennet. Wilde, who had supported Blumsky against her former colleague in the final weeks of the campaign, saw this clear mandate as an endorsement of her policies. But without any experience in public office, Blumsky struggled to cope: 'for the first year in particular I pretty much bumbled my way through'.[67] His inexperience showed weeks after his swearing in, as he reversed his policy that CEO Angela Griffin needed to put her job before her private consultancy business.[68] She agreed. Free weekend parking took a year to implement. Another moment of truth came midway through 1996, when Blumsky reversed his position towards selling the Council's majority share in Capital Power. The prospect of further asset sales inflamed community concern to such an extent that Blumsky agreed to a citizens' jury as a new tool for public consultation.

The jury's subsequent finding, in favour of public ownership, was promptly ignored. Economist Brian Easton was not surprised: 'The Wellington City Council, unlike its Christchurch counterpart, had no strategy of public ownership of key assets, such as local natural monopolies, and had been trapped into an invidious situation by the earlier sale of the minority holding.'[69]

Blumsky still believes that selling the rest of Capital Power was the right decision: 'I don't feel councillors should be running businesses. We weren't the right people and I didn't believe we had the skills to run it as a group. And so, after hearing the evidence, I changed my mind.'[70]

Economic development issues dominated the mid 1990s, as the outflow of corporate head offices continued and public sector employment remained static. The emphasis went on consultation, with the Council moving to calm community concerns about its decision-making processes. In 1996 Blumsky oversaw an elaborate series of 'vision' workshops and community forums, involving experts,

Building a Pacific presence

In 2001, Mayor Blumsky hosted a successful Pacific fono (gathering), attended by 80 people speaking for the main Pacific cultures in the city, including the Niuean, Samoan, Tokelauan, Fijian, Rarotongan, Tuvaluan and Tongan communities. The aims of the meeting were to establish a closer relationship between the City Council and local Pacific communities, and to encourage the latter's participation in decision-making.

The Pacific communities had finally gained a voice on Council in 1979, when Cr Tala Cleverley was elected. The profile of Pacific people in the city had continued to rise through the 1980s, with the establishment of the Pacific Islands Resource Centre in Willis Street, and the opening in 1984 of the Congregational Christian Church of Samoa in Newtown.

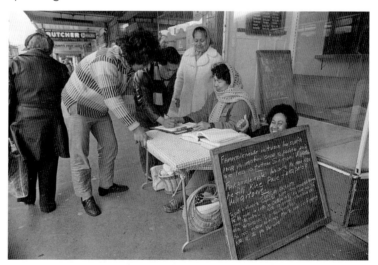

Cr Tala Cleverley (second from right), seen here during an earlier campaign to get more Polynesian people on the electoral roll.

ATL, Dominion Post Collection, EP/1977/3580/22

laypeople and scores of community groups. All grappled with the question: 'What could, or should, Wellington be like next century and beyond?' The resulting document, *Our City, Our Future*, was billed as the first strategic plan for a New Zealand city. Further surveys and countless focus groups attempted to answer the question: 'What will keep people here?' Quality of life and good jobs were identified as the two main issues. Blumsky saw things more simply:

> Ansett air hostesses working on the Mystery Weekend counters in Auckland … would be grumpy when they gave someone an envelope for Wellington. People hated it. My vision was to make them love working on that counter when they gave out envelopes for a weekend in Wellington. And I actually think we did it. The Council had $100,000 for tourism promotion; we made it $3 million. We created coffee culture, party culture. Changes to liquor licensing rules helped us encourage hotels, restaurants and bars. We did Blair, Allen, Wakefield Streets. We created a whole infrastructure to support people getting out and about. We did the Sunday shopping free parking. We organised events, events, events. And that created a great place to walk through, eat, drink, go out, have fun, meet people. That's what did it, using our strength and our size. We created a difference, and that was the Wellington brand.[71]

Carmen's cafe culture had finally arrived. And Blumsky's vision too would be realised as the number of domestic visitors to the capital more than doubled in fifteen years, from 1,152,000 in 1990 to 2,772,000 in 2005. International visitor numbers rose from 234,000 to 430,147 in the same period.[72] By the mid 1990s, the Courtenay Place precinct had emerged as the city's entertainment district. Crowds thronged the streets, gathering around buskers and other performers. Wall-to-wall cafes, restaurants and bars stayed open until all hours. Blumsky's own Wakefield Street apartment made him a symbol of the urban resurgence and the unprecedented boom in inner-city living. Within a decade, 'New York-style' apartments of varying quality became available by the hundred, in purpose-built blocks and revamped commercial buildings. The occupants ranged from young professionals and students to former suburbanites with grown-up children. Prendergast sees the apartment boom as having another important function:

> We had a city that was busy by day and dead at night. Fran could see that having 24-hour use meant you were using existing infrastructure. Your city is vibrant and alive and safe after dark. It is more efficient to use pipes

and footpaths, schools and parks that are already there than to do what Auckland has done and allow green-field development to keep marching out over the hills. They're now faced with congestion and all the other things that go with it.[73]

Continuing pledges to save money also saw the restructuring of the early 1990s making a comeback. Library services were seen as a soft target for savings, as Angela Griffin, in cost-cutting mode, promised better services by replacing people with computers. Librarians managed to fight off 'business process re-engineering', a brand of restructuring that stripped out both the Environment Division and Council Support Services. From the sidelines, Miramar Labour MP Annette King was sceptical of the promised gains:

> We were told [that] if we sold half of Capital Power, it would solve all our problems. Then if we sold all of Capital Power it would solve our problems. Now we are told if we lose nearly 200 jobs it will solve our problems. But what are the benefits?[74]

By the mid 1990s attention had turned to the waterfront, as construction proceeded on the massive Museum of New Zealand project. The Council-owned Lambton Harbour Management (LHM) earned praise in 1990 for constructing Frank Kitts Park, with its tree-lined promenades, amphitheatre and sweeping lawns. But its Queen's Wharf Events Centre, opened in 1995, was variously described as a 'Soviet ablution block' and an 'acoustic disaster'.[75] The size and ugliness of the building prompted Kelburn resident Helen Glasgow to form the lobby group Waterfront Watch. This group awakened public opposition to LHM's proposed 'wall of buildings' along the waterfront, which included a $120 million hotel and casino on Taranaki Wharf and a six-storey residential development on Chaffers Street. Michael Fowler had first raised the idea of a casino in 1978. Following public opposition and a Council moratorium on waterfront development, Blumsky decided the social cost would be too high:[76]

> I just felt it would have killed Courtenay Place. People said I did it because of the gambling. But a structure on the waterfront would have sucked the lifeblood out of Courtenay Place and the restaurants and the night life we were trying to create as a point of difference.[77]

Blumsky later posed for his official mayoral portrait with his jacket slung over his shoulder and the lights of Courtenay Place behind him. He gained an almost Kitts-like reputation for sheer mayoral visibility, later drawing criticism for a self-promoting leadership style.[78] But the 1998 local body elections brought him back with a bigger majority: 'When I was re-elected, I knew I was the mayor and I had a right to be there. I felt I knew what I was doing.'[79] Another milestone for Blumsky was his appointment as CEO of Garry Poole.

Wellington's economy remained shaky. Prendergast remembers how councillors realised that improving the 'quality of life' alone wouldn't stem the head office exodus:

> We all were devastated in Mark's second term when we found we were still losing the corporates. The research said it was about jobs. We got involved much more deeply in economic development and business clusters. Ultimately we set up Positively Wellington Business, making sure we supported the businesses that were going to fill the shoes of the big business that left the city.[80]

Blumsky made himself unpopular by talking about overhauling the Council. In 1996, he called for the city to have a ten-strong elected 'board of directors', on high salaries and performance contracts, rather than a mayor and councillors. He said it was frustrating to have 'no contract or legal right to bring people into line if it is ever needed'.[81] The sale of another Council asset underlined his point. The 'core services reviews' during Blumsky's first term that had prepared the ground for the sale of Capital Power had also questioned the city's ownership of 34 percent of Wellington Airport. Meanwhile, the Coalition government of Prime Minister Jenny Shipley prepared to sell its 66 percent shareholding in the airport to Infratil. In mid 1998, after public consultation, Blumsky was confident he had the numbers on Council for a sale. The news was conveyed to Cabinet. Cr Kent Clark, a bus driver, then caused confusion by switching sides after talking to his passengers on the 6.25 a.m. bus from Karori. In the resulting impasse, New Zealand First leader Winston Peters dissolved the Coalition with National. Looking back, Blumsky grimaces: 'I learned the power of the bus driver.'

In February 1998, the Museum of New Zealand Te Papa Tongarewa ('Our Place') opened on the waterfront near Taranaki Wharf. The imposing storehouse for the nation's treasures was an immediate success, attracting a million visitors by mid-year and more than justifying the Council's $10 million contribution. Meanwhile, across the inner harbour, a $50 million sports stadium resembling a water tank (or, more popularly, a cake tin) was emerging on disused railway land near Aotea Quay. The home of Wellington rugby was on the move. Late in 1999, a crowd of 30,000 watched the farewell Wellington Lions versus Otago match at Athletic Park. A century after spectators first trekked to Newtown to watch rugby and other sports, the stands were crumbling. Since 1991, when its owners, the Tenths Trust, had won the right to increase the peppercorn rental, the Wellington Rugby Football Union had increasingly found Athletic Park a financial burden. 'The Park' was later demolished to make way for a retirement village. The WestpacTrust stadium, designed by architects Warren and Mahoney, opened on New Year's Eve 1999.

Lambton Harbour Management's evolving plans for the waterfront continued to meet resistance in the late 1990s. The Civic Trust, set up in 1981 to monitor the city's development, joined the opposition to a major redevelopment of Chaffers Park. Meanwhile, the group Rangatiratanga Tuku Iho accused LHM chief executive Donald Best and his fellow directors of 'setting themselves up as gods' and not consulting adequately.[82] After a long series of public meetings, petitions, moratoria, consultations and resignations, the Council unveiled its so-called Variation 17 scheme, which involved twenty new buildings lining the waterfront, including two twelve-storey towers. At the end of 1999 Waterfront Watch, now headed by Lindsay Shelton, launched a campaign against the scheme that culminated in a packed meeting at the Town Hall:

> It was only after we filled the Town Hall with people protesting against the building plans that the Council backed down. I remember seeing Mayor Blumsky slumped in his chair at the back of the hall as speaker after speaker criticised the Council's plans. Within a few months, he announced that Variation 17 would be withdrawn.[83]

Blumsky recalls: 'I just sat in the audience. If the Events Centre had been a really neat building I don't think we would have had any of this. But because of that, there was huge distrust. And so I called for a "cup of tea".'[84]

The Mayor was listening. But after eight years as president of Waterfront Watch, Shelton had become sceptical about the sincerity of the Council's consultation processes, required under the RMA. His view was shared by many of the city's voluntary heritage, environment and community groups.

The city council was unable — even, it seemed to me, unwilling — to enter into genuine dialogue with organisations such as ours whose views differed from what it wanted to do. Only after we took extreme measures — a Town Hall meeting, an appeal to the Environment Court — was change achieved. Had the council been able to enter into a two-way dialogue, change should have been achieved without the need for our organisation to go to such extreme lengths to prove its case. The question now is whether voluntary organisations still have the strength to continue fighting the council. When I see the council's advertising inviting citizens to state their views on plans of all kinds, I think back on my own experience, which showed me that the council went through the motions of consultation but was unable to bring itself to factor public opinion into its final decision making.[85]

At the end of 2000, just eight years after its skewering by *North and South*, Wellington took the magazine's coveted 'Top Town' prize. For Blumsky, it was the high point of his mayoralty. In less than a decade, the capital had successfully re-invented itself, as the magazine acknowledged:

One only need visit the sleek new Wellington Stadium to watch the Hurricanes, Wellington's regional rugby team, play in the Super 12 series, and experience the intensely parochial fervour which fuses the crowd of 38,500 … [I]s this burst of civic pride justified? Well, yes, it seems so. The economy, while still vulnerable to the vagaries of the financial and government sectors, has warmed up considerably. Visionary town planning has, with the exception of one or two blunders, opened up the waterfront and provided public spaces, urban parks and public buildings of which city dwellers are justifiably proud. Ambitious projects — Te Papa, the stadium — and the sympathetic restoration of handsome old buildings [have] reinvigorated the downtown precinct. The city has remade itself and its citizens like what they see.[86]

Peter Jackson's decision to use his home town as a base for filming J. R. R. Tolkien's *Lord of the Rings* trilogy further lifted civic pride. Later, Jackson invested tens of millions of dollars in elaborate, high-tech facilities, thus laying permanent ground for a film-making industry in what some were now calling 'Wellywood'. Jackson's enterprise was seen as a perfect fit with an emerging vision of Wellington as the 'creative capital'. Early in 2001, Blumsky travelled to Los Angeles to promote Wellington as 'home of *Lord of the Rings*'.

Treasure from Middle Earth

On 11 October 1999, on a pine-needle-strewn track on Mt Victoria, film-maker Peter Jackson and his crew captured the first rough images of an epic enterprise. In the scene, a group of hobbits cower in fear beneath tree-roots, hiding from the Black Riders — a dramatic moment in the first of three films based on J. R. R. Tolkien's *Lord of the Rings* trilogy.

Blumsky poses in Midland Park with British actor Sir Ian McKellen, who played Gandalf in the *Lord of the Rings* trilogy.

WCA, 00521:5:16-10A

Over fifteen hectic months, Jackson and his crew travelled to locations around the country, using snow-capped mountains, forests and river plains to recreate the landscapes of Tolkien's fantasy world. The capital became the heart of the $250 million project, with interior scenes filmed at Jackson's Camperdown studios in Miramar. Outside locations included Seatoun's Fort Dorset and the Dry Creek quarry in Lower Hutt, where the battle of Helm's Deep was filmed.

The economic impact of the project was profound. Although Jackson worked under a cloak of secrecy, almost every Wellingtonian seemed to know one of the 300 crew or the estimated 15,000 extras. The millions of dollars injected into the local economy made businesses happy, and the local populace smiled indulgently as the stars shopped and socialised among them, even when it was disclosed that drunken hobbits had scaled the Cuba Mall fountain and urinated into it.

A mayor for the 21st century

Midway through 2001, Blumsky announced his retirement. Kerry Prendergast, his deputy over two terms, had a change of heart and decided to join the mayoral race. Her long-standing ambition for a parliamentary career had led her to stand for the National Party as a list candidate in the 1999 general election, but National's drubbing saw her miss out on a seat. In the 2001 mayoral election, however, Prendergast's middlebrow image and breadth of local body experience helped her clinch an election night victory with a majority of 8,685 votes. The new Council comprised nine women and eleven men. At her swearing-in, Prendergast announced that the mayoral robe would be worn at full Council meetings, with the mace being ceremonially carried in at the start of each meeting and out again at its conclusion. The new Mayor was putting her own stamp on the mayoralty, in a clear departure from the casual Blumsky style.

Late in 2001 came news that Wellington would host the Australasian premiere of *The Fellowship of the Ring*, the first film of the trilogy. Overnight, the city changed its name: municipal employees found they were now working for the Middle Earth City Council; the evening paper changed its masthead to *Middle Earth Post*, and carried the memorable headline 'City Embraces Hobbit Habit'; arrivals at Wellington Airport were greeted by a huge banner welcoming them to Middle Earth.

In 2002, standing in the middle of the new stadium, Jackson persuaded one-day cricket fans to become sound extras for the battle scenes at Helm's Deep. The combined efforts of 20,000 Wellingtonians stamping their feet, snarling and humming added so much sonic depth to the film that crowds at rugby games were also enlisted.

In 2003 Prendergast was instrumental in securing the right to host the world premiere of *The Return of the King*, the final film in the trilogy. On 1 December, an estimated 120,000 people choked the streets to cheer Jackson and his retinue of hobbits, orcs, elves and black riders as the parade passed by. At Courtenay Place, the stars paused for autographs and photographs as they strolled along 470 metres of red carpet to the Embassy Theatre, refurbished at a cost of $4.5 million, underwritten by Council.

Wellington was suitably dressed for the occasion, with the Cave Troll hanging off the old Corporation Building in Civic Square, Gollum glowering from the roof of a new airport terminal, and Legolas's arrow piercing the facade of Molly Malone's bar. A huge 'Fell Beast', a long-necked creature of fangs and menace, loomed above the Embassy. For the first time in its history, Wellington found itself at the centre of world attention.

Prendergast also aimed for the unifying leadership style that had worked for Fran Wilde. She enjoyed some of Wilde's success in lobbying councillors informally and keeping them too busy to make trouble. But in 2002 she faced controversy over the $278,000 Council bail-out of a golf tournament on the nearby Kapiti Coast featuring champion Tiger Woods. The spending was later justified on the grounds that this was the kind of event 'a vibrant and exciting' city should be promoting.[87]

At the end of 2002, the giant dairy company Fonterra announced it was shifting 400 head office jobs to Auckland. In response, Prendergast unveiled her vision for the city as 'Creative Wellington — Innovation Capital'. At its heart was a plan to foster creative 'clusters', embracing film, creative industries, software development and, appropriately, earthquake engineering. The *Dominion Post* was unconvinced:

Mayor Kerry Prendergast, photographed in 2004.

WCA, D02S0882

The string of major corporations that has left Wellington has become alarmingly long, and the new businesses that have arrived do not match, in size or prestige, those that have left. Having produced her vision, the hard work for Ms Prendergast must now begin, because so far it is hard to see in the strategy anything that will turn that tide.[88]

The Wellington crowd enjoys the carnival atmosphere of the Rugby Sevens at Westpac Stadium.

WCA, 45606:199

The Mayor and Council worked to make the vision tangible, increasing and funding to bodies such as Positively Wellington Tourism and Positively Wellington Business. Effort went into shoring up remaining businesses and attracting tourists, students and skilled migrants. Events and attractions of every stripe were championed as part of a conscious 'Events Capital' strategy. Over Waitangi weekend 2005, for example, the International Rugby Board Sevens tournament attracted an estimated 25,000 visitors to the capital, boosting the local economy and helping to create a carnival atmosphere. Over the same three days, the city hosted a Chinese New Year parade and fireworks, the annual 'One Love' Concert, the Global Yacht Challenge, a Waitangi Day family concert, and the ASB Tennis International. Diwali, the Hindu 'festival of lights', exemplified the range of community festivals supported as part of encouraging cultural expression. First celebrated in the city in 2000, Diwali has become an annual fixture, attracting thousands to Civic Square.

The Council worked hard to be 'business friendly' in order to attract business to the capital — and keep it here. Commercial rates were progressively reduced as part of a 'rates differential' programme introduced after the 1987 sharemarket crash to lessen the impact of falling commercial property values. In 2002 Prendergast said it was 'grossly unfair' that commercial ratepayers had until recently paid more than $7 for every $1 paid by residential ratepayers:

> Our commercial sector rates were the highest in the country and that was not the way to go. Over the next seven years we'll reduce that ratio to $1 for $2.80. It's a 10-year programme of gradually reducing the commercial sector impost, which of course gets put on the residential sector. But if we did it any quicker, the impost would be huge on the residential sector with the risk that not only I'd go but my council would as well. This way at least the commercial sector can bank on a market in seven years that'll be much more fair and reasonable.[89]

Wellington also remembered its past. In 2002, 3.2 ha of the central Town Belt land taken by the government in 1871 for education and hospital purposes was returned to the city. It was the culmination of a decade of discussion and lobbying by the Council and the Friends of the Town Belt group. Bounded by Alexandra Road to the east and Wellington Hospital, Government House and Wellington College to the west, the site included a fever hospital built after the 1918 influenza epidemic to isolate patients with infectious diseases such as scarlet fever and tuberculosis. The historic building's large windows, sun-porches and verandahs, and the park-like surroundings, reflected the medical wisdom of the time that open air was vital to restoring health. The Council subsequently restored the heritage building, and changed the District Plan to protect it. In the city centre, the Council was involved in the restoration of the old Bank of New Zealand and the St James and Embassy theatres.

In 2004, as the local body elections approached, Prendergast looked likely to secure a second mayoral term. Initiatives taken that year included the 'enhancing' of Oriental Bay with 27,000 tonnes of golden Takaka sand, and improving the seating and lighting in Manners Mall. Less glamorous issues such as water supply, sewerage and storm-water networks, rubbish and recycling were also addressed. A new 6.5 million litre reservoir was completed at Maupuia, and progress made on another new reservoir in Roseneath. A fundamental upgrade of the central city's storm-water system entailed the construction of 650 metres of new tunnels beneath Willis, Victoria, Bond and Harris Streets. The massive and protracted tunnelling effort followed a series of torrential downpours that raised questions about Wellington's changing weather patterns. The transport network also came in for attention as the Council implemented a Safer Roads project with the aim of reducing accident numbers by one-third by 2010.

Other issues proved divisive, including a proposal to build a national music school on the old Circa Theatre site in Harris Street, on the north-east corner of Civic Square; the restarting of development on the waterfront; and the still hotly contested inner-city bypass. The Council's consultation processes were described as a 'charade': for example, people were asked whether they wanted the music school, but not presented with alternative options for the land, including keeping it as open space. As the 2004 local body election approached, Prendergast brushed aside talk that she had a 'bullying style'; but she did concede that she could be 'sharp, and I don't suffer fools easily'.[90]

The October election proved the most turbulent in years. Delays in vote-counting procedures at a national level forced candidates to wait eleven anxious days to hear the final results. To compound the problem, Wellington City was holding its first-ever election under proportional representation, based on the single transferable vote (STV) system selected by a citizens' referendum in November 2002. The size of the Council was reduced and several of the Mayor's supporters missed re-election; her deputy, Alick Shaw, was only narrowly returned. An unusually scathing *Dominion Post* pointed to the 'deep-seated dissatisfaction of voters'.[91] The Mayor promised to do better: 'What I want to do is review what we've been doing, identify who we will consult, how we can eliminate duplication, how we can clarify what we are doing and engage with the community so we're all speaking the same language.'[92]

As her second term progressed, Prendergast made arts infrastructure a priority. Her Council refurbished properties in Abel Smith Street to create an Arts Centre, providing studios and rehearsal space for theatre groups, television producers, fashion designers, and dozens of other creative artists. Positively Wellington Business helped secure funding for a new state-of-the-art soundstage at Miramar's

Camperdown Studios, used by Peter Jackson for the filming of *King Kong*. Meanwhile, more public artworks brightened the city, as the Council worked with the Wellington Sculpture Trust on such dramatic pieces as Andrew Drummond's 'Tower of Light' on Cobham Drive, one of more than 20 sculptures erected around the city. The list of 'iconic' events lengthened as the World of Wearable Art shifted from Nelson to the capital in 2005, confirming Wellington's status as the cultural, arts and events capital of New Zealand.

The Council's sustained effort to promote Wellington was paying off. In 2004 the number of domestic tourists reached 3.1 million, compared with 1.1 million in 1990.[93] Population trends also improved. Wellington grew by 3.9 percent between 1996 and 2001, higher than the national average of 3.3 percent but no match for Auckland's 6.4 percent.[94] Long-term trends indicate that the northwards drift will continue. By 2021, Auckland is expected to have grown in twenty years by the equivalent of Wellington's 2003 population of 185,100.[95]

As early as 1865, commentators sensed that for Wellington, becoming the capital was 'the tide that leads on to fortune'.[96] And so it proved for a century. The city's economic life-support system did, however, go into shock after the massive restructurings of the 1980s, as civil service jobs, many of them based in Wellington, plummeted from 89,000 in 1986 to 30,355 in 2001. Since 2001, however, the number of permanent public service staff has risen to 40,325.[97]

Reclaiming the past

This book ends in 2005 where it began: down by the shoreline of Te Whanganui-a-Tara. Much has happened in 165 years. We have, however, only crossed the inner harbour from Pipitea Point to the bottom of Taranaki Street. Here on the edge of a bustling city, on land being cleared for yet another apartment block, pieces of the old Te Aro Pa are unearthed weeks before Christmas. Relics of the city's Maori past emerge from the rubble after being buried for a century and a half.

At 39 Taranaki Street, archaeologists have found remnants of traditional ponga-log whare (houses) that once sheltered 200 inhabitants, members of subtribes of Taranaki and Ngati Ruanui. The people living here in 1840 gathered seafood, cultivated gardens and sold the produce. In 2005, the site also yields an iron cannonball, an all-too-obvious symbol of the pressures exerted by settlers on these centrally located lands. Following an enforced sale of the land in 1865, the local authorities extended Taranaki Street in 1870 to provide access to the reclamation and what was to become Taranaki Wharf. By 1890, no trace of the pa or its people remained.

The surprise discovery arouses powerful feelings among local Maori. Over the summer of 2005/06, the Wellington Tenths Trust, the Historic Places Trust, the City Council and the anxious developer join forces to plan the preservation effort. The diggings are covered with white plastic tents and watched over by security guards. The available options include encasing the remains of the whare in glass for people to view, ideally on their present site. Cr Ray Ahipene-Mercer, who is leading the Council's contribution, shares the amazement of many when he views the diggings:

> The feeling was remarkable. It was a moving experience — to see the actual remnants of spaces that people lived in. Though the people were not my whakapapa, I feel a very powerful link as a Maori. As a city councillor, I think it's exciting. This is absolutely irrefutable evidence of the Maori history behind this place.[98]

Wellington has come a long way to this excavation on its former shoreline. A municipality that once helped to drive a road through the heart of Te Aro Pa is now working to rescue relics of its history. Past and present lie here side by side, stirred by a tangy summer wind.

Notes

Introduction

1. Malcolm McKinnon, (ed.), *New Zealand Historical Atlas: Ko Papatuanuku e Takoto Nei*, David Bateman/Historical Branch, Department of Internal Affairs, Wellington, 1997, plate 25.
2. Alan Mulgan, *City of the Strait: Wellington and its Province*, p.204.
3. Charles Wilson, *New Zealand Cities: Wellington*, p.37.
4. Nancy M. Taylor, *The Journal of Ensign Best 1837–1843*, Government Printer, Wellington, 1966, p.152.
5. *Evening Post*, 9 January 1954.
6. Dante, *The Divine Comedy: Cantica 1: Hell*, translated by Dorothy Sayers, Penguin Books, London, 1979, p.98.
7. Lauris Edmond, 'The Active Voice', in *50 Poems: A Celebration*, Bridget Williams Books, Wellington, 1999.
8. Louis Ward's *Early Wellington* (1929) is a quirky grab-bag of civic material, including details of the 1842 Borough Council, and the formation of the Wellington City Corporation in 1870. Alan Mulgan's centennial history, *City of the Strait* (1939), contains a chapter on the history and activities of municipal government. More popular was Fanny Irvine-Smith's readable and detailed *Streets of My City* (1948), with information about the municipality as it was in the 1930s. In the 1960s, Canadian postgraduate student George Betts celebrated the WCC centenary with *Betts on Wellington* (1970), a summary of his comprehensive academic survey of local politics and civic participation. Norman McLeod and Bruce Farland's contribution to the centenary was *Wellington Prospect: Survey of the City 1840–1970*, a collection of brief essays touching on civic topics. Terence Hodgson's essential *Colonial Capital: Wellington 1865–1910* (1990) is a pictorial work with essays on municipal enterprise. The sesquicentennial year also produced David Hamer and Roberta Nicholls' excellent *Making of Wellington, 1800–1914*, a collection of longer essays, some on civic matters. In 2003, David McGill published *Wellington: A Capital Century*, another heavily illustrated book tackling aspects of municipal governance. Chris Maclean's *Wellington: Telling Tales* (2005) also explores the City Council's role in shaping the city.

Chapter 1: Colonial Settlement to Borough Capital

1. Ian Wedde, *The Drummer*, Auckland University Press, Auckland, 1993.
2. David McGill, *Pioneers of Port Nicholson*, p.31.
3. Louis Ward, *Early Wellington*, p.34.
4. *Evening Post*, 2 March 1911. McKenzie always claimed that he and Ticehurst were the first Europeans to land on the site.
5. Dinah Priestley, *Old Thorndon*, p.12, and G.H. Scholefield(ed.), *A Dictionary of New Zealand Biography*, p.29.
6. Mairatea Tahiwi and Cushla Parekowhai, 'Ruhia Porutu', in Charlotte Macdonald, Merimeri Penfold & Bridget Williams (eds), *The Book of New Zealand Women: Ko Kui Ma Te Kaupapa*, Bridget Williams Books, Wellington, 1991, p.534.
7. Barnet Burns, *A Brief Narrative of the Remarkable History of Barnet Burns*.
8. *Nga Tupuna o Te Whanganui-a-Tara*, Wellington City Council & Wellington Tenths Trust, Wellington, 2001, pp.27–9.
9. *New Zealand Mail*, 24 April 1880.
10. *Evening Post*, 30 December 1904.
11. George Clarke, *Notes on Early Life in New Zealand*, pp.52–4.
12. Elsdon Best, 'Te Whanga-nui-a-Tara: Wellington in Pre-Pakeha Days', *Journal of the Polynesian Society*, p.153.
13. Malcolm McKinnon (ed.), *New Zealand Historical Atlas: Ko Papatuanuku e Takoto Nei*, pp.24–5.
14. Heritage Trail, 'Te Ara o nga Tupuna: The path of our ancestors', URL: http://www.wcl.govt.nz/maori/wellington/TeAra1.html
15. Waitangi Tribunal, *Te Whanganui a Tara me Ona Takiwa, Report on the Wellington District*, Wellington, 2003.
16. David Millar, *Once Upon a Village: A History of Lower Hutt, 1819–1965*, p.13.
17. Angela Ballara, 'Te Wharepouri, Te Kakapi-o-te-rangi (?–1842)', *Dictionary of New Zealand Biography*, updated 7 July 2005, URL: http://www.dnzb.govt.nz
18. Ballara, 'Te Wharepouri'.
19. Edward Jerningham Wakefield, *Adventure in New Zealand*, p.37.
20. *Nga Tupuna o Te Whanganui-a-Tara*, p.17.

21 A.R. Cairns, 'Ngatata, Wiremu Tako (?–1887)', *Dictionary of New Zealand Biography*, updated 7 July 2005, URL: http://www.dnzb.govt.nz/

22 John Wood, *Twelve Months in Wellington, Port Nicholson*, p.9.

23 Alexander Majoribanks, *Travels in New Zealand*, p.11.

24 Arthur Carman, *Birth of a City: Wellington, 1840–43*, p.5.

25 Wakefield, *Adventure in New Zealand*, p.82.

26 Wakefield, *Adventure in New Zealand*, p.92.

27 J.C. Beaglehole, *Captain Hobson and the New Zealand Company: A Study in Colonial Administration*, Department of History of Smith College, Massachusetts, USA, 1928, p.55.

28 Carman, *Birth of a City*, p.11.

29 J. Ward to W.M. Smith, 1 August 1839, NZC 102/1–2, Archives New Zealand (ANZ).

30 Wakefield, *Adventure in New Zealand*, p.149.

31 Hobson to Russell, 10 November 1840, *Great Britain Parliamentary Papers (GBPP)*, No.311, 1841, p.126.

32 Carman, *Birth of a City*, p.15.

33 J. Russell to W. Hobson, 9 December 1840, *GBPP*, No.311, 1841, p.26.

34 S. Revans to H.S. Chapman, Letters Vol.II, July 1841, p.165, Alexander Turnbull Library (ATL).

35 Kathleen Coleridge, 'Thriving on Impressions: The Pioneer Years of Wellington Printing', in David Hamer & Roberta Nicholls (eds), *The Making of Wellington: 1800–1914*, p.91.

36 *New Zealand Gazette*, Vol.I, No.11, 20 June 1840.

37 Diana Beaglehole, 'Political Leadership in Wellington, 1839–53', in Hamer & Nicholls (eds), *The Making of Wellington*, p.170.

38 Coleridge, 'Thriving on Impressions', p.94.

39 Wakefield, *Adventure in New Zealand*, p.253.

40 Wellington Borough Council Minutes, 10 November, 1842, Wellington City Archives (WCA).

41 *Wharenui — Wharewaka, Te Aro Pa — Taranaki Wharf*, Cultural Impact Report, Wellington Tenths Trust, Wellington, 2005, p.27.

42 Herbert Roth, *Trades Unions in New Zealand: Past and Present*, p.3.

43 'George Hunter (1788–1843)', in G.H. Scholefield (ed.), *A Dictionary of New Zealand Biography*, p.420.

44 Mary Swainson to her grandparents in England, 25 September 1842, Unpublished MS, ATL.

45 *Evening Post*, 2 October 1947.

46 *NZ Gazette*, 6 August 1843; *Spectator*, 18 August 1843.

47 *Illustrated London News*, 9 February 1850.

48 Ward, *Early Wellington*, p.286.

49 *Illustrated London News*, 9 February 1850.

50 *NZ Gazette*, 19 July 1845.

51 George Macmorran, *Some Schools and Schoolmasters of Early Wellington*, p.27.

52 Brad Patterson, 'A "Half Australian, Half American" Town', in J. McConchie, D. Winchester and R. Willis (eds), *Dynamic Wellington: A Contemporary Synthesis and Explanation of Wellington*.

53 *Independent*, 9 December 1848.

54 *NZ Mail*, 12 June 1907.

55 George Betts, *Betts on Wellington: A City and its Politics*, A.H. & A.W. Reed, Wellington, 1970, p.32.

56 Mary Taylor to Ellen Nussey, 14 October 1850, WS no.610, Brontë Parsonage Museum, Haworth, UK.

57 Mary Taylor to Charlotte Brontë, April 1850, WS no.550, Brontë Parsonage Museum, Haworth, UK.

58 Mary Taylor to Ellen Nussey, 9 February 1849, WS no.422, Berg Collection, New York Public Library.

59 *The Cyclopedia of New Zealand*, Vol.1, Cyclopedia Co. Ltd, Wellington, 1897, p.247.

60 *Evening Post*, 22 July 1876.

61 Wellington City Council Minute Books (WCCMB), WCA, Vol.57, p.374, 10 September 1949.

62 Ward, *Early Wellington*, p.177.

63 Kathleen A. Coleridge, 'Carpenter, Robert Holt (1819/20?–1891)', *Dictionary of New Zealand Biography*, updated 21 July 2003, URL: http://www.dnzb.govt.nz

64 Speech of His Honour the Superintendent on opening the Third Session of the Third Provincial Council of Province of Wellington, 24 April 1863, *Wellington Provincial Council Proceedings*, 1863–1865, ATL.

65 *Independent*, 4 March 1862.

66 *Independent*, 13 July 1865.

67 Wellington Town Board Minute Books (WTBMB), WCA, Vol.1, p.125, 20 March 1865.

68 WTBMB, WCA, Vol.1, p.142, 11 July 1865.
69 WTBMB, WCA, Vol.1, p.10, 3 October 1863.
70 WTBMB, WCA, Vol.1, p.11, 9 October 1863.
71 *NZ Spectator and Cook Strait Guardian*, 28 October 1863.
72 *NZ Spectator and Cook Strait Guardian*, 8 July 1863.
73 WTBMB, WCA, Vol.1, p.43, 19 January 1864.
74 WTBMB, WCA, Vol.1, p.62, 2 August 1864.
75 WTBMB, WCA, Vol.1, p.66, 2 September 1864.
76 This and subsequent calculations are provided by the Reserve Bank of New Zealand's CPI Inflation calculator. See www.rbnz.govt.nz.
77 *Independent*, 14 September 1865.
78 *Independent*, 14 September 1865.
79 *Evening Post*, 4 March 1865.
80 WTBMB, WCA, Vol.2, p.312, 22 June 1868.
81 WTBMB, WCA, Vol.2, p.386, 29 January 1869.
82 WTBMB, WCA, Vol.2, p.415, 18 June 1869.
83 WTBMB, WCA, Vol.2, p.245, 20 November 1867.
84 WTBMB, WCA, Vol.2, p.60, 26 January 1866.
85 WTBMB, WCA, Vol.2, p.66, 26 January 1866.
86 *New Zealand Parliamentary Debates (NZPD)*, Vol.4, 1868, p.334.
87 *NZPD*, Vol.4, 1868, p.335.
88 WTBMB, WCA, Vol.2, p.171, 14 September 1867.
89 *Evening Post*, 4 March 1867.
90 *Evening Post*, 12 March 1867.
91 R.E. Offer, *Walls for Water: Pioneer Dam Building in New Zealand*, Dunmore Press, Palmerston North, 1997, p.33.
92 WTBMB, WCA, Vol.2, p.432, 2 August 1869.
93 WTBMB, WCA, Vol.2, p.176, 14 May 1867.
94 WTBMB, WCA, Vol.2, p.196, 26 July 1867.
95 WTBMB, WCA, Vol.2, p.435, 30 August 1869.
96 WTBMB, WCA, Vol.2, p.472, 17 December 1869.
97 WTBMB, WCA, Vol.2, p.172, 14 May 1867.
98 *Independent*, 22 August 1868.
99 *Independent*, 16 August 1868.

Chapter 2: Dodge City on Sea

1 *Evening Post*, 8 July 1870.
2 *New Zealand Gazette*, 16 September 1870.
3 *Evening Post*, 8 July 1870.
4 *Evening Post*, 3 January 1948.
5 *Evening Post*, 9 July 1870.
6 *Independent*, 22 July 1869.
7 *Wellington Almanac*, 'Thomas McKenzie', Wellington, 1864.
8 Pat Lawlor, *Old Wellington Hotels*, p.38.
9 *Evening Post*, 3 January 1948.
10 Craig Press, 'The Role of Government in Developing the Colonial City: The Case of Wellington, 1840–1903', p.59.
11 William Sutch, *The Quest for Security in New Zealand, 1840 to 1966*, p.43.
12 *Evening Post*, 3 January 1948.
13 Jessica Rankin, unpublished diary 1867–1869, Pharazyn family.
14 Rankin diary.
15 Rankin diary.
16 F.L. Irvine-Smith, *Streets of My City*, p.43.
17 Gael Ferguson, *Building the New Zealand Dream*, p.20.
18 G.L. Meredith, *Adventuring in Maoriland in the Seventies*, p.18.

19 Heaphy memoranda and reports cited in *Te Whanganui o Tara me Ona Takiwa: Report on the Wellington District*, Waitangi Tribunal, Wellington, 2003, p.341.
20 Morris Love, 'Te Ati Awa of Wellington', *Te Ara: The Encyclopedia of New Zealand*, updated 17 March 2005, URL: http://www.teara.govt.nz/NewZealanders/MaoriNewZealanders/TeAtiAwaWellington/en
21 *New Zealand Parliamentary Debates (NZPD)*, Vol.7, 1870, p.395.
22 *Evening Post*, 21 July 1870.
23 *Evening Post*, 29 August 1870.
24 Wellington City Council Minute Books (WCCMB), WCA, Vol.3, p.2, 30 September 1870.
25 K.C. McDonald, *City of Dunedin: A Century of Civic Enterprise*, pp.121–3.
26 WCCMB, WCA, Vol.3, p.74, 28 March 1871.
27 City of Wellington: Reports and Proceedings of the City Council on a Water Supply to the City, 00030:1:1, WCA.
28 City of Wellington: Reports and Proceedings on a Water Supply, WCA.
29 Hector Report, 1871, 00030:1:2, WCA.
30 WCCMB, WCA, Vol.3, p.34, 18 November 1870.
31 *Evening Post*, 5 December 1873.
32 WCCMB, WCA, Vol.5, p.225, 30 October 1879.
33 WCCMB, WCA, Vol.3, p.182, 1 March 1872.
34 WCCMB, WCA, Vol.3, p.306, 25 September 1873.
35 WCCMB, WCA, Vol.3, p.401, 6 August 1874.
36 WCCMB, WCA, Vol.3, p.180, 1 March 1872.
37 *NZPD*, Vol.16, 1874, p.390.
38 *New Zealand Times*, 6 May 1879.
39 *New Zealand Times*, 11 July 1879.
40 WCCMB, WCA, Vol.3, p.68, 3 March 1871.
41 *New Zealand Times*, 3 January 1881.
42 WCCMB, WCA, Vol.3, p.62, 24 February 1871.
43 Leslie Verry, *Seven Days a Week: The Story of Independent Newspapers Ltd*, INL Print, Wellington, 1985, pp.17–22.
44 *Evening Post*, 11 December 1873.
45 *Evening Post*, 16 December 1873.
46 *Evening Post*, 17 December 1873.
47 *New Zealand Times*, 6 May 1879.
48 WCC Outwards Correspondence Letter Book No.1, 17 May 1872–12 March 1875, 00296:2:1, WCA.
49 *New Zealand Mail*, 11 April 1874.
50 WCCMB, WCA, Vol.3, p.242, 16 January 1873.
51 WCCMB, WCA, Vol.3, p.314, 9 October 1873.
52 WCCMB, WCA, Vol.3, p.91, 2 June 1871.
53 WCCMB, WCA, Vol.4, p.106, 20 January 1876.
54 George Betts, *Betts on Wellington: A City and its Politics*, p.36.
55 *NZPD*, Vol.20, 1876, p.403.
56 *NZPD*, Vol.35, 1880, p.162.
57 WCCMB, WCA, Vol.5, p.234, 27 November 1879.
58 WCCMB, WCA, Vol.5, p.119, 28 March 1879.
59 Chris Cochrane, 'Styles of Sham and Genuine Simplicity: Timber Buildings in Wellington to 1880', in David Hamer and Roberta Nicholls (eds), *The Making of Wellington, 1800–1914*, p.123.
60 WCCMB, WCA, Vol.4, p.172, 19 October 1876.
61 *New Zealand Times*, 16 November 1880.
62 Town Belt, 1861–1923, 00002:4:188, WCA.
63 *New Zealand Times*, 27 April 1882.
64 *New Zealand Times*, 3 May 1882.
65 Re Tramway Act — R. Somerville, 28 Nov 1878, 00233:2:1878/1351; Forwarding report re use of steam power by Tramway Company — Under-Secretary for Public Works, 04 Dec 1878, 00233:2:1878/1375, WCA.
66 WCC Outwards Correspondence Letter Book No.2, 12 March 1875–30 October 1876, 00296:2:2, WCA.
67 *New Zealand Mail*, 20 November 1875.
68 *New Zealand Mail*, 1 April 1876.
69 WCCMB, WCA, Vol.4, p.88, 24 June 1875.

70 *Te Whanganui a Tara me Ona Takiwa: Report on the Wellington District.*
71 *New Zealand Times*, 24 January 1878.
72 *New Zealand Times*, 28 October 1879.
73 David Johnson, *Wellington Harbour*, p.150.
74 *Evening Post*, 19 March 1881.
75 Johnson, *Wellington Harbour*, p.154.
76 *New Zealand Mail*, 14 March 1884.
77 *Evening Post*, 14 August 1884.
78 *Evening Post*, 28 April 1885.
79 G.T. Bloomfield, *New Zealand: A Handbook of Historical Statistics*, p.57.
80 *Hawke's Bay Herald*, 4 August 1880.
81 *Evening Post*, 9 September 1879.
82 John McKinnon, *John Plimmer and his Family, 1841–1991*, p.31.
83 Lawlor, *Old Wellington Hotels*, p.18.
84 *New Zealand Mail*, 10 November 1877.
85 *Evening Post*, 14 February 1880.
86 *Evening Post*, 21 November 1877.
87 *Evening Post*, 15 October 1876.
88 *Evening Post*, 24 December 1883.
89 WCCMB, WCA, Vol.5, p.271, 4 March 1880.
90 WCCMB, WCA, Vol.6, p.153, 8 November 1882.
91 *Evening Post*, 15 September 1882.
92 *The Cyclopedia of New Zealand*, Wellington, 1897, p.297.
93 WCCMB, WCA, Vol.5, p.348, 19 August 1880.
94 *New Zealand Times*, 26 October, 9 November 1883.

Chapter 3: Illuminations

1   David Hamer, *The Webbs in New Zealand, 1898*, p.47.
2   *Evening Post*, 21 June 1887.
3   *Evening Post*, 21 June 1887.
4   *Evening Post*, 17 June 1887.
5   *New Zealand Parliamentary Debates (NZPD)*, Vol.58, 1888, p.491.
6   *Wellington City Council Minute Books (WCCMB)*, WCA, Vol.7, p.486, 11 August 1887.
7   *Evening Post*, 13 August 1887.
8   *Evening Post*, 13 June 1887.
9   Luc Sante, *Low Life: Lures and Snares of Old New York*, p.184.
10 Re complaint supported by Mr Sommerville that Mr Loughman has been leaving his horses unattended in a public street while visiting houses of ill-fame (brothel) — Inspector of Nuisances, 00233:3:1879/1788, WCA.
11 WCCMB, WCA, Vol.5, p.427, 24 March 1881.
12 WCCMB, WCA, Vol.5, p.23, 29 August 1878.
13 Terence Hodgson, *Colonial Capital*, p.46.
14 Michael Bassett, *The Mother of All Departments: The History of the Department of Internal Affairs*, p.47.
15 *New Zealand Official Yearbook*, 1897, p.91.
16 James Belich, *Paradise Reforged: A History of the New Zealanders from the 1880s to the Year 2000*, p.525.
17 F.S. Maclean, *Challenge for Health: A History of Public Health in New Zealand*, p.249.
18 *New Zealand Times*, 24 March 1888.
19 See Craig Press, 'The Role of Government in Developing the Colonial City: The Case of Wellington, 1840–1903', MA Thesis, Victoria University of Wellington, 1995.
20 *The Cyclopedia of New Zealand*, Vol.1, Wellington, 1897, p.220; André Siegfried, *Democracy in New Zealand*, p.251.
21 Charles Wilson, *New Zealand Cities: Wellington*, p.12.
22 Rollo Arnold, *New Zealand's Burning: The Settlers' World of the mid 1880s*, p.204.
23 Arnold, *New Zealand's Burning*, p.196.
24 David Johnson, *Wellington Harbour*, p.161.

25 *Evening Post*, 1 August 1887.

26 WCCMB, WCA, Vol.8, p.272, 21 March 1889.

27 WCCMB, WCA, Vol.8, p.272, 21 March 1889.

28 Drainage at Government House, 00233:25:1889/1510, WCA.

29 *Evening Post*, 18 December 1889.

30 Ross Galbreath, 'Onslow, William Hillier (1853–1911)', *Dictionary of New Zealand Biography,* updated 16 December 2003, URL: http://www.dnzb.govt.nz

31 WCCMB, WCA, Vol.9, p.209, 16 April 1891.

32 G.H. Scholefield(ed.), *A Dictionary of New Zealand Biography*, Vol.II, p.376.

33 A.G. Bagnall, *Wairarapa: An Historical Excursion*, Hedley's Bookshop/Masterton Trust Lands Trust, Masterton, 1976, p.328.

34 *New Zealand Times*, 8 July 1885.

35 WCCMB, WCA, Vol.7, p.118, 18 August 1885.

36 WCCMB, WCA, Vol.9, p.79, 24 July 1890. The nineteenth-century theory of zymotic disease was that acute infectious illnesses such as typhoid were caused by a virus or organism acting like a ferment in the system.

37 Prevention of typhoid fever, Dr Chapple, 1892, 00233:34:1892/740, WCA.

38 WCCMB, WCA, Vol.10, p.427, 21 June 1894.

39 Re Melrose Road — H.M. Hayward, 1904–1906, 00233:107:1904/1640, WCA.

40 WCCMB, WCA, Vol.10, p.427, 21 June 1894.

41 Hamer, *The Webbs in New Zealand*, p.47.

42 WCCMB, WCA, Vol.13, p.74, 16 June 1898.

43 *Marlborough Express Weekly Edition*, 23 January 1886.

44 Arnold, *New Zealand's Burning*, p.98.

45 Water at the high levels: Report from the City Surveyor, 02 Feb 1894, 00030:1:3, WCA.

46 Water at the high levels: Report from the City Surveyor, 02 Feb 1894.

47 Alan Mulgan, *City of the Strait: Wellington and its Province*, p.214.

48 *Evening Post*, 12 June 1887.

49 WCCMB, WCA, Vol.9, p.11, 2 April 1890.

50 WCCMB, WCA, Vol.11, p.84, 25 February 1895.

51 Report of Staff Committee, 1889, 2003/6:1:1, WCA.

52 WCCMB, WCA, Vol.9, p.11, 2 April 1890.

53 WCCMB, WCA, Vol.9, p.179, 19 February 1891.

54 WCCMB, WCA, Vol.9, p.11, 2 April 1890.

55 WCCMB, WCA, Vol.9, p.327, 18 September 1891.

56 *Evening Post*, 8 August 1889.

57 Hilda McDonnell, 'Meech, Matilda (1825?–1907)', *Dictionary of New Zealand Biography*, updated 16 December 2003, URL: http://www.dnzb.govt.nz

58 WCCMB, WCA, Vol.24, p.236, 15 May 1913.

59 Mary Findlay, *Tooth and Nail: The Story of a Daughter of the Depression*, pp.77–78.

60 WCCMB, WCA, Vol.8, p.420, 29 November 1889.

61 McDonnell, 'Meech, Matilda'.

62 *Evening Post*, 9 January 1890.

63 *Evening Post*, 20 September 1887.

64 *Evening Post*, 23 January 1890.

65 *The Cyclopedia of New Zealand*, Vol.I, p.220.

66 WCCMB, WCA, Vol.11, p.16, 22 November 1894.

67 WCCMB, WCA, Vol.11, p.96, 14 March 1895.

68 *Evening Post*, 6 December 1889.

69 *The Cyclopedia of New Zealand*, Vol.I, p.220.

70 *Evening Post*, 9 January 1890.

71 *Evening Post*, 5 October 1889.

72 *Evening Post*, 22 January 1890.

73 *Evening Post*, 23 January 1890.

74 Sir Harold Beauchamp, *Reminiscences and Recollections*, p.180.

75 NZPD, Vol.101, 1898, pp.219-21.

76 Michael Bassett, note to author, 4 February 2005.

77 *NZPD*, Vol.101, 1898, p.225.
78 WCCMB, WCA, Vol.11, p.245, 26 September 1895.
79 *Evening Post*, 29 August 1896.
80 WCCMB, WCA, Vol.10, p.225, 17 July 1893.
81 WCCMB, WCA, Vol.10, p.48, 7 November 1892.
82 WCCMB, WCA, Vol.11, p.216, 1 August 1895.
83 WCCMB, WCA, Vol.11, p.379, 20 March 1896.
84 *NZPD*, Vol.101, 1898, p.220.
85 Hamer, *The Webbs in New Zealand*, p.47.
86 *Evening Post*, 15 August 1899.
87 *Evening Post*, 23 June 1898.

Chapter 4: A People's Municipality

1   Town Clerk's reports, 1902–1908, 00033:1:1, WCA.
2   Judith Burch, 'Getting to Karori: Before and After the Tunnel', *The Stockade*, Vol.33 (2000), pp.8–18.
3   *New Zealand Times*, 30 January 1900.
4   Burch, 'Getting to Karori', p.4.
5   Michael Bassett, *The Mother of All Departments: The History of the Department of Internal Affairs*, p.60.
6   *New Zealand Times*, 30 January 1900.
7   *New Zealand Times*, 30 January 1900.
8   *Evening Post*, 30 January 1900.
9   G.T. Bloomfield, *New Zealand: A Handbook of Historical Statistics*, pp.57–58.
10 Alan Henderson, *The Quest for Efficiency: The Origins of the State Services Commission*, p.31.
11 Charles Wilson, *New Zealand Cities: Wellington*, p.47.
12 *Evening Post*, 2 March 1911.
13 *New Zealand Official Yearbook, 1919*, p.461.
14 David Johnson, *Wellington Harbour*, p.243.
15 Wellington City Council Minute Book (WCCMB), WCA, Vol.13, p.25, 5 April 1898.
16 Chris Maclean, *Telling Tales*, p.12.
17 Pat Lawlor, *Old Wellington Days*, p.52.
18 WCCMB, WCA, Vol.22, p.133, 15 December 1910.
19 WCCMB, WCA, Vol.25, p.155, 2 April 1914.
20 WCCMB, WCA, Vol.27, p.65, 4 May 1916.
21 Wilson, *New Zealand Cities: Wellington*, p.37.
22 Wilson, *New Zealand Cities: Wellington*, p.13.
23 WCCMB, WCA, Vol.14, p.440, 21 March 1901.
24 WCCMB, WCA, Vol.14, p.484, 4 April 1901.
25 George Betts, *Betts on Wellington: A City and its Politics*, p.60.
26 Betts, *Betts on Wellington*, pp.39–40.
27 Betts, *Betts on Wellington*, p.131.
28 *New Zealand Times*, 17 April 1901.
29 *Evening Post*, 5 April 1900.
30 *Evening Post*, 23 February 1900.
31 Lawlor, *Old Wellington Days*, p.99.
32 Lynette Shum, 'Remembering Haining Street: With Both Eyes Open', *Chinese in New Zealand*, URL: http://www.stevenyoung.co.nz/chinesevoice/historical research/lynetteshumdec03.htm
33 *Evening Post*, 15 June 1887.
34 WCCMB, WCA, Vol.11, p.359, 27 February 1896.
35 David Millar, *Once Upon a Village: A History of Lower Hutt, 1819–1965*, p.103.
36 Mrs Stevenson and others Re Petition re unsatisfactory state of Houses in Haining Street, 00233:65:1900/43, WCA.
37 WCCMB, WCA, Vol.16, p.197, 30 March 1903.
38 WCCMB, WCA, Vol.16, p.176, 30 March 1903.
39 *Evening Post*, 5 April 1900.

40 WCCMB, WCA, Vol.14, p.48, 22 March 1900.

41 WCCMB, WCA, Vol.14, p.54, 29 March 1900.

42 WCCMB, WCA, Vol.14, p.234, 30 August 1901.

43 *Evening Post*, 9 June 1904.

44 *Evening Post*, 17 August 1900.

45 City Engineer, 00233:1901/298, WCA.

46 WCCMB, WCA, Vol.16, p.286, 2 July 1903.

47 *New Zealand Times*, 25 July 1902.

48 *New Zealand Times*, 28 July 1902.

49 *New Zealand Times*, 30 October 1903.

50 Lawlor, *Old Wellington Days*, p.77.

51 City Engineer's departmental correspondence, 1907 B-L, 1907, 00437:1:2, WCA.

52 *New Zealand Times*, 10 December 1903.

53 *New Zealand Times*, 12 December 1903.

54 *Evening Post*, 16 April 1902.

55 WCC Outwards Correspondence Letter Book No.30, 06 Feb 1902–04 Sep 1902, 00296:11:1, WCA.

56 *New Zealand Times*, 22 December 1903.

57 WCCMB, WCA, Vol.19, p.155, 14 February 1902.

58 00233:122:1907/361, WCA.

59 Graham Stewart, *End of the Penny Section: When Trams Ruled the Streets of New Zealand*, p.74.

60 WCCMB, WCA, Vol.14, p.328, 22 November 1900.

61 WCCMB, WCA, Vol.17, p.144, 2 June 1904.

62 WCCMB, WCA, Vol.19, p.196, 11 April 1907.

63 Stewart, *End of the Penny Section*, p.85.

64 WCCMB, WCA, Vol.23, p.35, 19 November 1911.

65 *New Zealand Parliamentary Debates (NZPD)*, Vol.153, 1910, p.1091.

66 *NZPD*, Vol.153, 1910, p.1102.

67 WCCMB, WCA, Vol.16, p.229, 13 April 1903.

68 *Evening Post*, 16 April 1902.

69 Adrian Humphris, 'Tramways and Suburban Growth: A Case Study of Kilbirnie', p.161.

70 *The Cyclopedia of New Zealand*, Vol.I, p.275.

71 Town Clerk's reports, 1902–1908, 00033:1:1, WCA.

72 00233:1910/1670, WCA.

73 Interviewing Mayor i.e. Pooling Wadestown Tramways, 00233:220:1913/1089, WCA.

74 Bathing, Lyall Bay beach — W.H. Morrah, 1905, 00233:114:1905/566, WCA.

75 WCCMB, WCA, Vol.21, p.159, 16 December 1909.

76 *Truth*, 1 January 1916.

77 Population Figures, City of Wellington, 1935–1987, 00009:522:34/7, WCA.

78 Millar, *Once Upon a Village*, p.114.

79 *Evening Post*, 7 December 1904.

80 Jane Tolerton, 'He Came, He Sang, He Stayed', *New Zealand Woman's Weekly*, 8 October 1984.

81 *New Zealand Mail*, 30 March 1902.

82 *New Zealand Times*, 8 December 1904.

83 *New Zealand Mail*, 24 October 1873.

84 *New Zealand Mail*, 3 December 1886.

85 *Cyclopedia of New Zealand*, Vol.I, p.218.

86 *New Zealand Mail*, 8 October 1903.

87 *New Zealand Mail*, 4 November 1903.

88 *New Zealand Mail*, 23 March 1904.

89 WCCMB, WCA, Vol.17, p.128, 19 May 1904.

90 *Municipal Handbook of New Zealand*, Government Printer, Wellington, 1911, p.73.

91 *New Zealand Times*, 13 December 1904.

92 WCCMB, WCA, Vol.18, p.40, 1 June 1905.

93 Lawlor, *Old Wellington Days*, p.81.

94 WCCMB, WCA, Vol.19, p.116, 12 December 1906.

95 Phillip Cleaver, 'The Pakeha Treatment of Death in 19th and 20th Century Wellington', Lecture to the Wellington Historical and Early Settlers' Association Inc, 15 February 1996, p.9.
96 *Municipal Handbook of New Zealand*, p.74.
97 *Maoriland Worker*, 9 February 1912.
98 *New Zealand Times*, 1 October 1898.
99 WCCMB, WCA, Vol.18, p.26, 14 May 1905.
100 Herbert Roth, *Trade Unions in New Zealand: Past and Present*, p.25.
101 *Evening Post*, 31 January 1912.
102 *Evening Post*, 21 December 1911.
103 *Dominion*, 2 February 1912.
104 WCCMB, WCA, Vol.23, p.116, 22 December 1911.
105 Enquiry re Inspector Fuller, 00233:196:1912/44, WCA.
106 *Evening Post*, 27 January 1912.
107 Roth, *Trade Unions in New Zealand*, p.32.
108 WCCMB, WCA, Vol.23, p.320, 16 May 1912.
109 WCCMB, WCA, Vol.23, p.357, 10 June 1912.
110 WCCMB, WCA, Vol.24, p.129, 27 February 1913.
111 Cr Tregear removing advertising boards from tramcars, 00233:228:1913/2016, WCA.
112 WCCMB, WCA, Vol.24, p.479, 6 November 1913.
113 Henry A. Wood, 'The Life of a Pioneer Farmer, 1873–1953', MS-2520, ATL.
114 Michael Bassett and Michael King, *Tomorrow Comes the Song: A Life of Peter Fraser*, p.60.
115 WCCMB, WCA, Vol.24, p.479, 6 November 1913.
116 WCCMB, WCA, Vol.25, p.19, 11 December 1913.
117 Kerry Howe, *Singer in a Songless Land*, p.193.
118 Robin Hyde, *The Godwits Fly*, Auckland University Press, Auckland, 1970, p.117.
119 WCCMB, WCA, Vol.26, p.473, 14 February 1916.
120 WCCMB, WCA, Vol.27, p.460, 31 May 1917.
121 *Wellington City Council Yearbook*, 1918/19, Whitcombe & Tombs Ltd, Wellington, 1918.
122 WCCMB, WCA, Vol.27, p.383, 22 March 1917.
123 WCCMB, WCA, Vol.27, p.476, 14 June 1917.
124 WCCMB, WCA, Vol.27, p.207, 24 August 1916.
125 WCCMB, WCA, Vol.28, p.128, 4 October 1917.
126 Town Clerk's reports, 1902–1908, 00033:1:1, WCA.
127 *Evening Post*, 7 April 1916.
128 WCCMB, WCA, Vol.28, p.269, 26 March 1918.
129 *WCC Yearbook*, 1918/19.
130 WCCMB, WCA, Vol.29, p.26, 17 October 1918.

Chapter 5: Convulsions

1 Medical orderly Alfred Hollows, quoted in Geoffrey Rice, *Black November: The 1918 Influenza Epidemic in New Zealand*, p.52.
2 Wellington City Council Minute Book (WCCMB), WCA, Vol.29, p.55, 2 December 1918.
3 *Dominion*, 5 November 1918.
4 Submission to Influenza Epidemic Commission, 1919, Health Department, H3/1, p.612 (Mayor Luke), ANZ.
5 *Evening Post*, 11 November 1918.
6 Rice, *Black November*, p.103.
7 *Dominion*, 19 November 1918.
8 Submission to Influenza Epidemic Commission, 1919, H3/1, p.612 (Mayor Luke), ANZ.
9 Rice, *Black November*, p.57.
10 Rice, *Black November*, p.143.
11 Michael Bassett and Michael King, *Tomorrow Comes the Song: A Life of Peter Fraser*, p.85.
12 Submission to Influenza Epidemic Commission, 1919, H3/1, p.612 (Mayor Luke), ANZ.
13 WCCMB, WCA, Vol.29, p.81, 19 December 1918.

14 Rice, *Black November*, p.46.

15 *New Zealand Parliamentary Debates (NZPD)*, Vol.183, 1918, pp.390–2.

16 'Report of the Influenza Epidemic Commission', *AJHR*, 1919, H-31A, p 38.

17 Graham Bush, *Local Government and Politics in New Zealand*, p.29.

18 Michael Bassett, *The Mother of all Departments: The History of the Department of Internal Affairs*, p.74.

19 Pat Lawlor, *Confessions of a Journalist*, pp.88, 252.

20 *Evening Post*, 7 April 1916.

21 Beryl Hughes, 'McVicar, Annie (1862–1954)', *Dictionary of New Zealand Biography*, updated 7 July 2005, URL: http://www.dnzb.govt.nz/

22 *Evening Post*, 29 April 1919.

23 WCCMB, WCA, Vol.31, p.301, 10 November 1921.

24 WCCMB, WCA, Vol.29, p.316, 25 July 1919.

25 WCCMB, WCA, Vol.31, p.332, 10 January 1922.

26 WCCMB, WCA, Vol.31, p.347, 2 February 1922.

27 WCCMB, WCA, Vol.34, p.288, 9 April 1925.

28 WCCMB, WCA, Vol.35, p.306, 7 July 1926.

29 WCCMB, WCA, Vol.29, p.116, 20 February 1919.

30 Michael King, *Te Puea*, Sceptre, Auckland, 1977, p.137.

31 WCCMB, WCA, Vol.40, p.144, 19 December 1929.

32 Ben Schrader, 'Modernising Wellington: The 1920s to the 1950s', in John Wilson (ed.), *Zeal and Crusade: The Modern Movement in Wellington*, p.15.

33 Wellington City Council Commission of Enquiry Evidence 3, 1932, 00512:1:4, WCA.

34 Patricia Grace, Irihapeti Ramsden and Jonathan Dennis, *The Silent Migration: Ngati Poneke Young Maori Club 1937–1948*, p.39.

35 WCCMB, WCA, Vol.381, p.107, 9 July 1928.

36 WCCMB, WCA, Vol.41, p.26, 28 July 1930.

37 *NZPD*, Vol.191, 1922, p.767.

38 *Dominion*, 4 June 1926.

39 Northland Tunnel Commission Inquiry, 00233:527:1926/456 pt2, WCA.

40 Sydney Street West, Damages, Claims for Compensation, 1926, 00523:36:71/1528, WCA.

41 WCCMB, WCA, Vol.32, p.82, 29 June 1922.

42 WCCMB, WCA, Vol.32, p.145, 31 August 1922.

43 WCCMB, WCA, Vol.37, p.211, 1 February 1927.

44 WCCMB, WCA, Vol.38, p.133, 9 July 1928.

45 WCCMB, WCA, Vol.40, p.448, 9 June 1930.

46 *Evening Post*, 10 January 1981.

47 WCCMB, WCA, Vol.47, p.402, 3 August 1936.

48 Eugene Grayland, *More Famous New Zealanders*, Whitcombe & Tombs, Christchurch, 1972, p.93.

49 *WCC Year Book*, 1931–1932, 00087:3:2, WCA.

50 Wellington City Council Commission of Enquiry Evidence 1, 1932, p.710, 00512:1:2, WCA.

51 WCCMB, WCA, Vol.41, p.324, 5 February 1931.

52 Rosa Coory, quoted in Martin Doyle, *Newtown: Community in a Wellington Suburb*, Wellington Safer Community Council, Wellington, 1998, p.21.

53 WCCMB, WCA, Vol.41, p.494, 4 June 1931.

54 WCCMB, WCA, Vol.42, p.234, 8 October 1931.

55 *Evening Post*, 16 September 1932.

56 WCCMB, WCA, Vol.41, p.54, 31 July 1930.

57 WCC Commission of Enquiry Evidence 1, 1932, p.752, 00512:1:2, WCA.

58 WCC Commission of Enquiry Evidence 1, 1932, p.819, 00512:1:2, WCA.

59 WCC Commission of Enquiry Evidence 1, 1932, p.60, 00512:1:2, WCA.

60 WCC Commission of Enquiry Evidence 1, 1932, pp.59–60, 00512:1:2, WCA.

61 WCC Commission of Enquiry Evidence 1, 1932, p.720, 00512:1:2, WCA.

62 WCC Commission of Enquiry Evidence 1, 1932, p.875, 00512:1:2, WCA.

63 WCC Commission of Enquiry Evidence 1, 1932, p.834, 00512:1:2, WCA.

64 WCC Commission of Enquiry Evidence 1, 1932, pp.825–6, 00512:1:2, WCA.

65 WCC Commission of Enquiry — Report and summary of recommendations, 1932, 00512:1:1, WCA.
66 *Evening Post*, 16 September 1932.
67 *Evening Post*, 8 January 1932.
68 *AJHR*, 1932, H-35, p.11.
69 Michael Bassett, *Coates of Kaipara*, p.176.
70 *Evening Post*, 8 January 1932.
71 John E. Martin, *Holding the Balance: A History of New Zealand's Department of Labour 1891–1995*, p.174.
72 William Sutch, *The Quest for Security in New Zealand, 1840 to 1966*, p.131.
73 WCCMB, WCA, Vol.41, p.404, 19 March 1931.
74 WCC Commission of Enquiry Evidence 1, 1932, p.76, 00512:1:2, WCA.
75 WCC Commission of Enquiry Evidence 1, 1932, p.16, 00512:1:2, WCA.
76 WCCMB, WCA, Vol.41, p.494, 4 June 1931.
77 *Evening Post*, 16 September 1932.
78 *Evening Post*, 8 January 1932.
79 WCCMB, WCA, Vol.42, p.342, 19 November 1931.
80 Tony Simpson, *The Sugarbag Years: An Oral History of the 1930s Depression in New Zealand*, p.98.
81 Rosslyn Noonan, 'The Riots of 1932: A Study of Social Unrest in Auckland, Wellington, Dunedin', p.129.
82 *Evening Post*, 8 January 1932.
83 *Evening Post*, 13 April 1932.
84 Margaret Thorn, *Stick Out, Keep Left*, p.60.
85 WCCMB, WCA, Vol.43, p.76, 12 May 1932.
86 Simpson, *Sugarbag Years*, pp.155–6.
87 WCCMB, WCA, Vol.43, p.20, 16 March 1932.
88 Simpson, *Sugarbag Years*, p.136.
89 *Evening Post*, 6 September 1932.
90 *Evening Post*, 16 September 1932.
91 WCCMB, WCA, Vol.43, p.76, 12 May 1932.
92 WCCMB, WCA, Vol.44, p.80, 3 April 1933.
93 *Evening Post*, 14 September 1932.
94 *AJHR*, 1934–5, H-35, p.16.
95 Graham Bush, *Decently and In Order: The Government of the City of Auckland, 1840–1971*, p.557.
96 Simpson, *Sugarbag Years*, p.194.
97 WCCMB, WCA, Vol.45, p.430, 14 September 1934.
98 WCCMB, WCA, Vol.46, p.288, 19 June 1935.
99 WCCMB, WCA, Vol.47, p.402, 3 August 1936.
100 WCCMB, WCA, Vol.49, p.290, 16 February 1938.
101 WCCMB, WCA, Vol.47, p.340, 14 June 1936.
102 WCCMB, WCA, Vol.48, p.245, 11 March 1937.
103 Gabor Toth, 'Café Culture in Wellington'.

Chapter 6: Centennial to Crusade

1 *Southern Cross*, 24 February 1948.
2 Wellington City Council Minute Books (WCCMB), WCA, Vol.55, p.343, 16 October 1946.
3 N.B. Palethorpe, *Official History of the New Zealand Centennial Exhibition*, p.35.
4 *Evening Post*, 21 January 1993.
5 Bernard Kernot, 'Maori Buildings for the Centennial', in William Renwick (ed.), *Creating a National Spirit: Celebrating New Zealand's Centennial*, p.69.
6 Palethorpe, *New Zealand Centennial Exhibition*, p.43.
7 Gavin McLean, 'Business as Unusual', in Renwick (ed.), *Creating a National Spirit*, p.29.
8 Palethorpe, *New Zealand Centennial Exhibition*, p.51.
9 WCCMB, WCA, Vol.51, p.339, 14 February 1940.
10 McLean, 'Business as Unusual', p.36.
11 *Dominion*, 27 June 1950.

12 Playground Salvage Correspondence, AG001:6:280, WCA.
13 WCCMB, WCA, Vol.51, p.271, 15 November 1939.
14 Peter Cooke, *Defending New Zealand: Ramparts on the Sea 1840–1950*, Part II, p.560.
15 WCCMB, WCA, Vol.51, p.351, 14 February 1940.
16 *Evening Post*, 16 May 1940.
17 WCCMB, WCA, Vol.52, p.9, 13 June 1940.
18 *Otago Daily Times*, 12 June 1940.
19 Damien Wilkins, *When Famous People Come to Town*, p.40.
20 Nancy Taylor, *The New Zealand People at War: The Home Front*, Vol.1, p.180.
21 *Evening Post*, 6 February 1940.
22 David Grant, *Out in the Cold: Pacifists and Conscientious Objectors in New Zealand during World War II*, p.58.
23 WCCMB, WCA, Vol.52, p.430, 6 October 1941.
24 *Evening Post*, 14 May 1941.
25 *Evening Post*, 18 May 1941.
26 *Dominion*, 19 May 1941.
27 *WCC Year Book*, 1941–1946, p.34, 00087:3:7, WCA.
28 *Press*, 22 December 1941.
29 *Evening Post*, 4 December 1941.
30 Cooke, *Defending New Zealand*, p.709.
31 WCCMB, WCA, Vol.52, p.339, 11 June 1941.
32 WCCMB, WCA, Vol.52, p.466, 15 October 1941.
33 *Press*, 6 February 1942.
34 *Dominion*, 17, 27 June 1942.
35 Taylor, *The Home Front*, Vol.II, p.1083.
36 David Millar, *Once Upon a Village: A History of Lower Hutt, 1819–1965*, p.162.
37 WCCMB, WCA, Vol.52, p.377, 4 August 1941.
38 Denial of Resources to Enemy, AC023:90:1, WCA.
39 David Johnson, *Wellington Harbour*, Wellington, p.320.
40 WCCMB, WCA, Vol.53, p.154, 10 June 1942.
41 WCCMB, WCA, Vol.53, p.287, 25 January 1943.
42 A.H. McLintock (ed.), *An Encyclopaedia of New Zealand*, Vol.III, Government Printer, Wellington, 1966, p.87.
43 *Dominion*, 19 November 1942.
44 WCCMB, WCA, Vol.53, p.393, 16 June 1943.
45 *New Zealand Woman's Weekly*, 20 August 1942.
46 F.B. Katene, chairman of the Ngati Poneke Tribal Committee to Hon. P.K. Paikea, Minister in Charge of the Maori War Effort, 16 November 1942, Nash Papers, Bundle 2067, Folio 446, ANZ.
47 WCCMB, WCA, Vol.53, p.401, 16 June 1943.
48 WCCMB, WCA, Vol.53, p.253, 11 November 1942.
49 WCCMB, WCA, Vol.54, p.233, 13 September 1944.
50 Director of Housing Construction to Defence Works Allocation Committee, 19 February 1943, Housing Division, Ministry of Works, HD 10/426/1, ANZ.
51 WCCMB, WCA, Vol.55, p.64, 14 November 1945.
52 *Evening Post*, 15 August 1945.
53 WCCMB, WCA, Vol.55, p.279, 5 August 1946.
54 WCCMB, WCA, Vol.55, p.231, 15 May 1946.
55 *Dominion*, 17 May 1944.
56 Ben Schrader, 'Modernising Wellington: The 1920s to the 1950s', in John Wilson (ed.), *Zeal and Crusade: The Modern Movement in Wellington*, p.19.
57 *Dominion*, 1 April 1964.
58 WCCMB, WCA, Vol.56, p.61, 18 June 1947.
59 WCCMB, WCA, Vol.55, p.456, 25 February 1947.
60 WCCMB, WCA, Vol.55, p.439, 12 February 1947.
61 WCCMB, WCA, Vol.55, p.468, 25 February 1947.
62 *NZ Truth*, 9 November 1949.
63 WCCMB, WCA, Vol.56, p.336, 21 April 1948.

64 WCCMB, WCA, Vol.56, p.415, 5 July 1948.
65 WCCMB, WCA, Vol.58, p.196, 3 July 1950.
66 WCCMB, WCA, Vol.58, p.205, 3 July 1950.
67 WCCMB, WCA, Vol.58, p.161, 14 June 1950.
68 Gerald O'Brien, note to author, 20 July 2005.
69 *Evening Post*, 17 March 1979.
70 WCCMB, WCA, Vol.58, p.446, 5 March 1951.
71 WCCMB, WCA, Vol.59, p.89, 13 June 1951.
72 WCCMB, WCA, Vol.59, p.201, 10 October 1951.
73 WCCMB, WCA, Vol.58, p.204, 12 July 1950.
74 WCCMB, WCA, Vol.60, p.250, 27 April 1953.
75 WCCMB, WCA, Vol.60, p.388, 12 August 1953.
76 *Evening Post*, 9 January 1954.
77 Jock Phillips, *Royal Summer: The Visit of Queen Elizabeth II and Prince Philip to New Zealand 1953–54*, p.67.
78 *Evening Post*, 12 January 1954.
79 WCCMB, WCA, Vol.61, p.63, 21 January 1954.
80 Phillips, *Royal Summer*, p.33.
81 *Evening Post*, 11 January 1954.
82 WCCMB, WCA, Vol.56, p.460, 11 August 1948.
83 *Evening Post*, 6 February 1952.
84 WCCMB, WCA, Vol.62, p.363, 14 December 1955; Vol.64, p.117, 13 November 1957.
85 Redmer Yska, *All Shook Up: The Flash Bodgie and the Rise of the New Zealand Teenager in the 1950s*, Penguin, Auckland, 1993, p.140.
86 WCCMB, WCA, Vol.61, p.107, 1 February 1954.
87 *Dominion*, 25 January 1957.
88 *Dominion*, 2 March 1940.
89 *Dominion*, 14 January 1941.
90 *NZ Listener*, 28 March 1958.
91 WCCMB, WCA, Vol.61, p.143, 29 March 1954.
92 WCCMB, WCA, Vol.64, p.302, 14 May 1958.
93 WCCMB, WCA, Vol.49, p.430, 15 June 1938.
94 Bond St, Premises Bethune Hunter, 1938–1958, 00009:1415:45/455/2, WCA.
95 *Evening Post*, 18 February 1957.
96 *Evening Post*, 28 March 1958.
97 Minutes of Deputation to the Mayor by Bethune's Exchange Building subcommittee, 11 August 1958, Series 8/6/1, New Zealand Historic Places Trust (NZHPT).
98 *Dominion*, 15 August 1958.
99 H.B. Wylde, 'The Capital City's Old Customhouse as a National Historic Place', unpublished MS in Series 8/6/1, NZHPT.
100 Wellington Airport, *Official Souvenir Brochure*, Wellington, 1959, author's collection.
101 WCCMB, WCA, Vol.62, p.78, 11 May 1955.
102 *Dominion*, 4 April 1959.
103 WCCMB, WCA, Vol.64, p.498, 15 October 1958.
104 WCCMB, WCA, Vol.65, p.193, 6 April 1959.
105 *Dominion*, 27 February 1959.

Chapter 7: Tar and Cement

1 Comment by American industrial designer J.O. Sinel, during a 1960 visit to New Zealand. *NZ Listener*, 11 June 1965.
2 *Evening Post*, 2 May 1964.
3 *Dominion*, 2 May 1964.
4 *Evening Post*, 11 March 1960.
5 *Evening Post*, 21 May 1959.

6   *Evening Post*, 19 November 1959.
7   Wellington Regional Planning Authority, *Report on the Development of the Wellington Region*, Wellington, 1959.
8   G.T. Bloomfield, *New Zealand: A Handbook of Historical Statistics*, p.58.
9   Alan Henderson, *The Quest for Efficiency: The Origins of the State Services Commission*, p.398.
10 Wellington City Council Minute Books (WCCMB), WCA, Vol.70, p.183, 11 September 1963; Vol.71, p.542, 17 March 1965.
11 David Johnson, *Wellington Harbour*, p.382.
12 WCCMB, WCA, Vol.69, p.352, 12 December 1962.
13 Bill Brien, comment to author, 16 March 1994.
14 *Evening Post*, 6 June 1964.
15 *Evening Post*, 22 June 1964.
16 WCCMB, WCA, Vol.71, p.226, 16 September 1964.
17 City Engineer's Department Annual Report for the year ended 31 March 1961, 00008:1:11, WCA.
18 WCCMB, WCA, Vol.70, p.42, 12 June 1963.
19 WCCMB, WCA, Vol.76, p.419, 4 October 1968.
20 Catherine Love, 'Love, Makere Rangiatea Ralph (1907–1994)', *Dictionary of New Zealand Biography*, updated 7 July 2005, URL: http://www.dnzb.govt.nz/
21 *New Zealand Parliamentary Debates (NZPD)*, Vol.321, 1959, p.2672.
22 *Evening Post*, 19 November 1959.
23 *Evening Post*, 2 June 1960.
24 Motorway: Foothills Motorway (General File), 00001:1232:35/1233 Pt 1, WCA.
25 Richard Miller, 'The Wellington Urban Motorway: The Parts Played by the Planning Authorities and the Bolton Street Cemetery Preservation Society', p.40.
26 *Evening Post*, 25 May 1959.
27 *Evening Post*, 14 May 1961.
28 WCCMB, WCA, Vol.66, p.530, 12 October 1960.
29 Town Planning, Master Transportation Plan for Wellington City, general, 1960–1962, 00001:2305:68/37 Pt 1, WCA.
30 Master Transportation Plan, 00009:1062:58/41, WCA.
31 Motorway, Foothills Motorway, general file, 1959–1963, 00001:1232:35/1233 Pt 1, WCA.
32 *Dominion*, 27 August 1928.
33 *Evening Post*, 23 August 1928.
34 Margaret H. Alington, *Unquiet Earth: A History of the Bolton Street Cemetery*, p.143.
35 *Dominion*, 23 August 1963.
36 *Evening Post*, 14 February 1964.
37 *Evening Post*, 6 July 1965.
38 *Evening Post*, 19 June 1964.
39 *Dominion*, 16 May 1964.
40 Bolton Street Cemetery Preservation Society, Minutes of the inaugural meeting, 27 October 1964, quoted in Alington, *Unquiet Earth*, p.158.
41 James Beard, 'Precinct Plan for Wellington', 1965, quoted in *Bobs and Cycles*, Open Space Society Monthly Opinions, Suppositions, Issues, Statements (OSSMOSIS), 1994.
42 Dennis Rose, interview with author, 8 July 2005.
43 *Evening Post*, 13 November 1964.
44 William Sutch, *Wellington: A Sick City*, p.14.
45 *Evening Post*, 14 November 1964.
46 *Evening Post*, 20 June 1968.
47 *Evening Post*, 13 October 1965.
48 Director of Roading, Submission no. 1557, 19 October 1965, National Roads Board, quoted in Miller, 'The Wellington Urban Motorway', p.61.
49 *Evening Post*, 30 October 1965.
50 *Evening Post*, 27 October 1967.
51 *Evening Post*, 28 October 1967.
52 *Evening Post*, 3 June 1965.
53 Rose, interview.
54 D.G. Porter, 'Housing the Citizen', in N.H. McLeod and B.H. Farland (eds), *Wellington Prospect: Survey of a City 1840–1970*, p.119.

55   George Betts, *Betts on Wellington: A City and its Politics*, p.219.
56   *Dominion*, 14 February 1964.
57   *Dominion*, 30 July 1964.
58   *Dominion*, 3 August 1964.
59   Gerald O'Brien, interview with author, 20 July 2005.
60   Ken Clark, note to author, 2 August 2005.
61   *Evening Post*, 5 May 1965.
62   *Evening Post*, 30 October 1965.
63   Capital City Planning Committee, Wellington City Councillors and Government Ministers of the Crown, general, 1965–1970, 00001:2134:60/4842 Pt 1, WCA.
64   Works and Planning Department Annual Report, 1968, 00008:2:2, WCA.
65   *Dominion*, 6 December 1968.
66   *Dominion*, 3 October 1968.
67   WCCMB, WCA, Vol.79, p.345, 20 April 1970.
68   WCCMB, WCA, Vol.73, p.369, 13 September 1966.
69   WCCMB, WCA, Vol.74, p.285, 12 April 1967.
70   Anneke Vooren-Hesp, 'No Commitments for Me, Please', in Stephen Levine (ed.), *New Zealand Politics: A Reader*, pp.190–2.
71   Ray Bradley and Allan Levett, 'The Housing Crisis: A Case Study in Group Behaviour', in Levine (ed.), *New Zealand Politics*, p.204.
72   *Dominion*, 31 July 1972.
73   WCCMB, WCA, Vol.83, p.41, 10 November 1971.
74   Frank McKay, *The Life of James K. Baxter*, Oxford University Press, Auckland, 1990, p.272.
75   James K. Baxter, *Collected Poems*, Oxford University Press, Auckland, 1995, p.530.
76   *Dominion*, 7 October 1971.
77   Geoffrey Debnam, *The Limits of Local Initiative: Imposed and Negotiated Planning in the Aro Valley*, p.11.
78   *Dominion*, 25 July 1973.
79   *Dominion*, 4 September 1973.
80   WCCMB, WCA, Vol.90, p.255, 10 September 1975.
81   *New Zealand Times*, 23 February 1902.
82   WCCMB, WCA, Vol.22, p.266, 6 April 1911.
83   WCCMB, WCA, Vol.86, p.310, 28 August 1973.
84   WCCMB, WCA, Vol.88, p.91, 12 June 1974.
85   Debnam, *Limits of Local Initiative*, p.3.
86   Works and Planning Department Annual Report, 1966, p.4, 00008:2:2, WCA.
87   Works and Planning Department Annual Report, 1968, p.39, 00008:2:2, WCA.
88   WCCMB, WCA, Vol.77, p.273, 9 April 1969.
89   WCCMB, WCA, Vol.82, p.337, 8 September 1971.
90   WCCMB, WCA, Vol.81, p.171, 10 February 1971.
91   J.T. Salmon, 'Conservation in the Development of the Wellington Region'.
92   WCCMB, WCA, Vol.84, p.99, 14 June 1972.
93   *NZ Herald*, 5 June 1973.
94   WCCMB, WCA, Vol.87, p.208, 3 February 1974.
95   *Evening Post*, 20 December 1969.

Chapter 8: Sea Change

1   Ray Ahipene-Mercer, submission on behalf of Wellington District Maori Council, 21 July 1986, in *Wellington Wastewater Management Options*, Wellington, 1986, p.15.
2   *Dominion*, 16 September 1975.
3   Wellington City Council Minute Books (WCCMB), WCA, Vol.90, p.411, 7 November 1975.
4   Paul Martin, *Carmen: My Life*, p.15.
5   John Hollings, interview with author, 24 August 2005.
6   David McGill, *Wellington: A Capital Century*, p.262.

7   Michael Fowler, interview with author, 3 August 2005.
8   *Dominion*, 28 October 1974.
9   Graeme Peterson, interview with author, 9 June 2005.
10 Fowler interview.
11 *Dominion*, 18 September 1975.
12 Fowler interview.
13 *Dominion*, 23 June 1975.
14 WCC Handbook, 1963, WCA, p.3.
15 *Dominion*, 18 September 1975.
16 *Dominion*, 16 September 1975.
17 WCCMB, WCA, Vol.91, p.108, 5 February 1976.
18 WCCMB, WCA, Vol.93, p.9, 5 November 1976.
19 Ian Lawrence, interview with author, 14 September 2005.
20 Operation Waterloo, Overseas Fund-raising Tour Report, 5 March — 13 April 1977, Fowler papers.
21 WCCMB, WCA, Vol.93, p.357, 13 April 1977; Vol.95, p.241, 15 February 1978; *Dominion*, 19 September 1983.
22 WCC Accounts: Government Audit, 1970–1981, 00001:1801:60/95/1 Pt 6, WCA.
23 Martin, *Carmen*, p.194.
24 Robert Jones, *Memories of Muldoon*, Canterbury University Press, Christchurch, p.71.
25 Lawrence interview.
26 *Dominion*, 5 October 1977.
27 *Dominion*, 7 October 1977.
28 WCCMB, WCA, Vol.97, p.86, 8 December 1978.
29 WCCMB, WCA, Vol.101, p.179, 27 January 1981.
30 WCCMB, WCA, Vol.104, p.187, 9 July 1982.
31 *Evening Post*, 26 December 1979.
32 Michael Fowler Centre, Opening Ceremony, General, 1983, 00001:397:6/5114/25 Pt 4, WCA.
33 WCCMB, WCA, Vol.106, p.134, 15 June 1983.
34 Michael Fowler Centre, Opening Ceremony, General, 1982–1983, 00001:396:6/5114/25 Pt 2, WCA.
35 *Dominion*, 18 August 1983.
36 *Evening Post*, 12 September 1983.
37 *Evening Post*, 9 April 1983.
38 *Dominion*, 16 September 1983.
39 WCCMB, WCA, Vol.106, p.13, 11 May 1983.
40 WCCMB, WCA, Vol.106, p.291, 9 September 1983.
41 *Dominion*, 19 September 1983.
42 WCCMB, WCA, Vol.92, p.372, 8 October 1976.
43 *Dominion*, 20 June 1977.
44 WCCMB, WCA, Vol.92, p.114, 14 July 1976.
45 Fowler interview.
46 WCCMB, WCA, Vol.94, p.398, 2 September 1977.
47 WCCMB, WCA, Vol.96, p.235, 16 August 1978.
48 WCCMB, WCA, Vol.100, p.146, 11 July 1980.
49 WCCMB, WCA, Vol.102, p.232, 11 September 1981.
50 Town Planning, Central Area, between Harbour, Cambridge Terrace, Motorway and Kaiwharawhara, 1975–1982, 00001:2311:68/55 Pt 1, WCA.
51 WCCMB, WCA, Vol.97, p.428, 31 May 1979.
52 WCCMB, WCA, Vol.98, p.15, 18 April 1979.
53 WCCMB, WCA, Vol.101, p.403, 15 April 1981.
54 Geoff Chapple, *1981: The Tour*, Reed, Auckland, 1984, p.147.
55 WCCMB, WCA, Vol.102, p.206, 7 August 1981.
56 Condition of Streets and Roads in Wellington, 1979–1982, 00001:1198:35/635 Pt 7, WCA.
57 Chris Maclean, *Wellington: Telling Tales*, p.182
58 WCCMB, WCA, Vol.106, p.231, 5 August 1983.
59 WCCMB, WCA, Vol.107, p.79, 16 November 1983.
60 WCCMB, WCA, Vol.107, p.255, 15 February 1984.

61 *Evening Post*, 9 February 1984.

62 John Marshall, *Memoirs, Vol. One: 1912 to 1960*, Collins, Auckland, 1983, p.50.

63 WCCMB, WCA, Vol.57, p.246, 18 May 1949.

64 Capital City Planning Committee, Wellington City Councillors and Government Ministers of the Crown, General, 1977–1987, 00001:2134:60/4842 Pt 3, WCA.

65 *Evening Post*, 26 February 1985.

66 *Dominion*, 1 October 1977.

67 Blincoe to City Engineer, 2 July 1986, in *Wellington Wastewater Management Options*, p.63.

68 Lawrence interview.

69 *Dominion*, 11 May 1985.

70 *Dominion*, 14 May 1985.

71 Lawrence interview.

72 WCCMB, WCA, Vol.109, p.293, 15 May 1985.

73 WCCMB, WCA, Vol.109, p.310, 7 June 1985.

74 *Evening Post*, 9 January 1986.

75 WCCMB, WCA, Vol.108, p.185, 15 August 1984.

76 *Dominion*, 12 November 1985.

77 *Dominion*, 30 August 1985.

78 *Evening Post*, 6 February 1986.

79 *Evening Post*, 10 May 1985.

80 *Evening Post*, 6 February 1986.

81 *Evening Post*, 8 February 1986.

82 Drainage, Sewerage System, General (Deed 12383, Contracts 2460, 2801, 2863), 1985, 00001:511:12/868 Pt 9, WCA.

83 WCCMB, WCA, Vol.111, p.205, 16 July 1986.

84 WCCMB, WCA, Vol.111, p.377, 8 October 1986.

85 *Evening Post*, 18 March 1986.

86 *Wellington Wastewater Management Options*.

87 WCCMB, WCA, Vol.111, p.337, 10 September 1986.

88 *Evening Post*, 7 October 1986.

89 WCCMB, WCA, Vol.111, p.412, 30 October 1986.

90 *Evening Post*, 22 October 1992.

91 *Dominion*, 13 August 1991.

92 Jim Belich, personal communication with author, 30 October 2005.

93 Rosemary McLeod, 'Capital Chaos: The Dubious Achievements of the Wellington City Council', *North and South*, July 1992, p.70.

94 *Dominion*, 20 April 1988.

95 WCCMB, WCA, Vol.113, p.163, 14 October 1987.

96 *Evening Post*, 28 May 1984.

97 *New Zealand Official Yearbook 1988–89*, Department of Statistics, Wellington, 1989, p.75.

98 Town Planning, Central Area, between Harbour, Cambridge Terrace, Motorway and Kaiwharawhara, 1975–1982, 00001:2311:68/55 Pt 1, WCA.

99 Peter Healey, note to author, 12 March 2004.

100 *Dominion* 20 April 1988.

101 *Dominion*, 20 April 1988.

102 WCCMB, WCA, Vol.114, p.66, 10 February 1988.

103 Prendergast interview with author, 11 November 2005.

104 Annual Plan, 1990–1991, 00081:1:1, WCA.

105 *Evening Post*, 15 April 1988.

106 *NZ Herald*, 14 April 1988.

107 *Evening Post*, 29 August 1986.

108 Statistics, Population of Wellington (file closed, see now AD 95/03), 1984–1992, 00001:1150:34/21 Pt 4, WCA.

109 *New Zealand Official Yearbook 1990*, Department of Statistics, Wellington, 1990, p.134.

110 City Planner to Mayor, 9 May 1990, 00001:2134:60/4842 Pt 4, WCA.

111 WCCMB, WCA, Vol.116, p.365, 10 May 1989.

Chapter 9: Sesqui City to Wellywood

1   *Evening Post*, 25 January 1990.
2   (A) Exposition: International 1990 hosted by the City of Wellington, (B) Wellington: 150th Anniversary (16 May 1990) (D.12230), 1989–1990, 00001:1648:50/217/1 Pt 6, WCA.
3   (A) Exposition: International 1990 hosted by the City of Wellington, (B) Wellington: 150th Anniversary (16 May 1990) (D.12230), 1990, 00001:1648:50/217/1 Pt 7, WCA.
4   (A) Exposition: International 1990 hosted by the City of Wellington, (B) Wellington: 150th Anniversary (16 May 1990) (D.12230), 1988–1989, 00001:1648:50/217/1 Pt 4, WCA.
5   (A) Exposition: International 1990 hosted by the City of Wellington, (B) Wellington: 150th Anniversary (16 May 1990) (D.12230), 1989–1990, 00001:1648:50/217/1 Pt 4, WCA.
6   (A) Exposition: International 1990 hosted by the City of Wellington, (B) Wellington: 150th Anniversary (16 May 1990) (D.12230), 1989–1990, 00001:1648:50/217/1 Pt 6, WCA.
7   *Evening Post*, 13 February 1990.
8   *Evening Post*, 24 February 1990.
9   *Evening Post*, 28 February 1990.
10 *Evening Post*, 23 March 1990.
11 *Evening Post*, 22 September 1990.
12 *Dominion*, 20 September 1990.
13 *Sunday Star*, 11 March 1990.
14 David McGill, *Wellington: A Capital Century*, p.288.
15 *Evening Post*, 23 March 1990.
16 *Evening Post*, 8 March 1990.
17 *Dominion*, 28 December 1990.
18 Wellington City Council Minute Books (WCCMB), WCA, Vol.119, p.81, 16 November 1990.
19 Kerry Prendergast, interview.
20 *Evening Post*, 13 May 1991.
21 *Dominion*, 14 May 1991.
22 Wellington City Council Structure and Operation Review, Independent Review Group, Wellington, 1991, p.92, 00066:1:2, WCA.
23 Jenny Fitzwater, comment to author, 6 December 2005.
24 *Evening Post*, 13 May 1990.
25 *Evening Post*, 14 May 1991.
26 *Losses of the Wellington City Council Abattoir 1987 to 1991*, Audit Office, Wellington, October 1991.
27 *North and South*, May 1991, p.79.
28 Jim Belich, personal communication with author, 2005.
29 Reserve, Corner of Manners Street and Dixon Street, 1990–1992, 00001:1036:31/222 Pt 4, WCA.
30 *Evening Post*, 28 November 1991.
31 *Evening Post*, 10 February 1992.
32 *Dominion*, 17 February 1992.
33 *Evening Post*, 6 May 1992.
34 Audit Office Report to WCC on Te Aro Park Redevelopment Project, 17 March 1992, WCA.
35 Condition of Streets and Roads in Wellington, 1982–1984, 00001:1198:35/635 Pt 8, WCA.
36 Premises, Owen Street, 1929–1991, 00009:1391:45/347, WCA.
37 *Evening Post*, 28 September 1992.
38 WCCMB, WCA, Vol.120, p.149, 11 September 1991.
39 Annual Plan, 1992–1993, 00081:1:3, WCA.
40 Rosemary McLeod, 'Capital Chaos: The Dubious Achievements of the Wellington City Council', *North and South*, July 1992, pp.70–80.
41 *Dominion*, 10 April 1992.
42 *Evening Post*, 10 April 1992.
43 *Evening Post*, 13 April 1992.
44 Belich, personal communication, 2005.
45 Prendergast interview.
46 *North and South*, July 1992, p.71.

47 Prendergast interview.
48 Fran Wilde, interview with author, 28 October 2005.
49 *NZ Herald*, 29 October 1992.
50 Wilde interview.
51 *National Business Review*, 28 May 2004.
52 Annual Plan, 1993–1994, 00081:1:4, WCA.
53 Wilde interview.
54 Prendergast interview.
55 *Evening Post*, 3 December 1993.
56 WCCMB, WCA, Vol.122, p.501, 19 October 1994.
57 *City Voice*, 30 March 1994.
58 *Dominion*, 24 March 1994.
59 *Evening Post*, 24 March 1994.
60 *Evening Post*, 21 March 1994.
61 Annual Plan, 1994–1995, p.6, 00081:1:5, WCA.
62 Wilde interview.
63 *Evening Post*, 4 March 1995.
64 WCC Annual Plan, 1994–5, p.10, WCA.
65 *Evening Post*, 16 October 1995.
66 Mark Blumsky, interview with author, 27 October 2005.
67 Blumsky interview.
68 *Dominion*, 8 November 1995.
69 *New Zealand Listener*, 7 September 1996.
70 Blumsky interview.
71 Blumsky interview.
72 Information provided by Positively Wellington Tourism, 2005.
73 Prendergast interview.
74 *Evening Post*, 24 July 1996.
75 *Evening Post*, 28 May 1996.
76 *Evening Post*, 9 June 1997.
77 Blumsky interview.
78 *Evening Post*, 28 March 2000.
79 Blumsky interview.
80 Prendergast interview.
81 *Evening Post*, 16 November 1996.
82 *Evening Post*, 19 April 1996.
83 Lindsay Shelton, note to author, 23 October 2005.
84 Blumsky interview.
85 Shelton, note.
86 Lauren Quaintance, 'Top Town, Wellington', *North and South*, December 2000, p.36.
87 Deborah Coddington, 'Kerry Prendergast, Face to Face', *North and South*, September 2002, p.80.
88 *Dominion Post*, 2 December 2002.
89 *North and South*, September 2002, p.36.
90 *Dominion Post*, 4 September 2004.
91 *Dominion Post*, 13 October 2004.
92 *Dominion Post*, 12 October 2004.
93 Wellington Visitor Statistics, Positively Wellington Tourism, 2004.
94 *Wellington City Community Profile*, Statistics New Zealand, Wellington, 2005.
95 *States of the Nation*, Massey University, November 2003.
96 *Independent*, 13 July 1865.
97 Human Resource Capability Survey of Public Service Departments as at 30 June 2005, State Services Commission, Wellington, URL: http://www.ssc.govt.nz.
98 *Dominion Post*, 10 January 2006.

Select Bibliography

Manuscripts and Archives

Wellington City Archives, Wellington (WCA)

MINUTES

00115:0:1	Minutes of the Wellington Borough Council, 1842–1843
00165:0:1, Vol. 1	Minutes of the Wellington Town Board, 1863–1865
00165:0:2, Vol. 2	Minutes of the Wellington Town Board, September 1865–August 1866, and Wellington Board of Works, September 1866–September 1870
00166:0:1, Vols 3–127	Minutes of meetings of the Wellington City Council, 28 September 1870–17 September 1997

FILES

00001:397:6/5114/25	Michael Fowler Centre, Opening Ceremony
00001:1198:35/635	Condition of Streets and Roads in Wellington
00001:1232:35/1233	Motorway: Foothills Motorway (General File)
00001:1648:50/217/1	Exposition: International 1990 hosted by the City of Wellington
00001:1801:60/95/1	WCC Accounts: Government Audit
00001:2134:60/4842	Capital City Planning Committee, WCC and Ministers of the Crown
00066:1:2	WCC Structure and Operation Review, 1991
00233:196:1912/44	Enquiry re. Inspector Fuller, 1912
00233:527:1926	Northland Tunnel Commission of Inquiry, 1926
00512:1:2	Wellington City Corporation, Commission of Enquiry, 1932
2003/6:1:1	Report of Staff Committee, 1889

Archives New Zealand, Head Office, Wellington (ANZ)

HEALTH DEPARTMENT (H)

Series 3/1   Commission of Inquiry into Influenza Epidemic, 1919

HOUSING DIVISION, MINISTRY OF WORKS (HD)

Series 10/426/1   McLeans Block Flats

NASH PAPERS (N)

Bundle 2067, Folio 446   Maori War Effort

NEW ZEALAND COMPANY (NZC)

Series 102/1–2   Principal Agent's Office, Wellington, Inwards Correspondence, 1839–40

Alexander Turnbull Library, Wellington (ATL)

Marshall, Mary Frederica, 1826–1854, letters of Mary Frederica Swainson to her grandparents in England, 1840–1854 (1960), qMS-1337–1339

Revans, Samuel, 1808–1888, copies of letters from Samuel Revans, principally to H. S. Chapman dated at sea and at Wellington, 20 September 1839–1 September 1842, qMS-1687–1689

Wood, Henry A., 'The Life of a Pioneer Farmer, 1873–1953', MS-2520

New Zealand Historic Places Trust (NZHPT)

Series 8/6/1   Bethune's Exchange Building

Miscellaneous

Rankin, Jessica, unpublished diary, 1867–1869, Pharazyn Family

Oral Sources and Personal Communications

Beard, James, architect, interviewed by author, 18 July 2005

Belich, Sir James, former Mayor of Wellington, correspondence with author, 30 October 2005

Blumsky, Mark, former Mayor of Wellington, interviewed by author, 27 October 2005

Clark, Ken, former Wellington City Planner, correspondence with author, 2 August 2005

Clark, Kent, former City Councillor, interviewed by author, 9 November 2005

Fantl, Robert, architect, interviewed by author, 8 July 2005

Fitzwater, Jenny, former WCC employee, correspondence with author, 6 December 2005

Fowler, Sir Michael, former Mayor of Wellington, interviewed by author, 3 August 2005

Hollings, John, earthquake engineer, interviewed by author, 24 August 2005

Lawrence, Ian, former Mayor of Wellington, interviewed by author, 14 September 2005

Michael, Gordon, former WCC employee, interviewed by author, 7 June 2005

O'Brien, Gerald, former City Councillor and MP, interviewed by author, 20 July 2005

Peterson, Graeme, former WCC employee, interviewed by author, 9 June 2005

Prendergast, Kerry, Mayor of Wellington, interviewed by author, 11 November 2005

Ritchie, Helene, City Councillor, interviewed by author, 18 June 2004

Rose, Dennis, former secretary, Bolton Street Preservation Society, interviewed by author, 8 July 2005

Shelton, Lindsay, former president, Waterfront Watch, correspondence with author, 23 October 2005

Wilde, Fran, former Mayor of Wellington, interviewed by author, 28 October 2005

Newspapers and Magazines

Auckland Star	*New Zealand Herald*
City Voice	*New Zealand Listener*
Dominion	*New Zealand Mail*
Dominion Post	*New Zealand Spectator and Cook's Straits Guardian*
Evening Post	*New Zealand Times*
Illustrated London News	*New Zealand Truth*
Maoriland Worker	*North and South*
Marlborough Express (weekly edition)	*Otago Daily Times*
National Business Review	*Press* (Christchurch)
New Zealand Gazette/New Zealand Gazette and Britannia Spectator/New Zealand Gazette and Wellington Spectator	*Southern Cross*
	Wellington Independent

Official Publications

Appendix to the Journals of the House of Representatives (AJHR)

Census of New Zealand

New Zealand Gazette (NZG)

New Zealand Official Yearbook

New Zealand Parliamentary Debates (NZPD)

Statistics of New Zealand

Books

Alington, Margaret H., *Unquiet Earth: A History of the Bolton Street Cemetery*, Wellington City Council/ Ministry of Works and Development, Wellington, 1978

Arnold, Rollo, *New Zealand's Burning: The Settlers' World of the mid 1880s*, Victoria University Press, Wellington, 1994

Barber, Laurie, and Roy Towers, *Wellington Hospital, 1847–1976*, Wellington Hospital Board, Wellington, 1976

Bassett, Michael, *Coates of Kaipara*, Auckland University Press, Auckland, 1995

——— *The Mother of All Departments: The History of the Department of Internal Affairs*, Auckland University Press, Auckland, 1997

Bassett, Michael, and Michael King, *Tomorrow Comes the Song: A Life of Peter Fraser*, Penguin, Auckland, 2000

Beauchamp, Harold, *Reminiscences and Recollections*, Thomas Avery & Sons, New Plymouth, 1937

Belich, James, *Paradise Reforged: A History of the New Zealanders from the 1880s to the Year 2000*, Allen Lane/The Penguin Press, Auckland, 2001

Betts, George, *Betts on Wellington: A City and its Politics*, A. H. & A. W. Reed, Wellington, 1970

Bloomfield, G. T., *New Zealand: A Handbook of Historical Statistics*, G. K. Hall, Boston, MA, 1984

Burns, Barnet, *A Brief Narrative of the Remarkable History of Barnet Burns*, Kiwi, Christchurch, c. 1998

Bush, Graham, *Decently and In Order: The Government of the City of Auckland, 1840–1971*, Collins, Auckland, 1971

——— *Local Government & Politics in New Zealand*, Auckland University Press, Auckland, 1995

Carman, Arthur, *The Birth of a City: Wellington, 1840–43*, A. Carman, Wellington, 1970

Clarke, George, *Notes on Early Life in New Zealand*, J. Walch, Hobart, 1903

Cooke, Peter, *Defending New Zealand: Ramparts on the Sea, 1840–1950*, Part II, Defence of New Zealand Study Group, Wellington, 2000

Debnam, Geoffrey, *Limits of Local Initiative: Imposed and Negotiated Planning in the Aro Valley*, New Zealand Institute of Public Administration, Wellington, 1986

Ferguson, Gael, *Building the New Zealand Dream*, Dunmore Press, Palmerston North, 1994

Findlay, Mary, *Tooth and Nail: The Story of a Daughter of the Depression*, Penguin Books, Auckland, 1974

Grace, Patricia, Irihapeti Ramsden and Jonathan Dennis, *The Silent Migration: Ngati Poneke Young Maori Club 1937–1948*, Huia, Wellington, 2001

Grant, David, *Out in the Cold: Pacifists and Conscientious Objectors in New Zealand during World War II*, Reed Methuen, Auckland, 1986

Hamer, David, *The Webbs in New Zealand, 1898*, Price Milburn/ Victoria University Press, Wellington, 1974

Hamer, David, and Roberta Nicholls (eds), *The Making of Wellington, 1800–1914*, Victoria University Press, Wellington, 1990

Henderson, Alan, *The Quest for Efficiency: The Origins of the State Services Commission*, State Services Commission, Wellington, 1990

Hodgson, Terence, *Colonial Capital: Wellington 1865–1910*, Random Century, Auckland, 1990

Howe, Kerry, *Singer in a Songless Land*, Auckland University Press, Auckland, 1991

Irvine-Smith, F. L., *The Streets of My City, Wellington, New Zealand*, A. H. & A. W. Reed, Wellington,1948

Johnson, David, *Wellington Harbour*, Wellington Maritime Museum Trust, Wellington, 1996

King, Michael, *Te Puea*, Sceptre, Auckland, 1977

Lawlor, Pat, *Confessions of a Journalist*, Whitcombe & Tombs, Auckland, 1935

——*Old Wellington Days*, Whitcombe & Tombs, Wellington, 1959

——*Old Wellington Hotels*, Millwood Press, Wellington, 1974

Levine, Stephen (ed.), *New Zealand Politics: A Reader*, Cheshire, Melbourne, 1975

Macdonald, Charlotte, Merimeri Penfold and Bridget Williams (eds), *The Book of New Zealand Women: Ko kui ma te Kaupapa*, Bridget Williams Books, Wellington, 1991

McDonald, K. C., *City of Dunedin: A Century of Civic Enterprise*, Dunedin City Corporation, Dunedin, 1965

McGill, David, *Pioneers of Port Nicholson*, Reed, Auckland, 1984

——*Wellington: A Capital Century*, Transpress, Wellington, 2003

McKinnon, John, *John Plimmer and his Family, 150 Years, 1841–1991*, Plimmer Family Reunion Committee, Wellington, 1991

Maclean, Chris, *Wellington: Telling Tales*, Whitcombe Press, Wellington, 2005

Maclean, F. S., *Challenge for Health: A History of Public Health in New Zealand*, Government Printer, Wellington, 1964

Macmorran, George, *Some Schools and Schoolmasters of Early Wellington*, S. & W. Mackay, Wellington, 1900

Majoribanks, Alexander, *Travels in New Zealand*, Smith Elder, London, 1850

Martin, John E., *Holding the Balance: A History of New Zealand's Department of Labour 1891–1995*, Canterbury University Press, Christchurch, 1996

Martin, Paul, *Carmen: My Life*, Benton Ross, Auckland, 1988

Meredith, G. L., *Adventuring in Maoriland in the Seventies*, Angus & Robertson, Sydney, 1935

Millar, David, *Once Upon a Village: A History of Lower Hutt, 1819–1965*, New Zealand University Press, Wellington, 1972

Mulgan, Alan, *City of the Strait: Wellington and its Province*, Reed Books, Wellington, 1939

Offer, R. E., *Walls for Water: Pioneer Dam Building in New Zealand*, Dunmore Press, Palmerston North, 1997

Palethorpe, N. B., *Official History of the New Zealand Centennial Exhibition*, New Zealand Centennial Exhibition Company, Wellington, 1940

Phillips, Jock, *Royal Summer*, Daphne Brasell Associates/Department of Internal Affairs, Wellington, 1993

Priestley, Dinah, *Old Thorndon*, Anchorage Press, Wellington, 1988

Reeve, Alan, *Lions and Lambs of Wellington: Well Known Citizens in Caricature*, Watkins, Wellington, 1932

Renwick, William (ed.), *Creating a National Spirit: Celebrating New Zealand's Centennial*, Victoria University Press, Wellington, 2004

Rice, Geoffrey, *Black November: The 1918 Influenza Epidemic in New Zealand*, Allen & Unwin/Department of Internal Affairs, Wellington, 1988

Roth, Herbert, *Trade Unions in New Zealand: Past and Present*, Reed Education, Wellington, 1973

Sante, Luc, *Low Life: Lures and Snares of Old New York*, Granta Books, London, 1998

Scholefield, G. H. (ed.), *A Dictionary of New Zealand Biography*, Whitcombe & Tombs, Wellington, 1940

Siegfried, André, *Democracy in New Zealand*, Bell, London, 1914

Simpson, Tony, *The Sugarbag Years: An Oral History of the 1930s Depression in New Zealand*, 2nd edn, Hodder & Stoughton, Auckland, 1984

Stewart, Graham, *The End of the Penny Section: When Trams Ruled the Streets of New Zealand*, Grantham House, Wellington, 1993

Sutch, William, *The Quest for Security in New Zealand, 1840 to 1966*, Oxford University Press, Wellington, 1966

—— *Wellington: A Sick City*, Sweet & Maxwell, Wellington, 1965

Taylor, Nancy, *The New Zealand People at War: The Home Front*, Government Printer, Wellington, 1986

Thorn, Margaret, *Stick Out, Keep Left*, Auckland University Press/Bridget Williams Books, Auckland, 1997

Waitangi Tribunal, *Te Whanganui a Tara me Ona Takiwa: Report on the Wellington District*, Legislation Direct, Wellington, 2003

Wakefield, Edward Jerningham, *Adventure in New Zealand*, reprinted by Golden Press, Auckland, 1975

Ward, Louis, *Early Wellington*, Whitcombe & Tombs, Auckland, 1929

Wellington City Council and Wellington Tenths Trust, *Nga Tupuna o Te Whanganui-a-Tara*, Wellington City Council/Wellington Tenths Trust, Wellington, 2001

Wellington Tenths Trust, *Wharenui — Wharewaka, Te Aro Pa, Taranaki Wharf*, Cultural Impact Report, Wellington Tenths Trust, Wellington, 2005

Wilkins, Damien, *When Famous People Come to Town*, Four Winds Press, Wellington, 2002

Wilson, Charles, *New Zealand Cities: Wellington*, Whitcombe & Tombs, Auckland, 1919

Wood, John, *Twelve Months in Wellington, Port Nicholson*, Pelham Richardson, London, 1843

Articles and Papers

Best, Elsdon, 'Te Whanga-nui-a-Tara: Wellington in Pre-Pakeha days', *Journal of the Polynesian Society*, Vol.26, part 1, 1917

Burch, Judith, 'Getting to Karori: Before and After the Tunnel', *The Stockade*, Vol.33, 2000

Cleaver, Phillip, 'The Pakeha Treatment of Death in 19th and 20th Century Wellington', lecture to the Wellington Historical and Early Settlers' Association Inc., 15 February 1996

Coddington, Deborah, 'Kerry Prendergast, Face to Face', *North and South*, September 2002

McLeod, Rosemary, 'Capital Chaos: The Dubious Achievements of the Wellington City Council', *North and South*, July 1992

Patterson, Brad, 'A "Half Australian, Half American" Town', in J. McConchie, D. Winchester and R. Willis (eds), *Dynamic Wellington: A Contemporary Synthesis and Explanation of Wellington*, Institute of Geography, Victoria University of Wellington, 2000

Porter, D. G., 'Housing the Citizen', in N. L. McLeod and B. H. Farland (eds), *Wellington Prospect: Survey of a City 1840–1970*, Hicks Smith, Wellington, 1970

Quaintance, Lauren, 'Top Town, Wellington', *North and South*, December 2000

Salmon, J. T., 'Conservation in the Development of a Wellington Region', in *Seminar on the Development of the Wellington Region, Victoria University of Wellington, 7–9 September 1970: Seminar Papers and Excerpts from Proceedings*, Victoria University of Wellington, 1970

Schrader, Ben, 'Modernising Wellington: The 1920s to the 1950s', in John Wilson (ed.), *Zeal and Crusade: The Modern Movement in Wellington*, Te Waihora Press, Christchurch, 1996

Theses and Research Essays

Humphris, Adrian, 'Tramways and Suburban Growth: A Case Study of Kilbirnie', MA Thesis, Victoria University of Wellington, 2003

Miller, Richard, 'The Wellington Urban Motorway: The Parts Played by the Planning Authorities and the Bolton Street Preservation Society', Research Essay, Victoria University of Wellington, 1969

Noonan, Rosslyn, 'The Riots of 1932: A Study of Social Unrest in Auckland, Wellington, Dunedin', MA Thesis, University of Auckland, 1969

Press, Craig, 'The Role of Government in Developing the Colonial City: The Case of Wellington, 1840–1903', MA Thesis, Victoria University of Wellington, 1995

Toth, Gabor, 'Café Culture in Wellington', Research Essay, Victoria University of Wellington, 2000

Websites

Dictionary of New Zealand Biography, URL: http://www.dnzb.govt.nz/dnzb/

Index

Page numbers in **bold** indicate principal reference. Page numbers in *italics* indicate illustrations.

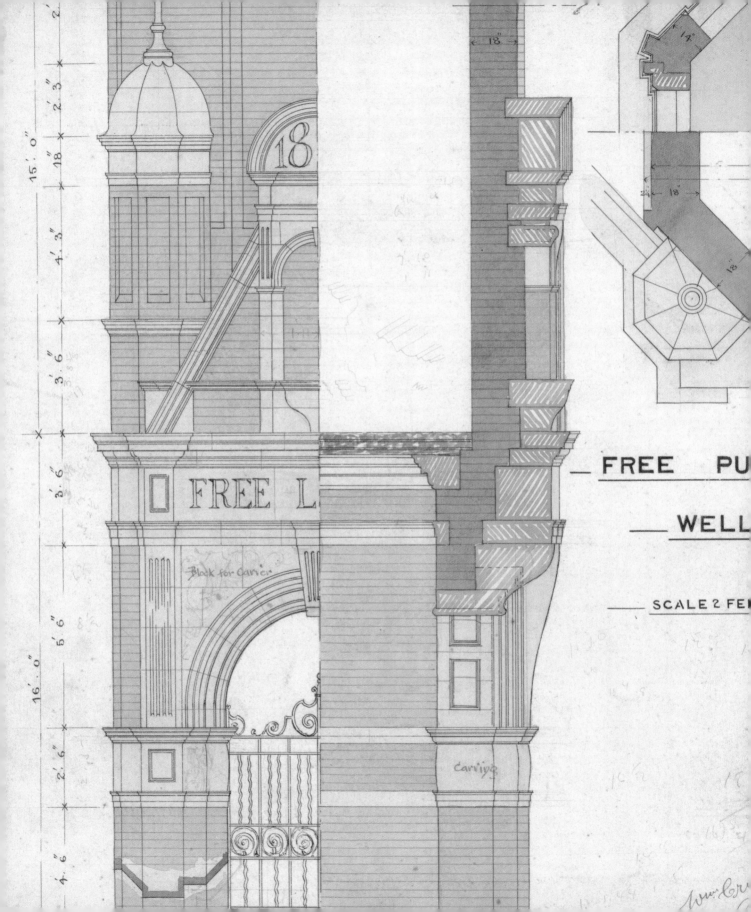

FREE LIBRARY

18

FREE PU

WELL

SCALE 2 FE

Block for Carver

Carving